Intimate JOURNALISM

To my daughter, Kyle.

Intimate JOURNALISM

The Art
and
Craft of
Reporting
Everyday Life

Walt Harrington

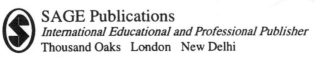

SAGE Publications
International Educational and Professional Publisher
Thousand Oaks   London   New Delhi

Also by Walt Harrington: *American Profiles: Somebodies and Nobodies Who Matter; Crossings: A White Man's Journey Into Black America; At the Heart of It: Ordinary People, Extraordinary Lives*

For information, address to:

 SAGE Publications, Inc.
2455 Teller Road
Thousand Oaks, California 91320
E-mail: order@sagepub.com

SAGE Publications Ltd.
6 Bonhill Street
London EC2A 4PU
United Kingdom

SAGE Publications India Pvt. Ltd.
M-32 Market
Greater Kailash I
New Delhi 110 048 India

Printed in the United States of America

Library of Congress Cataloging-in-Publication Data

Main entry under title:

Intimate journalism: The art and craft of reporting everyday life/
    editor, Walt Harrington
        p.   cm.
    Includes bibliographical references (p.   ).
    ISBN 0-7619-0586-3.—ISBN 0-7619-0587-1 (pbk.)
    1. Feature writing.   2. Journalism—United States
I. Harrington, Walt, 1950-
PN4784.F37I58   1997
070.4′4—dc21   96-45840

05 06 07 08   10 9 8 7

Acquiring Editor:	Margaret Seawell
Editorial Assistant:	Renée Piernot
Production Editor:	Astrid Virding
Production Assistant:	Denise Santoyo
Typesetter/Designer:	Marion Warren
Cover Designer:	Candice Harman
Print Buyer:	Anna Chin

Contents

Permissions

"The Job of Remembering for the Tribe," copyright 1997 by Walt Harrington.

"A Writer's Essay: Seeking the Extraordinary in the Ordinary," copyright 1997 by Walt Harrington.

"The Man Who Couldn't Read" by Gary Smith first appeared in *Esquire* in 1990. Reprinted by permission of the author.

"Shadow of a Nation" by Gary Smith first appeared in *Sports Illustrated* in 1991. Reprinted by permission of the author.

"The American Man at Age 10" by Susan Orlean first appeared in *Esquire* in 1992. Reprinted by permission of the author.

"The Last Housewife in America" by David Finkel first appeared in *Esquire* in 1990. Reprinted by permission of the author.

"TV Without Guilt" by David Finkel first appeared in *The Washington Post Magazine* in 1994. Copyright 1994 *The Washington Post*. Reprinted with permission.

"Mrs. Kelly's Monster" by Jon Franklin first appeared in *The Evening Sun* in 1978. Reprinted by permission of *The Baltimore Sun*.

"Missing Alice" by Pete Earley first appeared in *The Washington Post Magazine* in 1985. Copyright 1985 *The Washington Post*. Reprinted with permission.

"In These Girls, Hope Is a Muscle" by Madeleine Blais first appeared in *The New York Times Magazine* in 1993. Reprinted by permission of the author.

"Zepp's Last Stand" by Madeleine Blais first appeared in *Tropic Magazine, The Miami Herald* in 1979. Reprinted by permission of the author.

"Each Other's Mirror" by Jeanne Marie Laskas first appeared in *The Washington Post Magazine* in 1989. Copyright 1989 *The Washington Post*. Reprinted with permission.

Civilization is a stream with banks. The stream is sometimes filled with blood from people killing, stealing, shouting and doing the things historians usually record; while on the banks, unnoticed, people build homes, make love, raise children, sing songs, write poetry and even whittle statues. The story of civilization is the story of what happened on the banks.

—Will Durant

Prologue:
The Job of
Remembering for the Tribe

Writers are rememberers or nothing. That's why the tribe gives us that job.
                                                    —Pete Hamill

As journalists for the tribe, we remember many things well. Yesterday's weather, always. Michael Jordan's amazing 69-point tear against Cleveland. Instability in Istanbul. Insurgency in Peru. Politician caught in love nest. Celebrity gets married, celebrity gets divorced. The Dow. The death of an old man in Omaha, Nebraska. The birth of a baby girl on the same day in Taos, New Mexico. Hurricanes in Jamaica. Massacres in Rwanda. Revolution in Russia. The speeches—oh, the speeches. And elections far and wide.

The tribe is grateful.

But other things we remember for the tribe almost not at all. The *feeling* a child has when she takes the power of the Holy Spirit into her heart at first communion. The feeling an old farmer has when he latches his barn door for the last time on the night before his homestead is sold. The feeling a teacher has when a bad student becomes a good one. The feeling a mother has when her daughter pitches the winning game in the Little League championship. The feeling a father has as he buries his firstborn son. The feeling a man has when he learns that he has beaten the cancer. The feeling a woman has when she learns that she has not.

On the banks of the stream that is our civilization, these emotions are life. As sportswriter and novelist Dan Jenkins puts it, "Life its ownself." But to most journalists honored with the job of remembering the stories of the tribe, these momentous events of everyday life are virtually invisible. To most American journalists, such events are akin to the dark and unknown matter believed to make up 90% of the universe: We keep reporting the movement of the planets when the big news is the unseen matter in which they spin. At best, most journalists are oblivious to reporting the incredible human beauty and subtlety that surround them. At worst, they militantly oppose reporting what they are untrained to discern and describe. But either way, readers are being denied a look at much of the world they inhabit.

In the language of the craft, we're missing the story.

Intimate Journalism is meant as a corrective—as both a call for change and a how-to manual. It's long past time to ask, in an era defined by shallow celebrity reporting in magazines, whether readers demand that kind of journalism or if it is all that many magazine journalists are capable of providing. It's long past time to ask American newspaper editors and reporters to rethink what they consider "news." It was decades ago that Herbert Gans, in his classic study of the American press, wrote, "How ordinary people work, what they do outside working hours, in their families, churches, clubs and other organizations . . . hardly ever make the news." Changing that won't be easy.

Most magazines and newspapers rarely achieve the standard of the stories in this collection. Magazine journalists usually aren't trained in in-depth reporting techniques, and more and more magazine editors turn to stories on the famous and the infamous to attract readers. Newspaper journalists, on the other hand, have been born and bred in the tradition that "news" is to be found in the process and product of public policy formation—in the overt and covert actions of county zoning boards, statehouses, the EPA, the White House, the Supreme Court—or in acts of God or man that crash upon the scene, as in earthquakes or terrorist bombings.

I have no quarrel with that tradition. I revere it. But what's so baffling to me after 20 years as a newspaper and magazine journalist is why we can't include in our reports more of the everyday worlds in which we and all our readers live. For years, I believed this wrongheaded view was embedded in the honorable belief that journalism's role was to be the public's watchdog, not its muse or storyteller or keeper of the sacred flame.

But now, with many miles on my Chevy, I also wonder if a darker motive is not at play, because most newspaper journalists simply can't do the kind of reporting and writing on display in *Intimate Journalism*. When it comes to conceptualizing such stories to reporting them to writing them, these masters of their newsroom universes are back in third grade. I suspect that the old-heads of straight news fear consciously or unconsciously that if time, effort and space on the page are regularly given over to the journalism of everyday life, they will lose out in the newsroom struggle for resources and status, that the skills they have spent a lifetime learning will be less valuable, that their power will be diminished. There's probably truth in these fears. At every newspaper there simmers animosity between the "hard" and "soft" journalists—with the soft faction always holding less power.

It is a trivial, careerist dispute. And it always astonishes me to hear the argument against soft journalism from unreconstructed hard journalists who will jump like dark on night after bureaucrats bickering about their pay or status at the expense of the people they're supposedly serving, when the result of the hard newspeople's intransigence is the same: It's the readers they are supposedly serving who lose out. It's sad that American newspaper editors don't better understand the kind of journalism collected in these pages, because newspapers are a medium that could be leading the way in the form. Unlike magazines, most papers aren't dependent on newsstand sales that require celebrity cover stories. Unlike magazines, newspapers also don't need to target a specific demographic audience, which allows them to write stories on a wide range of people and topics. Newspapers could and should be a fountain of fine everyday-life journalism.

I believe that fair, accurate, in-depth, sophisticated, narrative reporting of everyday life is prima facie good for readers. They read it. They like it. They respond to it. I believe the reporting of everyday life is prima facie good for newspapers. It expands their mission. It touches their readers in the heart, as well as the head. In a recent one-year period, the *Washington Post* lost 12,029 daily subscribers, the *Philadelphia Inquirer* lost 15,321, the *New York Times* lost 16,344, the *Detroit News & Free Press* lost 20,616 and the *Buffalo News* lost 26,031. In the face of this frightening free-fall in readership and the mad scramble to save the industry with everything from better design to color pictures to more sports to better weather maps to "civic journalism" that's meant to stimulate public deliberation and participation in public affairs, the reporting of everyday life should be an obvious part of any response.

Reporting of everyday life preserves journalistic integrity, expands the report, connects readers emotionally to their newspapers and makes journalists seem less like the unfeeling, uncaring hit men many people wrongly believe them to be. Unfortunately, much of this negative image is deserved, growing from the traditional watchdog ethic gone over the edge. As philosopher and media ethicist Clifford Christians writes of journalists in his book *Good News*, "Public storytellers must know the good as much as they need a language to describe the bad."

In an era when people live harried, cynical and fragmented lives far worse than we could have imagined only a few decades ago, a journalism that honestly and accurately evokes and describes the everyday lives and interior worlds of a wide range of people is more than a strategy for selling newspapers. As Alan Jones writes in his book *The Soul's Journey,* "We need stories that take note of our frailty and foolishness and yet honor our deepest longings and highest aspirations . . . that will heal our wounded imaginations."

The journalism of everyday life is a way to repair the torn social fabric that journalism has undeniably helped to shred. It's a journalism that's needed today as much as reporting on greed, corruption and social injustice was needed at the turn of the century, perhaps more. American journalism must go beyond what has become an unofficial self-description of its role in society—"to comfort the afflicted and afflict the comfortable." As Christians writes, what's needed now is a journalism "calling for narratives that nurture civic transformation." Or as William Faulkner said in his famous address while receiving the Nobel Prize in Literature, "The poet's voice need not merely be the record of man, it can be one of the props, the pillars to help him endure and prevail." Journalism, too, should help us endure and prevail.

The stories of everyday life—about the behavior, motives, feelings, faiths, attitudes, grievances, hopes, fears and accomplishments of people as they seek meaning and purpose in their lives, stories that are windows on our universal human struggle—should be at the soul of every good newspaper.

Obviously, they're not.

Twenty-five years ago, Tom Wolfe wrote that most feature journalism in American newspapers was "totem journalism," a kind of feel-goodism aimed at reinforcing the most common beliefs of readers. It has improved only slightly. When I began teaching seminars on advanced feature journalism to staffers at the *Washington Post* a few years ago, I was surprised to discover that no anthology of intimate journalism articles existed for students and professionals—and, worse yet, that the journalistic form itself was still a rarity. With notable exceptions, what passes for everyday-life journalism is too often a mishmash of superficial stories about Aunt Sadie cooking pies, unlikely heroes who save people from drowning or drag them from burning buildings, the nice kid next door who turns out to be a serial killer and poor people who, against the odds, make it to the top. There's nothing wrong with such stories, except that too often they are the end point of everyday-life coverage, reported and edited with the left hand by people unschooled and unaware of the intricate assumptions and techniques of intimate journalism, which results in stories made superficial by both accident and design.

It's a failure of vision.

And, really, there's no excuse for it. The basics of what Norman Sims has dubbed "literary journalism" and what others call "creative journalism," "creative nonfiction" or "documentary narrative" are there for the taking. Newspaper journalists do use these various techniques. Yet the methods are most often applied to certain kinds of stories—those about poor people, people dying of AIDS and people who for some reason have broken into the public spotlight after, say, killing their parents or being killed by their parents. In short, these are stories about people in extreme situations. Giving the same depth of attention to people as they live their everyday lives, seeking out the extraordinary in the ordinary, is rare. Yet everyday life is the only real laboratory we have for understanding ourselves and our society, our values and our behavior. Even when examining the aberrant, it is what has become routine within those aberrant worlds that is often most revealing of human nature.

The stories collected here are of that cut. They are reported to uncover and structured to evoke the emotional texture of their subjects' lives. They make readers leave themselves momentarily and feel what it's like to *be* another person. In practical terms, the introductory essay, the stories themselves and the writers' insights about how they did their stories give journalists who write shorter features, news features or celebrity profiles considerable guidance in how to make their articles more human and humane, about what reporting assumptions and approaches they must question, and even abandon, to do fine everyday-life journalism. While living up to traditional journalistic standards of accuracy, these stories are written with the emotionally absorbing tone and narrative arc of a short story. Reading them is like reading a novel, seeing a movie or watching a play—they evoke the sensation of life happening before our eyes.

This is the achievement of Gary Smith's story about a high school teacher and businessman who for decades hid his illiteracy from the world, and his story about a basketball star from the Crow reservation in Montana, which won a National Magazine Award. It is the achievement of all the stories collected here: Susan Orlean's profile of a typical 10-year-old suburban boy. David Finkel's story about a contented suburban housewife and his story about a happy family that watches TV as much as 17 hours a day—a finalist for the Pulitzer Prize for feature writing. Jon Franklin's story about a brain surgeon laboring methodically to save the life of a patient, which won a Pulitzer Prize in feature writing. Pete Earley's story of recapturing the memory of his sister, who had died in a car accident when he was a boy decades earlier. Madeleine Blais's story about a girls' high school basketball team that won the state championship, and her story about an old man who for 50 years fought to win an honorable discharge from the Army—a Pulitzer Prize winner for feature writing. Jeanne Marie Laskas's story about twin sisters and the great joy each takes in knowing another human being as well as she knows herself. Richard Ben Cramer's story about a family clinging to life's edge in West Philadelphia. Mike Sager's story about crack heads in Venice, California. And my own stories about a homicide detective wrestling with the numbing inhumanity he sees every day, a woman trying to accept her aging father's place in her home and an honored poet in the throes of creation.

All are stories set not in the stream but on the banks of our civilization: people harboring secrets, facing demons and raising children, people saving lives and taking them, people maturing, changing and seeking their own place, people writing poetry.

"Life its ownself."

A Writer's Essay:
Seeking the Extraordinary
in the Ordinary

On *Thinking* About Intimate Journalism

It's the kiss of death for anyone aspiring to do intimate journalism to think of what he or she does as lighteners, brighteners or human interest stories. That is a newsperson's way of thinking. Too often, those of us aspiring to do intimate journalism work in isolation from the grand traditions that inform or should inform our work—the traditions of documentary nonfiction, qualitative social science and anthropology, the classic journalism of the *New Yorker,* the new journalism of the '60s and '70s, the literary journalism of the '80s and '90s and the best of travel and nature writing. That is our genealogy.

The artfulness required to do intimate journalism is not mostly a God-given skill, but craft. It's crucial to think that way. Otherwise, we make the mistake of assuming that some people just have the knack. Some people do have the knack, but much of artful journalism, whether or not it is about ordinary people, is simply hard work—craft. I know, because whatever artfulness exists in my journalism was acquired, not inherited. The ideas, insights and tricks of the trade that I share here

This essay is based on presentations given in advanced feature writing seminars the author taught at the *Washington Post.*

grow from two decades spent pursuing that acquisition. I came out of a social science background in college and graduate school and was poorly read in literature and "writerly" journalism. My plan was to do a kind of humanized public affairs journalism, a dumbed-down social science for the masses. But as I went along during my first few years, I realized that I couldn't make my stories capture the complexity and subtlety I saw in the events I was reporting. My stories were caricatures of reality, not portraits of reality, because I simply didn't have the skills to capture what I knew to be before me.

So I put myself on a program. I took courses in fiction and autobiography writing. I began to read fiction, particularly short naturalistic fiction, with an eye to what I could take away for my journalism. I read and studied the artful journalism classics—the new journalism of *Esquire* and *Rolling Stone,* the old new journalism of the *New Yorker,* the classic nonfiction of A. J. Liebling, E. B. White, Joseph Mitchell, Lillian Ross, John Hersey, Norman Mailer, Truman Capote, Tom Wolfe, Jimmy Breslin, Gay Talese, Susan Sheehan, John McPhee, Jane Kramer, Tracy Kidder and Joan Didion.* I went back to the kind of fiction cited as having influenced modern nonfiction: Stephen Crane's *Red Badge of Courage,* Daniel Defoe's *Journal of the Plague Years,* Ernest Hemingway's *In Our Time,* John Steinbeck's *Grapes of Wrath,* Robert Penn Warren's *All the King's Men.* I found my way to the nature writing of Edward Abbey, Aldo Leopold and Wendell Berry and the travel writing of Peter Matthiessen, Bruce Chatwin and William Least Heat Moon, with its intricate interplay between sensory detail and interpretive meaning. I discovered the oral history of anthropologist John Langston Gwaltney and Studs Terkel, the documentary cum social science of Robert Coles and Michael Lesy and the documentary cum literature of James Agee.

Linking this work with my training in sociology, I began to think of each story I did not as a little feature but as a journalistic case study,

---

*For a more complete discussion of what's called New or Literary Journalism, see Tom Wolfe's introductory essays in *The New Journalism* (1973), edited by Wolfe and E. W. Johnson; two books edited by Norman Sims, *The Literary Journalists* (1984) and *Literary Journalism in the Twentieth Century* (1990); a book edited by Sims and Mark Kramer, *Literary Journalism* (1995), particularly Kramer's introductory essay; a book edited by Ronald Weber, *The Reporter as Artist* (1974); and my own list of suggested readings at the end of my book *American Profiles* (1992).

which is a marvelous way to take your journalism seriously no matter how small your newspaper or magazine, no matter how obscure your outpost. If examining everyday life is your goal, every place is your laboratory. It was years before I thought of "intimate journalism" as a subgenre of literary journalism, which may or may not attempt to evoke the subjective realities of subjects, either famous or obscure, but which inevitably uses reporting and writing techniques aimed at giving nonfiction a more storylike quality.

The idiosyncratic beauty and power of Agee's famous documentary work, *Let Us Now Praise Famous Men,* stunned me, and I latched onto the documentary method's overarching goal, as explained by historian William Stott in his book *Documentary Expression and Thirties America*—to describe and evoke "felt life" or the "feeling of a living experience." Unlike some stylishly interpretive journalism that aims to impose the author's "attitude" on the subject, my goal—and that of the documentary approach and the social science exemplified by books such as Elliott Liebow's *Talley's Corner,* Michael Lesy's *Time Frames* and Robert Coles's *Privileged Ones*—is to be essentially self-effacing, to let interpretations arise from within the subjects themselves.

But these notions I kept to myself in the newsroom, where they would have been viewed as weird or "highfalutin," even subversive. Unfortunately, America's newsrooms are filled with men and women who know too little about artful journalism—its grand place in the journalistic scheme of things, its intricate reporting and writing methods, the sometimes idiosyncratic personalities of those who are or could be good intimate journalists and the time and work that it takes to make in-depth intimate journalism happen.

We all know news editors who instinctively salivate at a good news or investigative story but whose eyes, if you were to tell them that your goal was to render the "feeling of a living experience," would glaze over as they assigned you to the ranks of the muddleheaded. This attitude has consequences.

The kind of journalism we end up doing is shaped by the way we *think* about our mission. If we think that a vital part of our job is to uncover, describe and evoke the texture, tone and meaning—the warp and woof, as people say—of the everyday lives of our readers, then the crucial role of intimate journalism comes suddenly and inevitably to the fore. This kind of journalism often gives up something in breadth and on-high authority in return for something gained in evocation and humanity. It is not "news you can use," as the modern catchphrase goes but "news you can feel."

The simple goal of intimate journalism should be to describe and evoke *how people live and what they value.* That short phrase encompasses the full range of our lives—work, children, faith, anything that we do or that we believe important, everything ordinary and everything extraordinary in our lives.

I'm talking about a kind of story that rises and falls on narrative structure, the reporting of physical detail, the reporting of human emotion, on evocative tone and the pulling of thematic threads through the course of the story. It's a journalism rooted in descriptive realism. As in Nelson Algren's words, "I try to write accurately from the poise of mind which lets us see that things are exactly what they seem."

The basic techniques:

- *Thinking, reporting and writing in scenes.*

- *Capturing a narrator's voice and/or writing the story from the point of view of one or several subjects.* In other words, writing from inside the heads of our subjects, trying to evoke their emotional realities—their felt lives.

- *Gathering telling details from our subjects' lives,* details that evoke the "tone" of that life. This means gathering a full range of sensory details—trying to report through all five of our senses, which creates not "color," as some reporters would call it, but documentary detail that allows us to write, in Algren's terms, as if "things are exactly what they seem."

- *Gathering real-life dialogue.* It creates the sense of life happening before readers' eyes. A corollary to this is to keep in mind the goal of having as few quotes as possible from people who are speaking to no one *in* the story except the reporter—in other words, the narrator. In fictional stories, subjects do not talk to the omniscient narrator. When they do in artful journalism, it's the equivalent of disembodied, talking heads in TV news.

Remarks made to no one *in* the story keep readers from losing themselves in the telling, because it reminds them that events aren't really happening before their eyes but are being relayed secondhand through an interpreter. Quotes going out into the ether interfere with readers losing themselves in the self-referential boundaries you are trying to create in the story.

• *Gathering "interior" monologue*—what subjects are thinking, feeling, imagining, dreaming, worrying about or wondering to themselves. Intimate journalism focuses not only on the facts but on the *meaning* that the facts have for our subjects. As Mark Twain wrote, "What a wee little part of a person's life are his acts and words! His real life is led in his head."

• *Reporting to establish a time line* that will allow us to write, as Jon Franklin has written in his book *Writing for Story,* a narrative article that at its beginning posits a problem, dilemma or tension that will be resolved or relieved by the end of the story, with a resultant change— usually some form of redemption but at least some kind of change—in our main subject or subjects. This gives a story a beginning, a middle and an end.

• *Immersing ourselves temporarily in the lives of our subjects* so that they become relaxed in our presence and so that we can see real events unfold, develop and be resolved.

• *Gathering physical details of places and people,* along with descriptions of their tics and mannerisms, at specific points in conversation or scenes so they can be used at exactly those points in our story.

• *Always being aware that no matter how artful our stories may be,* how specific they are to the lives of our subjects, they are primarily meant to enlighten, caution, criticize or inspire, always resonate, in the lives of readers. The eternal verities of love, hate, fear, ambition, dedication, compassion are still our bread and butter. Always remember: Scene, detail and narrative bring a story to life, while theme and meaning imbue it with a soul.

• *Finally, the glue for all of this is the reader's belief that, as Tom Wolfe once said, All of this is true!* It's all true—the color of hair and eyes, the raising of an eyebrow or a pause in midsentence, the details of a private reverie. The standard of what is "writerly" in journalism is much lower than it is in fiction for exactly this reason: It's all true. We can't build composites or play with the facts to fit a moral.

Of course, none or even most of these goals will ever be met in any one story, because each story will have different requirements, limitations and opportunities. Different journalists have different styles: Gary Smith's "The Man Who Couldn't Read" has almost no quotes, no dialogue, which is common in his stories. Mike Sager's "Death in Venice" is replete with dialogue, which is common in his stories. Except for accuracy and fairness, no rule is immutable. But thinking in these grand terms means that a piece of intimate journalism is a creature all its own. It has certain internal needs, in the way that TV news requires action footage and magazine articles require good photos. The more of these needs you can meet, the better your story.

Remember also that a journalist doesn't become proficient in all these techniques at once. John McPhee has a collection of stories titled *Pieces of the Frame*. That's how an aspiring intimate journalist should approach the body of knowledge he or she must eventually master—build your frame one piece at a time. Remember that almost every esteemed nonfiction writer started out writing simple feature stories. When Mike Sager was a young journalist at the *Washington Post,* he wasn't given the time or space to do the kind of stories he hoped to write someday. So he did small stories that allowed him to focus on aspects of the craft—a story about a farmer preparing his farm for winter, a story about three men who got together once a week to play pool, a story about a high school football team preparing for Saturday night's big game.

Jon Franklin took much the same tack as a young journalist. Before writing "Mrs. Kelly's Monster," he wrote a story on one day in the life of a dogcatcher, a story about a severely retarded man and the nurse who cared for him and a story about workmen building a wall in the middle of a busy freeway. Both men were often frustrated by editors who didn't share their journalistic vision. But I believe it's important to educate those editors, explain the kind of journalism you hope to do someday, give them examples of work you admire. But most of all, live up to their standards of absolute reporting accuracy and never let sloppy reporting or writing be an editor's legitimate excuse for reining you in.

For those who will or do work in a newspaper newsroom, it's necessary to distinguish between a piece of intimate journalism and what are known in the newspaper business as "news feature" stories. A news feature, a worthy and noble form, is first and foremost an issue or trend story that is humanized with examples and quotes from real people.

A fine example of the news feature form is a story by the *Washington Post's* Barbara Vobejda that ran on the *Post's* front page. It's about the wrenching adjustment middle-class parents must make when their children fail to live out parental dreams and ambitions. Vobejda's story is humanized with wonderful detail and description, great and telling quotes. To make its point, the story intersperses human stories with quotations from experts. It begins with a nice anecdotal lead and ends with a touching, telling remark. It is the perfect news feature.

The story could also have been done as a piece of intimate journalism. But Vobejda would have had to make decisions very differently from the beginning. She would have had to first pick one family to represent all families going through these events. Ideally, she would have found a family going through the events *now*—in other words, a family in the midst of resolving these disputes. She'd want a family that probably wasn't too pathological so that it could represent what an average family might go through.

She'd need a family willing to have its intimate lives portrayed in headlines. She'd need a family in which the parents and child were bright and articulate and not shy about expressing their thoughts and feelings. She'd still have to interview experts to know the issues that she should be certain to talk about with her family, although she'd probably not quote them at all. Then she'd need to follow the family through the weeks of unfolding contention and eventual resolution. She'd collect each person's narrative. While the family would be like blind people touching the elephant, Vobejda would see the whole elephant.

Eventually, something would happen, the matter would take a turn or even be resolved, and she would be there to see it happen. Vobejda would nudge this process along by bringing the family together for interviews that would encourage them to discuss matters they might normally not discuss. She'd ask questions from her knowledge of each person that the people themselves would never ask of each other.

If she had gone this route, her story would have been different. Not necessarily better, but different. It would have had the quality of a real-life short story being played out before our eyes. Readers would have lost the breadth of many examples and the authority of the experts' quotations, but readers would have gained in human depth, texture and evocation.

This kind of journalism requires, I believe, a somewhat different ethical stance for journalists. In classic journalism, it's the reader who is identified as what media ethicist Stephen Bates calls the "client"—the person the journalist is serving above those he is writing about and above those who employ him. That makes sense because the institution of American journalism is justified and protected by the First Amendment, which is meant to serve neither journalists nor subjects but the public interest. Yet when writing about the intimate lives of ordinary people, I believe journalists must adopt a hybrid ethical outlook closer to the one Bates says anthropologists use when writing about their normally ordinary subjects: "The anthropologist must do everything within his power to protect their physical, social and psychological welfare and to honor their dignity and privacy."

But unlike anthropologists, journalists usually use real names in their stories. The first ethical rule of intimate journalism is to be completely honest with your subjects about what kind of story you are writing. No ambush articles. The next rule is to explain to subjects the journalistic protocol of "on the record" and "off the record." Subjects who aren't used to dealing with reporters should be encouraged to go off the record whenever they wish, just as any politician would routinely do. But the final rule is still never to write a story that omits information to protect a subject if that information would alter a reader's basic interpretation of the published story. Sometimes, that can mean changing the focus of an article or even killing a story.

The difference between news features and intimate tellings is the difference between the humanized overview takeout on, say, mainstreaming handicapped children in the public schools and telling the in-depth story of one handicapped child who has been mainstreamed for the first time. It is the difference between the overview takeout on the growing girls' sports movement in America and telling the story of one girls' basketball team, as does Madeleine Blais's "In These Girls, Hope

Is a Muscle." It's the story of how one poor family lives, as told in Richard Ben Cramer's "How the World Turns in West Philadelphia."

One of the key choices in this kind of journalism is knowing when less is more—when leaving out the statistics, experts, the heavy-handed "so what" paragraphs helps the story. Years ago at the *Washington Post Magazine* I edited a story about legendary Florida Congressman Claude Pepper, who was in the final downhill slide of his remarkable political career. It was really a piece about a once-powerful man facing the loss of power and the end of his life. From scene to scene, you saw the bittersweet truth of life in Washington played out. But in the middle of this, we inserted a good 30 inches of biography and background. When I read it in print, I realized that I'd forgotten the prime directive of intimate journalism: Less is more.

In Barbara Vobejda's story, the Claude Pepper story, any intimate story, the decision about how to proceed must usually be made at the start. Because if we are reporting only Pepper's final days, all our time and energy and attention and space can go into that rendering. That's why the way we think about stories is so important. The way we think about them unalterably determines their final shape. This is the point where newspeople, often without knowing they are abandoning an intimate story, elect the news feature form, unwittingly rejecting the insight of Henry Adams, who said that understanding is "not a fact but a feeling."

The goal of intimate journalism is simple: It is to understand other people's worlds from the inside out, to understand and portray people as they understand themselves. Not the way they *say* they understand themselves but the way they really understand themselves. The way, as a subject once told me, you understand yourself "when you say your prayers in a quiet room."

It is the motivation of the anthropologist and the novelist, not the judgmental journalist or the self-righteous crusader. Stephen Crane once said that his only goal in writing *Maggie,* his novella about the life of a poor 19th-century girl, was to accurately describe her world. That is the goal.

A warning about attitude—your attitude.

As journalists, we are wise to be skeptics. But cynicism—the refusal to take anyone at face value—is crippling for those who aspire to do

intimate journalism. A better mental pose is suggested by novelist Amy
Tan in her book *The Joy Luck Club,* where she writes that a wise person
must learn "to lose your innocence but not your hope." Remind yourself
of that once a week, because human truths must be pursued with an
open heart. As journalists of a different cut, we shouldn't have to
apologize for that.

On Reporting . . .

It's hard to lay out a set of rules for intimate reporting, because it
comes in so many different forms. Gary Smith's "The Man Who Couldn't
Read," about the mindscape of the man hiding his illiteracy, is much
different from Mike Sager's article on crack users in Venice, California,
which is much different from David Finkel's "The Last Housewife in
America," which is much different from my own piece, "The Shape of
Her Dreaming," about how Rita Dove, former U.S. poet laureate, writes
a single poem. But the various forms and these selected articles still
share many reporting methods—and we must be ready to borrow from
them all.

Naturally, the basic rules of news journalism apply to intimate
journalism—facts must be correct and context must be fair and accurate. But when it comes to intimate journalism, there's a whole other
realm of "facts" that must be collected if we are to achieve our goals—if
we are to evoke the worlds of the people we are writing about, describe
people and places in enough documentary detail that they seem somehow indisputably real, evoke and describe the inner lives of our subjects,
capture a tone in which the reader can, we hope, momentarily forget
that this is a story and have the sensation of felt life happening before
his or her eyes.

It's important to remember that, although detail and dialogue and
graphic description are often important for their own sake in rendering
our stories, the meaning of our collected details in the minds of our
subjects, the interplay between detail and meaning, is still at the heart
of intimate journalism.

A Fortunate Man, by John Berger and Jean Mohr, is a book about the
day-to-day life of an English country doctor. It begins with the doctor
driving fast to the scene of an accident where a tree has fallen on a man,

and he is hurt severely. Several miles before the doctor gets there, he begins beeping his horn constantly. It can be heard all over the country-side and could be seen as a rural version of an ambulance siren. But the authors ask the next question, which is why is the doctor beeping his horn. The doctor says he's doing it because he believes the man pinned under the tree may hear it, know that the doctor is on his way, be filled with hope and thus hang on to life until the doctor can arrive.

Naturally, the doctor's motives tell us a great deal about the doc-tor—his sensitivity and empathy, his desire to grasp even the slimmest advantage in his effort to save a life. Yet it's easy to imagine any fairly good journalist describing that scene but missing its dramatic and fully subjective meaning by forgetting to ask the last simple and obvious question: What does it mean?

A great deal of the best intimate journalism reporting is spent trying to determine such meanings, trying to turn emotions and feelings and sensations into reportable "facts" that meet all the standards of jour-nalism. The more layers of complexity the better. If the man pinned under the tree were to live, for instance, the questions to ask him are whether he heard the doctor's horn and what he thought if he did? Was he conscious and filled with hope, as the doctor had imagined? Or was he unconscious and the doctor's effort went for naught? Or did he hear the horn but have no idea that the blare and the doctor were linked? These layers of human meaning aren't simply nice touches meant to make the providing of information more palatable to the reader. These layers of human meaning are the story itself.

As print journalists, we have been too much influenced by our fear that television is taking over our livelihoods, and we too often believe that the answer to TV and film competition is to simply "let the camera roll"—to capture more detail, scene and description in the fashion of a movie camera. We forget our great advantage—we can play the narrator, moving in and out of people's heads, telling our readers what things mean to our subjects. It's our edge and we should take full advantage of it. So if a policeman you are profiling has a doodad of some sort stuck to his dashboard, you can simply report it as a piece of "color" or you can ask him where he got it—perhaps it isn't even his, was there when he inherited the squad car. But perhaps it was a gift from his mother on her deathbed or a good-luck charm of an old partner who was killed in action. You just never know.

While once doing a story on a fundamentalist family, I asked the mother to walk me through her house and tell me where she got each item on display. As she gave me the tour, it became clear that she and her husband had bought nothing with an eye to decorating their home. Nearly all the knick-knacks on the shelves were gifts from people for whom they had done kindnesses. To simply have described these things as "status" details, as Tom Wolfe once called them, would have missed the point. Mark Kramer, a respected author and literary journalist, writes that "truth is in the details." A still deeper truth is in the meaning of the details.

Unlike in news reporting, in intimate reporting everything is a potential piece of data—and the problem is that you often can't know what will be important and what won't while you're reporting, so you've got to try and get it all. Much of it is obvious: You've got to collect details about the way, say, the homicide cop in my story "True Detective" looks and sounds—his hair color, eye color, shape of his nose and mouth, skin color and tone; where his wrinkles are when his face is in repose and where they are when he's smiling or frowning; how he talks, how fast, slang, pitch of voice, does it rise or drop when he gets afraid or angry.

At various points in intimate reporting, it's valuable to just stop whatever you're doing and jot such observations in your notes or dictate them into your tape recorder. But that's the easy part. Then comes the context in which your subject exists: What does the street where the murder victim is sprawled dead look like? Or what does the room where the suspect is being questioned look like? Unfortunately, you can't know what will be important and what will not be important until later, when your story has taken shape, so you must get as much down as you can.

There's a scene in "True Detective" about the nature of detective work, but it could have been written about intimate reporting: "The details seem trivial, but a homicide detective's life is a sea of details, a collage of unconnected dots gathered and collated. In the end, most will turn out to be insignificant. But at the time, a detective cannot know the revelatory from the inconsequential. He must try to see them all, then hold them in his mind in abeyance until the few details that matter rise forth from the ocean to reveal themselves"

When I jotted in my notes that a rat scurried along the sidewalk and then dove into the bushes as my detective returned to headquarters at dawn after having arrested a murderer, I didn't know that I would later use that rat diving for cover to symbolize the victory of good over evil.

So write down everything and anything.

Remember to collect, in the moviemaker's parlance, not only long shots but tight shots. My father was an amateur painter, and he used to tell me that there were two ways to paint a picture—one was to stand back and squint your eyes and see shapes and colors emerge in a beautiful blur, and the other was to get down on your knees and examine the flower, petal by petal.

It's important to think of the details you're gathering in that way, because there will be times when you'll want to capture and describe the sweep of things—the long shot, the dreamy and impressionistic vision at the crime scene. There also will be times when you'll want to stop the action for a tight shot and describe the scene before you in a precise and surgical manner, in a kind of anatomical detail—petal by petal. While collecting details, always try to keep these two later writing needs in mind.

Remember also to collect facts through all your senses. I have a hard time with this myself, and I admire people like Gary Smith, Madeleine Blais, Richard Ben Cramer, Mike Sager and Susan Orlean, who seem to do this effortlessly, while I must resort to craftsmen's tricks. I try to consciously keep a counter running in my head reminding me to note something from all my senses in important settings: What does the air smell like? What does the wind feel like on the skin? What is the touch of the murder weapon? What is the sound of the siren? What is the taste of the coffee?

In collecting such material, you must be methodical. I remember reading that John McPhee was once asked how he could possibly have known the temperature of the river water in which he was canoeing at exactly the precise instant he had reported it. McPhee explained that he had hung a thermometer on a string over the side of the canoe and that every once in a while he had pulled it up and recorded the water temperature at exactly that instant.

That's not an artist, but a craftsman, at work.

The most obvious reportorial aid for the intimate journalist, other than the pen and notebook, is the tape recorder. Although Gary Smith, Susan Orlean and David Finkel rarely use tape recorders, I and other writers find them indispensable when time allows for their use. For sit-down interviews, tape recorders are obviously helpful, not only for the gathering of long and correct quotations but because you inevitably hear subtleties on second listening that you don't hear in person. The tape recorder in sit-down interviews also frees you to take elaborate notes on a subject's appearance, mannerisms and voice and to record his or her facial expressions at specific times, as well as the movement of hands and arms, telling pauses, sighs, hesitations.

But where the tape recorder really makes its mark is in the creation of scenes. In "True Detective," it would have been impossible for me to describe the dialogue during police raids or on-the-scene police interviews with suspects if my tape recorder hadn't been poked right into people's faces. I couldn't have said the detective knocked on the door *nine* times or that he waited *five* seconds before he knocked again. Events are happening too fast to write it all down, even to take it all in. Certainly, events are happening too fast to accurately capture idiosyncrasies of speech and dialect. You also can dictate the details and events of a scene into your tape recorder much faster than you can make notes.

Another, less commonly used feature reporting aid, is the camera. When reading James Agee's *Let Us Now Praise Famous Men*, it seemed to me quite possible that some of his descriptions were actually descriptions of Walker Evans's accompanying photographs. When I read William Least Heat Moon's American travelogue, *Blue Highways*, I noticed that some of his scenic descriptions also seemed like descriptions of the photos in his book. Knowing the author was also a photographer, I realized it was possible that any number of beautifully turned scenes in *Blue Highways* might have been written with the help of his unpublished photographs.

Before this, I'd often gone to the photographers who'd shot my stories and examined their pictures, including outtakes, just to rekindle my feeling for the story before writing. But after *Blue Highways*, I realized there was no reason for me to wait for the photographer, that I could take my own not-for-publication snapshots, which I started doing. For my book, *Crossings: A White Man's Journey Into Black America*, I ended up taking more than 1,500 photographs, which turned out to be invaluable for recapturing not only the feeling of people and places but also the documentary details of dress, appearance and scene.

In "True Detective," a paragraph describes the dingy boardinghouse room of a murder victim, and a *Washington Post* colleague complimented me for its use of detail. Unfortunately, I had to admit that it wasn't my great powers of observation that had allowed me to capture the details of that room, but the snapshots I had examined with a magnifying glass long afterward.

Intimate journalism is often accomplished by leaving out this kind of ugly reporting substructure. In his book *Looking for the Light,* about the life of Depression-era photographer Marion Post Walcott, Paul Hendrickson has a chapter titled "Ode to an Instrument." It is two pages that describe and evoke the beauty of the old Speed Graphic camera, which Walcott used. When you read it, you think, "Lord, this man can write!" But it is the in-artful substructure—the reporting—that Hendrickson leaves out of his telling that makes the artful possible.

What Hendrickson doesn't mention is that he went to the Smithsonian Institution and got copies of the original catalogues and publicity literature on the Speed Graphic. Then he bought an old Speed Graphic so he could examine it, hold it, feel it, run through its complicated mechanical routine, hear its clicks and whirs. Then he found a photographer—the *Washington Post's* Bill Snead—who had actually used a Speed Graphic decades ago. Hendrickson had him recall what it was like to use the camera in the field. Watching and hearing Snead talk about the Speed Graphic with awe and respect, Hendrickson told me, "was like poetry." Yet none of this gritty, laborious craft is in his chapter.

There's no end to the craft you must hide: to say in passing that the farm house sits below a 900-foot bluff, you will swing by the county soil conservation office and get a copy of the farm's geological survey map. To say in passing that someone has a vase of Vivaldi roses in his apartment, you will spend an hour on the phone interviewing rose experts. You will go back to the scene of the crime the next day and walk off distances and check heights and angles. You will check maps to determine north, south, east and west. You will check decades-old weather reports to be sure it actually rained on the day someone says it rained.

You can be sure that Jon Franklin knew more than he reported in "Mrs. Kelly's Monster." He interviewed Mrs. Kelly, who was preparing to undergo dangerous brain surgery. He knew where Dr. Ducker, the brain surgeon, went to medical school. But little of this is in his story. You can be sure that Mike Sager wasn't as much the fly on the wall as his "Death in Venice" article about crack users makes him seem. He was asking questions, checking to see that it really was lint on the floor that the crack-heads kept reaching for. You can be sure that David Finkel, for "TV Without Guilt," got a lot of information from Mrs. Delmar by asking question after question about what later appears as Mrs. Delmar's thoughts. As Finkel told me, "We ask the most annoying questions."

And they are different questions. Under the rule of "you don't know what matters until you know what matters," you ask questions about everything—depending on the story—from "Do you believe in God?" to "Where did those little white spots on your shirt come from?" But this dual role of invasive inquisitor and invisible observer is a hard pose of mind to create in ourselves, because it requires that we relax completely and be completely alert at the same time. In psychiatrist and documentarian Robert Coles's book *The Call of Service,* there's a chapter about the methods he has learned to employ—and that's the key, learned to employ, because it takes years to do so. His goal is not only to get people to open up to him, as most reporters would say, but for him—Coles, the observer, the reporter—to be able to hear what people are saying.

This is where straight journalism's outlook of skepticism, even cynicism, comes into play, because the intimate journalist must find a different place—a different mental posture from which to work. This is not fancy philosophical debate but a tactical necessity. Coles was once an apostle of poet and physician William Carlos Williams, and he describes the way Williams entered the homes of his patients, back in the days when doctors entered the homes of their patients, and how Williams had a poet's methodology for gathering clues to the meanings of their lives.

"I try to put myself in the shoes of others," Williams said, mundanely enough. But then he went on: "We're completely lost in our own world—egoists! Or maybe we're locked into ourselves, and even though we want to break out, we can't seem to do it. It takes someone else to help us, a person who breaks in or has a way of letting us out. Or we stumble into some moment, some situation, that wakes us up, gets us enough off track to open up our eyes, our ears, our musty minds!"

Coles argues that Williams was unknowingly describing the task of the psychiatrist, sociologist and anthropologist—and, I'd add, the task of the intimate journalist. Coles asks, "How do we place our mind (and heart and soul) in a position—a place both literal and symbolic—that encourages our eyes and ears to pick up what we might otherwise miss?" He answers his question with a remark from Williams: "I'll go on my rounds, and some days I'm behaving like an automaton! . . . I'm as impatient as I can be with anyone who tries to get in my way. . . . On the right day, though, I'm all eyes and all ears. And I go even further—I stop myself in my tracks, and I talk to myself, and I say, 'Try to be a fly on the wall, or try to disappear into the crowd so you're not right smack in the middle of things, and people are responding to *you*,' because when that happens it doesn't always mean they're being *themselves* . . . !"

On those right days, Williams arrived at the tenement apartments of the poor in Paterson, New Jersey, with a different mental pose. Before entering, he wrote on his clipboard: "Things I noticed today that I've missed until today." After each house call, he added to his list—an unusual phrase a patient used, what the family was cooking, any new furniture, curtains or glassware, a newspaper article cut out and posted on the wall, playing cards or a game of checkers left on a table.

On those right days, Williams got down on the floor and let the children listen through his stethoscope to their own heartbeats and to his. He let them use his neurological hammer on his knees. He pulled out Hershey's Kisses, put them on the floor and let the children find the nerve to pick them up—and then he asked if he, too, might have just one or two for himself. He asked the children if they wanted to give *him* any advice. This ritual wasn't meant only to get his subjects to relax so that he—or we, as reporters—could maneuver and manipulate them into telling their secrets but to help Williams listen to and hear not only himself but the people around him, his subjects, his characters. Here are a few lines from "Paterson," the epic poem Williams eventually crafted from those random jottings on his clipboard:

> Plaster saints, glass jewels
> and those apt paper flowers, bafflingly
> complex—have here
> their forthright beauty, beside:
>
> Things, things unmentionable,
> the sink with the waste farina in it and
> lumps of rancid meat, milk-bottle-tops: have
> here a tranquility and loveliness . . .

To keep ourselves open to what is before us, we must not become too obsessed with asking ourselves, "What's the story here?"—and thus fall victim to the reporter's paranoia that we've got to produce something out of this mess and we better figure it out fast. That undermines our ability to grasp the story, because it means we'll inevitably fall back on well-worn themes and observations—interpretive cliches—and not give ourselves the time or frame of mind to see anything beyond that. Williams was trying to avoid that trap, to do a better job of collecting the human facts he needed to be a better doctor and a better poet.

That's why an intimate journalist must approach his or her subjects with an open heart. It's not a matter of hard or soft journalism but a matter of creating a place within ourselves—a "place our mind (and heart and soul)," as Coles writes, can see and hear what people are really saying. It's not a luxury but a necessary tactic of intimate journalism reporting, a mental posture at once arrogant and humble. In the words of documentary photographer Walker Evans, "It's as though there's a wonderful secret in a certain place and I can capture it. Only I, at this moment, can capture it, and only this moment and only me."

All of this, finally, ties into interviewing. Because all the detail and dialogue and scene will add up to froth without some human heft behind them. That comes from interviewing. The most obvious difference between straight news and intimate interviewing is that in intimate interviewing you try to avoid the idea that the story *is* the interview. Many subjects, especially those written about before, will think this.

It's necessary to break that expectation by making your subjects realize you expect far more from them in return for a story that will do far more. I usually exaggerate what it will take from subjects just so I know they are committed to the job. I make it clear that an intimate story is a cooperative project between reporter and subject and it can't be done without a subject's enthusiastic involvement. I try to define their role as one of helping me to tell the story. In the case of the homicide detective, you would make it clear that you expect to ride in the cop car, eat what he eats, stay out all night when he stays out all night, interview his friends and family, as well as sit down and do formal interviews with him.

My own preference is that sit-down interviews occur before you get very far into the reporting. I try not to think of these as interviews but as conversations. I never have a list of questions but usually start out with, "So where were you born?" My goal is to let people simply ramble on about their personal histories and see where it goes, because you just don't know yet what's important. Cast a wide net. See what rises forth.

It's important to remember that a lot of detail in stories also comes from interviews—in the form of anecdotes. But to make these anecdotes fit the documentary feel of the material you are gathering in contemporaneous scenes, it's necessary to do a kind of invasive interviewing—stopping the subject often and asking him or her the year or day some event occurred, perhaps the time of day, the weather that day. You have to fill in the material that you will need to make an anecdote into a scene.

After a couple of rambling interviews, the themes of a subject's life often emerge. It was in these interviews that the homicide detective talked about how he was for the first time afraid on the streets, how he now felt out of his element with the new brand of criminals, how he was being torn apart emotionally by the murders and murderers he was confronting daily, how sometimes he even broke down and wept as he rode home late at night. But in the story, this information is woven into the narrative so it seems as if the subject is thinking it at that point in the story.

In intimate interviewing, it's often important not to ask a question only once and let it go at that but to ask the same questions over and over in different ways at different times. You will be *writing* your story, not just quoting your subjects, and to fill out the depth of their attitudes and beliefs you must go back again and again. Often you will glean a new insight each time.

In interviewing and in spending time with your subjects, I suggest you be yourself—if you don't like blood, admit to the cops that you don't like blood and let them laugh at you. Make yourself a real person, talk about your background, your friends, your wife or husband, kids, father and mother. This is strictly my intuition, but I think people are more open with those who are being open with them, that people are more willing to show their vulnerabilities to those who reveal their own vulnerabilities.

Try to use your emotional experiences as a vehicle for unlocking those of your subjects. If you're a mother interviewing a woman about having had a baby, share the emotions you felt in childbirth to spur her recall of her own emotions. If you're doing the Delmars, share the memories you have of watching TV as a child to help Mrs. Delmar recall her own memories. The key is to always maintain a natural tone, to be yourself, to be genuine.

One of the hardest things to do is to remember that, if you are to later write your story as a narrative, you must discover or create threads that will help move your story through to a conclusion. This is separate from a story moving through time, as in a day or a week in the life of someone. You must also look for ideas and tone-setting scenes that you will later pull like threads through your story. In the case of Mike Sager's piece on crack, it's the beginning scene in the youth's bedroom that is brought back around at the end, the novel idea that these kids were better off before crack when they were killing each other in gang retaliations and the surprising twist that even Big Gato, who hates that the young guys have lost their pride, will succumb to crack. In Jon Franklin's piece on the brain surgeon, he repeats the exact time and the constant "pop, pop, pop" of the heart monitor.

Finally, before you start writing, try to take time to find a work of fiction or artful nonfiction that helps you get in the right frame of mind for writing your story. For "True Detective," I read mystery novels, which made me recognize the gritty, tactile feel I wanted my story to evoke. For "When Daddy Comes Home," I read Doris Lessing's novel *A Good Neighbor,* one of the few books that eloquently describes the horror and perilous dignity of old age. For "The Shape of Her Dreaming," I re-read Alan Lightman's *Einstein's Dreams,* which so beautifully captures the precise yet dreamy sensation I hoped to capture in my story.

Remember that imitation is flattery and that James Agee borrowed and changed the poetry of Hart Crane to describe the pages of his sharecropper's family Bible as "leaves almost weak as snow."

Remember that most artful journalism is craft.

And that most artful journalists are craftsmen.

On Writing . . .

The poet and novelist Ishmael Reed says, "Writin' is fightin'." I'd also add that writing is thinking. Because the greatest challenge for any artful journalist is to get his or her mind wrapped around a story before beginning to write, and then to keep control of the material at the same time the material is allowed to take on a life of its own, to shape itself, emerge in the process of writing—in the same way that poet Rita Dove tries to listen to what her poem is telling her as she is writing it. As the afterword remarks of the writers collected here show, you won't know what you think about a story entirely until after you've written it—or, sometimes, until it has written itself. In stories that are supposed to evoke the sensation of felt life, it's necessary for the writer to first feel the story before he or she can make other people feel it. When Paul Hendrickson said that hearing and watching Bill Snead describe the Speed Graphic camera was like poetry, he was feeling his story. He wasn't trying only to think his way through his story.

Sitting down to write is probably when the only smidgen of magic in intimate journalism really comes into play. It's the one place—other than a required natural ability to be comfortable and relaxed with all sorts of people—where craft takes a momentary backseat to the role of intuition, your intuition. Sitting down to write is at once the hardest and the most exhilarating part of what we do. Nothing is scarier than staring at a blank screen and trying to see your way through all the junk you've collected to find not a lead but a story. It's a moment of supreme arrogance, because it's when you sit down and decide what you have to say—what you'll put in, leave out, emphasize or downplay.

It really is an act of creation.

I've mentioned the need to get yourself into a frame of mind that helps you conceptualize and report stories, and finding the proper frame of mind may be even more important in writing. Let's say that you've imagined your story and that you've reported it, keeping in mind and trying to gather—depending upon the story—scenes, physical detail, dialogue and emotional facts gleaned through in-depth interviewing. I've mentioned the importance of keeping in mind during reporting what might end up being the theme or themes of your story and watching for devices that might serve to bring resolution to the tensions that people in your stories are facing. Now you've got to select your themes and your tensions.

To help do this, you've got to step outside the mind-set of straight reporting. I suggest you stay at home one morning, pour a cup of coffee, put on classical music or gentle jazz, whatever your preference, sit down in a comfortable chair, stack all your notes to one side. On top of one legal pad, jot the word "themes" and atop another write "facts, quotes and details to use." Then start reading your notes, your transcripts of interviews, anything else you've collected—read from start to finish. List under "facts, quotes and details" what you're pretty sure you'll use.

As possible themes strike you, write them down. Remember that the best themes are simple themes: basketball as a stand-in for war as the symbolic male act in Crow culture in Gary Smith's "Shadow of a Nation" or the beauty of one's life reflected perfectly in the life of another in Jeanne Marie Laskas's "Each Other's Mirror." The eternal verities are, well, eternal.

Now, this may sound a little wacky, but as you read, try to let the material wash over you in the way, if you happen to be Catholic, that a Christmas midnight mass might wash over you. Or, if you are a mother or father, in the way that rocking your child to sleep late at night in a dark and quiet house might wash over you. Or, if you are a lover of jazz, in the way that hearing Sarah Vaughan live at Washington, D.C.'s Blues Alley amid the cigarette smoke and the clinking of ice in whiskey glasses might wash over you. Make a sensory and emotional connection with your story.

Search for "felt life." If you have taken photographs, examine them with a magnifying glass—look at how people fold their hands, at the books on their shelves, at the expressions on their faces. If you have borrowed your subject's photo album, take a few minutes to study the pictures. If you have collected private letters, read them—and examine the handwriting, the twirling flourishes or the staid block lettering. Imagine your subject writing them. Whatever you feel when you are going through this ritual—sadness, joy, a bittersweet blending of both, anger, affection, disgust, whatever—try to get that feeling in your story. Try to envision the tone that grows out of the feeling, because it's likely that tone is fitting to your subject—pure joy, pure sadness, bittersweet emotions, a slow and gentle or a wild and raucous voice. Then try to write your story in that tone.

I once did a profile of actress Kelly McGillis as she went through the process of creating a Shakespearean character for the stage, and while doing the article I learned something about what I do as a journalist that had never gelled for me. In following her, as she let herself go and tried to become her character, as she searched within herself for emotions that she could use to imbue her character with emotion, as she finally tried to forget all the self-conscious tricks of technique and craft and methodology and enter into an intuitive frame of mind with herself and her subject, I was struck by how similar McGillis's needs and methods were to my needs and methods in trying to portray her.

When I wrote that on stage at her best she was like a child at prayer, like Faulkner in conversation with his characters, like Joe DiMaggio at bat—at that place where intuition resides—I was drawing on my own less profound but real enough experience of feeling as if I'm off somewhere else, not exactly here, when the writing is going well. It's a bush league version of what I feel when I read, say, Cormac McCarthy's novels, *Blood Meridian, All the Pretty Horses* or *The Crossing*: When I read McCarthy's books I have the strongest feeling that McCarthy isn't with us when he's writing, as if he's crossed over and entered some ethereal domain—the place where intuition resides.

While doing the McGillis story, I took to joking about "method journalism," after her method acting. But in the joke, I was half serious. I'm not sure you can do memorable intimate journalism if you aren't the kind of person who becomes obsessed with your story as you reach the writing stage—if you don't think about it unwillingly when you should be thinking of other things, if you don't dream about it at night, if you don't do the right-brain, left-brain crossover. I don't believe for a minute that this is any kind of gift. It's simply an emotional and cognitive dimension of our craft. Just as working from what I called an open heart is a necessary tactic of intimate journalism, this method journalism is a tactic to get in touch with your material.

In his book *Solitude,* about the links between solitude and creativity, psychiatrist Anthony Storr talks about the role mental "incubation" plays in creativity—it's a kind of simmering that takes place in our brains after all the reading and studying and that occurs not only consciously but unconsciously. All the writers in this collection talk about how important it is that they take time after their reporting is done to let their material simmer. Storr says that time is a necessary prelude to creative "illumination"—the instant when people suddenly see clearly what was unclear before, when they're hit with that flash of insight. I'm talking about trying to create for ourselves a preparatory writing ritual and a frame of mind that maximize the chance that insight will befall us, so that our minds will, even unconsciously, connect the seemingly unconnected dots in the story before us.

After trying to soak up all your material, you'll still find sometimes that nothing will come out of your head. At those times, sit down and read sections from favorite books or articles that capture a tone similar to the one you hope to capture, to get yourself in the mood. The African American painter Allen Stringfellow once said, "I work by music—religious music when I'm doing religious things and jazz when I'm doing jazz pieces. They arouse in me the same inner feelings. They're both inspiring." One of Kelly McGillis's acting coaches once taught her to listen quietly to Chopin before she came on stage to perform particularly difficult scenes—to let the music help unlock her intuition, to put her in the mood, to inspire her.

Read these lines from Jeanne Marie Laskas's story on the twins: "Isobel and Betty wear identical clothes, hairdos, eyeglasses, wristwatches. They are pretty women with deep chocolate eyes, black cherry hair and creamy complexions; distinguishing between the two is not easy, at first. After a while, though, you might notice that Isobel has a slightly narrower face, a slightly tilted smile, and that Betty often holds her hands on her hips, that Isobel often fluffs up her puffed sleeves, and then, later, you might graduate to the finer details: Isobel has a glimmer of irony in her eyes, a way of twisting the world into a wholly humorous place. Betty is innocent, soft. Isobel is Lucy Ricardo. Betty is Ethel Mertz."

Or these lines from Richard Ben Cramer's "How the World Turns in West Philadelphia": "In the dark living room, Mrs. Monroe called to Rusty . . . She held her arms out to him and he climbed onto her, wrapping his arms tightly around her neck . . . Fifteen minutes later, a bleach commercial threw a shaft of bright white across the room and for a moment lit Mrs. Monroe's face as it leaned lightly against her child's warm head, her brow smooth, her lips just parted, her eyes, like his, now closed."

Or these lines from my own "When Daddy Comes Home": "The reverend sits in a tall, flowered wing chair . . . He crosses his thin left leg over his right leg at the knee, adjusts his wooden cane against his side, plants his elbows on the chair's armrests and steeples his fingers. He rubs his palms together softly, barely touching, then plays with the change in his pocket. For a moment, he taps his cane with the nail of his finger, then lightly rubs his thigh with his right palm. He does not squirm, but rather makes each move with a methodical, self-conscious elegance. He holds his hands at his chest and rubs them together slowly, as if working lotion into his skin. The hands are large, with long, expressive fingers that curl upward after their middle joints. On the bridge of each hand is a spider web of wrinkles that seems to record his many years like the rings of an old tree. But his palms are as smooth and glassy as pebbles drawn from a running creek."

Read. I promise. It will put you in the mood.

With all this done in anywhere from a few hours on a small story to a few days on a huge story, try one last metaphysical trick before getting down to the rock-breaking job of writing. Sit down at the computer, put up your feet, close your eyes, think about your story and see what flashes to mind. Far more often than not, whatever image or scene I see at that instant turns out to be my lead. I tell myself that the flashing image is me talking to myself, that whatever flashes in my head after all the hard work is probably the strongest single image I've got to offer.

Sadly, that's where the magic ends and craft again takes over. Everybody does it differently. David Finkel elaborately indexes his notes and then tacks all the pages up on the wall over his desk. Susan Orlean must write her story through from beginning to end, her first draft nearly her last draft. Jeanne Marie Laskas will write a middle section, then the end, then the beginning—then she'll move them all around. Richard Ben Cramer will sometimes write for days before he finally sees the story he wants to write. As for me, I never know where my story is going until the lead and foreshadowing sections are written. Then I briefly outline and jot down ideas or images I'll want to come back around on before the end of the story. But however you do it, you have to *write* your story—get in the flow of it. Don't stop and spend half an hour digging out a fact or a quote when you are on a roll. Get it later. Keep writing, trying to find the rhythm of your story.

So much of what we do now is the carrying out of the assumptions we made during reporting—write in scenes, don't run from quote-to-information, quote-to-information, don't quote for quote's sake. Keep out tangential quotes and characters that lend only traditional authority. Usually, be aware of moving your story through time through your scenes—and, as Mark Kramer has written, tell the rest of your story as digression.

Introduce tensions early that will be resolved by the end. If possible, let your subjects seem to gain insight and self-awareness in the course of your story. This sounds impossible, but with proper in-depth interviewing it happens much of the time. Of course, it won't just happen if you haven't anticipated and chronicled this growth or change while reporting.

Sometimes resolution is real, and sometimes it is an imposed dramatic device. In Madeleine Blais's "Zepp's Last Stand" the resolution is obviously real—the old guy wins his honorable discharge. But if he hadn't, Blais still would have found a way to bring dramatic closure to her story—perhaps she would have argued that by not getting his name cleared, Mr. Zepp continued to have a reason to live. In David Finkel's "TV Without Guilt" nothing is resolved, but you have the feeling of resolution, of a turning-point insight, when Finkel reveals Mrs. Delmar's deep fears of life beyond TV—the tip of all she is perhaps keeping at bay. Always remember: Scene, detail and narrative bring a story to life, while theme and meaning imbue it with a soul.

The best journalism stories—intimate or otherwise—have ideas that organize and drive them, that make sense of the material and that give us a scale for measuring the significance of various facts and details, a scale for weighing their importance in the story, for even deciding what to use or what not to use in your story. Remember the words of Cormac McCarthy in *The Crossing*: "For this world also which seems to us a thing of stone and flower and blood is not a thing at all but is a tale . . . All is telling. Do not doubt it." A story should be like a funnel—it begins at the wide end raising questions and inexorably leads the reader through a narrowing passage to insights and conclusions. The best story is a subtle argument. By its end, readers should be convinced.

There are, naturally, craftsmen's tricks:

Pacing. Especially in longer stories, it's often necessary to speed up or slow down the pacing from section to section, the way a roller coaster ride is arranged with slow climbs followed by wild descents. A scene moves gently and poetically—followed by digression, followed by a scene that zips along.

Remember to shift from long shots, sweeping impressionistic descriptions, to tight shots in which you stop-action, freeze-frame in the way that the camera slowly shows us the sled named Rosebud in *Citizen Kane*, in the way that James Agee describes a line of mules with precise grace in *Let Us Now Praise Famous Men:* "The mules loiter in a hooved muck of tattered water in a tract of brownlighted shadow slivered with sun, a sapling grove licked leafless within their reach, the trunks rubbed slick: very naked-looking and somehow shy without harness, as if they had not quite the right to nature, they stand, they drift, they wait, they glide, and lift back their cynical heads like flowers as the men who master their days lift open the gate and advance toward them."

Voice. It is the hardest thing to talk about because I fear that people must find whatever is their own natural voice. Different stories demand different tones, but unifying that difference is always a writer's own natural voice. My voice tends dangerously close to the melodramatic. David Finkel's tends toward gentle irony. Madeleine Blais's is gentle and a touch fantastic. Mike Sager's is hip and edgy. Gary Smith's is like a whisper.

The challenge is to mesh your voice with your story. The only practical suggestion I have for that—other than trial and error—is to read, not necessarily deeply but widely, being on the lookout for the kind of voice that speaks to you. When I was young, for instance, I admired the *New Yorker* and the John McPhees of the world for their method. But their voice, that casual, distanced voice, which I believe implies that we can think our way to understanding and insight, just left me cold while the more dramatically structured, visual and emotional journalism of *Esquire* spoke to me. You have to find your own path.

Think of your stories as pieces meant to be read out loud. Nothing can reveal the flaws in a story quicker than reading it out loud to yourself—looking for words that don't roll off the tongue, rhythms that clash, cliches that must be rephrased, language that is encrusted with the made-up words of bureaucrats and social scientists, attributions that give long, meaningless job titles instead of conversational descriptions such as "she runs the place," interest-group words such as "hearing-impaired" or "visually challenged," touching human stories that call people by their *last* names, ages given as if from a police blotter—"Little Joe Blow, nine, found his mother dead in a dumpster late last night."

Try to use implied attribution. When you've reconstructed dialogue that two participants confirm—or if one guy's dead and his remarks aren't controversial—leave out the attribution. When you have events that are undisputed among several participants, write these events as scenes without attribution. Whenever you can, layer in material that doesn't come from subjects but from your reporting—the temperature on the day little Joe Blow found his mother's body in the dumpster or the color of the dumpster or the width of the alley that holds the dumpster.

When possible, write from inside the heads of your characters. This often means turning long quotes from subjects into your own prose. Remember to try to keep your subjects talking to each other or seeming to think their quotes, rather than having them make their remarks to you, the reporter, unless you're a character in the story—as Pete Earley is a character in "Missing Alice" and as Susan Orlean is in "The American Man at Age 10." This helps ground a story within itself, creating a world readers can enter and where they can become momentarily lost.

Try to embellish your facts to help set an interpretive and poetic tone in your piece—not by changing the facts but by giving them an occasional tweak. You can say the sky is blue—or you can say the sky is so blue it looks as if it's going to disappear into itself. Or you can say the sky is so blue it looks somehow unreal, like a painted dome. Or take a trick from nature writer Edward Abbey who will say a flower or a cactus looks "like a swan" or "like a maiden"—or he'll add a touch of interpretive, personifying life to a sentence by describing a certain vegetable as "humble." Or as Madeleine Blais describes Edward Zepp's 83 years: "He is at the age of illness and eulogy." But remember that if this isn't your thing, nothing is necessarily lost: As Mark Kramer has written, literary journalism is defined by a "plain and spare" style, meaning a little flourish can go a long way.

Remember, reading is still the key to finding your voice, style and manner: classic nonfiction books, classic magazine literary journalism, naturalistic novels and short fiction, first-person memoirs and oral histories, documentary writing, nature writing and travel literature—all of which employ in different ways the approaches and techniques I've mentioned.

But don't read only for tone or voice but also to de-construct how Smith, Blais and Finkel do what they do. Before writing "The Shape of Her Dreaming," I re-read Madeleine Blais's "In These Girls, Hope Is a

Muscle." I didn't want my readers to be reminded that Rita Dove was talking to me, the reporter. I wanted to create the illusion that she was thinking this story out loud. So I studied how Blais had managed to quote her subjects with almost no attribution—as in "she says" or "he says"—and realized she had introduced most of her quotes with colons, allowing her to eliminate the attributions. I shamelessly cribbed the technique.

Don't read stories; study them. How did he get that particular piece of information? How did she use dialogue to break up runs of information? How did he combine quotation and description? When you read Cormac McCarthy's fiction, ask how you could report his scenes as nonfiction. In *All the Pretty Horses,* McCarthy has a hauntingly simple scene set at a rural Mexican barn dance: "At the band's intermission they made their way to the refreshment stand and he bought two lemonades in paper cones and they went out and walked in the night air . . . The air was cool and it smelled of earth and perfume and horses . . . They sat on a low concrete watertrough and, with her shoes in her lap and her naked feet crossed in the dust, she drew patterns in the dark water with her finger."

As an intimate journalist, ask yourself: Where would I have had to be physically to have reported McCarthy's barn dance scene as a piece of journalism? What techniques would it have taken for me to have become the third-person, nonfiction narrator and tell the same story? What details would I have had to collect? What would I have had to see, hear, smell? Which conversations could I have overheard and which could I have later reconstructed in interviews? In short, read to beg, borrow and steal.

A Final Thought . . .

If you yearn to do this kind of journalism, I suggest you demand it—of your newspapers and magazines, editors and reporters—but mostly of yourselves. That's what's so empowering about print journalism. You don't need elaborate equipment—no lights or cameras or sound booms. You don't need great resources—no grants or big advances. You often don't even need permission from The Powers That Be. You can go and assign the story. Or if you're a reporter, you can go report and write the story. Each time you do, the depth of response from your readers will amaze you, your confidence will grow and you will want to do it again because this kind of journalism is simply closer to human truth than what most journalists do. You will feel that closeness when you accomplish it. And once felt, you'll want to feel it again and again.

Read these stories. Then go see for yourself.

Gary Smith

Gary Smith has worked as a reporter for the *New York Daily News* and *Inside Sports*. In 1983, he joined *Sports Illustrated*. He has written for *Esquire, Rolling Stone* and *Life*. His stories have been nominated four times for the National Magazine Award for feature writing. His story "Shadow of a Nation" won that award in 1991. He lives in Charleston, South Carolina.

The Man Who Couldn't Read

Slowly, so the bed wouldn't creak, the millionaire who couldn't sleep rose and walked barefoot to the bookshelves. "Tonight," he whispered to himself. "Please let it happen tonight." He turned on the lamp. His eyes moved past the two framed rectangles of glass on the wall—past his college diploma, past his teaching certificate—and fell upon the book cover, the one filled by the angry black face. He stared into the rage and hurt in the author's eyes. He moved his fingers across the title, *Soul on Ice*. This man understands, the millionaire thought. This man, too, is a prisoner, an outsider; maybe this man will help me tonight. His thumb riffled the pages. Don't force it, he told himself. This man is screaming, this man writes words that jump into your ears and eyes; just stand here, very calmly, and let them come in. . . .

All his life? Is that how long he would have to play this game? He lay back down in bed and looked at his wife. No one else knew his secret. Not his two children, not his friends. Not his old college professors, not the high school students he had taught for 18 years, not the business associates in his multimillion-dollar real-estate-development company in Southern California. Only Kathy knew. They would take everything if they found out—the diploma and teaching certificate, the apartment complexes and shopping centers and rental properties, the Mercedes and the big house overlooking the ocean. Or they'd refuse to believe his secret, insist he was playing them for fools.

None of them understood what night sweat could do to a man. If he needed one badly enough, was there *any* charade a man couldn't play? John remembered a spring day back in fourth grade, back when the realization that he would be forever different from everyone else had begun to come over him. He had run out of class at 3:00 p.m., aching for some arena in which to prove he wasn't really the boy who sat at his desk, stupid and silent as a stone, and then had felt his legs moving toward the school's ball field, even though he was too young to play. Standing behind the batting cage with his glove on his hand, he watched the game with hungry eyes, noticing that neither team wore uniforms and there was no outfield fence, and how the big kid on the other school's team belted the ball over the right fielder's head his first two times up. Now there were two outs, the bases loaded, the big kid at the plate again, and John felt himself moving slowly, silently, out to deep right field. Then—*crack!*—the ball was arcing across the sky, and boys all over the field were shouting and running . . . and suddenly John Corcoran could feel it, snug and stinging inside the glove on his left hand! And the umpire signaled *out!* and all the players on his school's team were racing toward the bench and he was racing with them, heart thumping with excitement and fright—he was *in* the game now, how could he possibly get out? He kept stealing looks at the manager and the boys, waiting for them to call his bluff, to send him home. "You bat third this inning," barked the manager; he walked to the plate as if in a dream. Three fastballs hissed by him—*"Strike three!"* roared the ump—yes, there it was, the story of John Corcoran's life. He could play the part, trick the enemy, infiltrate the game. But at midnight, the moment of truth—then the millionaire stood alone in his pajamas with a book in his hands. . . .

Why hadn't he just refused to play? Why hadn't he just shoved away their books and diplomas and white-collar, upper-class dreams? Even now, at 52, he couldn't quite understand why he had stayed in a classroom for 35 years, why he had gone back for 80 more credits *after* he had graduated from college; why he hadn't fled academia the moment he had stolen his passport, received his degree. Like a Jew in Nazi Germany, he'd say, who gets off of a boxcar heading for the concentration camp—

and then gets back on. Crazy, he'd say, shaking his head. An absolutely crazy thing to do for a man who couldn't read or write.

That's how he spoke and thought, all analogy and metaphor, all intuition and unfinished sentences, sometimes bewildering, sometimes brilliant; the left side of his brain, the cool, logical lobe a man uses to arrange symbols in a sequence, had always seemed to misfire. Some words, in an obvious context, he had learned to memorize and master— STOP on a street sign, EXIT over a doorway—but tuck them into the middle of a sentence and they mocked him. Letters traded places, vowel sounds lost themselves in the tunnel of his ears . . . and yet. . . . His blue eyes fill with tears and his Adam's apple climbs up his throat a lot these days. If only someone had sat next to that little boy, put an arm around his shoulder and said, "I know you can't read, John. It won't be easy, but I'll help you. Don't be scared, it's going to be okay"—then he could have learned.

Instead, in second grade, in Santa Fe, New Mexico, they put him in the dumb row. Stubborn little brat. Just sits there when you ask him to read or write a sentence. We'll cure that. Open your hands, John. Open your hands! The ruler smacked against his palms. That'll teach him to read. His third-grade nun handed a yardstick to the children when John refused to read or write, ordered him to roll up his pants and let each student in his row have a crack.

Which was worse, he wonders now sometimes, the stinging flesh . . . or the never-ending silence? That was how his fourth-grade teacher had tried to cure him, by asking him to read and then letting one minute of quiet pile upon the next and the next until the little boy thought he must suffocate. And then passed him on to the next grade and to the next teacher. John Corcoran never failed a year in his life.

His parents? Perhaps they wondered why their son would arrange to have one of his sisters read the Community Chest cards in Monopoly. Or maybe his parents' search for a place to belong sucked all the time and energy for wondering out of them. Somewhere, they would find it, somewhere these two orphans who had married would find home. Somewhere, somehow, in St. Louis or Springfield or Santa Fe, in Amarillo or Abilene or Albuquerque, in Los Alamos or Roswell or Ajo or Parker or Blythe or Encinitas or just by moving to the other side of town, they would refind the magic of the days when they dated, back when he was a center for the Minneapolis Red Jackets professional football team and she was a Chicago fashion model. Pack up the six kids. Pack up the U-Haul trailer. The world would be a better place in the next town, and the next, and the next. By the time he graduated from high school, John had lived in 35 houses and attended 17 schools.

His dad was a teacher and a coach. He consumed words as if they were food: two newspapers a day and *Gone With the Wind* in a single sitting one night. How could a boy explain to a dad like him his nausea each Friday morning before the weekly spelling test, how could he say to him, "Dad, I can't read"? His father was always on the run, coming home at 6:00 p.m. from football or baseball practice, scrambling up some eggs for his five girls and little boy, running off to a second job teaching night school or selling cars or insurance. His mom had an asthmatic daughter on her mind or on her knee half the day, then rushed off at 3:00 p.m. to work the late shift at the local drugstore. They would go without furniture or new clothes or a Christmas tree, then rent a house for twice what they could afford, so that their children would grow up in the right neighborhoods, so that their dream, at least, would have the proper shingles and floorboards and beams.

That was the gift, and the curse, they gave to their little boy who couldn't read. An injustice? A lousy paycheck? Don't sit there. Take a night course. Reach for the stars. Head west. The Corcorans are winners, the Corcorans don't settle for second best. You break the news to your mother this time, John—it's a much better job, no way a man can turn it down. God knows, nobody wanted her to feel the way she did that day back in '45, when John was eight. That day Franklin Roosevelt died, and she looked around and saw her life once more packed up in cardboard boxes, and she cried, "Why don't we just turn on the gas?"

Sometimes, when the car was loaded and the kids were wedged in and another town was receding behind them, his sisters laughed and called themselves Irish Okies. Sometimes they cried. Not John, though. Each town was a new place to start over, to infiltrate the game. Who knew? Maybe the light would be different in Albuquerque or Los Alamos, maybe the letters wouldn't switch places and swim. Maybe he could stop beating his head against his pillow at night and promising to say a rosary to God every day from now to kingdom come in exchange for a miracle; maybe in the next town he could *read.*

He entered junior high. It was no longer a game. Now it was war, John Corcoran against the literate world. Now he had to change classes for each subject, to hide his secret from six teachers instead of one. All those dumb rows and yardsticks and awful silences, all those moves from town to town had taught him a few tricks, of course. How to read a human being and smell warmth or danger, how an illiterate with two good fists, a quick wit and a handsome smile could adapt and survive. No longer could he sit at his desk and wait for the humiliation to come—the stakes had grown too high now, the shame too steep. He had to walk into a classroom and size it up in a heartbeat, he had to somehow *influence* the people and the atmosphere inside it, he had to take control. *This* teacher, *this* subject, *this* school, what strategy would work best? Sit in the front row, clean the erasers, become the teacher's pet? Slink toward the back of the room and look for someone wearing glasses to cheat off? Or choose a seat in the middle, remain pleasant, silent, become the invisible man? Quickly, John, make a decision. Which teachers to talk sports with, which to stare down, which to act so goddamn crazed in front of that they would be afraid to call his name. "Don't laugh at John," a ninth-grade teacher ordered her class. "There's something wrong with him." *Yes, there is, there is!* he wanted to scream. Instead, he stood and walked like a spastic across the room, threw them far off the scent, grinned as everyone roared. Couldn't any of them *see*? He yearned to be his church's altar boy, but he couldn't read the prayers; he longed to be his school's crossing guard, but they dismissed him for poor grades; he ached to be the all-American boy, not the class clown or the discipline problem. But any label was better than the dreaded one, the unspeakable one: *He can't even read!*

Manipulate. He never liked that word. It sounded cruel, it sounded evil—my God, he was just a frightened teenager with raging hormones trying to get by. *Orchestrate.* That was better. Orchestrating girls to help him write essays. Orchestrating pals to read him the math problem or whisper the instructions for the next assignment in typing class. What's wrong, Corky, can't you read? they would ask in jest now and then. "*Duhhhhh* . . . no . . . I can't read," he would say, his jaw hanging stupidly, making them laugh. His senior year of high school, he would be voted homecoming king, go steady with the valedictorian and star on a basketball team en route to the state championship game . . . only to have to move 60 miles away at midseason.

He would never say, "Read this for me," when he needed to know what was written on a page. "What does this mean to you?" he would say, or "What do they want here?" He wouldn't say, "Write this for me," when he needed to turn in a paper. He'd say, "Let's work on this together," start pacing and thinking out loud, leave his buddy sitting there with the paper and the pen. No one felt orchestrated by John. No one felt used. He would pick you to play on his team even if everyone knew you were a clod, present your case to a pretty girl, stand by your side in a fight. And before you knew him well enough to catch the fear in his eyes, he was packed and gone.

In 10th grade, he made the conscious decision. He would bury his shame forever, play out the masquerade, never let down his guard. Keep watching from the edge of his eye when the others were reading silently in class, to see when he should turn the page. Scribble something, *anything,* inside his notebook when the others were taking notes, mimic even their facial expressions, then cover his page so no one would see. Stare down at his right hand, make sure again and again he hadn't fallen back into his bad habit of holding his pen between his third and fourth fingers. One mistake could be fatal. Any moment, any corner he turned, who knew what threat might arise? "Try again, John. You're sure you can't see that letter on the screen?" the eye doctor asked when he was in 11th grade.

(Yes, of course I can see it, I just don't know what letter it is!) "Uh . . . no sir, I'm sorry . . . I can't." That was how John got his first pair of glasses.

His mom kissed him when he graduated. And kept talking about college. His 52-year-old dad took a job as a hotel night clerk in order to attend summer school for a California teaching credential; morning sessions at San Diego State, afternoons at the University of San Diego. Well, why not, John? Reach for the stars, son, you can be anything you want; education, that's the key. These were his role models, people who never doubted the American Dream, no matter how deftly it dodged them—it was always just a few more credits or miles away.

But . . . *college?* March right into the belly of the beast? He was 6′ 4″, could dunk a basketball, had been selected All-Conference and offered a scholarship by the University of Wyoming—but no, it would be *insane* to consider, pure suicide.

But . . . what about junior college? He spent a year and a half at Riverside Community College, in California; then one semester at Palos

Verdes, sat next to the right girls, stole the right answers, smiled the right smiles and somehow survived. Cheating? Was it really cheating? His mind grasped concepts quickly, understood math intuitively; he was smarter than half the damn kids in the room, willing to work twice as hard—should he be shut out just because a couple of wires in his brain were crossed? The University of Texas at El Paso (then Texas Western) offered him a basketball scholarship. His spirits soared. His heart sank. He was *in* the game now, how could he possibly get out?

He took a deep breath, closed his eyes . . . and recrossed enemy lines. Welcome to campus, John—how 'bout a beer? He would take the can, walk into the bathroom, empty it in the sink and refill it with water. No, the stakes were too high now, not even a sip, not even for a second could he afford to lose control. His eyes roamed every room he entered, searching for the newspaper or magazine or pen that could betray him, the nitpicker that could trip him up, the escape hatch he could use to slip away. He quizzed each new friend: Which teachers required papers, which gave essay tests, which gave multiple choice? He studied the seating configurations and the faces in every classroom: Which students might slip him an answer, which might squeal? (Wrinkles, always sit behind people with wrinkles—older students were most likely to rat.) He registered for seven classes a semester, dropped the two most difficult during the 6-week grace period. The minute he stepped out of a class, he tore the pages of scribble from his notebook, in case anyone asked to see his notes, returned to his room and shredded them. He stared at thick textbooks in the evening so his dormitory roommate wouldn't doubt, then joined a fraternity, drank can after can of water in order to tap the treasure chest of old term papers and old tests, in order to feel as if he finally belonged. He watched classmates in chemistry memorize the element chart in an hour; it took him 15.

And he lay in bed, listening to the clock chew away the night, exhausted but unable to sleep, unable to make his whirring mind let go. Thirty straight days, God. Thirty straight days he'd go to mass, crack of dawn, he *promised,* if only God would let him get this degree. . . .

U.S. Government 101-102. Two-semester class, four essay tests, *required* for graduation: the Monster. No way to use the finger signals from his buddy that he had used to get through Educational Statistics. No cheat sheets on narrow adding-machine paper scrolled up his long-sleeved shirt this time, no old tests, no clue what the questions would be.

He took a seat in the back, slid against the wall with the open window. Carefully, with no idea what he was writing, he copied the questions from the blackboard into his blue book. His eyes stole around the room. Silently . . . slowly . . . his hand moved toward the window. The blue book fell to the grass. The smart, skinny kid, the one John was setting up a date for, scooped it up, sat beneath a tree and began writing. John began scribbling in a second blue book, watching the clock, the teacher, the window, the other students, sweat running down his ribs. The book slid back in the window. Bingo! Four times, never caught! Thirty straight days, God, that's a promise! No, that's *not* cheating, not when you don't have any choice, that's *not* a sin . . . is it? . . . Is it?

He staggered into the doctor's office one day, a bundle of frayed nerves. "Tension," the doctor diagnosed. "Not enough sleep." For his cure, the doctor laid in John's hands a book on how to handle stress.

"Read it," the doctor said.

An odd thing happened. He got the diploma. He gave God His 30 days of mass. Now what, John, now what? Maybe he was addicted to the edge, maybe he was panting too hard for his father's love, maybe the thing he felt the most insecure about—his mind—was the thing he needed most to have admired. Maybe that's why, in 1961, John became a teacher.

A teacher. The perfect inconceivability for an illiterate. The perfect cover. He called his father from El Paso. Dad, he said, I had the application sent to your house, but I don't know if I'll be home in time to turn it in. Think you could fill it out? Thanks!

He taught world history for two years at Carlsbad High in California and then for one at Corcoran High; he had Robert Martinez, the only student in class he could depend on to recognize every word, stand each day and read the textbook to the class. "Again?" Robert finally complained. "Can't anybody else here read? I don't even think the teacher can!"

"Ha-ha, Robert. Very funny."

He gave the students standardized tests, used a form with a hole punched next to each correct answer and laid it right over the students' exams; any dolt could do it. He lay in bed for hours on weekend mornings and wondered why he felt depressed. He met a woman. A woman who had lived in the same town in California all her life, gone to the same high school as her mother had, grown up in a house with four generations of her Portuguese-Azorean family. A straight-A student, a nurse. Not a leaf, like John. A rock. "There's something I have to tell you, Kathy," he said one night in 1965 before their marriage.

"There's something I have to tell you, too," she said.

"Kathy, I . . . I can't read. . . ."

He's a *teacher*, she thought. He must mean he can't read *well*. "Well," said Kathy. "I am Rh-negative."

The subject was dropped, the two secrets dismissed. John didn't understand Kathy's until five years later, when their day-old baby died. Kathy didn't understand John's until two and a half years later, when she overheard him struggling to read a children's book to their 18-month-old daughter.

He began teaching social studies and sociology. He began to turn the old rules upside down. All his tests were oral, he brought in films and videos and guest speakers by the score. Let's move our desks into a circle, he told his students. Let's talk about ourselves and each other, about how we feel. Or he'd douse the lights, put a match to a candle, have everyone huddle around him and pretend they were in a cave on the verge of collapsing (oh, if only they knew!). Then say: Maybe one or two of you can make it out. Who should go? Convince us, tell us why.

He became known as an innovator. His timing—the late '60s and the '70s, when the humanities were flowering in American high schools—was perfect. His state—California, that lover of the latest trend—was perfect, too. Besides, how could the administration question him? He volunteered to take on the school's toughest kids and slowest learners, the Mexicans and Samoans and blacks whom traditional methods had failed. And he broke through those kids' walls, he fired their curiosity, he honest-to-God cared. He could reach a teenager's anger and hurt . . . because it was *his*.

But his vigil, would it ever, ever end? That book you've been carrying around all week, Mr. Corcoran what's it about? Here, read it, tell me what you think. He was a spy with phony papers, an actor on a rickety stage. . . . While I've got you here in the office, Mr. Corcoran, can you fill in this employee insurance form? Sorry, have to take it home with me, got a conference with a parent in two minutes. Here, John, can you read this mimeograph and give me some feedback? Sorry, just got back from the ophthalmologist, my eyes are dilated, can't. Always in a hurry, always a little distracted, always forgot his glasses, always burying pens under paper so the moment wouldn't come. Always tossing a dictionary at students who were stuck on a word. Funny, not just one dictionary in Mr. Corcoran's room, but 20 or 30, in case, somehow, one day, everyone got stuck on a word.

The morning bulletin? He let a student read it. A discipline problem? He handled it himself—if it went to the principal, he'd have to write a report. A stomachache, a fever? He went to school anyway, so he wouldn't have to write the substitute a lesson plan. He arrived early, stayed late, hung out in the library more than any other teacher, hauled in boxes of secondhand books he had bought at flea markets and dispensed them to the kids—my God, who could ever even remotely consider that . . . ?

It was all in the air he gave off, as if reading a birthday card out loud at a family gathering, glancing at a menu or filling in his medical history at the doctor's were a little beneath him. How coolly he could hand them to his wife, pick up a magazine and leaf through it. Kathy was a good girl, she filled out his forms, read and wrote his letters.

Why, then, people would ask years later when his long ruse was finished, why didn't he simply ask *her* to teach him to read and write? No! He couldn't humble himself before her that way, he couldn't truly believe that anyone could teach him that. Why didn't she simply insist? No! He could be a powerful, dominating man, a master of orchestration—maybe, almost subconsciously, she needed to hold that one thing over him, to keep the scales of their marriage from tipping. And if that moment ever came, that nightmare when the literates locked the door, encircled him, stuck a book before him and screamed, *Read!* John Corcoran had a contingency plan even for that: Fake a heart attack. A stroke. That's how much the masquerade meant.

And he was pulling it off, he had it almost down to a science . . . so *why?* he wonders sometimes now. Why was he still starved for something more tangible to assure him he was okay? At age 28, he borrowed $2,500, bought a second house, fixed it up and rented it. Bought and rented another and another. Purchased some land, had a few houses built, started visualizing things that men who used the other half of their brains couldn't see. He worked harder and harder, his business got bigger and bigger, until he needed a full-time secretary to read him his correspondence, a full-time lawyer to read his contracts, a partner—his wife's brother—to oversee the office. And then one day his accountant told him he was a millionaire. Damn, his teaching colleagues said, never realized Corcoran could be so shrewd, so good at taking risks—how'd that ever happen?

A millionaire. Perfect. Who'd notice that a millionaire always pulled on the doors that said PUSH or paused before entering public bathrooms, waiting to see from which one the men walked out? Who'd notice that he got lost when you gave him directions, that he had his subcontractors write in their own names when he issued checks, that he hardly had any *close* friends?

He quit teaching in 1979. His staff grew to 20 people. Taiwanese-American investors began to back him, 25 limited partnerships joined his stable. He deserved this . . . didn't he? Hadn't he overcome twice as many obstacles, hyperventilated twice as hard as anyone else? Wasn't he hyperventilating still? Yes, this was the horror: The more land he bought, the more apartments and motels and housing developments he built, the more construction loans he signed his name to, the wealthier and more successful he became . . . the more and more the man who couldn't read had to lean upon *them*, the literates. The ones he had never really trusted, the ones who had smacked his palms, whipped his calves, condemned him to the dumb row.

But he was home free—why did he feel more and more scared? The walls of each room in his house began to vanish, covered by shelf after shelf of books. He spent hours during vacations sitting in a bookstore in a stuffed chair by the fireplace, gazing at pages. He stared at two or three network-news programs each evening and then down at his newspaper, hoping, *please,* to connect the words he heard with the hieroglyphics. He went to two classes of a speedreading course, a desperate lunge for magic. Magic or miracle—he was convinced now that it would take something superhuman to solder the short circuit in his head. The Bible! he thought on some nights. Wouldn't a just God let him read the Bible? He grabbed the book, opened it to the first page—no? Well, then, he'd punish God, refuse to believe in him, erase him from the cosmos. And then come yo-yoing back in a cold sheen of Irish-Catholic sweat. . . .

Stop. Up with the houselights. Move to the back of the theater now, stand behind the very last row. From here you can see it, see all that the award-winning actor cannot see. The deepening resentment of the wife.

The growing tension of the overworked father. The gradual erosion of family life. The mounting anxiety of his partner, Kathy's brother, because John can't seem to stop risking, expanding. The inevitable screech of the national economy and the California real estate market. . . .

In 1982, the bottom began to fall out, the charade to shatter. His properties began to sit empty, his creditors to call, his financial backers to evaporate. Sell, John, his wife's brother urged. Take a loss, sell *now*. Impossible, he couldn't. He began laying off employees so he could pay the interest on his loans, whittling his staff from 20 to three, working 16 hours a day to compensate. The Taiwanese-Americans pulled out. A zillion documents were piling on his desk, nearly all the front men he had gathered around himself to intercept them were gone, threats of foreclosures and lawsuits began tumbling out of envelopes. File bankruptcy, his wife's brother urged, go Chapter 11, *now*.

No. Never. Please, Kathy, did he have to get down on his knees and beg? He needed her more and more to write and read letters for him, but she was working long hours with terminal-cancer patients at a clinic and had nothing left, at 9:00 p.m., to give. His son's grades went to hell all at once—my God, what if the boy can't read, what if John had passed it along in his blood? His driver's license was about to expire again—who had time anymore to memorize which box to check for 25 questions on *each* of the written test's five possible versions? Every waking moment, it seemed, he was pleading with bankers to extend his loans, coaxing builders to stay on the job, negotiating with lawyers to settle out of court, trying to make sense of the pyramid of paper. His wife's brother walked away, sued him for $10 million; Kathy got ripped this way and that. Another man sued him, then another and another; his shoulder and neck muscles bunched up like fists. He couldn't sleep; he lay on the floor some nights, spread his arms and begged God to save him. They were ganging up on him, the bastards, they were tearing down the facade plank by plank. And they wouldn't stop until he was alone and penniless and they had him on the witness stand, sworn to the truth under threat of perjury, and the man in black robes said: The truth, John Corcoran. Can you not even read?

In the fall of 1986, at the age of 48, he did two things he swore he never would. He put up his house as collateral, to obtain one last construction loan. And he walked into the Carlsbad Library and told the woman in charge of the tutoring program, "I can't read." He cried. He filled with dread. He was certain it was hopeless.

He was placed with a 65-year-old grandmother named Eleanor Condit. Strange, how she didn't seem horrified by his true face. Strange, how she just encouraged him to go on. She sat with him through a TV series on how words came to be, on the history of the English language, and the Monster began losing its snarl. And painstakingly—letter by letter, phonic by phonic, the way it might have been done 40 years ago—she began teaching him to tame it. Within 14 months, John Corcoran's land-development company began to revive. And John Corcoran could read.

The next step was confession, a speech before 200 stunned businessmen in San Diego. To heal he had to come clean, he had to give all those years of pain a *reason*. He was placed on the board of directors of the San Diego Council on Literacy, began traveling across the country to give speeches and lobby legislators on the need to attack America's invisible epidemic, the one that afflicts a staggering 85% of its juvenile delinquents, 75% of its citizens without jobs. "Illiteracy is a form of slavery," he would cry. "A form of child neglect, child abuse. We can't waste time blaming anyone. As a country, we need to become *obsessed* with teaching people to read, *now*!"

He could sleep, now that each next minute of his life didn't need to be controlled. He read every book or magazine he could get his hands on, every road sign he passed, out loud as long as Kathy could bear it—it was glorious, it was like singing!

And then one day it occurred to him, one more thing he could finally do. Yes, that dusty box in his office, that sheaf of papers bound by ribbon. . . . A quarter century later, John Corcoran could read his wife's love letters.

▪ Author's Afterwords . . .

An editor called me with the idea of doing a piece on John Corcoran. For me, the central question from the beginning was how a person could pull off such an incredible deceit. I try not to anticipate too much before I start a story, but getting the details of that deceit was foremost in my mind—along with what it did to John to live that way and how the lie radiated into other parts of his life. I figured this story would be intensely internal.

John was open and good about providing details. We talked every day for about a week, maybe five or six hours a day. Pretty soon, I realized how vast a secret and a lie he'd lived. I asked him a million questions about every little thing. "What book did you pick up when you were trying to find the magic book that would allow you to finally read? Why that book?" All kinds of situational things. For instance, he's got a book in his hands in school—what does he do if someone asks him what he thinks of that book? He has to find a way out of it, so he flips them the book and says, "You tell me what you think about it." Or what happens, as a teacher, when he's sick and has to write a lesson plan for his substitute?

I needed to know all those precise situations that a person who's pulling off this large a lie would be confronted with again and again and to know how he squirmed out of each and every one of them. By compiling so many examples, I was able to keep pouring them out all over the piece. The sheer accumulation of them forces readers to feel John's growing desperation—and to keep wondering what's coming next and how's John going to get out of it, to have that same uneasy feeling of eternal vigilance John had to have.

Obviously, he had to cheat a great deal to get through college. So I asked, "What was the most intricate cheating scheme you ever had to pull off?" He started talking about a particular essay test, so I asked every possible detail about that day, about the room and how he had done it. I asked him what the desperation and fear felt like. The smaller the detail, the better, but you don't want to use details just to prove you've done a good job of reporting. You want to select details that will help make readers feel that they're almost living that moment with the subject, that they're experiencing it too.

I'm not as big on using scenes that I happen to observe while I'm interviewing the person, unless they're particularly revealing. Often in a magazine story, writers rely largely on those kinds of scenes and then strain to make them stand for something. I'd rather find the moments in a subject's past that really did stand for something and re-create them as if I was there. I'm emphasizing the person's quest, the movement of his or her life, more than the random scenes that I might or might not happen to chance upon when I'm visiting that person.

John, for example, was a man so desperate to hide his illiteracy that he had an emergency plan: If he was really up against the wall, if he really needed to, he planned to fake a heart attack! If you don't get readers to feel the extent of that fear, they'll never know what his reality was like. I don't want to judge what he did. I want to understand it and then transfer that to readers so they understand the context and feelings that led to John's actions. In this story, I try to throw the question back in readers' laps: Is John really cheating on that essay test? It's like a poor man who's starving to death—is it stealing for him to take the fruit off someone else's table? But if you don't make readers feel John's desperation, it's easy for them to make a judgment against him.

Somewhere in a story, though, it's important to let readers see how the subject's internal reality plays out for the people around him. I wrote about John's wife and friends, how and why they were swept up in his deceit. You shouldn't overlook the objective reality in your attempt to reveal a person's inner reality—it's important to show how your subject's way of being and feeling ripples out and affects the world.

But I don't do that by quoting a lot of people saying this or that about the subject. I try to get a sense of how he affects people—often it's in very opposite ways—and to compress that into a narrative that gives off smoke signals of both perceptions. Character traits that seem to be opposites are usually just the flip side of one another, and that is what I try to get across. In this story, I wanted to quickly get readers inside John's inner world, to make them feel how scary it was for him. The time when a man's alone at night, facing himself, is usually when those feelings are most intense, so that's where I started.—G. S.

Shadow of a Nation

---

*I have not told you half that happened when I was young. I can think back
and tell you much more of war and horse stealing. But when the buffalo
went away the hearts of my people fell to the ground, and they could not lift
them up again. After this nothing happened. There was little singing
anywhere.*

Plenty Coups
Chief of the Crows, 1930

Singing. Did you hear it? There was singing in the land once more that day.
How could you not call the Crows a still-mighty tribe if you saw them on the
move that afternoon? How could your heart not leave the ground if you were
one of those Indian boys leading them across the Valley of the Big Horn?

It was March 24, 1983, a day of thin clouds and pale sun in southern
Montana. A bus slowed as it reached the crest of a hill, and from there,
for the first time, the boys inside it could see everything. Fender to
fender stretched the caravan of cars behind them, seven miles, eight—
they had made the asphalt go away! Through the sage and the buffalo
grass they swept, over buttes and boulder-filled gullies, as in the long-ago
days when their scouts had spotted buffalo and their village had packed
up its lodge poles and tepee skins, lashed them to the dogs and migrated

in pursuit of the herd. But what they pursued now was a high school basketball team, 12 teenagers on their way to Billings to play in a state tournament. The boys stared through their windows at the caravan. There was bone quiet in the bus. It was as if, all at once, the boys had sensed the size of this moment . . . and what awaited each of them once this moment was done.

In one seat, his nose pressed to the window, was one of Hardin High's starting guards, Everette Walks, a boy with unnaturally large hands who had never known his father. In a few weeks he would drop out of school, then cirrhosis would begin to lay waste his mother. He would wind up pushing a mop at 2:00 a.m. in a restaurant on the Crow reservation. In another seat sat one of the forwards, an astounding leaper named Miles Fighter. He, too, had grown up with no father, and recently his mother had died of cirrhosis. In just a few years, he would be unemployed and drinking heavily.

Not far away sat the other starting guard, Jo Jo Pretty Paint, a brilliant long-range shooter, a dedicated kid—just a few minutes before a game at Miles City, his coach had found him alone, crouched, shuffling, covering an invisible opponent in the locker room shower. In two years Pretty Paint would go out drinking one evening, get into a car and careen over an embankment. He would go to his grave with a photograph of himself in his uniform, clutching a basketball. Hunched nearby, all knees and elbows and shoulders, was Darren Big Medicine, the easygoing center. Sixteen months after Pretty Paint's death, he would leave a party after a night of drinking, fall asleep as he sped along a reservation road, drive into a ditch and die.

And then there was Takes Enemy. . . .

Weeping. Did you hear it? There was weeping in the land that day. Sobs for those missing from that glorious caravan, those decaying in the reservation dust, for Dale Spotted and Star Not Afraid and Darrell Hill and Tim Falls Down, Crow stars of the past dead of cirrhosis and suicide and knife-stabbing and a liquor-fogged car wreck. Sobs for the slow deaths occurring every night a mile from Jonathan Takes Enemy's high school, where an entire squad of jump shooters and dunkers and power forwards from the past could be found huddling against the chill and sprawled upon the sidewalks outside the bars on the south side of Hardin. Jonathan's predecessors. Jonathan's path-beaters. "Good Lord!" cries

Mickey Kern, the computer-science teacher and former basketball score-keeper at Hardin High. "How many have we lost? How *many?*"

But Takes Enemy—he would be the one who escaped, wouldn't he? That was what the white coaches and teachers and administrators at his school kept telling him. His mind was sharp, his skill immense; the destiny of all those others needn't be his. Brigham Young wanted him. Oregon State and Arizona State had sent letters. O. J. Simpson would shake his hand in New York City and present him with a crystal cup for being named Montana's Outstanding Athlete of 1984. He was 6' 2", he could twirl 360 degrees in the air and dunk the ball, he could shoot from distance. He loved to take a rebound with one hand and bring it to his other palm with a resounding *slap,* make a right-angle cut on the dribble at a velocity that ripped the court wide open, then thread it with a blind running pass, an orange blur straight from the unconscious. "Watching him play," says Janine Pease-Windy Boy, the president of Little Big Horn College, the junior college on the Crow reservation, "was like watching clean water flow across rocks."

Young Indian boys formed trails behind him, wearing big buttons with his picture on their little chests. They ran onto the court and formed a corridor for him and his teammates to trot through during pregame introductions, they touched his hands and arms, they pretended to *be* him. The coaches had to lock the gym doors to start practice. Girls lifted their pens to the bathroom walls: "I was with Jonathan Takes Enemy last night," they wrote. "I'm going to have Jonathan Takes Enemy's baby." He was a junior in high school. Already he was the father of two. Already he drank too much. Already his sister Sharolyn was dead of cirrhosis. Sometimes he walked alone in the night, shaking and sobbing. He was the newest hero of the tribe that loved basketball too much.

Takes Enemy felt the bus wheels rolling beneath him. The sun arced through the Montana sky. The circle was the symbol of never-ending life to the Crows—they saw it revealed in the shape and movement of the sun and moon, in the path of the eagle, in the contours of their tepees and the whorl of their dances. As long as the people kept faith with the circle, they believed, their tribe would endure. Jonathan settled back in his seat. Sometimes it seemed as if his life were handcuffed to a wheel, fated to take him up . . . and over . . . and down. . . .

Somewhere behind him on the highway, his first cousin would soon be getting off his job on the reservation's road crew and joining the

exodus to the ball game in Billings—*the* legendary Crow player, some
people said; the best player, *period,* in Montana high school history, said
others; the one who ignited his tribe's passion for high school basketball
back in the 1950s and seemed to start this dark cycle of great players
arising and vanishing: Larry Pretty Weasel. The one whose drinking
helped drive him out of Rocky Mountain College in Billings and back to
the reservation in 1958, just a few days before the NAIA's weekly bulletin
arrived proclaiming him the best field-goal percentage shooter in the
country.

Horns honked in the caravan behind Takes Enemy, passengers waved.
In the long-ago days before white men had brought their horses or guns
or cars or liquor, his people had chased buffalo in this same direction,
across these same valleys, stampeding them over cliffs near the land
where Billings would one day arise. This same creature whose skull the
Crows would mount on a pole and make the centerpiece of their religious
Sun Dance . . . they would drive over the edge of the cliff and then
scramble down to devour.

The bus ascended another hill. Takes Enemy looked back at his
people one more time.

One winter night in 1989, the custodian at Lodge Grass High on the
Crow reservation forgot to flick off a switch. When the team bus pulled
into the parking lot after a road game nearly four hours away, the lights
above six of the 17 outdoor baskets that surround the school were still
burning. It was 2:00 a.m. It was snowing. Two games of five-on-five were
being played.

Somehow, in the mindless way that rivers sculpt valleys and shame
shapes history, the Montana Indians' purest howl against 100 years of
repression and pain had become . . . high school basketball. Yes, the
Crows' 8,300 people were racked by alcoholism and poverty, 75% of them
were unemployed, the attrition rate for those who went to college was
95%, and their homeland, through cheating, broken treaties and sell-
outs, had dwindled from the 38.8 million acres guaranteed them by the
U.S. government in 1851 to the present-day 1.1 million—*however,* just
let them lace on sneakers and lay their hands on a basketball. Though
Indians constituted but 7% of Montana's population, their schools would
win 10 Class A, B and C state high school basketball titles between 1980
and 1990.

To the north and northwest of the Crow reservation lay the reservations of the Blackfeet, Sioux, Flathead, Assiniboine, Gros Ventre, Chip-
pewa, Cree, Salish, Kootenai and Pen D'Oreilles; to the east lay the
Cheyenne. These tribes, too, loved to run and shoot and jump. At
tournament time in Montana, Indian teams were known to streak onto
the floor for layup drills in war headdress, their fans to shake arenas with
chants and war cries and pounding drums as their boys raced up and
down the floor at speeds few white teams could sustain. Old women
wrapped in blankets were known to pound the bleachers in unison with
their canes, to lose their cool and swing the canes at the calves of enemy
players; a few, back in the 1940s, even jabbed opponents with hat pins
as the boys ran up the sidelines. Their children spent their days shooting
at crooked rims and rotting wooden backboards. Their young men drove
for days to reach Indian tournaments all across America and came home
to strut the dusty streets in the sheeny jackets they had won there.

Of all the perplexing games that the white man had brought with
him—frantic races for diplomas and dollar bills and development—here
was the one that the lean, quick men on the reservations could instinctively play. Here was a way to bring pride back to their hollow chests and
vacant eyes, some physical means, at last, for poor and undereducated
men to reattain the status they once had gained through hunting and
battle. Crow men had never taken up the craftwork, weaving or metal-
lurgy that males in other tribes had. They were warriors, meat eaters,
nomads whose prestige and self-esteem had come almost entirely from
fulfilling an intricate set of requirements—called "counting coup"—
while capturing enemy horses or waging battle. A man could count coup
by touching an enemy, by seizing a bow or a gun in a hand-to-hand
encounter, by capturing a horse in a hostile camp or by being the pipe
carrier (which signified leadership) on a successful raid. Only by counting coup, some say, could a man marry before the age of 25; only by
counting coup in all four categories could he become a chief. Children
were named after the exploits of warriors; men starved themselves for
days and slept alone in the mountains to invite dreams that would guide
them on raids; a woman attained honor by the number of scalps and the
war booty captured by her man, tokens of which she brandished when
she danced.

And then the white men hunted the buffalo nearly to extinction and
banned intertribal warfare. "It castrated the Crow male," says Ben Pease,

a tribal elder who played basketball for Hardin High in the 1940s. "It created a vacuum. During World War I we still weren't citizens, so our men couldn't gain prestige from that war. People began living off the war deeds of their ancestors, depending on them for their status. Some Crows fought in World War II, and for a while these men, especially those who came back with wounds or proof of bravery, became our leaders, and our ceremonies often revolved around them. But time passed, and there weren't enough wars or war heroes; there was a void that needed to be filled. In the late '50s Larry Pretty Weasel emerged at Hardin High, and our basketball players began to be noticed in the newspapers. That continued through the '60s and '70s; more and more of our children began to play. Something had to take war's place, some way had to be found to count coups. It was basketball."

Old Crow rituals had warm blood and fresh drama again. Some players tucked tiny medicine bundles—little pouches that might contain tobacco seeds or small pieces of bone or feather—inside their socks or tied them to their jerseys, the way warriors once had tied them to their braids before entering battle. Some burned cedar and prayed before big games. The same drum cadence and honor songs used 200 years ago to celebrate the seizing of a dozen horses or the killing of three Sioux now reverberated through gymnasiums and community halls at the capture of a basketball trophy.

"For us, a victory in a high school basketball game is a victory over everyday misery and poverty and racism," says Dale Old Horn, who heads the department of Crow studies and social sciences at Little Big Horn College. "But it's not a *real* victory. It doesn't decrease bigotry. It doesn't lessen alcoholism. It doesn't remove one Indian from the welfare rolls or return a single acre of our land. It gives us pseudo pride. It hasn't led us on to greater things."

No Indian has ever played in the NBA. Only one, Don Wetzel of the Blackfeet, ever came off a Montana reservation to play for an NCAA Division I team (the University of Montana, 1967-71). Trophy cases in the lobbies of Indian schools throughout the state are filled with gleaming silver . . . and with black-bordered dedications to the dead. This is not just the Crows' tragedy. Two months after graduating from Browning High on the Blackfeet reservation in 1987, 6' 3" All-Stater Gary Cross Guns packed his car to go to a junior college in Kansas. One last night out was all he wanted. The next morning his sister went for a horseback ride. She found her brother's car and his body in Cut Bank Creek.

Wetzel, who once coached basketball at Browning and is now super-intendent of schools in Harlem, Montana, could bear it no longer. In the three years since Cross Guns's death, he has traveled 14,000 miles and talked to 12,000 kids, "trying," he says, "to make people see how scary this whole situation has become."

Every now and then, a lesser player left the Crow reservation and quietly, with no scholarship or fanfare, got his degree. But as best as anyone can figure, since 1970 only one prominent Crow player, Luke Spotted Bear, has received a college scholarship and graduated (from Mary College in Bismarck, North Dakota)—and Spotted Bear often felt that his people held this *against* him. "Some of them say I'm too good for them now," he says. "If possible, they don't want to be around me."

College recruiters stopped coming to the reservation, opportunities disappeared. "Well, I tried to work with Indians," says Herb Klindt, coach at Rocky Mountain College for 37 years. "I tried to keep them in college. But I got to a point where I just threw up my hands in disgust and gave up, and most of the other coaches did, too."

The game that was a highway into mainstream America for black men . . . was a cul-de-sac for red ones. Something happened to their heroes when the drum beats died, when the war whoops faded, when the faces in the audience were not like theirs. Something in the Crows' love for basketball was toxic.

And along came a boy who was asked to change all that. Along came a nice, shy kid—Jonathan Takes Enemy.

His people understood his significance. They sent him off to do battle with all the spiritual might they could muster. Before big games a medicine man would receive a cigarette from the Takes Enemy family, take it outside their house just in front of the Little Big Horn River in the town of Crow Agency, light it and pray to the Great Spirit for Jonathan. Once, the medicine man wafted cedar smoke and an eagle feather over the gold chain that Takes Enemy carried with him to games for good luck. He warned Takes Enemy not to shake his opponents' hands before a game, so they could not drain away his power. All these steps were meant to protect Jonathan from harm, but he couldn't quite trust them. How could he escape the reservation and take up the solitary quest for success in the white world if he let himself think in the old way? How could he escape the dark fate of Spotted and Not Afraid and Falls Down if he believed that a man's destiny hung upon a puff of smoke in the wind?

When members of the tribe invited players on Jonathan's team to join them in sweat baths before the division and state tournaments, in order to purify their bodies and spirits in the ritual way their ancestors had before battle, Jonathan had refused; it was simply too hot in the sweat lodge. Jonathan's coach at Hardin, George Pfeifer—in his first year of coaching Indians and curious about their rituals—consented to do it. On a 20°-day on the banks of the Little Big Horn, a powdery snow falling from the sky, the short, stout white man followed the example of eight Crow men and stripped off his clothes. "Go in, Brother George," directed one of them. Brother George got on his knees and crawled behind them into a low, dome-shaped shelter made of bent willows and covered by blankets. Inside, it was so dark that Brother George could not see the hand he held up in front of his face.

Someone poured a dipper of water over sandstones that had been heated in a bonfire for hours. Steam erupted from the rocks, hissed up and filled the sweat lodge with heat more intense than any sauna's. Sitting cheek to cheek, the men put a switch in Brother George's hand, expecting him to beat himself upon the back and legs to make it even hotter. In the darkness he heard the others thwacking themselves, groaning and praying for his team in the Crow tongue. He gave up all pretense, flopped onto the floor and cupped his hands around his mouth to find a gulp of cooler air.

A half hour passed like this. A couple dozen more dippers of water were poured onto the scalded rocks. At last the sweat-soaked men crawled out into the frigid daylight and promptly leapt into the icy river. Brother George's legs refused. He stood there, trembling with cold, about to be sick for three days.

"You're not going to dive in the river, Brother George?" one cried.

"No way."

"That's all right, Brother George. No goddam magic in that."

But here was the difference: In a few weeks Pfeifer would laugh and tell anecdotes about the day that he left his world and entered another. Jonathan could not. Sometimes he felt the suspicious eyes of whites upon him, felt his tongue turn to stone, his English jumble, when he tried to express to them his feelings. He had but to utter that name to white ears—Takes Enemy—to feel his own ears begin to turn red.

All day and night as he grew up, the television had been on in his home, floating images into his head of white men who drove long cars and lived in wide houses, of Indians who were slow-witted and savage and usually, by the movie's end, dead. One day, when he was in junior high, he saw a movie about Custer's Last Stand. He couldn't help himself; in his stomach he felt thrilled when the Indians rolled over the hills and slaughtered every white man. It bewildered him, a few years later, to learn that it was the Sioux and Cheyenne who had slain Custer's troops—that several Crow scouts had ridden *with* Custer. Everything was muddy, nothing ran clean. It was whites who made him speak English most of the day when he entered first grade, rather than the Crow language he had grown up speaking; whites who hung a dead coyote from the outside mirror of Plenty Coups High School's team bus; whites who sang "One little, two little, three little Indians" at his brothers when they played away games in high school. And yet it was Hardin's white athletic director and assistant principal, Kim Anderson, who sometimes drove far out of his way to make sure Jonathan made it to school in the morning; white teachers who offered him encouragement and hope when he passed them in the halls.

Sometimes he would bicycle up the steep incline to the Custer Battlefield, a mile and a half from his home, to sit alone near the markers that showed where each of the white men had fallen, and to stare off into the distance. From here the world stretched out and waited for him to touch it; from here he could see land and a life beyond the reservation. In the daydream he often had here, it would be *he* who was walking from the wide house to the long car, *he* waving a cheery goodbye to his wife and kids, *he* driving off down the well-paved road to the well-paid job, *he* acting out the clichéd American dream he saw on the TV screen. What choice had he? There no longer existed an Indian success cliché to dream of.

An hour or two later he would fly back down the hillside from the battlefield, barely needing to touch his pedals, determined to make the dream come true. It was only when the long hill ran out, when he labored back into his town, that the heaviness returned to his legs.

One evening a few months after his senior season, in which he averaged 28 points a game and shattered a Montana record by scoring

123 points in three state tournament games, his mother, Dorothy, held a "giveaway" in his honor. She was suffering from diabetes, which in a few years would force the amputation of her right leg below the knee and lash her to a kidney dialysis machine three days each week, yet she was determined to thank God and her tribe for the greatness of her son. Jonathan, her seventh surviving child (two had died shortly after birth), had been born with a crooked face and a too-large nose, and so in her hospital bed Dorothy had lifted the infant above her eyes and turned all her fears for him over to God. "Here, Lord," she whispered, "raise him up, he's all yours." The Lord's day care center turned out to be a basketball court; from the age of three, all Jonathan did was dribble and shoot. On dry, frigid days he would play for so long that the ball would chafe away his skin, and he would come home at dusk with bloody fingers for his mother to bandage. Dorothy's eyes still shone when she stared at the Mother's Day card he had drawn in crayon for her in second grade: three yellow flowers in a blue vase, a snowcapped mountain beneath the sun—and a man slam-dunking a basketball. And just look how the boy had turned out, with a face straight and well proportioned, a body long and strong, a name that the wind had carried across the Big Horn and Wolf mountains, had whispered into the ears of the Cheyenne and Sioux, even laid upon the tongues of the pale skins. If only the boy's eyes would leave his shoes. If only the boy would stop stumbling home at 4:00 a.m. with the same stink on his breath as her husband, Lacey. . . .

In the giveaway ceremony, Jonathan's exploits were to be celebrated in the same manner in which Crows once commemorated a successful raid. Besides all the cousins and uncles and aunts and nephews and nieces who gathered, Jonathan's other "family," his clan, was there. (There are 10 clans in the Crow tribe, some consisting of as many as a thousand members; at birth one automatically becomes a member of the same clan as one's mother.) First Jonathan was to dance in a circle as singers sang his honor song, then he was to stand to the side as an "announcer" gave an account of his deeds, and finally he was to give away packages that consisted of four gifts to his clan uncles and aunts. It is a lovely ritual, one in which the hero, in a reversal of the white man's custom, showers his community with gifts in gratitude for the support and prayers that enabled him to succeed. Jonathan's family, just barely getting by on his father's meager salary as a custodian in the reservation hospital, couldn't possibly afford all these gifts, but in keeping with tradition his relatives had contributed so that the giveaway could take place.

Jonathan dreaded the stares that would be drawn to him if he wore the ritual Indian clothing, but he couldn't bear to disappoint his people. Slowly he pulled on the ribbon shirt, the buckskin vest, the colorful beaded armband and the war bonnet. They felt so odd upon him; he felt like no warrior at all. The first horse he had ever ridden had flung him from its back; the first bullet he had ever fired at an animal had slain a dirt clod far from its target. One of his great-great-grandfathers, known simply as Fly, had been a powerful warrior, a possessor of six wives. Another, Red Bear, had been a medicine man so potent that he simply had to fill his peace pipe and hold it toward the sun and all the tobacco in it would burn. Their home had been the river-fed valleys and shimmering plains, their roof the sky, their walls the snow-topped mountains a week's walk away. Jonathan? His home was a cramped three-bedroom box in which as many as 15 siblings and cousins often vied for sleeping space, sometimes on the floor beneath the kitchen table or even in the driveway, in the backseat of a car. Jonathan's bed, until he was seven, was a mattress jammed between the beds of his mom and dad.

With his family and his clan trailing behind him, he lowered his eyes and led them into the Little Big Horn College building for the giveaway. Rather than tokens of scalps or war booty captured from the enemy, Dorothy wore a huge orange shawl with large black letters stitched upon it that listed his coups: JONATHAN TAKES ENEMY, STATE CLASS A MVP, ALL-STATE 1ST TEAM, ALL-CONFERENCE 1984, CONVERSE BASKET-BALL ALL-AMERICA HONORABLE MENTION, HERTZ AWARD, ATH-LETE OF THE YEAR. Beneath were sewn four white stars; four is the Crows' sacred number. Jonathan was supposed to lead the assembly in a dance, but his feet could not quite bring themselves to do it. Almost imperceptibly he shifted his weight from one foot to the other, leading everyone around the room again and again in a plodding circle as the big drum pounded and the 11 singers in the center lifted their voices to his glory—and reminded him of his obligation to those around him.

> Outstanding man
> Look all around you
> Nothing lasts forever
> Look all around you
> Share your talent and knowledge

Share what? All he had to divvy up, it sometimes seemed, were self-doubt and pain. One day in ninth grade, at the end of basketball practice, his family had come to the school and told him that his sister had died at the age of 24, after years of hard drinking. He turned to the wall and broke down. Just a few weeks later his girlfriend told him she was pregnant. Terrified, he dropped out of school for the rest of the year, hid from his teachers on the streets, sometimes even hid from his own family—and reached for the same poison as his sister had.

He knew the danger he was wooing. The night he learned he had made the varsity, a rare honor for a freshman, he and a few friends went out in a pickup truck to drink beer. A tribal police car pulled up to the truck. Alcohol was banned on the reservation, but Crow policemen sometimes looked the other way. "Go home," this cop ordered the teenagers, but the kid at the wheel panicked, jammed the accelerator and roared away. Suddenly, Takes Enemy, a boy who was afraid even on a sled, found himself hurtling down a curving country road at 100 mph, four police cars with flashing lights and howling sirens just behind him. One came screaming up beside the truck, trying to slip by and box the teenagers in. Instead of letting it pass, Jonathan's friend lurched into the other lane to cut the car off. The pickup truck skidded off the road, toppled onto its roof and into a ditch. Takes Enemy limped out, somehow with just a badly bruised hip.

He vowed not to drink again. He remembered how uneasy he had been as a child, awakening on the mattress between his parents' beds to see the silhouette of his father stagger into the room. Even in an alcoholic haze, his father was a gentle man, but, still, that silhouette was not Dad—it was a stranger. Then, too, there was what alcohol had done to his cousin the legend, Pretty Weasel. So many fans thronged gymnasiums to watch Pretty Weasel play for Hardin High that his team had to crawl through windows to get to its locker room. He could shoot jump shots with either hand, fake so deftly that he put defenders on their pants and, at 5' 10," outjump players a half-foot taller. It was almost, an opponent would muse years later, "as if you were playing against a kind of enchanted person." Pretty Weasel's younger brother Lamonte got drunk and died in a car accident. Then Pretty Weasel partied his way out of a four-year college scholarship and onto a reservation road crew.

But Jonathan couldn't keep his vow. He felt as if he were locked in a tiny room inside his body, and it was only when he was playing basketball or drinking that he could break out of it. The first time he was drunk had been in seventh grade at Crow Fair, the weeklong celebration every August when the field on the edge of his town became the tepee capital of the world. Hundreds of tepees were erected, and Indians from far away came to dance and drink and sing with his people deep into the night. Jonathan slipped the bootlegger $4 for a half-pint of whiskey, poured it down—and out poured the talking, laughing Jonathan he had always yearned to be. His mother came and found him at the fair at 3:00 a.m. Dorothy, a sweet, passive woman dedicated to the Pentecostal Church, began yelling that he would end up just like his father . . . but that was all. In many homes across the reservation . . . that was all.

His sophomore year he moved in with his girlfriend and her parents, to help her bring up their baby daughter. Four months after his girlfriend delivered, she had news for him. She was pregnant again. His whole life seemed hopeless, his daydream of escaping snuffed out. Was it his fault? No matter how hard Jonathan thought about it, he could never be sure. So many things had happened to his people that *were* beyond their control, it had become almost impossible to identify those that were *not*. He watched three brothers go to college and quickly drop out. He watched all three of them take turns with the bottle.

There were no movie theaters or bowling alleys or malls on the reservation. When it became too dark to see the rim on the courts behind the elementary school, Jonathan and his friends would drive up and down the main street of Crow Agency—from JR's Smokehouse to the irrigation supply yard and back again—seeing the same people, the same mange-eaten dogs and rust-eaten cars, until the monotony numbed them. Then someone would say, "Let's go drinking." It was a ritual that had become a display of solidarity and shared values among his tribe, so much so that to say no was to mark oneself as an alien. None of the teenagers had enough money to buy liquor, but all of them had Indian wealth—relatives. Uncles and aunts, cousins and grandparents are as close to most Crows as parents and siblings are to a white child; a boy can walk into five or six houses without knocking, open the refrigerator without asking, eat without cleaning up the crumbs. Jonathan and his friends would each ask a relative or two for a buck, and all of the sharing and family closeness in which the Crows pride themselves would boomerang. Each kid would come up with a few dollars to pitch into the pot, and off they'd go to the liquor stores that waited for them half a hiccup past the reservation borders. It wouldn't take long to see someone they knew who was of drinking age—the boys were related by blood or clan, it seemed, to everyone. They whisked their beer or whiskey back onto the reservation, where the statutes against juveniles drinking were less severe, and began gulping it as if they were racing to see who could sledgehammer reality quickest, who could forget his life first.

Jonathan's absences from school mounted. That was how he responded to trouble. He disappeared. His parents wanted him to get an education, but to make the house quiet for two hours each night and insist that he study, to pull him out of his bed when the school bus was rolling up the road—no, they couldn't quite do that. Each of them had dropped out after the ninth grade, but there was more to it than that. Almost every Crow parent had a close relative who had been forcibly taken from his home by white government agents in the early 1900s and sent off to a faraway boarding school, where his hair was shorn, his Indian clothes and name were taken away, and he was beaten for speaking his own language. How many Indians could chase an education without feeling an old pang in their bones?

On intelligence alone, Takes Enemy had made the honor roll in junior high, but now he fell behind in class and was too ashamed to ask the white teachers for help. He lost his eligibility for the first half-dozen games of both his sophomore and junior seasons, regained it after each Christmas and started dropping in 25 or 30 points with a dozen assists a game, leading his teammates flying up and down the floor. His coaches called it Blur Ball. His people called it Indian Ball. And his brothers, three of whom had also been stars at Hardin High, would whip the crowd to wildness, reaching back into imaginary quivers on their backs, loading their make-believe bows and zinging invisible arrows at the other teams; vibrating their hands over their mouths to make the high, shrill *wooo-wooo* battle cry that once froze frontiersmen's hearts; shouting themselves hoarse, making Takes Enemy feel as if he could simply lift up his legs and let his people's ecstasy wash him up and down the hardwood.

He scored 49 points in a state tournament game his senior year and was named the tournament's MVP. The outside walls of his house literally vanished, swathed in posters of congratulation from his fans. "A great major college prospect," said then BYU coach Ladell Andersen.

Do it, teachers urged him. Do it so *they* could once more believe in what they were doing, do it so *all* the Crow children whose eyes were on him could see how it was done. "Just *one*," they kept saying to him. "If just one great basketball player from here could make the break and succeed, it could change everything. College recruiters would start coming here, other kids would follow your example. You can be the one, Jonathan. You can be the breakthrough."

He was flown to BYU. He stared at the 26,000 white faces strolling across campus. He stood at the top of the basketball arena and looked down, his eyes growing wider and wider, the court growing tinier and farther away. He had never heard of anyone like himself playing in a place like this; he couldn't even fathom it. "He said almost nothing the whole time," recalls Andersen. "I asked him a few questions. He was nodding his head yes when he should have been shaking it no."

The stack of letters from universities grew at his home. Jonathan never replied. His senior year was ending, his sun descending toward the hills. In the long-ago days a Crow hero could go on doing what he did until an arrow or a bullet found him, then let the breeze carry off his soul to the Other Side Camp. But in the 20th century the hero's bullet was high school graduation—and then he had to go on living. "Where are you going to college?" people asked Jonathan everywhere he went. "He'll be home by Thanksgiving," they told each other. "Like crabs in a bucket, that's how we are," says Dell Fritzler, the coach at Plenty Coups High. "Whoever tries to get out, we yank him back down." Even Jonathan's own Indian name—bestowed upon him during his senior season after it had come to the medicine man in a dream—tugged downward at the boy. Iiwaaialetasaask, he was called. Does Not Put Himself Above Others. Go off to college? That would Definitely Put Himself Above Others. No, white people couldn't understand this; Jonathan himself could barely grasp the code: It was okay for an Indian to clench his teeth and compete as part of a team, especially an Indian team. But to do it alone, to remove yourself from the dozen people in your living room at midnight and go sit over a chemistry or algebra book—in many families, that tainted you. "We want our young people to go off and show the world how great a Crow can be," says Fritzler, "but as soon as someone does, as soon as anyone starts trying or studying too hard, a lot of us say, 'Look at him. He's trying to be a white man.' "

Takes Enemy's head spun. There were just too many mixed signals, too many invisible arrows from the audience whizzing by. Like most Crows, he'd been brought up not to make autonomous decisions but to take his cues from his immediate family, his extended family, his clan and his tribe. If *they* hadn't decided whether to assimilate into the white man's world or to recoil from it—how could he? And then, his two little children—he couldn't just walk away from them. The small living room he grew up in, with its 65 photographs of family members on the wall—a warm, happy place that the people in those pictures would flow into with no invitation, sit around sipping coffee and exchanging the sly puns and double entendres that his people excelled at, talking until there was nothing left to talk about and then talking some more—he couldn't just leave that behind. "Why?" he remembers wondering. "Why do I have to do it the white man's way to be a success in this world?" Why did all the human wealth he had gathered in his life, all the close friends and relatives, count for nothing when he crossed the reservation borders; why did material wealth seem to be the only gauge? And then his eyes and whys would turn the other way: "Why am I so important to my people? Why do *I* have to carry the hopes of the Crows?" All he had really wanted to do, ever since taking apart a stereo in the 10th grade and staring in wonder at all the whatchamacallits inside, was to go to a vocational school and learn electronics. But no, the herd was rolling, the people were waving and shouting him on, his legs were pulling him closer and closer to the ledge. He drank to close his eyes to it. One night at a school dance an administrator found out he was drunk. The next day he was ordered to take a chemical-dependency class.

Where were the people in his tribe who had lived through this? Why weren't they at Takes Enemy's door? Myron Falls Down, a prolific scorer for a Crow independent team in the 1970s, heard the rumors and wondered if he should do something. Six years earlier it had come to Falls Down like thunder through a hangover: That the addiction sucking the life from him and his people went beyond the beer they drank at night after playing ball, beyond the pills some ingested and the weed they puffed, beyond the Aqua Velva and Lysol and fingernail-polish remover some of them swilled; that *basketball,* the way the Crows were using it, had become a drug too. One morning in 1979, at the age of 27, he stood up from the bed where he slept every night with his ball. He went to the two glass-enclosed cases in the living room where his 50 trophies were displayed, and he began throwing them into cardboard boxes. "What are you doing?" cried his mother. She and Myron's nieces raced to unscrew the little figurines from their wooden bases before he could sweep all of them away. He grabbed the five jackets he had won in tournaments, loaded them and his trophies into his car, drove to the dumpster on the edge of Lodge Grass and heaved them all in. He would never take another drink or drug after that day. He would never play, or go to see, another basketball game—not even, 10 years later, the junior high school games of his 13-year-old son. "If there was a connection between education and basketball on this reservation, there would be nothing wrong with basketball," says Falls Down, now a tribal health administrator. "But right now there is none. Basketball is an escape from reality for us. But I never did speak to Jonathan. I felt he or his family would have approached me if they wanted to hear my message."

Pretty Weasel—where was he? The man named Montana's Outstanding Athlete 27 years before Takes Enemy, the one recruited by the University of Utah, Texas A&M and Seattle University, the cousin caught in this same crossfire eight years before Jonathan was born. Relatives and friends had sat at Takes Enemy's dinner table to spill their guts and offer counsel, but the man who with one look or word might have given Jonathan a glimpse at the ledger, at the remorse and relief in the soul of a man who has walked away from his greatness, had signaled nothing. Pretty Weasel stood in the shadows at basketball games, refused invitations to giveaways, belittled his own legend. "Never saw myself play," he said. "Can't picture myself being able to play with those black boys." Years later, at the age of 51 and no longer a drinker, he would wish that he had gotten his degree, explored the borders of his talent. "But I don't give advice," he says. "I guess I feel more like the whites do. That every man can be as good as he wants to. That every man does it on his own."

Graduation day came. Jonathan still hadn't decided. Barely, just barely, he got his diploma. As the teachers watched him carry it across the stage, Anderson, the assistant principal, turned and said, "I hope we're not looking at the first day of the end of his life."

***

> When the dance is over, sweetheart,
> I will take you home in my one-eyed Ford.

That sloppy man with the red-rimmed eyes and the puffy face, taller than the others. . . . That whiskered man with the slurred speech and the thick belly and the slumped shoulders, standing on the riverbank near Two Leggins Bridge . . . that's him. That's Jonathan Takes Enemy.

It's 1989. It's 3:00 a.m. When the bars close in Hardin, Jonathan and his friends often come here to sing and laugh and drink and dance until the sun comes up. At dawn somebody often hits somebody, and somebody's brother or cousin jumps in to help, and there's a whole pile of them in the dirt. And then they go home to sleep. There's no work for most of them to do.

But the sky's still dark, they all still feel good. They're singing "49" songs, native chants interspersed with English lyrics, sad-happy tunes to the beat of a drum. Takes Enemy still can't bring himself to dance or sing, but he's thumping out the drumbeat on a car hood. "Way-la-hey-ley, way-la-hey-ley . . . ya-hey-oh-way-la-hey . . . ," his companions croon. "When the dance is over, sweetheart, I will take you home in my one-eyed Ford."

The dance is over. It ended four years ago, as soon as it began. Six games into Jonathan's freshman season at Sheridan College, the Wyoming school whose scholarship offer he grabbed at the last minute because it was just an hour's drive from home, he quit. It's all still a blur to him: Hiding from everyone when it was time to leave home. Reporting to college two days late and only because Anderson found him and took him there. Being stopped in the yard as he left, asked by his teary-eyed mother, "Are you *sure* you want to go, Jonathan? They aren't *forcing* you?" Trying to go from a world where it's disrespectful to look someone in the eye into one where it's disrespectful *not* to. Sitting alone in his dorm room for days, walking alone to the cafeteria, eating alone. Telling none of the white people about his fear and loneliness. Being guided by no one through the bewildering transition from reservation to white world. Knowing before his first game that something was wrong, because he had done something he could never do the night before a high school game—sleep. Knowing that the feeling he had had at Hardin—that he was on a mission, playing for his people—was gone. Returning to the reservation three straight weekends and not coming back in time for Monday practice. Two weekends later, not coming back at all. Walking away from the No. 1-ranked junior college team in the nation . . . but whose nation, *whose?*

"Crawled back under the blanket," said the whites. They've seen Indians do it so often that they have a cliché for it. "Every Indian that leaves has a rubber band attached to his back," says Jonathan's brother James. The Crows have seen their people do it so often that they only shrug. In some strange way, by going away to college and then by quitting, too, Takes Enemy has managed to fulfill everyone's expectations.

Somewhere, perhaps upon the hilltop at Custer Battlefield, his daydream still exists. More and more, he bicycles back there, as if in search of it. After all, he is only 24, he tells himself, his life is just beginning—or already half over, according to Crow life-expectancy charts. His pockets are empty. He bums beer money from his dad, who has stayed clean since entering an alcohol rehabilitation program recently. No one will hire Jonathan. No one will buy him drinks at the bars in Hardin the way they did when he was in high school. Sometimes he walks out of the bars and onto the streets, sees a teacher from the school driving by and slinks into the shadows. He's not a bum, he's *not.* Twice he has been thrown into the reservation jail for drinking, lain on the floor all night in a cell with 30 other drunk men, listened to them moan and retch.

He has gained more than 20 pounds. He still plays ball, lumbering up the floor in Indian tournaments held across the state and the country. After games the team goes drinking—and sometimes, even right before them. He signs up for courses at the reservation's junior college; some he completes, some he doesn't. He has a new girlfriend, Trudi Big Hair, and two more children, Jonathan and Tashina. The four of them sleep in a small room at his parents' house, and no one ever hints that it's time he moved out. Sometimes in the morning the children jump on him in bed and shout, exploding his hangovers. He drifts back to sleep until noon, goes to a class or two, kills a few hours staring at the TV or picking up his welfare check, plays pickup basketball with his friends until dark . . .

and then often starts all over again. Each time he drinks, Trudi etches an X on the calendar. Day by day, Jonathan watches his life get crossed out.

Once or twice he has gone to see his old school play. He doesn't go inside. He watches from a half-open door. It's not his court anymore, not his domain. A new hero has arisen, a boy at Lodge Grass High named Elvis Old Bull. Old Bull took his team to state titles in '88 and '89, was named tournament MVP both years, noticed kids beginning to dress and cut their hair like he does, heard himself called a major college prospect. He has a child, but isn't married; he skips school too much; he drinks too much; his eyes are haunted. Sometimes Jonathan feels as if there is something he could tell the boy—but no, he can't, he *can't*. Old Bull enters a rehabilitation center just after his junior season. The treatment fails. He misses far too many days of school to remain eligible for his final season, but the people need that third straight title too much, and school administrators can't quite bring themselves to sit him down. "You're going to end up just like Jonathan Takes Enemy," people in the tribe keep telling him. He leads his team to the third state title, wins his third tournament MVP trophy, then simply stops going to school. He watches his classmates graduate through eyes swollen from a car wreck from another night's drinking. And the sun arcs across the Montana sky, and the eagle wheels, and the circle remains unbroken.

Autumn 1990. The sun drops behind the Big Horn Mountains. An orange 1980 Mustang turns onto the highway and bears north across the reservation, toward Billings. There is no caravan behind him. Takes Enemy goes alone. His face is clean-shaven, his clothes are neat, his cheekbones have bloomed again. He is 25, but he looks like that boy in those high school pictures once more. All summer he has jumped rope, slipping into his backyard to do it at midnight when no one on the reservation could see.

He presses the accelerator. Just a short visit home today; he cannot dally. He needs to get off the reservation by nightfall and back to his apartment in Billings, to Trudi and little Jonathan and Tashina, back to his new life as a student and a basketball player at Rocky Mountain College. Because when the darkness comes and his friends come. . . . "To do this," he says, "I can't be near them. I *miss* them. But I have to be alone." He hasn't had a drink in months. He hears that Old Bull has made a change too, moving to Bozeman with hopes of fulfilling his high school requirements and getting a shot at college ball.

"It's *my* decision to go to college this time," Jonathan says. "I finally realized that I was running out of time. It's not that the reservation is a bad place. There are many good people there. But it's just not a place where you can become what you want to become. It's not a place where you can achieve your dreams."

Last spring he convinced Luke Gerber, the coach at Hardin High, that he was serious. Gerber called Jeff Malby, the coach at Rocky Mountain College, and Malby remembered how the clean water had once flowed across the rocks. He offered Takes Enemy a scholarship to the liberal arts college in Billings, with 810 students. So far, it fits Jonathan just right.

He passes the reservation border, glances into his rearview mirror. He knows that some people back there are now calling him an "apple"— red on the outside, white on the inside. He knows what he is leaving behind, what he is losing. Knows it in the morning when he passes his new neighbors in Billings and they just barely nod. Knows it when it's midnight and he and Trudi are buried in textbooks, and the apartment is silent. "It's just too quiet here," he'll say. "We're so isolated." And when he lies in bed at night and thinks of his sick mother, he knows it then, too.

His eyes move back to the windshield. Ahead of him, over the rolling hills, across the sage and buffalo grass, he can just make out the soft electric glow of Billings. He's starting to get an idea of what lies this way. He's passing all four of his classes. He's averaging 19.8 points and 4.6 assists for his new team. He's just getting his bearings, but his coaches say that he'll soon establish himself as the best player in Montana and that he's destined to be an NAIA All-America before he's done.

Everything's still so new to him. Paying his own rent each month from the grant money allotted to him by the tribe and the Bureau of Indian Affairs, paying electric bills, buying his own food. Studying until 1:00 a.m., making sure that Trudi gets off to Eastern Montana College in the morning, that his kids get off to day care and preschool, living in the white man's world, in a hurry, on a schedule.

He wants to go back to the reservation someday and help kids to take the risk, to see both the beauty and the danger of the circle. But he may never live there again. He rolls down his car window. He listens to the air. There is no singing in the land. There is only a quiet, sad-happy song inside a young man's heart.

■ Author's Afterwords . . .

An editor had read a short piece about another Crow basketball player and asked me to look into it. There was a lot of potential in that story and a lot of misery, too. I didn't want my story to be an unrelentingly dark piece. I talked to people for three or four days on the phone, and somebody finally mentioned Jonathan Takes Enemy. Jonathan said it was all right to come visit, and so I went to Montana for nine or 10 days.

I hooked up with him at college in Billings, spent a couple days there, but he was reticent to go back to his reservation. I said, "This is where your life was, and we can't amputate the first 20-some years." Finally, I convinced him to ride back with me and show me where he'd hung out, tell me about the people and introduce me to his family. We were there a day. Then I went back on my own and picked up a lot of the pieces he hadn't tied up for me.

I don't use tapes. I use legal pads to take notes. When I start talking to someone for a story, I don't have a lot of fixed objectives. Mostly, I'm sending out a lot of fishing lines and seeing what comes back. When I sense that I'm on to something important, I'll keep coming back to that with questions from all angles. But at first I'm just trying to get comfortable and get the subject comfortable. It wasn't easy with Jonathan. He was very shy. I had to keep coming back at him with questions to find out how he felt in each of the moments of his life that came up. He wouldn't just hand anything to me.

He would say, "We played a lot of basketball." And I'd say, "What kind of court did you play on? What were the rims made out of? How many hours did you play in a day? Where was the court? Would you play in the snow?" When I'd sense that something he referred to was important, that I could use a scene like that to suggest something larger about his life, I'd ask every possible question so I'd have a wealth of details, the kind that would allow me to put the reader in the moment, almost like fiction.

I want to have the freedom of a fiction writer, who can make up whatever details he needs to create that feeling. But the only way I can come close as a journalist is to collect a vast amount of factual details in the interviewing, and then choose the right ones when it's time to write. Once I start to form an instinct about a person, I probe to make sure my instinct is correct. A lot of my reporting comes from asking a question three different ways. Sometimes the third go at it is what produces the nugget, but even if the answers aren't wonderful or the quotes usable, they can still confirm or correct my impressions.

On the reservation, a man invited me to go into a sweat lodge with him, and so I went. I would've done it just for the hell of it, but it also made people see that I was open to their ways. I was on the reservation about five days, just walking around observing, talking to people, talking to Jonathan's family. They were shy, but I just let it play out, tried not to force it.

I interviewed maybe 35 people. When I'd come back from the reservation to Billings, I'd go to Jonathan and ask for more details to help me re-create the scenes people were telling me about. The Indian chants—the "49" songs, they called them—which they sang when they were drinking at night, for instance. I'd pick his brain to find out how it felt, that pull of brotherhood on the reservation that felt so warm but yet kept holding him back whenever he tried to pursue his dreams or ambitions.

After reporting, I usually take about a week to organize my material, go through the notes and put information into categories. I'll use different colors of pens, and all the important stuff I'll rewrite on new pages of notes under category headings. Then, when I'm reaching for a detail as I'm writing, I can go right to that category instead of wading through seven or eight note pads.

I'll often spend a day or two just walking around and thinking about a story. If you've come up writing for newspapers, this is where you have to be careful. There's a great urge to get to the typewriter and start producing something. I used to be that way. At first you begrudge that time of thinking, figuring out structure, what you really want to say with your story. But you shouldn't. You're not losing time, you're saving it, because you're going to spend a lot more time if you get a third of the way into your story and realize you don't really know where you're going.

Sometimes I want to start a story by putting the reader right inside the subject, right at the heart of the psychological dilemma. Other times I'll pull the microscope way back and look from a thousand miles away, then try to come closer and closer. It's hard to put any kind of formula on it. It's a feel for each situation, and a lot of it depends on how deep inside the subject has allowed you to look. As a writer, you can't set up camp inside a subject's guts if he hasn't let you in there. If it's not authentic, the strain in the writing will show.

Once I get that first couple of pages down, I've usually established a rhythm and a tone for the story. Sometimes I'm barely conscious of that rhythm and tone, but in this story I was. I'd probably read five books about the Crow Indians, and when I came across that quote from Plenty Coups that I used at the top, I knew I wanted to start with it and play off of it. The tone just followed from there.—G. S.

Susan Orlean

Susan Orlean has worked as a contributing editor for *Rolling Stone* and *Vogue* and written articles for the *Boston Globe, New York Times Magazine, Spy* and *Esquire*. She is the author of two books, *Red Socks and Blue Fish* (1989) and *Saturday Night* (1990). In 1992, she became a staff writer for the *New Yorker.* She is at work on a third book, *Passion,* about a fanatical orchid collector and poacher in South Florida. She lives in Manhattan.

The American Man at Age 10

If Colin Duffy and I were to get married, we would have matching superhero notebooks. We would wear shorts, big sneakers and long, baggy T-shirts depicting famous athletes every single day, even in the winter. We would sleep in our clothes. We would both be good at Nintendo Street Fighter II, but Colin would be better than me. We would have some homework, but it would never be too hard and we would always have just finished it. We would eat pizza and candy for all of our meals. We wouldn't have sex, but we would have crushes on each other and, magically, babies would appear in our home. We would win the lottery and then buy land in Wyoming, where we would have one of every kind of cute animal. All the while, Colin would be working in law enforcement—probably the FBI. Our favorite movie star, Morgan Freeman, would visit us occasionally. We would listen to the same Eurythmics song ("Here Comes the Rain Again") over and over again and watch two hours of television every Friday night. We would both be good at football, have best friends and know how to drive; we would cure AIDS and the garbage problem and everything that hurts animals. We would hang out a lot with Colin's dad. For fun, we would load a slingshot with dog food and shoot it at my butt. We would have a very good life.

Here are the particulars about Colin Duffy: He is 10 years old, on the nose. He is 4′ 8″ high, weighs 75 pounds and appears to be mostly leg and shoulder blade. He is a handsome kid. He has a broad forehead, dark eyes with dense lashes and a sharp, dimply smile. I have rarely ever seen him without a baseball cap. He owns several, but favors a University of Michigan Wolverines model, on account of its pleasing colors. The hat styles his hair into wild disarray. If you ever managed to get the hat off his head, you would see a boy with a nimbus of golden-brown hair, dented in the back, where the hat hits him.

Colin lives with his mother, Elaine; his father, Jim; his older sister, Megan; and his little brother, Chris, in a pretty pale-blue Victorian house on a bosky street in Glen Ridge, New Jersey. Glen Ridge is a serene and civilized old town 20 miles west of New York City. It does not have much of a commercial district, but it is a town of amazing lawns. Most of the houses were built around the turn of the century and are set back a gracious, green distance from the street. The rest of the town seems to consist of parks and playing fields and sidewalks and backyards—in other words, it is a far cry from South-Central Los Angeles and from Bedford-Stuyvesant and other, grimmer parts of the country where a very different 10-year-old American man is growing up today.

There is a fine school system in Glen Ridge, but Elaine and Jim, who are both schoolteachers, choose to send their children to a parents' cooperative elementary school in Montclair, a neighboring suburb. Currently, Colin is in fifth grade. He is a good student. He plans to go to college, to a place he says is called Oklahoma City State College University. OCSCU satisfies his desire to live out west, to attend a small college and to study law enforcement, which OCSCU apparently offers as a major. After four years at Oklahoma City State College University, he plans to work for the FBI. He says that getting to be a police officer involves tons of hard work, but working for the FBI will be a cinch, because all you have to do is fill out one form, which he has already gotten from the head FBI office. Colin is quiet in class but loud on the playground. He has a great throwing arm, significant foot speed and a lot of physical confidence. He is also brave. Huge wild cats with rabies and gross stuff dripping from their teeth, which he says run rampant throughout his neighborhood, do not scare him. Otherwise, he is slightly bashful. This combination of athletic grace and valor and personal reserve accounts for considerable popularity. He has a fluid relationship to many social groups, including the superbright nerds, the ultrajocks, the flashy kids who will someday become extremely popular and socially successful juvenile delinquents and the kids who will be elected president of the student body. In his opinion, the most popular boy in his class is Christian, who happens to be black, and Colin's favorite television character is Steve Urkel on *Family Matters,* who is black, too, but otherwise he seems uninterested in or oblivious to race. Until this year, he was a Boy Scout. Now he is planning to begin karate lessons. His favorite schoolyard game is football, followed closely by prison dodge ball, blob tag and bombardo. He's crazy about athletes, although sometimes it isn't clear if he is absolutely sure of the difference between human athletes and Marvel Comics action figures. His current athletic hero is Dave Meggett. His current best friend is named Japeth. He used to have another best friend named Ozzie. According to Colin, Ozzie was found on a doorstep, then changed his name to Michael and moved to Massachusetts, and then Colin never saw him or heard from him again.

He has had other losses in his life. He is old enough to know people who have died and to know things about the world that are worrisome. When he dreams, he dreams about moving to Wyoming, which he has visited with his family. His plan is to buy land there and have some sort of ranch that would definitely include horses. Sometimes when he talks about this, it sounds as ordinary and hard-boiled as a real estate appraisal; other times it can sound fantastical and wifty and achingly naive, informed by the last inklings of childhood—the musings of a balmy real estate appraiser assaying a wonderful and magical landscape that erodes from memory a little bit every day. The collision in his mind of what he understands, what he hears, what he figures out, what popular culture pours into him, what he knows, what he pretends to know and what he imagines, makes an interesting mess. The mess often has the form of what he will probably think like when he is a grown man, but the content of what he is like as a little boy.

He is old enough to begin imagining that he will someday get married, but at ten he is still convinced that the best thing about being married will be that he will be allowed to sleep in his clothes. His father once observed that living with Colin was like living with a Martian who had done some reading on American culture. As it happens, Colin is not especially sad or worried about the prospect of growing up, although he sometimes frets over whether he should be called a kid or a grown-up; he has settled on the word *kid-up.* Once, I asked him what the biggest advantage to adulthood will be, and he said, "The best thing is that grown-ups can go wherever they want." I asked him what he meant, exactly, and he said, "Well, if you're grown-up, you'd have a car, and whenever you felt like it, you could get into your car and drive somewhere and get candy."

Colin loves recycling. He loves it even more than, say, playing with little birds. That 10-year-olds feel the weight of the world and consider it their mission to shoulder it came as a surprise to me. I had gone with Colin one Monday to his classroom at Montclair Cooperative School. The Coop is in a steep, old, sharp-angled brick building that had served for many years as a public school until a group of parents in the area took it over and made it into a private, progressive elementary school. The fifth-grade classroom is on the top floor, under the dormers, which gives the room the eccentric shape and closeness of an attic. It is a rather informal environment. There are computers lined up in an adjoining room and instructions spelled out on the chalkboard—BRING IN: (1) A CUBBY WITH YOUR NAME ON IT, (2) A TRAPPER WITH A 5-POCKET ENVE-LOPE LABELED SCIENCE, SOCIAL STUDIES, READING/LANGUAGE ARTS, MATH, MATH LAB/COMPUTER; WHITE LINED PAPER; A PLAS-TIC PENCIL BAG; A SMALL HOMEWORK PAD, (3) LARGE BROWN GROCERY BAGS—but there is also a couch in the center of the classroom, which the kids take turns occupying, a rocking chair and three canaries in cages near the door.

It happened to be Colin's first day in fifth grade. Before class began, there was a lot of horsing around, but there were also a lot of conversations about whether Magic Johnson had AIDS or just HIV and whether someone falling in a pool of blood from a cut of his would get the disease. These jolts of sobriety in the midst of rank goofiness are a 10-year-old's specialty. Each one comes as a fresh, hard surprise, like finding a razor blade in a candy apple. One day, Colin and I had been discussing horses or dogs or something, and out of the blue he said, "What do you think is better, to dump garbage in the ocean, to dump it on land, or to burn it?" Another time, he asked me if I planned to have children. I had just spent an evening with him and his friend Japeth, during which they put every small, movable object in the house into Japeth's slingshot and fired it at me, so I told him that I wanted children but that I hoped they would all be girls, and he said, "Will you have an abortion if you find out you have a boy?"

At school, after discussing summer vacation, the kids began choosing the jobs they would do to help out around the classroom. Most of the jobs are humdrum—putting the chairs up on the tables, washing the chalkboard, turning the computers off or on. Five of the most humdrum tasks are recycling chores—for example, taking bottles or stacks of paper down to the basement, where they would be sorted and prepared for pickup. Two children would be assigned to feed the birds and cover their cages at the end of the day.

I expected the bird jobs to be the first to go. Everyone loved the birds; they'd spent an hour that morning voting on names for them (Tweetie, Montgomery and Rose narrowly beating out Axl Rose, Bugs, Ol' Yeller, Fido, Slim, Lucy and Chirpie). Instead, they all wanted to recycle. The recycling jobs were claimed by the first five kids called by Suzanne Nakamura, the fifth-grade teacher; each kid called after that responded by groaning, "Suzanne, aren't there any more recycling jobs?" Colin ended up with the job of taking down the chairs each morning. He accepted the task with a sort of resignation—this was just going to be a job rather than a mission.

On the way home that day, I was quizzing Colin about his world views.

"Who's the coolest person in the world?"

"Morgan Freeman."

"What's the best sport?"

"Football."

"Who's the coolest woman?"

"None. I don't know."

"What's the most important thing in the world?"

"Game Boy." Pause. "No, the world. The world is the most important thing in the world."

Danny's pizzeria is a dark little shop next door to the Montclair Cooperative School. It is not much to look at. Outside, the brick facing is painted muddy brown. Inside, there are some saggy counters, a splintered bench and enough room for either six teenagers or about a dozen 10-year-olds who happen to be getting along well. The light is low. The air is oily. At Danny's, you will find pizza, candy, Nintendo and very few girls. To a 10-year-old boy, it is the most beautiful place in the world.

One afternoon, after class was dismissed, we went to Danny's with Colin's friend Japeth to play Nintendo. Danny's has only one game,

Street Fighter II Champion Edition. Some teenage boys from a nearby middle school had gotten there first and were standing in a tall, impenetrable thicket around the machine.

"Next game," Colin said. The teenagers ignored him.

"Hey, we get next game," Japeth said. He is smaller than Colin, scrappy and, as he explained to me once, famous for wearing his hat backward all the time and having a huge wristwatch and a huge bedroom. He stamped his foot and announced again, "Hey, we get next game."

One of the teenagers turned around and said, "Fuck you, *next game,*" and then turned back to the machine.

"Whoa," Japeth said.

He and Colin went outside, where they felt bigger.

"Which street fighter are you going to be?" Colin asked Japeth.

"Blanka," Japeth said. "I know how to do his head-butt."

"I hate that! I hate the head-butt," Colin said. He dropped his voice a little and growled, "I'm going to be Ken, and I will kill you with my dragon punch."

"Yeah, right, and monkeys will fly out of my butt," Japeth said.

Street Fighter II is a video game in which two characters have an explosive brawl in a scenic international setting. It is currently the most popular video-arcade game in America. This is not an insignificant amount of popularity. Most arcade versions of video games, which end up in pizza parlors, malls and arcades, sell about 2,000 units. So far, some 50,000 Street Fighter II and Street Fighter II Championship Edition arcade games have been sold. Not since Pac-Man, which was released the year before Colin was born, has there been a video game as popular as Street Fighter. The home version of Street Fighter is the most popular home video game in the country, and that, too, is not an insignificant thing. Thirty-two million Nintendo home systems have been sold since 1986, when it was introduced in this country. There is a Nintendo system in seven of every ten homes in America in which a child between the ages of eight and 12 resides. By the time a boy in America turns 10, he will almost certainly have been exposed to Nintendo home games, Nintendo arcade games and Game Boy, the handheld version. He will probably own a system and dozens of games. By 10, according to Nintendo studies, teachers and psychologists, game prowess becomes a fundamental, essential male social marker and a schoolyard boast.

The Street Fighter characters are Dhalsim, Ken, Guile, Blanka, E. Honda, Ryu, Zangief and Chun Li. Each represents a different country, and they each have their own special weapon. Chun Li, for instance, is from China and possesses a devastating whirlwind kick that is triggered if you push the control pad down for two seconds and then up for two seconds, and then you hit the kick button. Chun Li's kick is money in the bank, because most of the other fighters do not have a good defense against it. By the way, Chun Li happens to be a girl—the only female Street Fighter character. I asked Colin if he was interested in being Chun Li. There was a long pause. "I would rather be Ken," he said.

The girls in Colin's class at school are named Cortnerd, Terror, Spacey, Lizard, Maggot and Diarrhea. "They do have other names, but that's what we call them," Colin told me. "The girls aren't very popular."

"They are about as popular as a piece of dirt," Japeth said. "Or, you know that couch in the classroom? That couch is more popular than any girl. A thousand times more." They talked for a minute about one of the girls in their class, a tall blonde with cheerleader genetic material, who they allowed was not quite as gross as some of the other girls. Japeth said that a chubby, awkward boy in their class was boasting that this girl liked him.

"No way," Colin said. "She would never like him. I mean, not that he's so . . . I don't know. I don't hate him because he's fat, anyway. I hate him because he's nasty."

"Well, she doesn't like him," Japeth said. "She's been really mean to me lately, so I'm pretty sure she likes me."

"Girls are different," Colin said. He hopped up and down on the balls of his feet, wrinkling his nose. "Girls are stupid and weird."

"I have a lot of girlfriends, about six or so," Japeth said, turning contemplative. "I don't exactly remember their names, though."

The teenagers came crashing out of Danny's and jostled past us, so we went inside. The man who runs Danny's, whose name is Tom, was leaning across the counter on his elbows, looking exhausted. Two little boys, holding Slush Puppies, shuffled toward the Nintendo, but Colin and Japeth elbowed them aside and slammed their quarters down on the machine. The little boys shuffled back toward the counter and stood gawking at them, sucking on their drinks.

"You want to know how to tell if a girl likes you?" Japeth said. "She'll act really mean to you. That's a sure sign. I don't know why they do it, but it's always a sure sign. It gets your attention. You know how I show a girl I like her? I steal something from her and then run away. I do it to get their attention, and it works."

They planned four quarters' worth of games. During the last one, a teenager with a quilted leather jacket and a fade haircut came in, pushed his arm between them and put a quarter down on the deck of the machine.

Japeth said, "Hey, what's that?"

The teenager said, "I get next game. I've marked it now. Everyone knows this secret sign for next game. It's a universal thing."

"So now we know," Japeth said. "Colin, let's get out of here and go bother Maggie. I mean Maggot. Okay?" They picked up their backpacks and headed out the door.

Psychologists identify 10 as roughly the age at which many boys experience the gender-linked normative developmental trauma that leaves them, as adult men, at risk for specific psychological sequelae often manifest as deficits in the arenas of intimacy, empathy and struggles with commitment in relationships. In other words, this is around the age when guys get screwed up about girls. Elaine and Jim Duffy, and probably most of the parents who send their kids to Montclair Cooperative School, have done a lot of stuff to try to avoid this. They gave Colin dolls as well as guns. (He preferred guns.) Japeth's father has three motorcycles and two dirt bikes but does most of the cooking and cleaning in their home. Suzanne, Colin's teacher, is careful to avoid sexist references in her presentations. After school, the yard at Montclair Cooperative is filled with as many fathers as mothers—fathers who hug their kids when they come prancing out of the building and are dismayed when their sons clamor for Supersoaker water guns and war toys or take pleasure in beating up girls.

In a study of adolescents conducted by the Gesell Institute of Human Development, nearly half the 10-year-old boys questioned said they thought they had adequate information about sex. Nevertheless, most 10-year-old boys across the country are subjected to a few months of sex education in school. Colin and his class will get their dose next spring. It is yet another installment in a plan to make them into new, improved men with reconstructed notions of sex and male-female relationships. One afternoon I asked Philip, a schoolmate of Colin's, whether he was looking forward to sex education, and he said, "No, because I think it'll probably make me really, really hyper. I have a feeling it's going to be just like what it was like when some television reporters came to school last year and filmed us in class and I got really hyper. They stood around with all these cameras and asked us questions. I think that's what sex education is probably like."

At a class meeting earlier in the day:

Suzanne: "Today was our first day of swimming class, and I have one observation to make. The girls went into their locker room, got dressed without a lot of fuss and came into the pool area. The boys, on the other hand, the *boys* had some sort of problem doing that rather simple task. Can someone tell me what exactly went on in the locker room?"

Keith: "There was a lot of shouting."

Suzanne: "Okay, I hear you saying that people were being noisy and shouting. Anything else?"

Christian: "Some people were screaming so much that my ears were killing me. It gave me, like, a huge headache. Also, some of the boys were taking their towels, I mean, after they had taken their clothes off, they had their towels around their waists and then they would drop them really fast and then pull them back up, really fast."

Suzanne: "Okay, you're saying some people were being silly about their bodies."

Christian: "Well, yeah, but it was more like they were being silly about their pants."

Colin's bedroom is decorated simply. He has a cage with his pet parakeet, Dude, on his dresser, a lot of recently worn clothing piled haphazardly on the floor and a husky brown teddy bear sitting upright in a chair near the foot of his bed. The walls are mostly bare, except for a Spiderman poster and a few ads torn out of magazines he has thumbtacked up. One of the ads is for a cologne, illustrated with several small photographs of cowboy hats; another, a feverish portrait of a woman on a horse, is an ad for blue jeans. These inspire him sometimes when he lies in bed and makes plans for the move to Wyoming. Also, he happens to like ads. He also likes television commercials. Generally speaking, he likes consumer products and popular culture. He partakes avidly but not indiscriminately. In fact, during the time we spent together, he provided a running commentary on merchandise, media and entertainment:

"The only shoes anyone will wear are Reebok Pumps. Big T-shirts are cool, not the kind that are sticky and close to you, but big and baggy and long, not the kind that stop at your stomach."

"The best food is Chicken McNuggets and Life cereal and Frosted Flakes."

"Don't go to Blimpie's. They have the worst service."

"I'm not into Teenage Mutant Ninja Turtles anymore. I grew out of that. I like Donatello, but I'm not a fan. I don't buy the figures anymore."

"The best television shows are on Friday night on ABC. It's called TGIF, and it's *Family Matters, Step by Step, Dinosaurs* and *Perfect Strangers*, where the guy has a funny accent."

"The best candy is Skittles and Symphony bars and Crybabies and Warheads. Crybabies are great because if you eat a lot of them at once you feel so sour."

"Hyundais are Korean cars. It's the only Korean car. They're not that good because Koreans don't have a lot of experience building cars."

"The best movie is *City Slickers*, and the best part was when he saved his little cow in the river."

"The Giants really need to get rid of Ray Handley. They have to get somebody who has real coaching experience. He's just no good."

"My dog, Sally, costs $72. That sounds like a lot of money, but it's a really good price because you get a flea bath with your dog."

"The best magazines are *Nintendo Power*, because they tell you how to do the secret moves in the video games, and also *Mad* magazine and *Money Guide*—I really like that one."

"The best artist in the world is Jim Davis."

"The most beautiful woman in the world is not Madonna! Only Wayne and Garth think that! She looks like maybe a . . . a . . . slut or something. Cindy Crawford looks like she would look good, but if you see her on an awards program on TV she doesn't look that good. I think the most beautiful woman in the world probably is my mom."

Colin thinks a lot about money. This started when he was about nine and a half, which is when a lot of other things started—a new way of walking that has a little macho hitch and swagger, a decision about the Teenage Mutant Ninja Turtles (con) and Eurythmics (pro) and a persistent curiosity about a certain girl whose name he will not reveal. He knows the price of everything he encounters. He knows how much college costs and what someone might earn performing different jobs. Once, he asked me what my husband did; when I answered that he was a lawyer, he snapped, "You must be a rich family. Lawyers make $400,000 a year." His preoccupation with money baffles his family. They are not struggling, so this is not the anxiety of deprivation; they are not rich, so he is not responding to an elegant, advantaged world. His allowance is $5 a week. It seems sufficient for his needs, which consist chiefly of quarters for Nintendo and candy money. The remainder is put into his Wyoming fund. His fascination is not just specific to needing money or having plans for money: It is as if money itself, and the way it makes the world work, and the realization that almost everything in the world can be assigned a price, has possessed him. "I just pay attention to things like that," Colin says. "It's really very interesting."

He is looking for a windfall. He tells me his mother has been notified that she is in the fourth and final round of the Publisher's Clearinghouse Sweepstakes. This is not an ironic observation. He plays the New Jersey lottery every Thursday night. He knows the weekly jackpot; he knows the number to call to find out if he has won. I do not think this presages a future for Colin as a high-stakes gambler; I think it says more about the powerful grasp that money has on imagination and what a large percentage of a 10-year-old's mind is made up of imaginings. One Friday, we were at school together, and one of his friends was asking him about the lottery, and he said, "This week it was $4 million. That would be I forget how much every year for the rest of your life. It's a lot, I think. You should play. All it takes is a dollar and a dream."

Until the lottery comes through and he starts putting together the Wyoming land deal, Colin can be found most of the time in the backyard. Often, he will have friends come over. Regularly, children from the neighborhood will gravitate to the backyard, too. As a technical matter of real-property law, title to the house and yard belongs to Jim and Elaine Duffy, but Colin adversely possesses the backyard, at least from 4:00 each afternoon until it gets dark. As yet, the fixtures of teenage life— malls, video arcades, friends' basements, automobiles—either hold little interest for him or are not his to have.

He is, at the moment, very content with his backyard. For most in-tents and purposes, it is as big as Wyoming. One day, certainly, he will grow and it will shrink, and it will become simply a suburban backyard and it won't be big enough for him anymore. This will happen so fast that one night he will be in the backyard, believing it a perfect place, and by the next night he will have changed and the yard as he imagined it will be gone, and this era of his life will be behind him forever.

Most days, he spends his hours in the backyard building an Evil Spider-Web Trap. This entails running a spool of Jim's fishing line from every surface in the yard until it forms a huge web. Once a garbage-man picking up the Duffys' trash got caught in the trap. Otherwise, the Evil Spider-Web Trap mostly has a deterrent effect, because the kids in the neighborhood who might roam over know that Colin builds it back there. "I do it all the time," he says. "First I plan who I'd like to catch in it, and then we get started. Trespassers have to beware."

One afternoon when I came over after a few rounds of Street Fighter at Danny's, Colin started building a trap. He selected a victim for inspiration—a boy in his class who had been pestering him—and began wrapping. He was entirely absorbed. He moved from tree to tree, wrapping; he laced fishing line through the railing of the deck and then back to the shed; he circled an old jungle gym, something he'd outgrown and abandoned a few years ago, and then crossed over to a bush at the back of the yard. Briefly, he contemplated making his dog, Sally, part of the web. Dusk fell. He kept wrapping, paying out fishing line an inch at a time. We could hear mothers up and down the block hooting for their kids; two tiny children from next door stood transfixed at the edge of the yard, uncertain whether they would end up inside or outside the web. After a while, the spool spun around in Colin's hands one more time and then stopped; he was out of line.

It was almost too dark to see much of anything, although now and again the light from the deck would glance off a length of line, and it would glint and sparkle. "That's the point," he said. "You could do it with thread, but the fishing line is invisible. Now I have this perfect thing and the only one who knows about it is me." With that, he dropped the spool, skipped up the stairs of the deck, threw open the screen door, and then bounded into the house, leaving me and Sally the dog trapped in his web.

▓ Author's Afterwords . . .

Esquire called and asked me to do a story on Macaulay Culkin. I said I didn't want to profile him, but if the point was to profile someone his age, I'd be game. The first challenge was to find a 10-year-old who was an individual and someone symbolic of his species. I asked friends of friends and finally was introduced to Colin. I didn't want a kid whose life was exceptional. I figured a boy who lived in the suburbs was more typical than a Manhattan kid, and Colin's parents were schoolteachers, which seemed perfect.

I'm a proud banner bearer of the idea of being completely unprepared. I say this knowing that all journalism professors will shudder. When you're writing about a politician or a celebrity who has an agenda, it's important to be prepared because you're in an adversarial role. But when you go in to write a story that requires empathy and curiosity, the less preconception you bring the more genuine your empathetic connection will be. For me, the best way to do this is to put myself in a sort of emotional danger, to go in vulnerable. The fact is, I *am* vulnerable—I am the stranger, the one who's awkward and out of place. It's important for me to keep that emotion, to remember that I'm the one who doesn't know what's going on. It makes me ask better questions, because I need to understand through their eyes, not through what I've boned up on.

I spent two weeks, day and night with Colin. I'd go to his house in the morning without a plan, go to school with him, hang out with him after school. I can't tell you how self-conscious I felt the day I began. Colin didn't talk to me for the first three days. I thought, I can't do this story—I can't even get him to talk to me! I didn't ask him a lot of questions because I thought if I started pestering him, he would avoid me more and more. I could tell he was embarrassed going to school with this big girl tagging along. On the third day, he apparently decided I was okay, and that day after school he said, "Do you want to come over and see my room?"

At some point on every story I find myself thinking that I don't know what I'm doing. I don't know where the story is going, and my reporting feels like just a bunch of scattered moments. Being worried that I've lost track keeps me sharp. I wait until I'm finished reporting to figure out the story. Sometimes, as I'm reviewing my notes or writing, a tiny detail suddenly takes on weight. I'm often thoroughly surprised. A story really is a creature, and the creature always has arms and legs I didn't expect it to have. That's why I'm a fanatical over-reporter. I don't know what's going to be useful, so everything is important.

I use note pads and not a tape recorder. I don't like dealing with technology while I'm trying to pay attention, and I hate transcribing. When I'm through reporting, I type up my notes as a way of reviewing them. Then I sit down and highlight important material. The Colin story was written as if from inside his mind. When I re-read it, I laughed because it's as much in his voice as mine. The way the world appeared to him was so divine and eccentric. It was a teeny bit realistic and a lot imaginary. His voice was the perfect way to capture his complicated sense of the world. The way I saw things as an adult didn't seem important.

When I finally do sit down to write, I'm ready. It sounds a bit mystical, but I don't exactly know where the writing comes from. I often look at a lead after I've written it and think, Where did that come from? And it seems like the only lead I could have possibly written. Often when I'm writing, the story starts having a voice that seems very natural. It's not deliberate. I get a little hypnotized by the sound of the people I'm talking to, and it fills my head. I fall into a rhythm with it. Before I get to that, I usually suffer through a few days of torture when instead of writing I wash lots of dishes and make the bed over and over and get my shoes polished, just to distract myself while I'm letting all this reporting cook. When I feel ready to write, it's because something has risen to the surface. I feel it and hear it when I sit down and start writing.

I took about 10 days to write Colin. It simmered for about three days before I started. On every story, I worry that this is the one I can't write. I used to interpret my anxiety as a premonition—this really is the one I'm going to screw up. But if you get nervous every time you fly, you realize after a while that you're not having a premonition that the plane will crash: You just get nervous every time you fly.

Sometimes, when a sentence I've written is musical, I'm just so happy. When I think of an analogy that seems really fresh and different, I'm just delighted. To create something that's separate from me—a thing that exists out in the world—gives me intense pleasure. I'm as excited as if I had pulled a rabbit out of a hat. I'm an unspiritual person, so I'm embarrassed to say it's a spiritual sensation. But it's a passion to express, and that is spiritual. The only way to create is to acknowledge that and savor it.—S. O.

David Finkel

David Finkel has worked as a reporter for the *Tallahassee Democrat* and the *St. Petersburg Times*. In 1990, he became a staff writer for the *Washington Post Magazine*. He is the winner of the distinguished writing award from the American Society of Newspaper Editors. His article "TV Without Guilt" was a finalist for the Pulitzer Prize for feature writing. He lives in Silver Spring, Maryland.

The Last Housewife in America

To find where the Stewart family lives, start from Cincinnati and work south down the interstate. Even when the sky is starless, it's easy to find the way. First comes the sign welcoming you to Kentucky. Next comes the city of Covington. Soon comes the town of Florence, which has two exits and a mall. The road at the second exit is wide and glossy until a certain curve, when the bright store signs fade and the suburbs come to an end. There are lights ahead, but they are different—no longer fluorescent and concentrated, but scattered yellow pinpoints on the far rim of a field. They are the porch lights of houses on a street called Red Clover Court, which is about to come awake. The street is a cul-de-sac. The houses are new. The first interior light, a bedroom lamp, is switched on before 6:00 a.m., followed by lights in the bathroom, the hallway, the kitchen. Before long, up and down the street, more lights come on as people hurry to shower, dress, assemble children, feed babies, pack diaper bags, load cars, get on their way. By sunrise, the migration has begun. Lights go off, doors are locked, garage doors rise, cars pull away. The rush is toward the highway and downtown Cincinnati, and as the last car turns out of sight, Red Clover Court seems suddenly abandoned.

At one house, however, a woman still stands by the front door. Her name is JoAnn Stewart, and she is waiting for her husband, Scott, who is coming down the hallway in a charcoal suit, his shirt wrinkle-free, his red tie knotted tightly, his briefcase in hand.

"Bye, honey," she says, rubbing him on the back.

Next comes her son Ben, blond and fresh, who will take the school bus to first grade.

"Use your manners," she says, kissing him on the cheek.

Then comes her other son, Brian, a big, happy boy, who will spend the morning in preschool.

"You have a good morning, okay?"

The door closes, and JoAnn is alone, and with no hesitation, she sets out to do what she does every day, what her mother used to do, and her grandmother before that. She sets out to be a housewife. She clears the breakfast dishes. She reaches for the vacuum. She reaches for the dustcloth. She reaches for the laundry. There is a smile on her face, and soon she begins to whistle.

In every life, days unfold in particular ways. Mostly they are steered by a watch: a succession of precise minutes and seconds, of deadlines and adjustments, of calculations and trade-offs in which a lingering morning kiss can mean a 10-minute wait for the next train. For JoAnn Stewart, days follow a different pace, one that is an anomaly. They are guided not by devices but by more forgiving measures—the length of a wash cycle, or the time it takes to bake a potato, or the type of light coming in through the kitchen windows. There are clocks in JoAnn's house, but when she is alone, they are unnecessary. When it's bright out, she knows, it's time to think about lunch. When the light begins to fade, it's time to think about dinner. Hers is an imprecise life with one precise aspect: Even though she knows being a housewife is an aberration, that is exactly what she wants to be.

JoAnn is 34 years old, a year younger than Scott, who works in public relations for Procter & Gamble. She has a relaxed grace and an effortless smile, and she talks in a way that makes Scott and the boys want to wake up and see why she is so happy. Her voice is the thing. There is a melody to it, a lilt—not Southern, exactly, which is so often twitters and sighs—but excited and uplifting. "Look," Brian will say, handing her an old feather he has brought in from outside. "Where did you find that?" she will ask, as if the feather were the most precious thing in the world.

She is like this all the time. Most nights, she is the last one to fall asleep. She will get into bed, turn out the lights and listen in the dark to the final sounds of a vanishing day. She will hear Scott's quiet breathing and the boys down the hall, turning under their covers. Sometimes the sounds lull her to sleep; other times she remains awake, sifting through her life. She thinks of growing up, how she used to come home from dates, fix herself a bowl of cereal and talk to her mother, who always waited up for her. She thinks of what life is like now. Just in the paper today there was a story about a woman who gave birth, put the baby in a plastic bag and threw the bag in the trash. Just threw a baby away!

Occasionally, one of the boys stirs with a bad dream. "Stop it," Ben will holler sharply, or, inexplicably, as on one night, "Purple." She gets up to check on him. He is sprawled across the sheets, eyes closed, one leg bent at the knee, the other hanging down in the space between the bed and the wall. The nightmare, whatever it was, is gone. She gets back into bed. She thinks of the house. She can visualize every inch of it, every corner, every blemish, every smudge. It's so ordinary, she sometimes thinks of her life. It's a thought that carries no hint of regret.

Monday. Cleaning day. She always starts with the beds. Hospital corners are adjusted. Sheets are tucked tight. Bedspreads are smoothed. Pillows are fluffed. The beds always go quickly, but from there on, the morning gets harder. After breakfast and dishes, she is vacuuming Ben's room. A minute later, she is on to Brian's, then the upstairs hallway, then her bedroom. From vacuuming, she sorts through the laundry, empties the trash, straightens the closets. In her closet, she finds a stray ball and tosses it toward Brian's room. "Whoops," she says as it ricochets off a wall, but she doesn't pause. She dons yellow gloves, picks up a sponge and sprinkles Comet in the bathroom sink. "I've tried some other ones. It's one of those things. My mom used Comet," she says. She pours Pine Sol into the toilet. "There's a big difference. I've tried the cheaper ones, the no-name ones. You don't have to use as much of this, and the smell is better."

She tackles the mirrors with Windex and a paper towel, although frequently she uses a coffee filter instead. "I was at Hardee's, and I saw someone using one on the windows. I went up, 'What are you doing?' He said, 'What do you mean? Washing the windows.' 'No, I mean with the coffee filter.' 'They have us use it. No lint.' I've used them ever since. They do work. On car windows, too."

From there, it's on to the first floor, the vacuum bumping down the stairs, the dustcloth flying over the bookcases, more Comet, more Pine Sol, more Windex. By late morning, she is done with the heavy work, at least until Friday, when she will do it all again. In the interim, she will straighten up, adjust, arrange, cook meals, run errands, wipe counters, do laundry, work in the garden and begin every day by throwing together the beds. She makes 21 beds a week. She washes and folds 100 pounds of laundry and goes to the grocery store at least twice. She serves 28 breakfasts, 15 lunches and 24 dinners. Plus drinks. Plus snacks. Plus, she mows the lawn and shovels the sidewalk and has taken charge of the landscaping and is thinking of painting the house.

"I don't know. I look at my mom," JoAnn says one afternoon, trying to explain why she has chosen to live such a life. Brian is on the floor watching TV. Ben is on the couch. She is making them cinnamon toast. "I think she's happy. I see her as someone who accomplished the major goal she had. I don't think she's regretful."

"Mom," Ben calls.

"I think I'm a reflection of her thinking," JoAnn goes on. "What Scott and I are doing, what's important to us . . ."

"*Mom!*"

"I think of her as a stable force . . ."

"Mom!"

"A kind of . . ."

"Mom, look at my moustache!"

"How can I put this?"

"Mom, I'm a shark!"

"You know, there are some women who work their whole life, who look back and realize the world goes on, and think, What good am I?" The toast pops up in the toaster. She puts it on a plate, smooths on some butter, sprinkles on the cinnamon. "I don't know. We're not as important as we think we are," says JoAnn. "I can think of people we know, and they work and work, and that's all they do."

Later, when Scott comes home, he walks into a house that seems new. The floors have been mopped, the teak furniture oiled, the fireplace mantel dusted. There is nothing thick or stale in the air; rather the smell is of lightness, of lemons and clear water. Scott goes upstairs to change, where the bedroom carpet is still lined with the brush of the morning's vacuum. JoAnn starts to assemble dinner and allows herself to wonder whether Scott knows how much she has done. "Probably not," she says. "But I don't know everything he does, either."

What he does is drive his Toyota Camry, the budget version with the stick shift, the one he had to borrow money from his in-laws for, out of the neighborhood. He drives past the spot on the highway where sometime last year a child was hit by a car and the chalk outline of the body took three months to fade. He turns onto the interstate, drives across the Ohio River and into downtown Cincinnati, where he parks under an overpass and heads on foot toward the edifice that is Procter & Gamble.

Especially in the morning, the sensation is of thousands of people hurrying in from every point of the compass. Scott is 6′ 5″, and his stride is long. He climbs a steep hill and walks past the different Procter & Gamble divisions, past Market Research, past Chemicals, past Corporate, past a man named Bob, who is P&G's liaison to bottlers across the country. "Hi, Bob," says Scott. "Morning, Scott," says Bob. Scott walks to the oldest building in the compound, shows his badge to security, takes the elevator to the fifth floor, turns the first corner and ducks into a small office with a nameplate by the door that reads, T. S. STEWART.

He likes to be at his desk by 7:30 a.m., before his boss, before the secretaries. "Just to get a jump on the day," he says, but the truth is he loves his job, and he loves P&G "Tide, Cheer, Dash, Bold, Era. You're talking about everything on the shelf," he says with pride. "It's just phenomenal. Oxydol, Comet, Top Job, Mr. Clean, Spic and Span. Coast, Camay, Safeguard, Lava." He spots a bottle of fabric softener on his desk. "And, of course, Downy."

The bottle of Downy is next to a photograph of Ben, Brian and JoAnn, which is next to a report entitled *P&G Statement Regarding Proposed Vermont Ban on Disposable Diapers*. For the past year, the ruckus over disposable diapers has been Scott's specialty, and he has traveled across the country to persuade journalists that P&G is as concerned as anyone about the environment. "It's exciting work," he says. "I can't think of anyplace else I'd rather be." He tries to call home as often as he can. Late last year, when he was in New York, he was walking along when he realized he was outside Macy's. Macy's of New York. Macy's of *Miracle on*

34th Street, one of JoAnn's favorite movies. He couldn't get to a pay phone fast enough.

"Guess where I am?" he said.

"Where?" she said, trying to hear him over the honking in the background.

"Someplace you'd like to be."

"Give me a hint."

"It has to do with shopping and Christmas."

"Macy's!"

Later he called again, after he had been inside. "Do you believe they have wooden escalators?"

He is on the phone a lot, once or twice a day to home and much of the rest of the time to any reporter who wants to know Procter & Gamble's position on diapers and recycling. A call comes in from Canada. Scott invites a new member of the Public Relations division into his office to listen. He shuts the door and talks to the Canadian reporter about the health benefits of disposable diapers, of the lack of leakage, of the recycling experiments P&G is conducting. He hangs up. The new employee, a woman, stares at him in amazement.

"It just flows out of your mouth!" she says to him. "It's so clear! I knew just what was being asked by your answers. Your bridges to the larger issues!" She shakes her head in disbelief. "I'm so impressed."

"Well," Scott says, a little embarrassed. "Thanks."

She leaves. He looks at his watch and tries to imagine what JoAnn is up to.

"Probably doing housework," is his guess.

Actually, at the moment, she is running errands. She goes her way, Scott goes his, and at night they sit on the couch, her feet on his lap, or his feet on hers, and talk about what the day was like.

She asks, "How was work?"

He asks, "How were the kids?"

They both answer, in detail. Beyond such talk, however, their worlds rarely collide. His job doesn't take them to a lot of parties, and besides, she only owns a couple of dresses, which are surrounded in her closet by endless sweaters and blue jeans. That's the way they both prefer it. Sometimes, though, some function comes along that they need to go to, and before they even arrive, they know what's bound to happen. Like at a Christmas party last year. They were in the kitchen with five or six other people when one of them, a woman, turned to JoAnn and said, "What do you do?"

"I stay home," JoAnn said. "I have two sons."

The woman chewed on this for a moment, as if tasting old cabbage. "Well, you *do* work then," she finally said.

The inclination was to walk away, or to fume a bit over such condescension, or at the very least to stop smiling, but JoAnn didn't. Maybe it was because she had heard those things enough times over the years to let them pass without a ripple. Or maybe she had come to realize that other people, especially women who own rows of dresses and eel-skin appointment books, don't know what to make of her.

"It kind of sounds shallow," she acknowledges of her life. "It sounds Victorian. It sounds boring. But it's not. Not to me."

Nor to Scott. It is what they wanted from their first date, back in November of 1978. Both had just graduated from college. He took her to the revolving bar on top of the Louisville, Kentucky, Hyatt. He ordered a daiquiri, and she ordered a gin and tonic, and at some point, when they felt comfortable enough with each other to share some dreams, she mentioned that if she married and had children, she would want to stay home. That's nice, he said, that's great. The bar kept spinning, past 11:00 p.m., past midnight, and every so often, when the table faced toward the west, they could see across the river to Indiana, where they had both grown up in families much like the kind they were talking about now.

He was raised in New Albany, in a brick split-level; she in a nearby town called Floyds Knobs, in a brick-and-glass house surrounded by woods. After college, he took a job running New Albany's job-training program, and she became director of the city's Parks department. Which is why they met. She employed a lot of the people he trained. So one day, he went to see her. Twelve years later, he can still remember what she looked like that day, and what she said about marriage, and most everything since.

"You remember the date of our first kiss?" he asks JoAnn one night.

She looks at him blankly.

"November 4, 1972; 2:02 a.m."

She thinks about that, and then she thinks about how long ago that was. In the time since, she has grown up. She went from being a daughter to a wife to a mother, leaving behind an empty room in a house that her parents eventually moved out of and sold. That house, the one she had lived in from childhood to college, had meant everything to her. Her parents had made it a wonderful place for a child to grow up, just as she is trying to do now.

She should have stayed away from that house. But one time she went back. It was last year, a hot day in September. She drove out with her parents and her brother Jon. They went as much for reminiscence as anything, and when the house appeared, so did all kinds of memories. Then they walked in the front door. Jon, sensing immediately that the house had changed, froze. JoAnn made it down a hallway before realizing the same thing. She turned around and excused herself. She walked back toward Jon, who whispered to her, "I'm going to be sick."

"I know," she whispered back.

"I can't believe it."

"I know."

They went outside, walked around a nearby pond, came back to the house. Their mother was out front, pacing aimlessly.

"Where'd you go?" she asked them.

"Couldn't take it," was all Jon could manage to say.

"I know," she said. "It makes you kind of sick."

Their father came out. They got in the car and drove off. "Time goes on," he said, laughing. Then he stopped laughing, and a long stretch of silence descended.

One time, when JoAnn was 16, a boy she knew died in the course of a day. He was slightly younger than she, the son of her parents' best friends. He was playing baseball, and as he stood at the plate, the catcher somehow misfired the ball. Maybe he was holding the ball too tightly, or maybe he was off-kilter. In any event, the ball didn't arch back toward the pitcher as it should have, but went fast and straight into the back of the boy's head. He was wearing a helmet, but it didn't matter. He went home a little dizzy, developed a fever in the evening and died soon after from a blood clot. It was 2:00 a.m., JoAnn remembers, when the phone in her house rang.

"I remember the moon was real bright. I couldn't make out any of the conversation, but you could tell by the voices. I can remember seeing the headlights pulling out of the driveway, and I ran up and saw the note they left, and I went back to my room and just lay there."

That was when JoAnn, who had grown up with no real misfortunes in her life, learned that people can die before they're ready. After that, she learned that they can die deliberately, in ways both indifferent and resigned. There was a friend in college. One night, they ordered some pizza, and the friend went back to her room to wait, and when JoAnn went to get her a few minutes later, she was sitting on her bed with one wrist slit open, casually watching the flow of blood as if it were science, not suicide.

Later, after college, when JoAnn worked at the Parks department, the acts of distress weren't as methodical, but the results were the same. There are housing projects in New Albany—not like a large city's, but projects nonetheless—and a lot of the young girls who lived there got pregnant. There was one girl, JoAnn remembers, barely 15, who treated pregnancy as a financial equation—one baby meant so much money a month, two babies meant that much more. Another girl she remembers would talk about how the boys were accusing her of being a lesbian because she wouldn't sleep with them. The girl was determined to hold out, though. She had plans to finish high school and go on to college. But then word came back that she had given in, that she was several weeks along, and JoAnn was overcome by a suffocating feeling, a realization that some lives are carved from a lack of choice and guided solely by disenchantment.

Self-esteem, she decided after that, is what's missing in a lot of children. Which is why, on the night when she got a little dreamy with Scott, she said that when she became a wife and mother, she would very much like to stay home.

Wednesday. JoAnn drives Brian to preschool and stays for a while. She knows Brian better than anyone does, and yet when he stands next to the other children, she is struck by how fast he is growing. "Look at his feet and hands," she marvels. "Like paws on dogs."

Next she goes to Ben's school to eat lunch. He is glad to have her there, just as she used to like it when she would climb onto a school bus for a field trip, and there, among the volunteers, would be her mother. She and Ben walk to the cafeteria, past the school lobby where a JUST SAY NO banner is hanging, past the office of the school counselor who conducts a weekly class for children whose parents are divorcing, past the office of the school psychologist who treated two elementary-school children last year after they'd threatened to kill themselves. The day's lunch selection is pizza. JoAnn sits across from Ben and three of his friends. Everyone is yelling, and it's hard to hear, but at one point JoAnn catches the word *therapy*. She turns to the little girl who is sitting next to her, and the girl leans forward, presses her face close and hollers, "I'm in therapy."

"Oh," JoAnn says. She smiles at the girl, and the girl smiles back, and they both return to their pizza, and JoAnn thinks to herself, Well, why not?

She heads home. It isn't far. Nothing is, actually. It's two miles from the house to the school, three to the grocery, three to the toy store, three to the mall. Dinner that night is pork chops, potatoes, green beans, salad and rolls made from scratch.

"These are good rolls, Mom," Ben says reaching for more.

Meanwhile, across the street at the Cooper residence, dinner hasn't even been started. In fact, Casey Cooper and his wife, Terri, are still unwinding from work. He has been up since 6:30 a.m. She has been up since 5:00. They both have full-time jobs, and their children, twin 15-month-old girls, go to day care.

"We had a choice between me working or having a small house in a neighborhood we didn't like," says Terri. "For me, it was more important to have this. I grew up in a neighborhood like this, and I want my kids to have it, too."

"We're exhausted a lot of the time," Casey says. "We come home, we've both already worked eight hours, and we have everything to do. The worst is when the kids are sick."

"It's hard. I miss the kids, I miss seeing the little things they do," Terri says. "I get a break at work and think, I wonder what they're doing?"

Down the street, at Dave and Joyce Crail's house, life is much the same. They get up at 6:00, give a bottle to their baby, Andrew, dress while he drinks it, pack his diaper bag, leave by 7:00, drop Andrew off at day care, get to downtown Cincinnati by 7:45 and grab breakfast from a vending machine. Dave usually has soda and cookies, Joyce usually has soda and Cheez Doodles. They are always tired. Once, when Andrew woke up early, Joyce went to comfort him, lay down on the floor, shut her eyes for a moment and awakened 12 hours later.

"There's times when I wish I could stay home," Joyce says. "But then, we wouldn't have this house. But then I think material things shouldn't be that important . . ." She lets out a sigh. "It's pretty resolved."

"No question," Dave says to her. "You quit, we move."

Next door at Tom and Judy McMeans's, the talk is of the time that Judy did stay home.

Tom: "When Judy didn't work, I got 'I'm going nuts. The kids are driving me crazy. I need to talk to an adult.' "

Judy: "He was my only release."

Tom: "I was tired of hearing it."

Judy: "I can't imagine what JoAnn's life is like."

JoAnn, on the other hand, can easily imagine theirs. She sees the rush of cars in the morning and the returning tide at night. She hears their stories and knows how hard it must be. She knows also that as much as she believes in what she's doing, they believe in what they're doing, as well. And who's to say who's right? There are no guarantees, not about anything. Scott wasn't the only one who passed by the chalk outline of the dead child. She did, too. And the children who do make it through childhood, and through ordinary games of baseball, and the pressures of adolescence, and the first days of college—she knows they can end up bleeding alone on a bed.

Who can say what will happen to Ben? Or Brian? Or her? She has known other women who stayed home, and she saw how they soured, grew lethargic, watched TV, wore their bathrobes most of the day. She thinks that in a few years she will probably want to do something else to keep her life interesting, maybe some volunteer work, maybe something like art lessons, but who knows? Who, for that matter, can say what will happen to her and Scott?

In their 10 years of marriage, they've had their share of fights. A few times she fled the house and went for long, long drives; one time she got out a suitcase and began to pack. But even as she was packing, she knew it was for show, that she could never leave for good. But marriages, even good ones, can fall apart. She knows that, too. One afternoon a few months ago, she and Scott found a message on their answering machine from an old friend who, like JoAnn, had chosen to remain home for her

husband and children, and had done just that for 15 years. The message
was that her husband was gone. The friend began to cry. The message
ended. JoAnn called back, of course, and asked what in the world had
happened, and the friend said her husband had suddenly announced he'd
had enough. "I don't love you," he'd said. She had looked at him,
uncomprehending. "I don't *like* you," he'd gone on. "I haven't loved you
for a long time."

"And?" JoAnn said, trying to imagine how such words must feel.

And, the friend said, she'd tried to wave off what he was saying as
nothing more than silliness. He was probably tired. He'd probably had a
bad day. "I'll start dinner," she had said to him. "Your favorite."

And?

He'd left.

So it is on a Saturday that JoAnn goes for a visit.

The friend is inside her house, waiting. Her husband, she says, came
back, but only for a few minutes. This time, she got angry and slapped
him, and he grabbed her around the neck, and the children, who had
been watching, came at him, hitting him until he ran off. Now he was in
an apartment, and she had no idea what to do. Fifteen years without
working is a long time, she reminds JoAnn.

There is nothing JoAnn can really do except listen, and she does that
through the afternoon and into the evening. When she leaves, it is dark.
"It will be okay," she tells her friend. Then she gets into her car, heads
toward the highway, and begins to cry, not only for her friend but also
for more general reasons, for the way so many lives work out. The miles
go by. She fiddles with the car radio awhile, turns it loud, shuts it off.
She is not really paying attention to the highway signs, but at one point
she realizes she is more than halfway home. And with that, a feeling of
anticipation comes over her, an ache to get back. She begins to go faster.
She is absolutely buoyant. She pulls into the driveway and hurries inside,
where Scott is awake, waiting. "Tell me about it," he says. She does, but
first she throws her arms around him.

"Ben. Brian. Come on."

It is the following Saturday, 21 beds and 100 pounds of laundry later.
JoAnn, Scott thinks, could use a day to herself, so he loads the two boys
into the car and heads toward Indiana. The morning is foggy, but as he

swings over the Ohio River, the fog has lifted enough for a glimpse of some old buildings on the far bank. "New Albany," Scott announces, "and Floyds Knobs is somewhere over there in the clouds."

He drives through downtown, past a furniture store with a sign in the window that reads CLEARANCE. "That sign has been there since I was growing up," he says. He goes past the place where he and JoAnn had their wedding reception ("It's bankrupt, the owner had a cerebral hemorrhage"), past one of the houses where he grew up ("The woman next door has cancer now"), to the Green Valley Convalescent Center, where his father, sick with Parkinson's disease, is being fed lunch.

"How's Dad?" Scott asks his mother, who visits the nursing home every afternoon.

"He had a bad night three nights ago," she says.

"Hallucinations?"

"They had to give him a shot."

Scott puts his arm around his father's shoulder and says, "Everything's going fine," slow and loud. His father looks at him and starts to say something, and Scott moves closer, so his ear is next to his father's mouth. He waits, not at all impatient. Sometimes the words come out, sometimes they don't. This time, they don't, so Scott moves away, smiles and says, "Everything's going well."

He looks at his mother. She is a woman who has been taking care of somebody or something since she became an adult. First she took care of her children, then, 18 years ago, her husband got sick and she began taking care of him. Sometimes, as he grew sicker, friends would ask her out, but she would say no, she had to be home with her husband, he depended on her. Every morning she would make him breakfast, every afternoon she would wash his hair, and every night she would put him to bed and worry about the day when he would be so sick he would no longer be able to stand. Eventually the day came. His legs gave out, and he fell, cutting open his head. So she put him in the nursing home and has been coming every day since, feeding him lunch, leaving with his dirty laundry, showing up the next day with the laundry cleaned, in time to feed him lunch again.

Scott imagines that his mother has some regrets about how her life has gone, but he has never asked. The closest he came was a day last winter. "When Dad dies, where do you want to go?" he said. "What do you want to do?"

At first she didn't answer, but then, sounding suddenly tired, she did. "I don't care to go anywhere," she said. "I just want to be able to go to the mall."

That was the end of it. Now, on a Saturday afternoon, she reaches for a box of tissues that she uses to wipe off the corners of her husband's mouth. She takes out several and puts them on the edge of the bed, within her husband's reach. "Your dad has trouble pulling Kleenexes out of these boxes," she says. Scott looks at the box and sees they're not Kleenexes at all, but Puffs, a Procter & Gamble product. "There's a toll-free number you can call and complain," he says. He looks at his father. "Well, what do you think?" he says. He leans close. This time, the words do come out.

"Nothing different," his father says.

There is a recurring vision JoAnn has, not a dream exactly, but something she likes to imagine. It is 15 or 20 years down the road, and her sons are getting married. Scott is there, of course, stoic as ever, and she is next to him, a little teary and proud that everything worked out. Or is it relieved? Regardless, the boys say their vows to women she can't quite make out, lift veils of lace, leave the church, turn the corner and are gone. That's what she sees. What she can't see is what comes next. But she has some ideas.

The boys, and their wives, and their children, live nearby and always stop by to visit. She and Scott grow old together, without sickness or wheelchairs or regrets. Her days wind down as gently as they built up, so that when her last moments are at hand, she is able to look back with contentment at the kind of life it has been. She leaves behind a wonderful home, a home important to the people she loved, so much so that if ever they came back to visit, they would be startled by any change.

For now, though, it is late Saturday afternoon on Red Clover Court, where a woman adrift in time is waiting for her husband and children to return. Her house is quiet. Quiet and clean. Quiet and clean and smelling like winter air. Everything is in place. Everything is perfect. The only thing missing is a family. Five o'clock comes and goes. So does 6:00. It gets dark. She waits. Finally, she hears a car. A moment later, the front door bursts open.

"Hey, Mom!"

She turns. She smiles.

"Hey, Ben!"

Author's Afterwords . . .

The housewife story was one of the first magazine pieces I ever did, and I was pretty nervous about the form. I must have seen statistics somewhere about how few households were left with the man working and the woman staying home. I wanted to find a woman who didn't seem conflicted about her role as a stay-at-home wife and mother. I wanted to examine her decision to be a housewife rather than any conflict she felt about staying home.

I found JoAnn through a friend who had grown up with her. I called her up and she was great. I liked her voice. She wasn't ambivalent about staying home. There were things going on in her mind. She was happy with her life.

I had spent years by then writing about the fringe of society, and I was tired of it. It's easy to do, and I wasn't learning that much new about life itself. One of the nice things about journalism is we get to take the measure of ourselves as we're learning about other people. This kind of journalism lets me immerse myself in the lives of other people who are engaged in things I'm curious about.

I was probably with JoAnn about a week and a half. I stayed in a hotel nearby. I was around as long as she could stand me being around. I knew I had to be there early and late and in between. But you can only be around a person so long before they want you gone. So I'd stay for a while, go away and come back.

I didn't go in with a story written in my mind. I didn't figure out the story until after I'd taken my last note. I only knew I wanted to begin with her as a stereotype and for her to go beyond stereotype in the story to become a dignified individual. You can't be more stereotypical than a lead that mimics the beginning to the old *Donna Reed Show* on TV, as JoAnn stands at the door and kisses the family goodbye as they all go on their way, and she's left there smiling. And then she cleans. But slowly, section by section, she becomes an admirable individual.

In any reporting, you want to write down everything you can because you don't know what you're going to use later. Anything that pertains to any sense I feel at any moment, I write down. My notebook is always out. I get people used to it. Then things relax from there. If you spend enough time, you're not so much the interviewer as somebody who's having a conversation. It takes time for people to stop answering in ways they think you want to hear. It takes going back and going back and going back.

This was one of my first attempts to write about the ordinary rather than the out-of-the-ordinary in life. To do that, I had to pay attention to different things. I had to pay attention to the sameness, to the poetry of it. To get in the mood to write the story, I read Anne Tyler novels to remind me of what's possible when you're writing about domestic life. I read *Dinner at the Homesick Restaurant* to remind myself what a detail can do.

I had come out of newspapers and my inclination was to fill the story with a lot of statistics. But my editor said, "Just tell us a story." I think that was good advice. The story starts with a tension for the reader—how can this woman possibly be happy? And it resolves that tension. The view today is that anyone who's a housewife must be an idiot. Well, JoAnn's not an idiot.

JoAnn didn't like some of the reaction to the story. *Esquire* ran a photo of her cleaning a toilet. She seemed not to be bothered by it. But most of the calls and letters were critical of her for allowing herself to be photographed cleaning a toilet—and smiling while she did it. But she was okay with that response, because she's comfortable with who she is. The piece got that across.

I think the conflict in the piece is the tension felt by most women who have made the decision to work and have children. The story allowed those women a look at what many of them dismiss out of hand. Not to tell them they're wrong for working, but just to say, "Here is the 3-D version of what you dismiss."—D. F.

TV Without Guilt

The first TV to come on is the one in the master bedroom, a 13-inch Hitachi. The time is 8:20 a.m. The alarm clock goes off, and Bonnie Delmar opens her eyes and immediately reaches over to the night stand for the remote. Her husband, Steve, has already left for work. The children are still asleep. The house is quiet. On comes CBS because Bonnie was watching the *David Letterman Show* when she drifted off the night before. She watches *This Morning* for a few minutes, catching up on what has happened in the last seven hours in the world beyond her Gaithersburg, Maryland, home and then she switches to NBC in time for the weather and Willard Scott. Later in the day, she will tell about a dream she once had. "I dreamt I was married to Willard Scott," she will say. "I was going to my 10th high school reunion, and I was excited that everyone was going to see that I was married to a celebrity, but then I wasn't excited because it was Willard Scott. You know?"

The second TV to come on is the 19-inch Zenith in the bedroom of Bonnie's daughter, Ashley, age seven years and 10 months. The time is now 8:45, 40 minutes before school begins, and Ashley and her younger brother, Steven, get dressed while watching *The Bozo Show*. The Zenith is the newest TV in the house, purchased a few weeks before to replace the 26-inch Sony console that had been in Ashley's room until the color picture tube went bad. "She threw a fit when the console broke," Bonnie says of Ashley's initial reaction. "She was, like, 'I won't watch TV in my

77

room anymore,' so Steve and Steven went out and got her a new TV, and she wasn't at all happy about it. I mean, she went in her room and cried about it. She actually cried. She wanted a big screen. I actually laughed at her. I said, 'You've got to be kidding,' and that made her more furious. She was saying, 'How can you give me such a small TV?' But, anyway, that's over. She's fine now." On the screen this morning, Bozo is standing next to a child who is attempting to throw a Ping-Pong ball into a succession of six buckets. She does this and wins several prizes, and Ashley and Steven jump around the bedroom cheering while Bonnie, who has been watching with them, claps her hands. "Wow!" she says. "What a great day."

The third TV to come on is the 27-inch Hitachi by the kitchen table. It's now a few minutes after 9:00, time for *Live—Regis & Kathie Lee.* This Hitachi has an especially complex remote, but Steven has mastered it, despite being only six. He picks it up and changes the channel to *Barney and Friends.* "I love you, you love me," the *Barney* theme song begins, but Steven sings his own variation, learned from Ashley, who learned it at school. "I hate you, you hate me," he sings, "let's kill Barney one two three, with a great big knife, stab him in his head, pull it out and then he's dead." "Steven!" Bonnie says, laughing. "How's it really go?" "I don't know," Steven says. He picks up the remote again and switches to cartoons, while Bonnie, who wants to watch *Regis & Kathie Lee,* goes over to the counter by the sink and turns on the five-inch, black-and-white, battery-powered Panasonic.

It is now 9:10 a.m. in the Delmar house. Fifty minutes have gone by since the alarm. Four TVs have been turned on. It will be another 16 hours before all the TVs are off and the house is once again quiet. By the sink, Bonnie continues to watch *Regis & Kathie Lee.* At the table, Ashley and Steven watch Speedy Gonzales in *Here Today, Gone Tamale.* Looking at them, it's hard to imagine three happier people.

"Mom," Ashley says later, after she has gone to school and come home and resumed watching TV, "I'm going to watch TV in Heaven."

"You're going to watch TV in Heaven?" Bonnie says.

"Yeah," Ashley says.

"Well," Bonnie says, "let's hope they have it on up there."

Of all the relationships of modern civilization, none is more hypocritical than the relationship between an American family and its television set.

We say we don't watch TV except occasionally, and yet, according to Nielsen figures, we have it on an average of seven and a half hours a day. We worry that TV causes violent behavior, and yet we keep watching violent shows. We complain that TV is getting too graphic, and yet we are buying sets with sharper pictures and larger screens. We insist we have better things to do than watch TV, and yet every night, on every street, shooting through the gaps in closed blinds or around the edges of drawn curtains is the electric blue glow that is the true color of our lives. TV is our angst. TV is our guilt. We watch it. We worry about it. We blame it. We watch it some more. We feel bad about how much we really watch it. We lie.

Except for the Delmars.

"I just don't buy it that too much TV is bad for you," says Steve, 37, the chief financial officer of a company that makes automated telephone answering systems, who gets home from work around 7:00, eats dinner while watching Dan Rather and Connie Chung, settles down in the den by the 19-inch Sony, watches a few hours of sports, goes back to the bedroom, turns on the Hitachi and falls asleep with it on because Bonnie can't fall asleep if it's off. "Nobody wants to admit they watch television—it's got the connotation: 'the boob tube'—but all these people, what are *they* doing? I'm not sure if they have any more intellect. It's not like they're all going to the Smithsonian or anything."

"Let's see," says Bonnie, 35, a housewife and former restaurant hostess with a bachelor's degree in elementary education, totaling up how much TV she watches a day. "It just depends on if I'm home or not. Almost always, the TV is on from four o'clock to the end of *David Letterman*. It depends, though. If I'm home, I'm watching. Probably nine hours a day is average. There are some days I might actually watch 16, 17 hours, but there are some days I'm out and about, and I don't get to watch as much."

At the Delmars', there are six TVs, counting the old Sony console that is now in the guest room, and plans are to refinish the basement and add two more. At the Delmars', not only is TV always on, it is virtually a member of the family, part of nearly every significant moment in their lives. Bonnie remembers her honeymoon. "The cable went out," she says. "It wasn't out for long, six hours maybe, but I was pretty mad." She remembers Steven's birth. "Steven was born during the halftime of a Redskins game," she says. "It was a Monday night, *Monday Night Football*, a big game. I was actually pushing, and Steve and the doctor were watching the game right down to the last second." She remembers Ashley's birth. "I cut out the TV guide the day she was born," she says. "I thought that would be interesting." She gets Ashley's baby book. "Look—*Webster* was on, in first run. *Mr. Belvedere. Diff'rent Strokes. Falcon Crest. Fall Guy. Miami Vice. Dallas. Dynasty. Knight Rider.* God, can you believe it? Wow." She remembers when Ashley and Steven were conceived. "I don't watch TV during sex, if you want to know," she says, laughing. "I'm capable of turning it off for five minutes." But not much longer than that. Certainly not for an entire day, Bonnie says. In fact, she says, she can't remember the last time a day passed without her watching something. "It would be very hard for me to make it through a day," she says. "It's almost an automatic reflex at this point."

The same goes for the kids, who, until recently, were allowed to watch as much TV as they wanted. Then came the night when Steve awakened well after midnight—Bonnie says it was toward 4:00 a.m.— and found Ashley sitting up in bed watching the Cartoon Network. Now the rule for the kids is no TV after 11:00 p.m. on school nights, but other than that, anything goes. "The kids watch everything from *Barney* to *Beavis and Butt-head,*" Bonnie says. There is no embarrassment in the way she says this, not even the slightest hint of discomfort. There is nothing other than brightness and happiness, for that is what she feels about TV.

"I love it. I love it. I can't help it. I love it," she says. "Why should I be ashamed of saying that?"

Three p.m. The 27-inch Hitachi is on. Time for *Maury Povich.* So far this day, Bonnie has watched parts of *Regis & Kathie Lee, Jerry Springer, Broadcast House Live, Geraldo, American Journal, Loving, All My Children, One Life to Live* and *John & Leeza,* and now she is watching Povich talk from his New York studio to a woman named Happy Leuken who weighs more than 600 pounds and is in a Boston hospital weight-loss program. "God, it's so sad," Bonnie says, looking at Happy, who is spread over her hospital bed like raw dough, chatting away. Now she and the rest of the viewing audience see what Happy can't, that Happy's hero, exercise guru Richard Simmons, is standing outside the door to Happy's room, poised to dash in and surprise her with a bouquet of flowers. "Watch," Bonnie says. "He loves to cry. He'll come in. He'll cry. She'll cry. The audience will cry. I might cry, too." In he runs. Happy looks surprised. The studio audience applauds. He embraces her. The studio audience cheers. He kisses her big neck. The cheers get louder. She kisses him on the lips. "There he goes," Bonnie says. "He's working up to it. He's starting to blink."

She keeps watching. "Did you know he was on *General Hospital?*" she says. "It was years and years ago. He was running an exercise class. There was one character, a heavyset character, who was in the class, and I thought they were going to transform her into something beautiful, but I guess she wouldn't lose any weight because they dropped the story line." Bonnie not only knows this about Richard Simmons, she knows everything about everybody. To her, TV is more than entertainment, it's a family of actors who share histories and links.

Earlier in the day, when she was showing off some school lunch boxes she has collected over the years, she got to the *Get Smart* lunch box and found herself thinking about Dick Gautier, who played Hymie the Robot, and Julie Newmar, who she thinks played opposite Gautier in one or two episodes and definitely played Catwoman in *Batman,* as did Eartha Kitt and Lee Meriwether, who was also in *The Time Tunnel* and whose daughter was a model on *The Price Is Right.* "Kyle. Kyle Meriwether," she said. "She used to substitute when one of the other girls, like Janice, couldn't make it." A little later, when the soap opera *Loving* came on, Bonnie said of an actress: "That woman is married to Michael Knight, who plays Tad in *All My Children,* and she *was* married to David Hasselhoff, who played a character named Michael Knight in that show *Knight Rider.* Isn't that weird?" Now, looking at Maury Povich, she says, "Can you believe Maury Povich is married to Connie Chung?"

So of course she knows about Richard Simmons, who is now sitting on Happy's bed, congratulating her on the 50 or so pounds she has lost, absently rubbing his thumb up and down her exposed lower leg. Over the years, there's been all kinds of research done on the effects of television on viewers, including, fairly recently, a study on the effects of the TV set itself, which showed that the bigger the screen is, the more involved a viewer feels. It also noted that people are buying bigger TVs all the time, something that Steve, who has looked at a 35-inch Mitsubishi, is considering for the basement. For now, though, the 27-inch Hitachi is the biggest screen in the house, which, as Simmons keeps rubbing Happy's leg, rubbing it, rubbing it, rubbing it, seems plenty big enough. "That kind of grosses me out," Bonnie says, and she leaves the house to pick up the kids from school.

The school is just down the street. In fact, lots of things in Bonnie's life are just down the street: the toy store where she buys Ninja Turtle dolls for Steven and *Beverly Hills, 90210* dolls for Ashley; the pizza place that is always advertising two pizzas with up to five toppings each for $7.99; the grocery store where she buys Cap'n Crunch, and Flintstone Push Ups in Yabba Dabba Doo Orange, and all the other things the kids want after seeing them on TV. The school is closest of all, so close that when Bonnie has the windows open and the TV volume down, she can hear the kids squealing and laughing on the playground.

She is back in a few minutes. The TV is still on, and as the car doors open and close, Happy Leuken is still chatting away, talking now about how the hospital allows conjugal visits. Now Happy's husband is talking about their own conjugal visit, about how exciting it was that, for the first time in years, his wife was able to lift her legs onto the bed by herself, and how much he's liking her body, really, *really* liking it—and that's what Ashley and Steven come home to.

They run into the house, stop by the TV, listen. Some parents might worry about this, but not Bonnie. She simply goes into the kitchen and begins getting out snacks. If the kids have a question, she figures, they'll ask it, and if they don't they'll probably get bored and change the channel. Sure enough, Steven picks up the remote and changes to cartoons. He and Ashley sit at the kitchen table. Bonnie pours them sodas. She gets them Rice Krispies treats. She defrosts some Ball Park Fun Franks—"Michael Jordan endorses these," she says—and serves them with potato chips, which Ashley dips in ketchup. The kids keep watching. Eating. Watching. Then they run back to Ashley's room to watch cartoons on her TV, and Bonnie changes the channel to Sally Jessy Raphael, where the topic is "moms who share their daughters' boy-friends."

"Don't you love watching this?" she asks during a commercial. "Can you tell me you're not enjoying this? I love seeing how people live." Even the worst shows, she says, have value if for no other reason than she gets to see what other lives are like. "Lesbians. Homosexuals. Transvestites," she says, listing people she has met through TV. "Spiritualists. Occult-ists. Teenage runaways. Teenage drug addicts. Teenage alcoholics. Child stars who are in trouble. Politicians. Bald men. People with physical problems. Cancer survivors. Siamese twins." Now she will learn about moms and daughters who share the same boyfriends, and tomorrow, according to a commercial, she will meet "a man who had his private parts enlarged—on the next Maury." She agrees it's a strange group of people. Nonetheless, she keeps watching as one of the moms on the show says she and her daughter run a phone-sex line and pretend to have orgasms while actually eating donuts and painting their nails.

"You know, TV really does open up your eyes about how many people in the world there are, and how different they are," Bonnie says. "I mean without TV, who would exist? Just these middle-class people I see every day. I wouldn't know anything else was going on." She watches to the end. Then, with the kids, she watches *Full House*. Then they watch *Saved by the Bell*. Then she watches the local news. Then Steve comes home and the entire family eats dinner and watches Dan Rather and Connie Chung. Then, sometimes with Steve, sometimes with the kids, sometimes by herself, Bonnie watches *Jeopardy, Mad About You, Wings, Seinfeld, Frasier,* the *Mary Tyler Moore Show,* the *Dick Van Dyke Show,* the *Tonight Show* and the *Late Show With David Letterman.* Toward the end of *Letterman* she falls asleep, awakens long enough to turn off the TV and falls back asleep until 8:20 a.m., when she reaches woozily for the remote and starts all over again.

Not that TV is the only thing Bonnie does. "I don't just sit and watch TV," she says. "I'll clean while I watch. I'll read the paper. I'll work on crafts. I like making doll-house furniture with Ashley. I'll fold laundry." She also reads books, volunteers at the school several times a week and works on the yard. But almost all of this involves TV, at least peripherally. The crafts are done in front of the Hitachi, and whenever she cleans the house she takes the portable Panasonic along to the rooms that don't have a TV. The book she is reading at the moment is by Howard Stern, and the book she's reading with Ashley, which came from a school book club, is about Stephanie, one of the characters on *Full House*.

From time to time, her friends poke fun at her about all of this, but she doesn't mind. Sometimes Steve does, too—"the walking TV Guide," he calls her—but she doesn't mind that either. They've been married nearly 10 years now, and even though she once turned down a free weekend in Jamaica with Steve in part because the hotel room didn't have a TV, he says of her, "If everybody was like Bonnie, the world would be a helluva lot better place."

"I'd definitely like to have a perfect family," she is saying one evening.

"She'd like to have the Beaver Cleaver family," says Steve.

"I would. You know I've had people tell me that Steven looks like Beaver," she says, adding that she always tells them, "Thank you."

"You do?" says Steve.

"Yeah," says Bonnie. "It's a compliment."

"Bonnie's life tends to be dictated by what she sees on television," Steve says, rolling his eyes.

"You think a lot of stuff on television is ridiculous," Bonnie says to him.

"Yeah, I do. For instance, talk shows. Why would anyone want to watch these shows all the time?"

"You learn a lot," Bonnie says.

"Like what?"

"About everything."

"Like enlarged sex organs?"

"Yeah," Bonnie says.

"It's like the *National Enquirer,*" Steve says. "Pretty soon there'll be a show on two-headed cabbages."

"But you know what?" Bonnie says. "I always have something to talk about at parties."

"That's true," Steve says.

"For instance," Bonnie says, "do you know how many women the average man sleeps with in his lifetime?"

"What's your source for this?"

"Geraldo."

"The man who put skin from his butt on his head?"

"Seven. The answer is seven," Bonnie says. "Don't you find that interesting?"

So there is conversation in the Delmar house, too, as well as family time, when everyone watches a show together. "We all watch *Home Improvement,*" Bonnie says. "We all watch *Seinfeld.*" They also watch *Married . . . With Children,* a show that has been called sexist, misogynous, soft pornography and worse. But it also has about 20 million regular viewers, including the Delmars, who try to watch it every week. This week, however, Bonnie announces she wants to watch a special on CBS, "a show that was on when I was little, and I want to watch it very much."

"What is it?" Steve asks.

"*The Waltons Reunion,*" Bonnie says.

"Oh, God. I thought they died," Steve says.

"I *loved* that show," Bonnie says.

"But Mom . . ." Ashley says.

"Mom . . ." Steven says.

"If you want to sit quietly, you can sit here and watch," Bonnie says. "But be quiet. Mommy wants to watch this."

And so Ashley and Steven go off to watch *Married . . . With Children* by themselves.

"Channel Two Five," Bonnie calls to them as they run down the hallway, so they'll know what to press on the remote.

They go to Ashley's room, a room in which they spend a couple of hours every day, just them and whatever they want to watch. Steven has his own bedroom a few steps away, but because he doesn't yet have a TV he is in Ashley's room more than his own, usually falling asleep and spending the night in her queen-sized bed. The bed has a heart-shaped pillow on it with a picture of Zack, from *Saved by the Bell,* along with the inscription "Sweet Dreams." "Ashley loves Zack," Steven says about that. "He's her love muffin." There is also a dresser drawer filled with video-tapes of children's movies—"We probably have 100," Steven says—as well as a Super Nintendo game, a VCR, a videotape rewinder, a cable outlet and, of course, the new 19-inch Zenith, on which Al Bundy, one of the *Married . . . With Children* characters, is saying to his wife, Peg, as their neighbor Marcy listens, "I'm telling you, Peg, I'm so hot, if Marcy wasn't here I'd take you on the floor right now." To which Peg says, "Get out, Marcy."

To which Ashley and Steven, hearing every word of this exchange, say nothing. They just keep listening as Al and Peg get in an argument about sex, and Peg says to Al that TV is the "only thing you've turned on in 20 years," and Al says to Peg, "Well, if you came with a remote and a mute button, I might turn you on, too." Wordlessly, Ashley and Steven watch the show until it ends and then run back out to Bonnie. "How was it?" she asks, and that's all she asks—not so much because she doesn't care what her children watch, but because she and Steve don't see any reason to worry about it.

"You know why?" Bonnie says the next day, when the kids are in school and she is making them a surprise for when they get home, a concoction of cereal, pretzel sticks, butter and brown sugar. "Because I really trust my kids. If there's anything bad, they'll tell me about it." She puts the pan in the oven. On the Hitachi, Maury Povich is about to show a videotape of a convenience store clerk being shot during a robbery. "It's so graphic, you might not want to watch," he warns.

If TV's so bad, Bonnie says, why are her kids doing so well? If it's so bad, why is Steven so happy, and why is Ashley excelling in school? Just the other day, at a parent-teacher conference, Ashley's teacher called her a terrific student and concluded by saying to Bonnie, "You will be seeing great things from Ashley"—and to Bonnie's way of thinking TV is one of the reasons why. As she said after the conference, "I have friends who think it's terrible that I let my kids eat candy, that I let my kids watch TV, that I don't have a lot of rules, but I'll tell you what: Set my kids and their kids in the same room and see who's better behaved. They're really, really sweet kids. And a lot of these parents who try to do everything right—no TV, lots of reading, lots of rules, trying to do everything perfectly—let's face it. Their kids can be real pains in the neck." The smell of melting butter and brown sugar fills the kitchen. On the Hitachi, the convenience store clerk is on the ground, bleeding, yelling for help. "I think they're doing good," she says of her kids. "I don't think TV has corrupted them at all. Who knows, you know? We won't know for 15, 20 years. But right now, they seem okay."

3:20. Time to go pick them up.

Once, last year, when Ashley was in first grade and Steven was still at home, Bonnie decided to let Ashley walk to school, just as she had done when she was a child growing up. That's when she lived in suburban Wheaton, Maryland, in a split-level, in a time when she and everyone else felt absolutely, unquestionably safe. Year after year she would walk to school, walk home at lunch time to eat a peanut butter sandwich and watch *The Donna Reed Show*, walk back to school, walk back home. The first day Ashley did this, though, the very first day, she came home with a note alerting parents that a man in a van had been seen loitering near certain bus stops, taking photographs of little children. So that was the end of that. For some reason the world has changed, Bonnie says, although she doesn't think the reason is TV.

The kids run in and plop down at the kitchen table. At this time of day, the decision about what to watch on the Hitachi is theirs, and they switch to Daffy Duck as they dig into the cereal-and-pretzel mix. Another day, they decide to stick with *Maury Povich*. "That lady is so skinny you can see her bones," Ashley says as the camera focuses on a woman who is almost skeletal.

"That lady has an eating disorder," Bonnie says.

"What's an eating disorder?" Ashley asks.

And so, because of TV, Ashley and Steven learn about eating disorders. Later, they watch *Beverly Hills, 90210*, in which the plot revolves around a boy who forces himself on a girl. And so Ashley and Steven learn about date rape.

Eleven o'clock comes. Time to turn off the Zenith, according to the new rule of the house. The night before, Ashley cried when Bonnie did this—"It's not *fair*," she yelled—but this night, in the darkened room, Bonnie sits on the edge of the bed and traces her fingers over her children's faces in light, lazy circles, and soon their eyes are shut.

And so Ashley and Steven learn to go to sleep without TV.

Thirty years ago: Bonnie is small. The TV is black and white. There is one TV in the entire house, no cable, no remote, no VCR, just a TV in the corner of the living room with an antenna on top and Red Skelton on the screen, and Bonnie is laughing so hard she is rolling around on the carpet. She is allowed to stay up as late as she wants, and watch as much TV as she wants, and there has never been a happier child.

Thirty years later: Ninety-eight percent of American households have TV, according to Nielsen Media Research; 66% have at least two TVs; 77% have at least one VCR; 62% get cable; and TV is under scrutiny by everyone from politicians who are proposing ratings for TV shows and video games, to academicians and sociologists who produce study after study about its dulling effects on developing brains, to a group of 20 worried women who come together one evening at an elementary school in Silver Spring, Maryland, not far at all from the neighborhood where Bonnie grew up.

Bonnie isn't among them. Bonnie, in fact, would never go to such a meeting, and neither would Steve, who says of such things, "These people who get so rabid, they should be taking it easy." The women, though, feel exactly the opposite. Members of a loosely organized group called the Mothers Information Exchange, they have come to hear about the effects of TV from Amy Blank, who is with the Maryland Campaign for Kids' TV, an organization that monitors children's programming on area TV stations. All of the women have children. All see TV as something to be concerned about. Several of the women go so far as to say they feel truly afraid of what TV might be doing to their children, and what they hear over the next 90 minutes doesn't make them feel any less anxious.

"As we'll learn this evening, we have an incredible relationship with that box over there," says Blank, an edge of direness in her voice, motioning toward a TV that is hooked up to a VCR. "We can't remember when we didn't have it in our lives. That's really profound. We don't have people in our lives this long, some of us. We've had this thing in our lives all our lives. It's incredible." She asks the women how many TV sets they own.

"We have five."

"We have four."

She asks how many hours a day the TVs are on.

"Six."

"Three-and-a-half."

"Oh God, this is embarrassing."

"Are you including *Barney* videos?"

"Do you have to include your husband?"

She turns on the TV and shows a videotape, in which the announcer says that "in a typical television season, the average adolescent views 14,000 instances of sexual contact or sexual innuendo in TV ads and programs." She turns on an opaque projector and shows a chart that says: "Most children will see 8,000 murders and 10,000 acts of violence before they finish elementary school." "They won't do any other thing, other than eat or sleep, that many times," she says. "That's what we're teaching them. It's okay to kill 8,000 people. It's okay to hurt or maim 10,000 people. It's okay. TV does it, so it's okay." She shows another chart of what parents should do, a list that includes limiting the amount of time children watch TV.

"I think we're seeing tremendous effects on our kids and on our society," she says. "I mean, we're a broken society. We really are. We're struggling. There's so much incredible pain out there. And many of us just don't know where to hide, and don't know what to do. I want to show you one last thing," she says, and on the TV comes a clip from *The Simpsons,* a show she detests so much that, earlier in the evening, when one of the mothers said she thought *The Simpsons* could be funny at times, she said, "Bart should be shot." This clip, though, she likes. It is of Marge Simpson, the mother, writing a letter to a TV station.

"Dear Purveyors of Senseless Violence," Marge begins. "I know this may sound silly at first, but I believe that the cartoons you show to our children are influencing their behavior in a negative way. Please try to tone down the psychotic violence in your otherwise fine programming. Yours truly, Marge Simpson."

"Dear Valued Viewer," the station manager writes back. "In regards to your specific comments about the show, our research indicates that one person cannot make a difference, no matter how big a screwball she is."

"I'll show them what one screwball can do!" Marge says to that.

Blank snaps off the TV.

"Well," she says, "I don't think any of us are screwballs," and with those words and the vision of 8,000 murders in their minds, the women head off into the darkness of prime time.

Meanwhile, back in Gaithersburg, where the Delmars are watching TV, life is as untroubled as usual. Thursday, 8:00 p.m. Time for *The Simpsons.* But it's also time for *Mad About You,* which Bonnie, Steve and Steven want to watch, so Ashley goes back to her room by herself. She turns on her TV. She sits at her desk, takes out some paper and pastels and starts to draw. Five minutes go by. Ten minutes. On the screen, a character named Krusty the Klown is reciting a limerick: "There once was a man from Enis . . ." Now Bart is sticking the leg of a chair in the garbage disposal, turning it on and riding it like a bronco. Now he is talking about how something "sucks."

But Ashley doesn't notice. She is completely involved in getting what she sees at the moment in her mind down on paper. She draws some white clouds in a blue sky. Now she draws a flower with blue petals and a pink center, and now she writes under the flower, "This is Steven." She puts down her pastels, looks at what she has done, holds it up, explains the title: "I think he looks like a flower." She runs out to the kitchen table and climbs onto the lap of Bonnie, who is, of course, busy watching TV, but not so busy that she can't give her daughter a hug, and in this way another evening passes by. Around 9:00, Ashley lies on the floor in front of the TV and does her spelling homework. At 10:00, she is back on Bonnie's lap. "I love you," she says to Bonnie as 10:30 comes and goes. "Kiss me."

Sometimes, Bonnie says, she thinks her life could be a TV show, although she isn't quite sure what kind of show it would be. She knows it wouldn't be a drama, she says, not yet anyway, because not enough dramatic things have happened, at least not directly to her. There have been friends with cancer, friends with bad marriages, friends who have suffered all kinds of traumas, but the only drama in her own life came a few years ago, when she found herself engaged in an escalating internal dialogue about mortality. For reasons she is still unsure of, she would make a dentist's appointment and wonder if she would live long enough to go, or she would buy milk and wonder if she would make it through the expiration date. Finally, in tears one day, she told her mother about this, and gradually the thoughts went away, bringing an end to a time that was certainly interesting, Bonnie says, and even momentarily disturbing, but hardly the stuff of TV.

So it wouldn't be a drama, she says, and neither would it be a talk show. There is, of course, plenty of talking in the Delmar house, but it's the talk of any family rather than of TV. The phone rings. It's Steve. "Hi," Bonnie says. "What time will you be home?" At the table, Steven takes a big bite out of a sandwich. "Chew carefully," Bonnie says. "Peanut butter can make you choke."

There are, on occasion, longer, deeper, more philosophical discussions, but those, too, are internal dialogues that usually come into her mind late at night, when everyone is asleep except Bonnie, who's trying one more time to go to sleep without being lulled there by TV. "I think that's the reason I have to have the TV on," she says. "If it's not on, I think. I think, I think, I think." About? "Everything. I know this sounds weird, but I think about ways the economy could be solved. Really. I think about NAFTA. I think about how my life could be better. I think about TV. It's an intense thing. I won't think about one solution, I'll think about 20. I get into all these ideas, and then I think I'll write a letter to Bill Clinton, or to Dear Abby, or someone else. And then . . . then I'll think no one wants to hear what I'm thinking, so I'll just turn the TV on, and eventually I'll drift off. That's the thing about TV, you don't have to think."

So: not a drama, not a talk show.

Obviously, then, it would have to be a situation comedy, which Bonnie says is fine with her because, after all, "isn't everybody's life a sitcom kind of life?" True enough, a lot of what goes on at the Delmars' seems exactly that. Days almost always begin brightly and end with hugs, and in between there's no telling what exactly will happen. Like the time Bonnie went out to mow the lawn, got on the rider mower, started picturing Eddie Albert "bouncing on that tractor" and began singing the theme song to *Green Acres*. Not once did she sing it, not twice, but over and over, for more than an hour, until she realized the kid across the street was looking at her like she was from another planet. Which is why whenever she has mowed the lawn since, she has hummed.

Or how about the time she was actually on TV? It was right after Ashley was born, and she had to make a fast trip to the grocery store. She grabbed a sweat shirt out of the dryer, hurried through the store with her baby and was in line to pay, thinking how big and unattractive she must look, when she noticed the checkout guy kind of smiling at her. How nice, she thought, suddenly feeling better about herself. "And then I came home and realized I had a pair of underwear and a sock stuck to my back," she says. "Static cling. I had walked through the whole store that way. Well, okay, I can handle that. But the next week one of the local TV stations had some cameras in the store, and they asked if they could talk to me and film me walking with my baby, and I said sure, and I'll bet all the Giant people were watching that night, and the checkout guy said, 'Hey! That's the lady who had the underwear stuck to her back!' "

So: a situation comedy.

"*Life With the Delmars,*" Bonnie says it could be called, and it would have four characters:

The dad.

"He'd be hard-working," she says. "He'd be a character who's in and out, one of those characters where you don't see too much of him, but funny. And fun."

The son.

"Kindergarten student. Enthusiastic. Mischievous. Rambunctious."

The daughter.

"Definitely precocious. She'd act like a teenager, a teenager wannabe. Stubborn. Funny."

And the mom.

"Let's see," she says. "Who am I?" She thinks. Thinks some more. Can't come up with a description, so she thinks instead about who might watch such a show.

"*I'd* watch it," she says.

Author's Afterwords . . .

I wanted to write a story about the relationship between a family and its television set. I planned to find a family that has the TV on the American average of seven-and-a-half hours a day. Then I came across the Delmars, who have multiple TVs on 17 hours a day. They didn't fit the original idea. They were extreme, but a pretty terrific extreme to explore. I originally thought I'd find conflict within the family about how long the TV should be on—"Oh, should we be watching TV or should we be bird watching?" But there was no angst, and isn't that interesting?

So I hung out with them for a couple of weeks. By the end, I was just somebody else watching TV in the house. It got to the point where sometimes Bonnie would be saying something, and I'd think, "Quiet, Bonnie, there's something interesting on TV." I wasn't in the house when she woke up, and I wasn't there when she went to sleep. Those scenes were methodically reconstructed question by question, detail by detail. I asked the most annoying questions—Where do you sleep in the bed? Who wakes up first? Do you wake up to the TV? What channel was it on? What show was on? What were they saying?

What made some of the reporting interesting was that during the day-time talk shows I noted what Bonnie was watching and what was being said on TV as she was doing something. Then I got the transcripts from the shows to fold in the quotes accurately. On shows where there weren't transcripts, I set up my tape recorder near the TV to pick it up while I took notes on what she said.

I often think I see where my story is going while I'm reporting it. Then I write a lead and realize the lead could be the ending. And then I'm completely lost and don't know where I'm headed. I may have an idea, but the story rarely sticks to that idea. Before I write, I make an index of everything that's in my notebooks—in notebook one, page eight, it says such and such. That way I don't have to spend a lot of time searching for things in my notes. I might do an outline on the back of an envelope—list seven or eight sections and the point of each. My aim is to decide where I want to begin and what I want to achieve by the end of the story. I stick to the outline about half the time.

As always, it took me a few days to get the first section down and then after that it went pretty quickly, a week-and-a-half probably. I come back with so much garbage in my notebooks and interesting stuff hidden in the garbage. You know the saying, "You can tell 100 stories badly, but you can only tell one story well." You can't ever tell the whole story. But there's always one story you can tell, and you have to decide what it is.

The reaction to this piece was remarkable—people liked her and hated me, people liked me and hated her. Every variation possible. Usually, I get three or four letters. I got 60 or 70. Bonnie called me in tears the afternoon it appeared. People were calling saying she shouldn't be allowed to have children, they should be taken away and put in foster homes. I told her to filter her calls with an answering machine and if the calls seemed threatening to call the police. And then I apologized for people's reactions. The next day, she called in a much better mood, because the lead of the story is about the weatherman Willard Scott and a dream Bonnie had about going to her high school reunion with him. He sent her flowers saying, "Will you go to the prom with me?" She thought that was wonderful, and she was okay after that.

The Delmars watch a lot more TV than I'm ever going to watch, but I've seen a lot worse families in my time. TV hadn't destroyed them. If the point of a good story is to get people to think a little, this one was successful like no story I've done. People just wanted to talk and talk and talk about this story. Who knows how her kids are going to turn out? But when I was there, they were okay. And the TVs were always on.

Yet the end of the story isn't completely happy, with Bonnie saying how she knows TV keeps her from thinking about more serious things, that it's an escape. When she said that, I knew I'd reached a level of intimacy where I didn't have just a surface story. The TV is always on, the family is happy, but there's an undercurrent. When I found it, that's what elevated the story.—D. F.

Jon Franklin

Jon Franklin has worked as a reporter for the U.S. Navy's *All Hand's Magazine* and Baltimore's *Evening Sun,* where his article "Mrs. Kelly's Monster" won a Pulitzer Prize for feature writing. He later won a second Pulitzer Prize for explanatory journalism. He is the author or coauthor of five books, including *The Molecules of the Mind* (1987) and *Writing for Story* (1986). He and his wife, Lynn, are working on a history of the misunderstanding of psychology. He a professor at the University of Oregon.

Mrs. Kelly's Monster

In the cold hours of a winter morning Dr. Thomas Barbee Ducker, chief brain surgeon at the University of Maryland Hospital, rises before dawn. His wife serves him waffles but no coffee. Coffee makes his hands shake.

In downtown Baltimore, on the 12th floor of University Hospital, Edna Kelly's husband tells her goodbye. For 57 years Mrs. Kelly shared her skull with the monster: No more. Today she is frightened but determined.

It is 6:30 a.m.

"I'm not afraid to die," she said as this day approached. "I've lost part of my eyesight. I've gone through all the hemorrhages. A couple of years ago I lost my sense of smell, my taste. I started having seizures. I smell a strange odor and then I start strangling. It started affecting my legs, and I'm partially paralyzed. Three years ago a doctor told me all I had to look forward to was blindness, paralysis and a remote chance of death. Now I have aneurysms; this monster is causing that. I'm scared to death . . . but there isn't a day that goes by that I'm not in pain, and I'm tired of it. I can't bear the pain. I wouldn't want to live like this much longer."

As Dr. Ducker leaves for work, Mrs. Ducker hands him a paper bag containing a peanut butter sandwich, a banana and two Fig Newtons.

Downtown, in Mrs. Kelly's brain, a sedative takes effect.

Mrs. Kelly was born with a tangled knot of abnormal blood vessels in the back of her brain. The malformation began small, but in time the vessels ballooned inside the confines of the skull, crowding the healthy brain tissue.

Finally, in 1942, the malformation announced its presence when one of the abnormal arteries, stretched beyond capacity, burst. Mrs. Kelly grabbed her head and collapsed. After that the agony never stopped. Mrs. Kelly, at the time of her first intracranial bleed, was carrying her second child. Despite the pain, she raised her children and cared for her husband. The malformation continued to grow.

She began calling it "the monster."

Now, at 7:15 a.m. in operating room 11, a technician checks the brain surgery microscope and the circulating nurse lays out bandages and instruments. Mrs. Kelly lies still on a stainless steel table. A small sensor has been threaded through her veins and now hangs in the antechamber of her heart. The anesthesiologist connects the sensor to a 7-foot-high bank of electronic instruments. Oscilloscope waveforms begin to build and break. Dials swing. Lights flash. With each heartbeat a loud speaker produces an audible popping sound. The steady pop, pop, popping isn't loud, but it dominates the operating room.

Dr. Ducker enters the O.R. and pauses before the X-ray films that hang on a lighted panel. He carried those brain images to Europe, Canada and Florida in search of advice, and he knows them by heart. Still, he studies them again, eyes focused on the two fragile aneurysms that swell above the major arteries. Either may burst on contact. The one directly behind Mrs. Kelly's eyes is the most likely to burst, but also the easiest to reach. That's first.

The surgeon-in-training who will assist Dr. Ducker places Mrs. Kelly's head in a clamp and shaves her hair. Dr. Ducker checks to make certain the three steel pins of the vice have pierced the skin and press directly against Mrs. Kelly's skull. "We can't have a millimeter slip," he says.

Mrs. Kelly, except for a six-inch crescent of scalp, is draped with green sheets. A rubber-gloved palm goes out and Doris Schwabland, the scrub nurse, lays a scalpel in it. Hemostats snap over the arteries of the scalp. Blood spatters onto Dr. Ducker's sterile paper booties.

It is 8:25 a.m. The heartbeat goes pop, pop, pop, 70 beats a minute, steady.

Today Dr. Ducker intends to remove the two aneurysms, which comprise the most immediate threat to Mrs. Kelly's life. Later, he will move directly on the monster.

It's a risky operation, designed to take him to the hazardous frontiers of neurosurgery. Several experts told him he shouldn't do it at all, that he should let Mrs. Kelly die. But the consensus was that he had no choice. The choice was Mrs. Kelly's.

"There's one chance out of three that we'll end up with a hell of a mess or a dead patient," Dr. Ducker says. "I reviewed it in my own heart and with other people, and I thought about the patient. You weigh what happens if you do it against what happens if you don't do it. I convinced myself it should be done."

Mrs. Kelly said yes. Now Dr. Ducker pulls back Mrs. Kelly's scalp to reveal the dull ivory of living bone. The chatter of the half-inch drill fills the room, drowning the rhythmic pop, pop, pop of the heart monitor. It is 9:00 when Dr. Ducker hands the two-by-four-inch triangle of skull to the scrub nurse.

The tough, rubbery covering of the brain is cut free, revealing the soft gray convolutions of the forebrain.

"There it is," says the circulating nurse in a hushed voice. "That's what keeps you working."

It is 9:20.

Eventually Dr. Ducker steps back, holding his gloved hands high to avoid contamination. While others move the microscope into place over the glistening brain, the neurosurgeon communes once more with the X-ray films. The heart beats strong, 70 beats a minute, 70 beats a minute. "We're going to have a hard time today," the surgeon says to the X rays.

Dr. Ducker presses his face against the microscope. His hands go out for an electrified, tweezer-like instrument. The assistant moves in close, taking his position above the secondary eyepieces.

Dr. Ducker's view is shared by a video camera. Across the room a color television crackles, displaying a highly magnified landscape of the brain. The polished tips of the tweezers move into view.

It is Dr. Ducker's intent to place tiny, spring-loaded alligator clips across the base of each aneurysm. But first he must navigate a tortured path from his incision, above Mrs. Kelly's right eye, to the deeply buried Circle of Willis.

The journey will be immense. Under magnification, the landscape of the mind expands to the size of a room. Dr. Ducker's tiny, blunt-tipped instrument travels in millimeter leaps.

His strategy is to push between the forebrain, where conscious thought occurs, and the thumblike projection of the brain, called the temporal lobe, that extends beneath the temples.

Carefully, Dr. Ducker pulls these two structures apart to form a deep channel. The journey begins at the bottom of this crevasse. The time is 9:36 a.m.

The gray convolutions of the brain, wet with secretions, sparkle beneath the powerful operating theater spotlights. The microscopic landscape heaves and subsides in time to the pop, pop, pop of the heart monitor.

Gently, gently, the blunt probe teases apart the minute structures of gray matter, spreading a tiny tunnel, millimeter by gentle millimeter, into the glistening gray.

"We're having trouble just getting in," Dr. Ducker tells the operating room team.

As the neurosurgeon works, he refers to Mrs. Kelly's monster as "the AVM," or arterio-venous malformation. Normally, he says, arteries force high-pressure blood into muscle or organ tissue. After the living cells suck out the oxygen and nourishment the blood drains into low-pressure veins, which carry it back to the heart and lungs.

But in the back of Mrs. Kelly's brain one set of arteries pumps directly into veins, bypassing the tissue. The unnatural junction was not designed for such a rapid flow of blood and in 57 years is slowly swelled to the size of a fist. Periodically it leaked drops of blood and torrents of agony. Now the structures of the brain are welded together by scar tissue and, to make his tunnel, Dr. Ducker must tease them apart again. But the brain is delicate.

The screen of the television monitor fills with red.

Dr. Ducker responds quickly, snatching the broken end of the tiny artery with the tweezers. There is an electrical buzzzzzt as he burns the bleeder closed. Progress stops while the blood is suctioned out.

"It's nothing to worry about," he says. "It's not much, but when you're looking at one square centimeter, two ounces is a damned lake."

Carefully, gently, Dr. Ducker continues to make his way into the brain. Far down the tiny tunnel the white trunk of the optic nerve can be seen. It is 9:54.

Slowly, using the optic nerve as a guidepost, Dr. Ducker probes deeper and deeper into the gray. The heart monitor continues to pop, pop, pop, 70 beats a minute, 70 beats a minute.

The neurosurgeon guides the tweezers directly to the pulsing carotid artery, one of the three main blood channels into the brain. The carotid twists and dances to the electronic pop, pop, popping. Gently, ever gently, nudging aside the scarred brain tissue, Dr. Ducker moves along the carotid toward the Circle of Willis, near the floor of the skull.

This loop of vessels is the staging area from which blood is distributed throughout the brain. Three major arteries feed it from below, one in the rear and the two carotids in the front.

The first aneurysm lies ahead, still buried in gray matter, where the carotid meets the Circle. The second aneurysm is deeper yet in the brain, where the hindmost artery rises along the spine and joins the circle.

Eyes pressed against the microscope, Dr. Ducker makes his tedious way along the carotid.

"She's so scarred I can't identify anything," he complains through the mask.

It is 10:01 a.m. The heart monitor pop, pop, pops with reassuring regularity.

The probing tweezers are gentle, firm, deliberate, probing, probing, probing, slower than the hands of the clock. Repeatedly, vessels bleed and Dr. Ducker cauterizes them. The blood loss is mounting, and now the anesthesiologist hangs a transfusion bag above Mrs. Kelly's shrouded form.

Ten minutes pass. Twenty. Blood flows, the tweezers buzz, the suction hose hisses. The tunnel is small, almost filled by the shank of the instrument.

The aneurysm finally appears at the end of the tunnel, throbbing, visibly thin, a lumpy, overstretched bag, the color of rich cream, swelling out from the once strong arterial wall, a tire about to blow out, a balloon ready to burst, a time-bomb the size of a pea.

The aneurysm isn't the monster itself, only the work of the monster, which, growing malevolently, has disrupted the pressures and weakened arterial walls throughout the brain. But the monster itself, the X rays say, lies far away.

The probe nudges the aneurysm, hesitantly, gently.

"Sometimes you touch one," a nurse says, "and blooey, the wolf's at the door."

Patiently, Dr. Ducker separates the aneurysm from the surrounding brain tissue. The tension is electric.

No surgeon would dare go after the monster itself until this swelling killer is defused.

Now.

A nurse hands Dr. Ducker a long, delicate pair of pliers. A little stainless steel clip, its jaws open wide, is positioned on the pliers' end. Presently the magnified clip moves into the field of view, light glinting from its polished surface.

It is 10:40.

For 11 minutes Dr. Ducker repeatedly attempts to work the clip over the neck of the balloon, but the device is too small. He calls for one with longer jaws. Soon that clip moves into the microscopic tunnel. With infinite slowness, Dr. Ducker maneuvers it over the neck of the aneurysm.

Then, in an instant, the jaws close and the balloon collapses.

"That's clipped," Dr. Ducker calls out. Smile wrinkles appear above his mask. The heart monitor goes pop, pop, pop, steady.

It is 10:58.

Dr. Ducker now begins following the Circle of Willis back into the brain, toward the second, and more difficult, aneurysm that swells at the very rear of the Circle, tight against the most sensitive and primitive structure in the head, the brain stem. The brain stem controls vital processes, including breathing and heartbeat.

The going becomes steadily more difficult and bloody. Millimeter, millimeter after treacherous millimeter the tweezers burrow a tunnel through Mrs. Kelly's mind. Blood flows, the tweezers buzz, the suction slurps. Push and probe. Cauterize. Suction. Push and probe. More blood. Then the tweezers lie quiet.

"I don't recognize anything," the surgeon says. He pushes further and quickly finds a landmark.

Then, exhausted, Dr. Ducker disengages himself, backs away, sits down on a stool and stares straight ahead for a long moment. The brain stem is close, close.

"This is a frightening place to be," whispers the doctor.

In the background the heart monitor goes pop, pop, pop, 70 beats a minute, steady. The smell of ozone and burnt flesh hangs thick in the air. It is 11:05 a.m., the day of the monster.

The operating room door opens and Dr. Michael Salcman, the assistant chief neurosurgeon, enters. He confers with Dr. Ducker, who then returns to the microscope. Dr. Salcman moves to the front of the television monitor.

As he watches Dr. Ducker work, Dr. Salcman compares an aneurysm to a bump on a tire. The weakened wall of the artery balloons outward under the relentless pressure of the heartbeat and, eventually, it bursts. That's death.

So the fragile aneurysms must be removed before Dr. Ducker can tackle the AVM itself. Dr. Salcman crosses his arms and fixes his eyes on the television screen, preparing himself to relieve Dr. Ducker if he tires. One aneurysm down, one to go.

The second, however, is the toughest. It pulses dangerously deep, hard against the bulb of nerves that sits atop the spinal cord.

"Technically, the brain stem," says Dr. Salcman. "I call it the 'pilot light.' That's because if it goes out . . . that's it."

On the television screen the tweezer instrument presses on, following the artery toward the brain stem. Gently, gently, gently, gently it pushes aside the gray coils. For a moment the optic nerve appears in the background, then vanishes.

The going is even slower now. Dr. Ducker is reaching all the way into the center of the brain and his instruments are the length of chopsticks. The danger mounts because, here, many of the vessels feed the pilot light.

The heartbeat goes pop, pop, pop, 70 beats a minute.

The instrument moves across the topography of torture, scars everywhere, remnants of pain past, of agonies Mrs. Kelly would rather die than further endure. Dr. Ducker is lost again.

Dr. Salcman joins him at the microscope, peering through the assistant's eyepieces. They debate the options in low tones and technical terms. A decision is made and again the polished tweezers probe along the vessel.

Back on course, Dr. Ducker works his tunnel ever deeper, gentle, gentle, gentle as the touch of sterile cotton. Finally the gray matter parts.

The neurosurgeon freezes.

Dead ahead the field is crossed by many huge, distended ropelike veins.

The neurosurgeon stares intently at the veins, surprised, chagrined, betrayed by the X rays.

The monster.

The monster, by microscopic standards, lies far away, above and back, in the rear of the head. Dr. Ducker was to face the monster itself on another day, not now. Not here.

But clearly these tangled veins, absent on the X-ray films but very real in Mrs. Kelly's brain, are tentacles of the monster.

Gingerly, the tweezers attempt to push around them.

Pop, pop, pop . . pop . . . pop . . . pop.

"It's slowing!" warns the anesthesiologist, alarmed.

The tweezers pull away like fingers touching fire.

. . . pop . . . pop . . . pop, pop, pop, pop.

"It's coming back," says the anesthesiologist.

The vessels control blood flow to the brain stem, the pilot light.

Dr. Ducker tries to go around them a different way.

Pop, pop, pop . pop . . pop . . . pop . . .

And withdraws.

Dr. Salcman stands before the television monitor, arms crossed, frowning.

"She can't take much of that," the anesthesiologist says. "The heart will go into arrhythmia and that'll lead to a . . . call it a heart attack."

Dr. Ducker tries a still different route, pulling clear of the area and returning at a new angle. Eventually, at the end of a long, throbbing tunnel of brain tissue, the sought-after aneurysm appears.

Pop, pop, pop . pop . . pop . . . pop . . .

The instruments retract.

"Damn," says the neurosurgeon. "I can only work here for a few minutes without the bottom falling out."

The clock says 12:29.

Already the gray tissue swells visibly from the repeated attempts to burrow past the tentacles.

Again the tweezers move forward in a different approach and the aneurysm reappears. Dr. Ducker tries to reach it by inserting the aneurysm clip through a long, narrow tunnel. But the pliers that hold the clip obscure the view.

Pop, pop . pop . . pop . . . pop . . .

The pliers retract.

"We're on it and we know where we are," complains the neurosurgeon, frustration adding a metallic edge to his voice. "But we're going to have an awful time getting a clip in there. We're so close, but . . ."

A resident who has been assisting Dr. Ducker collapses on a stool. He stares straight ahead, eyes unfocused, glazed.

"Michael, scrub," Dr. Ducker says to Dr. Salcman. "See what you can do. I'm too cramped."

While the circulating nurse massages Dr. Ducker's shoulders, Dr. Salcman attempts to reach the aneurysm with the clip.

Pop, pop, pop . pop . . pop . . . pop . . .

The clip withdraws.

"That should be the aneurysm right there," says Dr. Ducker, taking his place at the microscope again. "Why the hell can't we get to it? We've tried, 10 times."

At 12:53, another approach.

Pop, pop, pop . pop . . pop . . . pop . . .

Again.

It is 1:06.

And again, and again, and again.

Pop . . . pop . . . pop, pop, pop . . . pop . . . pop-pop-pop . . .

The anesthesiologist's hands move rapidly across a panel of switches. A nurse catches her breath and holds it.

"Damn, damn, damn."

Dr. Ducker backs away from the microscope, his gloved hands held before him. For a full minute, he's silent.

"There's an old dictum in medicine," he finally says. "If you can't help, don't do any harm. Let nature take its course. We may have already hurt her. We've slowed down her heart. Too many times." The words carry defeat, exhaustion, anger.

Dr. Ducker stands again before the X rays. His eyes focus on the rear aneurysm, the second one, the one that thwarted him. He examines the film for signs, unseen before, of the monster's descending tentacles. He finds no such indications.

Pop, pop, pop, goes the monitor, steady now, 70 beats a minute.

"Mother nature," a resident growls, "is a mother."

The retreat begins. Under Dr. Salcman's command, the team pre-pares to wire the chunk of skull back into place and close the incision.

It ends quickly, without ceremony. Dr. Ducker's gloves snap sharply as a nurse pulls them off. It is 1:30.

Dr. Ducker walks, alone, down the hall, brown paper bag in his hand. In the lounge he sits down on the edge of a hard orange couch and unwraps the peanut butter sandwich. His eyes focus on the opposite wall.

Back in the operating room the anesthesiologist shines a light into each of Mrs. Kelly's eyes. The right pupil, the one under the incision, is dilated and does not respond to the probing beam. It is a grim omen.

If Mrs. Kelly recovers, says Dr. Ducker, he'll go ahead and try to deal with the monster itself, despite the remaining aneurysm. He'll try to block the arteries to it, maybe even take it out. That would be a tough operation, he says without enthusiasm.

"And it's providing that she's in good shape after this."

If she survives. If. If.

"I'm not afraid to die," Mrs. Kelly had said. "I'm scared to death . . . but . . . I can't bear the pain. I wouldn't want to live like this much longer."

Her brain was too scarred. The operation, tolerable in a younger person, was too much. Already, where the monster's tentacles hang before the brain stem, the tissue swells, pinching off the source of oxygen.

Mrs. Kelly is dying.

The clock on the wall, near where Dr. Ducker sits, says 1:40.

"It's hard to tell what to do. We've been thinking about it for six weeks. But, you know, there are certain things . . . that's just as far as you can go. I just don't know . . ."

He lays the sandwich, the banana and the Fig Newtons on the table before him, neatly, the way the scrub nurse laid out the instruments.

"It was triple jeopardy," he says finally, staring at his peanut butter sandwich the same way he stared at the X rays. "It was triple jeopardy."

It is 1:43, and it's over.

Dr. Ducker bites, grimly, into the sandwich.

The monster won.

▮ Author's Afterwords . . .

It seemed to me that journalism often covered the stuff that was easy and traditional, while the really important stuff was happening in everyday life. So I asked myself, "How do you report that?" I was a science writer, but I really did features. I was interested in science and technology as it was being lived by real people. I'd been conscious of trying to make my stories read like short fiction for about two years before "Mrs. Kelly's Monster." When I grew up in Oklahoma, the library had a lot of old books on how to write from the '20s, '30s and '40s. That was the period of structuralism. The last great book written on that subject is *The Professional Story Writer and His Art*, by Robert C. Meredith and John D. Fitzgerald, published in 1963.

Borrowing from the classic short story structure, I wanted my stories to have a main character, a character complication, a development, a point of insight and a resolution. I had the idea that these things should work in nonfiction as well as they did in fiction. The only trick was you had to find stories you could actually put in the form while observing all the journalistic niceties. Usually a reporter has a story and figures out a way to do it. I had a way of doing the story and went out and looked for stories that fit that way of doing it. I practiced. I did a story about a day in the life of a dog catcher. I did a day in the life of a profoundly retarded man. I did a story about a bunch of guys building a wall in the middle of a freeway.

When I did the Mrs. Kelly story, I started out assuming the surgery would be a success. I interviewed her and her husband for about an hour ahead of time and interviewed her daughter. I interviewed the surgeon and then showed up for the operation. By then, I knew all the gimmicks and recognized that pacing was a big thing for this story. My pacing devices were keeping track of the exact time and the repeated "pop, pop, pop."

This sounds awful, but when I found out Mrs. Kelly had died, I thought I'd lost my story. A happy ending was the only ending I could conceive of doing. It took two or three hours for it to percolate through my head, and I began to realize that, sad as it was, the story was better because she had died. The story I had to tell was the story through Dr. Ducker's eyes.

I did a total of about two days of reporting, and then I wrote the story in two days. I had one notebook full of notes. That was it. I roughed the story out in one day, and the next day I reworked it all day. Along toward the end of the day, something started happening that had never happened to me before. John Steinbeck talks about holding fire in his hands, and I never knew what that meant. I started reading the story through and I noticed that my heart was racing. The piece was having a physiological effect on me. Whatever the hell it was, it was a moment you do not forget when you get a feeling from your own piece. God, it was fun.

Then I got scared. It was like stage fright. I knew I was going to put it out there and call a lot of attention to myself. This one was going to move people. So I did something I never do. I called Dr. Ducker and read parts to him. When I got done, there was a long silence and he said, "Well, Jon, that's pretty much how it was." I went in the next day and made some minor changes. It was like hitting a baseball. It happened that fast.

To be a fine writer, intelligence is important. But I think the real game is to perceive reality correctly. The writing part is technically how we do it, the lens through which we see. But you've got to be able to see reality when it's not what you expected, and when you know it's not what other people want to see. You've got to be able to stare right at it. It takes courage to let yourself go blank and see what really is there.—J. F.

Pete Earley

Pete Earley has worked as a reporter for the *Tulsa Tribune* and the *Washington Post*. He is the author of five books, including two best-sellers, *Family of Spies* (1988) and *The Hot House* (1992). His book *Circumstantial Evidence: Death, Life, and Justice in a Southern Town* (1995) won the Robert F. Kennedy Memorial Book Award for Social Justice. His most recent book is *Confessions of a Spy: The Real Story of Aldrich Ames.* He lives in Reston, Virginia.

Missing Alice

Midway across Ohio, the man beside me on the DC10 asked where I was going.

"Fowler, Colorado. A little town of about a 1,000 near Pueblo."

"Why would anyone go to Foouuller?" he asked, grinning as he exaggerated the name.

"A death. My sister."

"Sorry," he mumbled and turned away.

I was relieved. I didn't have to explain that my sister had been dead 19 years.

Alice was killed when I was 14. She was two years older and we had been inseparable as children. I couldn't talk about her death at first. My voice would deepen, my eyes would fill with tears. My parents would cry at the mention of her name, and we rarely spoke of her. Then it seemed too late. After I left home, my mother would phone me each February 13 and remind me that it was my sister's birthday. Year after year, I would forget—and find myself angry with my mother's insistent reminders.

It was just before last Christmas, as I shuffled boxes in the basement, that I ran across Alice's picture and a clipping describing her death. "A tragic accident Tuesday, June 14, about 7:05 p.m., took the life of Alice Lee Earley . . ."

I sat down on the concrete floor, closed my eyes and tried to picture her. I couldn't. I tried to focus more sharply: Alice eating Sugar Pops beside me at the breakfast table, Alice washing the green Ford Falcon, Alice stepping on my toes while singing in church. The events I recalled vividly. Alice's face I recalled not at all. I could only see the girl in the photograph—an image I had never liked, the face being without joy or expression. But in my mind I found no other. For the next week, I seemed to think of Alice constantly. One night I awoke in bed, turned to my wife and said: "Alice, are you there?" It took me an instant to realize what I had done. When I called my parents, now living in South Dakota, and told them I was returning to Fowler, my mother said: "Good, everyone always acts like Alice never existed."

I was at church camp when Alice died. The camp director shook me awake in the middle of the night and said my father was in his office. I padded barefoot on the barrack's cool concrete floor toward a yellow sliver of light escaping from beneath a closed door. Inside, my father was crying. I had never seen him cry.

I liked camp and I hated to leave, but I rode home quietly in the front seat between my parents. My mother sobbed. My father was silent, though once he smacked his palm fiercely atop the steering wheel. I tried to remember the last thing I had said to Alice, but I couldn't. So I thought of the girl I had met at camp the day before, about how I had hoped to sit next to her at evening vespers tomorrow, about how my friend, Eddie, would take my place. I knew the camp director would announce at breakfast that my sister was dead: Everyone would feel sorry for me. Maybe the girl would write me a letter.

On the way home we stopped at the house of the woman driving the car that had struck Alice. Flora Ledbetter came out of the bedroom in a white terry cloth robe, her eyes red. She sobbed. My father, a Disciples of Christ minister, said she was not to blame. Mr. Ledbetter put his arm around my shoulder. My mother hugged Mrs. Ledbetter. I felt sorry for her.

People came to the parsonage all that day. With each new wave, my parents repeated how Alice had died. "This is part of some greater plan," one woman offered.

I escaped to the garage, where I found my Honda 50—its front wheel bent, its spokes snapped, its battery case cracked. Alice's blood dotted the gas tank. I loved that scooter. On summer mornings, I would slice through the steam above the warming country blacktop, my shirt unbuttoned and whipping my back. The Mexicans picking cucumbers, cantaloupes and watermelons in the fields would pause and glance as I passed at full throttle, 45 miles an hour. When my father found me in the garage, I'd cleaned off everything but the blood and was trying to straighten the mangled wheel with a hammer.

"I think I can fix it," I said. The next day it was gone.

Fowler is nine miles west of Manzanola, 18 miles west of Rocky Ford and 28 miles west of La Junta. No planes, no trains, no bus stations. The Arkansas River keeps the flat, rocky land around Fowler, population 1,241, rich for watermelons, sugar beets, sweet corn and cantaloupes. Fowler is nine blocks square. I think of it as home.

My family had moved six times by my 14th birthday, the year we arrived in Fowler. The constant migration made Alice and me close, as did the nearness in our ages. Our brother, George, was six years older than I. Alice was alive for only the first year we lived in Fowler, and most of my memories of the town do not include her. But walking the streets of Fowler again helped me remember: Alice working behind the soda fountain at Fowler Drug, mixing me 15-cent cherry Cokes, Alice walking to the Fowler swimming pool with me on hot afternoons, Alice assisting me in my incarnation as Dr. Sly, child magician and escape artist. I remembered the time she and I convinced our Sunday school teacher that all of the students should read their favorite Bible stories aloud. The others read David and Goliath or Noah. I read Judges 5, Verse 26, how Jael pounded a tent peg into the head of Sisera, the heathen. Alice read Second Samuel 11, how David spied Bathsheba naked and dispatched her husband to the front lines to be slaughtered.

I drove to Fowler's First Christian Church, where my father had been pastor. The four chandeliers my parents donated in memory of Alice still hang from the white roof of the sanctuary. My mother's painting of a girl lighting candles at an altar still decorates the east wall. I sat in a wooden pew and stared above the communion table at the stained-glass window of Christ praying in the Garden of Gethsemane. I had taken collections, said prayers and read announcements beneath that window 100 times. They called me "the little preacher." I closed my eyes: *I am a lanky boy*

with buzz-cut hair and glasses mended with Scotch tape. My mother
wears her most colorful hat and we walk down the church aisle together
holding hands as the mourners' heads turn in unison at our passing. We
step to the first row in front of Alice's open coffin. She is in heaven and
we are witnessing: "Alleluia! Where O Death Is Now Thy Sting?"

"I did the first portion of your sister's funeral service," said pastor
Charles Whitmer when I asked him for his memory of the funeral. "When
I finished, your father walked up next to the casket and began talking
about Alice. He talked about his relationship with her and how much all
of you loved her and he kept his composure the entire time. I remember
thinking that no one could do that, no one could have kept his composure like he had, unless Christ was with him."

During the prayer, I search for Flora Ledbetter, who sits near the back
of the church. She is sobbing. Her husband sees me and lowers his eyes.
She is not to blame, my parents had said. I look at my mother, my father,
my brother. Their eyes are closed. My parents are holding hands, tightly.
I look at Alice. They have put too much makeup on her. She hates makeup.
I had kissed her goodbye, the night before, and her skin felt hard. My father
had called her "Our Sissie." I raise my head and look at the window of
Christ in the Garden. The morning sun has turned his robe blood red.
Alice's faith was always so complete. She had once promised that if the
communists took over, she would die a martyr.

I opened my eyes, walked to the altar, and knelt to pray, but I
couldn't. I waited, and it didn't come. I looked up at the stained-glass
window of Jesus. "Damn you!" I whispered. They were the words of a
14-year-old boy.

I drove to Jones Corner from Fowler by the route Alice had taken that
night. Then I drove Ledbetter's route, three times. On the last trip I
jammed on my brakes, imagining that I had just seen Alice on the
scooter. The car swerved as it entered the intersection, its headlights
cutting a swath across an empty field. I got out of the car and began
pacing. In the four years I lived in Fowler after Alice died, I had never
visited Jones Corner.

I stepped from the road into the ditch where Alice had been thrown.
It was steeply sloped, several feet deep, patched with snow. I stepped on
a beer bottle. An old magazine was frozen to exposed grass. I tried to

picture the scene: Ledbetter's car in the center of the road, my motor scooter thrown 66 feet to the side, my sister at my feet.

"I remember your sister was lying in the bar ditch about here," Wes Ayers, Fowler's deputy sheriff, had told me earlier in the day as he marked the spot on a piece of paper. "At the time, state troopers filed reports only if there was a fatality, and I asked the state trooper if he was going to do a report on your sister. He said, 'No.'

" 'Don't you see that big cut on that little girl's leg?' I asked. 'Well, it ain't bleeding at all and that can only mean one thing: she's got to be bleeding inside.' After I told him that, he got out his clipboard."

The thought of Alice lying among strangers as they speculated about the odds of her living enraged me. It had taken almost an hour after the accident to get Alice to the 37-bed Pioneer Memorial Hospital, only 22 miles away. The emergency room report, brief and routine, didn't explain the long time gap; it said she died of shock. She arrived at 8:00 p.m., awake and complaining of pain: "Pt ventilating when first seen. B/P 90/60—gradually dropped. Given Demerol 75 mg. for pain. Pt went into shock & coma." After Alice lapsed into unconsciousness, they finally started IVs in her right arm and ankle, suctioned her throat, massaged her heart, gave her adrenaline. "Pt never regained consciousness. Expired 9:30 p.m."

Years before my sister died, I shot a rabbit a few yards from the Fowler Cemetery, east of town and set amid towering Chinese elm trees. I had spooked the cottontail from a woodpile and it ran up an embankment, where it froze. I blasted its entrails across the snow. I thought about the rabbit and my clear memory of it when I drove into the cemetery. But I could not recall a single detail of my sister's graveside service.

It was almost midnight and the moon illuminated the tombstones. It was snowing gently. I walked to the headstone I believed was my sister's, but it wasn't. I slowly walked row by row, examining each headstone, seeing the names of people I had known in Fowler. Clouds began to block the moonlight and it seemed to get colder. It is embarrassing to say, but I suddenly felt afraid, as if I were intruding. For two decades I had lived without thinking of Alice. I thought: "I knew her only 14 years. She has been here for 19. They are her family now."

I couldn't find the headstone, so I shined my car's headlights into the cemetery. It was so cold now that I began to speed up my search. It struck me that Alice would not let me find her! I ran, faster and faster, glancing at each name. A sense of desperation shot through me. Suddenly, I caught myself. The image of me, frightened and racing through the Fowler Cemetery at midnight, was ludicrous. I would return tomorrow.

That night, voices outside my motel door awakened me from a dream. I lay in bed afraid to move, an emotion I had not felt since childhood. In my dream, I had been jogging. It was dark and a car began to follow me. It forced me down an alley blocked by a tall chain link fence. A gang of boys got out of the car. They pulled knives from their coats. I scrambled up the chain link fence, but as I reached the top it curled backward slowly, lowering me toward them. Just as they were about to reach me, they turned and grabbed someone else from the shadows. They stabbed and stabbed and stabbed, until the person was dead. Then they turned and pointed their bloody knives toward me.

I found Alice's grave without trouble the next day. "Alice Lee Earley. February 13, 1949. June 14, 1966. A lovely Daughter." I wanted to talk to her, but I felt foolish. If all there ever was of Alice was still in that grave, she would not hear me anyway. If life and death are miracles, though, I could have talked to her as easily from Washington as Fowler. I placed a bouquet of daisies before her headstone. A farmer drove by in a pickup. He glanced at me; I was ashamed at my embarrassment. I stood for the longest time. I wanted a sign. Some little miracle—hearing Alice's voice in my head, perhaps. But I heard only the silence that reaffirmed her refusal to welcome me. I thought that the daisies would freeze that night. I hoped the caretaker would leave them at least through tomorrow. Alice gets flowers so seldom, I thought.

A sadness came to me: My trip was for nothing. But as I returned to the car, the anger rose in me again—this time anger at Alice. I walked back to her grave and placed my hands on the stone. I drifted between talking and thinking. "Okay, you died, but things weren't so great here either."

I did move into your room. I got your dresser. I got your guitar. But things changed after you died. Night after night I lay in your bed listening to Mom and Dad cry: "If only we had bought her a car! If only we hadn't bought the Honda!" When they started the tranquilizers, I was terrified they, too, would die. "You left me, Alice!" You died on *my* motorcycle!

You always were so careful! I was the reckless one, everyone knew that! Why didn't I take the Honda's keys with me to church camp?

I began to cry: "Why did you have to die, Alice? Why not me?" I turned to leave, but as I walked to the car I felt a calm. I returned to the grave and sat in the snow. Eventually, I began to talk. I told Alice that I had left Fowler for college, that I had married at 20. I talked of the newspapers where I had worked, my house in Virginia, my three children. I said my oldest son, Stephen, had scored four points in last Saturday's basketball game. I told her that I teach Sunday school, but that the "little preacher" had died with her. Even today, I think of her and a naive rage at God wells up. My faith is unclear to me. I told her that my three-year-old daughter Kathy looks a lot like her, which makes me happy. At the times when I have been the happiest, however, I have sometimes looked at Kathy and felt suddenly sad at the inevitability of despair. I talked until I had nothing left to say and then I sat. I reached down and touched her grave marker. It wasn't enough. I kissed the stone.

"I love you, Alice. I always have."

I tracked Flora Ledbetter to the western slope of the Rockies. She and her husband, a teacher at Fowler High, had left Fowler a year after the accident. He was later killed in an airplane crash. Her second husband died of cancer. She married again and moved here. I wondered if her husband knew.

"I don't know if you will remember me or not," I said.

"I remember you," she answered. "What do you want?"

What I wanted from Ledbetter was remorse. I wanted her to say she was sorry. I wanted her to accept the blame I had assigned to her for 19 years. It turned out she wanted absolution from me. The accident had devastated her at the time, she told me. She wondered why she had lived and Alice had died. She sobbed for days; she couldn't sleep. Three days after the accident, she returned to Jones Corner. By then a stop sign had been installed on the road Alice was traveling.

"If anyone was to blame," Ledbetter said, "it was your sister. That's where the state put the sign, didn't they? . . . The worst part was that your parents sued me. The Bible says Christians shouldn't sue each other. Your father knew that. I didn't care about the money, but they were trying to prove that I was responsible. That wasn't fair."

I had not expected this. Like me, Ledbetter was angry—but at the state, at Alice and at my parents for filing a $25,000 wrongful death suit against her. Suddenly, I was on the defensive. I told her my parents sued because her insurance company had harassed them repeatedly and claimed that Alice's life was worth only $500. The case was eventually settled out of court for about $10,000, without Ledbetter admitting or denying guilt. I still remember the talk around town: My father, the minister, profiting from Alice's death. "Blood money," one Fowler gossip called it.

"The state trooper told me that this was one of those truly unavoidable accidents," Ledbetter said. "Your folks sued me anyway."

My tone changed. "I drove to that corner," I said coldly. "I retraced your steps and I could see *perfectly.*"

"There were weeds there and a big mound of dirt back then that made it hard to see. I think there was an irrigation well, too. I can't remember."

"I hated you when I was growing up. I covered your husband's photograph in the school yearbook with white tape."

She was quiet. "How do you feel now?"

I hesitated. "I don't hate you anymore. It was an accident. I guess it was no one's fault."

"I'm glad we talked," she said.

I went to a bar.

My mother had put the family scrapbooks out for my arrival. She was eager to talk about Alice. My father was reluctant. Late that night, we finally began.

"We were in the emergency room with Alice," my mother said. "She kept saying to me, 'Mamma, Mamma, I'm gonna die. It hurts. I'm gonna die,' and I said, 'No, darling, it's okay. They are going to save you. You are going to be okay.' " My mother took off her glasses and wiped her eyes.

"They didn't do a thing for her," my father said. "They cut her foot and put some kind of line in it, but it was leaking out all over the floor. Then they got into an argument because one of them didn't want to put a tube down her throat. She would have been just as well off if they had left her in the ditch, maybe better. The ambulance ran out of gas on the way to the hospital." That explained the delay in Alice's arrival at the hospital.

I thought of my parents standing helpless as Alice died. "Why didn't you sue them?" I demanded.

"Who?" asked my father.

"All of them!"

"I'm sure that they did all that they could," said my mother. "They didn't know as much then as they do now."

"But you sued the Ledbetters."

There was a long silence. "The last time I saw Mrs. Ledbetter," my father said, "she said it was 'God's will' that Alice died."

"It was just so unfair," my mother said. "Here was this big insurance company and we were so little . . . Do you know when Ledbetter's first husband died? He was killed February 13—on your sister's birthday. When I first heard it, I felt it was retribution. Your father never felt that way, but I did. Then I decided that was wrong."

"Everything that could have gone wrong did," my father said. "Both doctors in Fowler were out of town that night."

"Alice was supposed to be at work," my mother said. "But she had traded hours with another girl. I got so mad at that girl that I couldn't stand seeing her. I was mad at the Ledbetters. I was mad at the superintendent's wife because she didn't come to the funeral. I was mad at the sheriff's wife for not calling us when the accident happened so we could have gotten there in time to send Alice to Pueblo. I was mad at the doctors. But after a while, you realize that it doesn't help. Nothing can bring Alice back."

"How about God?" I asked. "Did you blame Him?"

My father shook his head. "No, I never felt that way."

On my first night home in Washington, Kathy woke me in the night and I carried her downstairs to the rocking chair. We sat long after she fell asleep and I thought of Alice. "She's gone," my mother had said. "What's the use in blaming?" I had told Flora Ledbetter that I didn't blame her for Alice's death. And I had meant it. Still, if she had left a minute earlier, taken a different route, Alice would be alive. I don't blame Ledbetter, but I do blame Ledbetter.

Job demanded of God: Why are the innocent slaughtered? "Then the Lord answered Job . . . Where were you when I laid the foundation of the earth? Tell me, if you have understanding."

I don't, I thought. I don't understand.

I closed my eyes and thought of Alice: *My mother, father, brother, Alice and I are in our backyard in Fowler. It is a summer Sunday night, near dusk. My mother sits in the brown lawn chair next to my father in his folding chaise. I sit with my brother a few steps away in the long grass holding our dog, Snowball. Alice stands at the grill, her back to us. She wears navy blue shorts and a white blouse. She is barefooted. Smoke and the scent of cooking hamburgers rise from the grill. Alice turns. The sun has reddened her face. The wind has uncurled her hair. She looks at me, and she is laughing.*

▧ Author's Afterwords . . .

I have a hard time reading this article even today. It's still painful, because it was such a personal journey. It's a story that came from inside me and wanted to be told, although I had no idea where it would go. I had mentioned to one of my editors that I was having these weird dreams about my dead sister. He said I should write about it. I wasn't sure I should. What was the story? But he convinced me. From the beginning, I had to divide myself between being the subject of the story and the writer. I'm not normally an introspective guy, in life or in my writing. I let the facts speak for themselves. So I did the story by going back and reporting my sister's death and recording my experiences and feelings.

Obviously, I wanted to find out what had happened and why her death was still bothering me 20 years later. So I did a kind of free-fall into the story, not knowing where it would go. And that's scary. I tried to let the story lead me. I had no idea what I'd find once I got to Fowler or to Alice's grave. I just knew I needed to put myself in these situations and see what happened. Even when I was in the graveyard and the church, I didn't know I'd include these events in the story. My only feeling then was confusion. I just wanted to get it all down and then go back and try to put it together, make sense of it as I wrote.

When I read the article years later, I'm struck by how short and simple the sentences are. I like that because it's a story that could be easily overwritten. I also like that it's written in almost all scenes with little analysis. It's not me on the couch trying to figure myself out. It's got action. I tell what happened to me and let readers draw the meaning for themselves. I'm not even sure I could tell you what the *meaning* really is. When I'm running all around the graveyard looking for Alice's grave, losing it, what does that mean? I've no idea. But it happened. And it somehow figures in, even though it can't be tied up with a neat ribbon of explanation. It's the same with the dream scene.

One editor wanted to delete the dream because he said he didn't know what it was supposed to mean and because it made me look mentally unhinged. He said readers would think I was crazy. But I *was* mentally unhinged for some moments while I was doing this story. Readers had to know that. It was right to leave it in.

As I wrote the story, it took on a life of its own. I opened a door and other doors seemed to keep opening on their own. I felt like I was floating along with the writing, not making it happen. It was happening to me. I don't want to sound too mystical, but I was caught up in this story and carried along by it.

After it appeared, I got tremendous reaction. People called and told me stories about deaths in their own families. It seemed to help people. I'd plugged into a whole world of buried emotions. If I'd done the story in a more traditional way, gone out and interviewed a dozen experts on death and dying, included their opinions and anecdotes about their patients, I probably would've found that my experiences weren't that unusual—the typical stages of grief. But giving over our stories to the "experts" strips them of their authenticity and narrative power. It's odd, but telling one person's story is somehow more universal.—P. E.

Madeleine Blais

Madeleine Blais has worked as a staff writer for the *Miami Herald's Tropic Magazine,* where her article "Zepp's Last Stand" won a Pulitzer Prize for feature writing. She has written articles for the *Boston Globe, Washington Post Magazine* and *New York Times Magazine.* She is the author of *The Heart Is an Instrument: Portraits in Journalism* (1992) and *In These Girls, Hope Is a*

123

Muscle (1995), which was a finalist for the National Book Critics Circle nonfiction book award. She is a professor of journalism at the University of Massachusetts and lives in Amherst, Massachusetts.

In These Girls, Hope Is a Muscle

The voice of the coach rises above the din of shuffling footsteps, loud greetings, the slamming of metal, the thud of books. "Listen up. I want you to check right now. Do you have your uniforms? Your shoes and your socks? Do you have any other items of clothing that might be needed?"

Coach Ron Moyer believes it's possible to pack abstractions along with one's gear, intangibles like "intensity" and "game face" and "consistency" and "defense." As the members of the Amherst Regional High School girls' basketball team prepare to board the Hoop Phi Express on their way to the Centrum in Worcester more than an hour away for the Massachusetts state championship, he tells them, "Today, I want you to pack your courage."

The team is 23-1 going into this game, losing only to Agawam, which, like the Haverhill team they are facing this evening, has some real height. Haverhill, known for aggressive ball, nothing dirty but just short of it, has two girls over six feet nicknamed Twin Towers. Moyer has prepped his team with a couple of specialized plays, the Murphy and the Shoelace, and he tells them: "Expect to play a little football." Amherst girls have a reputation for being afraid to throw their elbows, but this year they have learned to take the words "finesse team" as an insult. Although Coach has been careful to avoid saying "state championship" to goad his team, last fall he did tell one aging gym rat in town: "I have the two best guards in the state and probably the nation, but it all depends on the girls up front. There's an old saying: 'Guards win games, but forwards win championships.' We'll have to see."

At 6' 6", Moyer looms over his players. With a thick cap of graying brown hair and bangs that flop down over his forehead, he resembles a grizzly bear on spindly legs. The girls are more like colts. For Moyer, turning them into a team has nothing to do with breaking their spirit and everything to do with harnessing it.

As Jen Pariseau listens to Coach before leaving for Worcester, her legs can't stop twitching. One of the six seniors on the team playing high-school hoop together for the last time, she has thick, dark eyebrows and long, lanky limbs. For her, tonight's game is the perfect revenge, not just against Haverhill but also against some of the rebuffs she suffered as an athlete on the way up. For three years, she played on one of Amherst's Little League teams, the Red Sox. She was pitcher, shortstop and first baseman. When it was time to choose the all-star league, she was told her bunts were not up to par.

Jen's teammates are just as hyped up. Half of them are giving the other half piggybacks. There are lots of hand-slapping and nudges. They swirl around one another, everyone making a private point of touching Jamila Wideman, Jen's co-captain, as if one dark-haired, brown-eyed girl could transmit the power of her playing to all the others. Jamila is an all-America, recipient of more than 150 offers of athletic scholarships. On the court, the strong bones of her face are like a flag demanding to be heeded; she is a study in quickness and confidence, the ball becoming part of her body.

Jen Pariseau is two-time all-Western Mass, and together the two guards delighted fans all season with the way they delivered the ball to each other, sometimes in a dipsy doo behind the back or between the legs, often in an open shot. JennyandJamila. In Amherst, it's one word.

Coach pauses. He looks as though he is about to rebuke the girls for all the squirming, but he shrugs and gives a big smile. "Let's go." Then, perhaps more to himself than to them: "While we're still young."

Shortly after 5:00 in the evening, the sky is thick and gray and hooded, the cloud cover a welcome hedge against what has been a bitter New England winter. The bus the girls board is different from the usual.

"Hooked up and smooth," says Jen Pariseau, admiring the special features, including upholstered seats, a toilet, four television sets and a VCR mounted on the ceiling—a definite step up from the yellow tin cans they have taken to every other game. There are some cheerleaders on the bus as well as Tricia Lea, an assistant coach with her own high-school memories about what it was like to go up against those Hillies from Haverhill in their brown and yellow uniforms with the short shorts. "Haverhill. I don't know what they eat up there, but they can be slightly ruthless. Sportsmanship does not run very deep in that town."

A few years back, Coach had trouble convincing players and their families of the seriousness of the commitment to girls' basketball. JennyandJamila remember playing in varsity games five and six years ago when the gym would be empty of spectators except for their parents and maybe a few lost souls who had missed the late bus. Coach remembers girls who would cut practice to go to their boyfriends' games, and once during the playoffs, a team captain left to go on a school-sponsored cultural exchange for three weeks in the former Soviet Union. As far as he's concerned, the current policy could not be clearer: You want cultural exchange? You can have it with Hamp.

Tonight, Amherst is sending three "pep" buses to the game, unprecedented support for an athletic event, boys' or girls'. Amherst is a place that tends to prize thought over action, tofu over toughness. It prefers to honor the work of the individual dedicated to a life of monastic scholarship rather than some noisy group effort. But this season, there were sellout crowds. There was even that ultimate badge: a wary cop on the premises for the first time in the history of a girls' event.

Amherst is a college town, with the usual benign ineffectuality that makes most college towns as maddening as they are charming and livable. When the Chamber of Commerce sponsored a contest for town motto, Moyer submitted one that he still thinks should have won: "Amherst: Where sexuality is an option and reality is an alternative."

Amherst is, for the most part, smoke free, nuclear free and eager to free Tibet. Ponchos with little projectiles of fleece have never gone out of style. Banners stretch across South Pleasant Street at the town common, including the vintage "Spay or Neuter Your Pet, Prevent Abandonment & Suffering." This is a town that saves spotted salamanders, creating love tunnels (at taxpayers' eager expense) so that they can all descend from the hills in early spring and migrate to the marshy areas for sexual assignation without being squashed on Henry Street. There's a new band called Salamander Crossing; heavy metal it's not. A famous local headline: "Well-Dressed Man Robs Amherst Bank." Amherst is an achingly democratic sort of place in which tryouts for Little League, with their inevitable rejections, have caused people to suggest that more teams should be created so that no one is left out. There are people in Amherst who still think "politically correct" is a compliment. The program notes for the spring musical *Kiss Me, Kate* pointed out politely that *The Taming of the Shrew,* on which it is based, was "well, Shakespearean in its attitude toward the sexes."

The downtown area seems to support pizza joints, Chinese restaurants, ice-cream parlors and bookstores and not much else. It's hard to find a needle and thread, but if you wish you can go to the Global Trader and purchase for $4 a dish towel with a rain-forest theme. The surrounding communities range from the hard and nasty inner-city poverty of Holyoke, the empty factories in Chicopee and the blue-collar scrappiness in Agawam to the cornfields and asparagus patches in Whately and Hatfield and Hadley and the shoppers' mecca that is Northampton. They tend to look on Amherst with eye-rolling puzzlement and occasional contempt as the town that fell to earth.

The girls on the Hurricanes know they live in a kindly, ruminative sort of place. Sometimes they joke about how if they weren't playing ball, they'd be "tipping cows"—a basically useless activity necessitated by the unfortunate tendency of cows to sleep standing up.

With the playoffs looming, the six senior girls—JennyandJamila, Kathleen Poe, Kristin Marvin, Patri Abad and Kim Warner—were treated to a late lunch by Jamila's father, John Edgar Wideman, winner of two PEN/Faulkners as well as numerous other awards, and author of the nonfiction meditation *Brothers and Keepers; Philadelphia Fire,* a fictional visitation of the Philadelphia MOVE bombing in 1985; and *The Homewood Trilogy,* about growing up black in Pittsburgh.

It was at that lunch that the team's center, Kristin, in trying to sum up the peculiar, almost consoling, lack of outward drama in a town like Amherst, confessed that the night before she had had a dream. "My mom and I, we went to Stop and Shop and while we were there, we went down, you know, all our usual aisles in the regular order, picking out all the things we usually buy, and after that we got in line to check out."

"That's it?" said the other girls.

Jamila's father thought maybe the dream had another layer and so he tried a gentle psychoanalytic probe. He has a quicksilver face, his expression changing in a flicker from stormy to melancholy to soft and forgiving. Now it was contemplative.

"Did you run into any unusual people?"

"No."

"How about money? Did you run out of money or anything?"

"No."

"Kristin," said her teammates, "that's so sad."

Kathleen, who is in the top 10 academically in her class of 250, told Jamila's father that she tried reading a collection of his short stories, "the one called *Jungle Fever.*"

"I'm not Spike Lee. It was just *Fever.*"

"Mr. Wideman, I tried reading it," said Jen Pariseau, also in the top 10 academically. "I found the shortest story I could, and you know what? I think I understood it. I can't guarantee it, but I think I did."

He looked at his guests at the table, a blur of happy faces and ponytails. Their teasing was a joy. He is a former basketball player for the University of Pennsylvania and a Rhodes scholar who played at Oxford, and his passion for the game is such that Jamila tells people she was born playing basketball. Girls' basketball is not boys' basketball being played by girls. It's a whole new game. There's no dunking. They can't jump as high. They can't play above the rim. But they can play with every bit as much style. And there's that added purity, that sense of excellence for its own sake. It's not a career option for girls; after college the game is over, so there is none of the desperate jockeying for professional favor.

As a black man, Wideman knows only too well the shallow triumph of token progress. He had told Kathleen's father, "This is just one team in one season." It alone cannot change the discrimination against girls and their bodies throughout history. But here in these girls, hope is a muscle.

"Here's to the senior girls," he said, looking at all of them.

They hoisted their ritual glasses of water.

"This is," he said, "as good as it gets."

To look at them, these six seniors on the team, who all appear to be lit from within, one would assume that their lives have been seamless journeys. In fact, as Jen Pariseau puts it, she does not come from a "Dan Quayle kind of family"—and neither do most of the others.

Whatever sadness or disruption they've been dealt, an opposite force follows them onto the court. JennyandJamila have not gone it alone; they have had Kathleen's strong right hand, an almost irresistible force heading toward the basket. She never wastes a motion: the ball is in her hands one second, then quietly dropping through the hoop the next, without dramatics, almost like an afterthought. There's Kristin. Her flushed cheeks are not a sign of exhaustion but of some private fury. When the ball comes curling out of the basket, more often than not it is Kristin who has pushed and shoved her way to the prize.

The only underclass starter, Emily Shore, is so serious about her chance to play with the famous JennyandJamila that she spent the bulk of her summer lifting weights and battling in pickup games on Amherst's cracked and weather-ravaged outdoor courts with a succession of skeptical and then grudgingly appreciative young men.

They have become what every opponent fears most: a team with a mission.

As good as it gets. That is, of course, the exact sentiment the girls feel toward their fancy bus.

"Fasten your seat belts," says Coach. "Beverage service will commence shortly after takeoff. There'll be turbulence coming to Haverhill when the Hurricanes hit Worcester." Then he announces the people to whom he would like them to dedicate the entire season. "And that's to the 140 girls who are now playing youth basketball in Amherst for the first time this year."

Jen Pariseau says she wants to read a letter from Diane Stanton, the mother of Chris Stanton, the star of the boys' basketball team. "Jenny and Jamila," the letter began. Diane Stanton said she was addressing them because she knew them best, but the letter was for the whole team. "Your existence as a team represents a lot of things to a lot of women like me. . . . As a young girl I remember standing outside the Little League fence and watching the boys and knowing that I could hit and catch better than at least a third of them. When our high-school intramural field hockey team and softball team asked for leagues, we were told flatly NO, because there was no money. . . . When this group of girl athletes got together to form an intramural basketball team, we were subjected to ridicule and anger from some of the student body. . . . I lost courage, I'm embarrassed to admit, in my junior year and would no longer play intramural sports. Part of it was a protest against the failure of my school . . . to recognize that we needed to play as much as boys. I know the struggle."

Coach gives the driver a signal and the vehicle starts to roll.

A police car just ahead suddenly activates its lights and in a slow ceremony leads the vehicle to the corner of Main and Triangle Streets, where another officer has been summoned to stop traffic. Coach is beaming and silently thanks his old pal, Captain Charlie Scherpa, over in the Police Department for coming through. In addition to being a guidance counselor, Moyer has been the girls' coach off and on since 1981, a task he enjoys because unlike with boys, whose arrogance and confidence often have to be eroded before he can get the team to work, this is all constructive. The way to build a girls' team is to build their individual self-confidence.

The bus heads down Main (a street that is most famous for being the site of the house where Emily Dickinson was born, where she lived, died and wrote her poetry) to the corner of Northeast, where they get to run a red light, turning in front of Fort River Elementary School, then heading out to Route 9, where the escort lasts all the way to the town line. In an instant, the sign that says "Entering Pelham" appears, and in another instant a new one looms ahead that says "Entering Belcher-town."

The girls watch the film they had chosen unanimously to pump them for the game—*A League of Their Own*. The six seniors are lost in their own thoughts.

Kim Warner knows her mother, who works in personnel at the University of Massachusetts, will be at the game, plus her two sisters, plus her boyfriend's family. Her father lives in Florida, and although she sends him news accounts of all the games, he has never seen her play. She hasn't seen him since the 10th grade. She plans to go to Westfield State and major in early childhood education. On the way to the game,

Kim writes a fantasy letter in her head: "Dear Dad, At long last a lot of hard work paid off."

Patri Abad's mother, a bilingual teacher, has to be at work, and although Patri will miss her, she knows she can count on a large cheering section of friends. She almost didn't get to play this year. During her junior year, she had moved to Chicago with her mother and her new stepfather. Patri, who is Cuban on her father's side and Puerto Rican on her mother's, prayed incessantly to the Virgin. She received constant mail from teammates like Lucia Maraniss, back when Lucia was a gushing eighth-grader "Patri, I will always remember you as one of the wisest, most caring and compassionate people I've ever met. I'm going to miss you very, very, very, very, very, very, very, very, very, very, very, very, very, very much."

Whether it was divine intercession or that 14th "very" from Lucia, the resolve of Patri's mother to stay in Chicago eventually vanished. They returned to the Happy Valley, as Amherst is called, and Patri could finish her senior year as a member of the Hurricanes. She has been accepted at Drew, Clark and the University of Massachusetts, pre-med.

Kristin Marvin, also known as Jolly, Jolly Green and Grace (her teammates have misinterpreted her tenacity as clumsiness), is going to Holy Cross College, pre-med. She likes medicine because it has a strong element of knowability. Her parents were divorced when she was young and she lived with a lot of uncertainty. Her mother has since married a builder whose first wife married Kristin's father, who works in Connecticut and often rushes to the games after work in his business suit. The marital realignment has created a circumstance in which the daughter of her stepfather and stepmother is Kristin's double stepsister.

Coach calls Kathleen Poe his silent assassin—the girl with two distinct personalities. The demure senior with the high grades, with applications at Williams, Haverford, Duke and Dartmouth, is Kathleen; the girl on the court is her ferocious twin, Skippy. He concocted the dichotomy because when Kathleen first started playing she said "Excuse me" all the time and would pause to pick her opponents up off the floor. She wants to be like Jamila: someone you don't want to meet on the court but who will be a good friend off it.

Jamila plans to study law and African-American studies at Stanford. Like her mother, Judy Wideman, who is in her second year of law school, she hopes to be a defense attorney. As a child of mixed races, she has

told interviewers she identifies not with being black or white but with
being herself. Still, her bedroom has pictures of Winnie Mandela, Jesse
Jackson and the children of Soweto. After the riot in Los Angeles, she
wrote several poems that reflected her feelings.

In "Black," she wrote:

> I walk the tightrope between the fires
> Does anyone know where I fall through?
> Their forked daggers of rage reflect my eye
> Their physical destruction passes me by
> Why does the fire call me?

Jen is known locally as the best thing that ever happened to Pelham,
which is that little twinge on the highway on Route 9. Since Jen was two
and her brother, Chris, was four, they have lived with their father, who is
a manager of reservoirs and water treatment in Amherst. She is planning
to play ball for Dartmouth and to major in engineering. She turned down
Princeton, especially after the recruiter, who made a home visit, would
not let her father, who has a stutter, talk.

The door to her room is plastered with Nike inspirational ads. She
calls the wall above her bed her "strong women wall," and it is filled with
pictures of her favorite role models, including Ann Richards and Toni
Morrison. By her bedside, she keeps a clothbound book—given to her
by her teammate Rita Powell—in which she writes favorite quotes, a
customized Bartlett's.

Marilyn Monroe: "If I'm going to be alone, I'd rather be by myself."
Colette: "You will do foolish things, but do them with enthusiasm."
Zora Neale Hurston: "The dream is the truth."

The team bonding among these six seniors and the 10 younger girls is
one reason they have played so well: the sisterhood-is-powerful quest for
unity. They have a team song, "Real Love," and they have team trinkets
(beaded necklaces with their names and plastic rings and scrunchies
with basketballs), team teddy bears, team towels. At team dinners,
Jamila's mother carbo-loads them with slivered chicken cooked in garlic
and oil and lemon and served on a bed of noodles. The meals often
conclude with a dozen or so girls linking arms in a tight circle; swaying,
singing, shouting, *"Hoop Phi!"*

To witness adrenalin overload at its most frenetic, nothing beats the atmosphere on one of those yellow buses on the return home after a victory over Hamp. Northampton is a fine town, birthplace of Calvin Coolidge, home of Smith College. But, as Jen Pariseau says: "Something happens when we play Hamp. Both teams become brutes." Hamp fans are always trying to demoralize JennyandJamila with the scornful chant: "You're overrated; you're overrated."

A victory against Hamp, especially on their territory at Feiker gym, especially in front of at least 1,000 people with several hundred more turned away at the door, was a great moment to whoop and cheer the whole way home, to sing Queen's famous anthem, "We Are the Champions," to slap the ceiling of the bus, to open the windows and to shout:

> Who'll rock the house?
> The Hurricanes will rock the house.
> And when the Hurricanes rock the house
> They rock it all the way down.

But even though they beat Hamp in the Western Mass Regional finals, they weren't really champions—not yet. Do they have what it takes, these sweet-looking girls reared in maple syrup country on land that includes the Robert Frost trail? Playing before a few thousand fans in what is almost your own backyard is nothing compared with a stadium that seats 13,800, where real pros play. Rocking Feiker is one thing, but the Centrum?

When the bus finally pulls in front of the Centrum and it is time to leap off, the girls have faces like masks. To the world, they are a bunch of teenage girls; inside their heads, they are commandos. To the world, these teenagers have pretty names: Patri, Kristin, Jen, Kathleen, Kim, Jamila, Sophie, Jade, Emily J., Emily S., Jan, Lucia, Carrie, Rita, Jessi, Julie. But as far as the girls are concerned, they are the codes that encapsulate their rare and superb skills, their specialty plays, their personal styles. They are Cloudy and Cougar and Jonesbones and Gumby and Grace and Skippy. They are warriors.

The girls crowd into a locker room. With much less commotion than usual, they dress in their baggy knee-length uniforms. They slap hands and stand tall. Meanwhile, the arena is redolent of hot dogs, popcorn, sweat and anticipation, one side of the bleachers filled with their people and the other side with the fans from Haverhill.

The girls walk out wordlessly. They look up.

You have to live in a small town for a while before you can read a crowd, especially in New England, where fences are deep in the soil. But if you've been in a town like Amherst for a while, you can go to an out-of-town game, even one in as imposing and cavernous a facility as the Centrum, and you can feel this sudden lurch of well-being that comes from the soothing familiarity of faces that are as much a part of your landscape as falling leaves, as forsythia in season, as rhubarb in June. You scan the rows, and for better, and sometimes for worse, you know who's who. You know whose parents don't talk to whom else and you know why. You know who has had troubles that never get discussed.

You see the lawyer that represented your folks or one of their friends in a land dispute or a custody case. You see the realtor who tried to sell a house next to the landfill to the new kids in town. You see the doctor who was no help for your asthma and the one who was. You see the teacher who declared your baby brother a complete mystery and the teacher who always stops to ask what your remarkable brother is up to now. You know which man is the beloved elementary school principal, now retired. You recognize the plump-cheeked ladies from the cafeteria who specialize in homemade cinnamon buns for 65¢. You see your family and you see the fathers and mothers and stepfathers and stepmothers of your teammates. You know whose brother flew in from Chicago for the game; whose step-grandparents came from Minnesota.

But what is most important about all this is how mute it is. The commonality is something that is understood, as tacit as the progression of the summer to fall to winter to spring, and just as comforting.

Usually there is a buzz of cheering at the start of a game, but this time the Amherst crowd is nearly silent as the referee tosses the ball.

The Haverhill center taps the ball backward to her point guard. She comes down the court, swings the ball to the wing, who instantly dishes it inside to the center. Easy layup. Amherst blinks first. Two-nothing. In the Haverhill stands, the crowd cheers. It is the only pure cheer they will get.

Within a few seconds, the score is 6-4 Amherst, and something truly remarkable takes place. The Hurricanes enter into a zone where all of them are All-Americans. It's a kind of controlled frenzy that can overtake a group of athletes under only the most elusive of circumstances. It's not certain what triggers it: perhaps it's Jamila's gentle three-pointer from the wing or, more likely, when Jen drives the baseline and as she swoops beneath the basket like a bird of prey releases the ball back over her head, placing it like an egg against the backboard and through the hoop. It may have been 10 seconds later when Jamila steals the ball, pushing it down court in a three-on-one break, makes a no-look pass to Jen, who just as quickly fires the ball across the lane to Kathleen for an uncontested layup. Whatever it is that started it, there is nothing Haverhill can do to stop it, and time-outs repeatedly called for by their hapless coach only fuel Amherst's frenzy further.

Even the sportscasters can't remember a 37 to 0 run in a state championship game. The halftime score is 51-6.

An astonished Amherst can hardly even cheer. One Amherst fan shouts: "Where's Dr. Kevorkian?" Another makes the very un-Amherst comment: "They should bring on the Haverhill boys for the second half."

Among the spectators is Kathleen's father, Donald Poe, an associate professor of psychology at Hampshire College, who saw how her defense, along with that of Kristin and Emily Shore, kept Haverhill's score so low. When his son, Chris, was an infant, Donald Poe tried to teach him to say "ball" as his first word, until he was told that "b" is a hard sound for a baby. He expected a son to be an athlete, and when Kathleen came along he didn't have that expectation. Yet whenever they go into the yard and she pitches a ball to him, it takes only five minutes before his hand hurts. She throws a heavy ball.

To him, what's important is not that Amherst wins, but that the spirit of girls' sports endures. Next year, it doesn't have to be Amherst; it might be Westside in Springfield. Its junior varsity is undefeated. When he was in W. T. Woodson High School in Fairfax, Virginia, the girls were not allowed to use the boys' gym, which was fancy and varnished with a logo in the middle of the floor. The girls had a little back gym, without bleachers. After a game, whenever he saw the little kids asking his daughter for autographs, he was glad to see the girls, pleased that they now had models. But he was just as glad to see the boys asking; to him their respect for the girls' team was just as important.

The final score is 74-36.

After receiving the trophies and after collapsing in one huge hysterical teenage heap, they all stand up. First they sing "Happy Birthday" to Kristin Marvin, who turns 18 this day. Then they extend their arms toward their parents, teachers, brothers, sisters, even to some of those

140 little girls whose parents have allowed them a school night of unprecedented lateness, and in one final act as a team, these girls shout, in the perfect unison that has served them so well on the court, *"Thank you."*

Back in the locker room, Kristin Marvin sucks on orange slices and sloshes water on her face. She then stands on a back bench, raises her right fist, turns to her comrades and shouts "Holy #@&*! We're the *@#&*@# champions!" And then she loses it! For the next half-hour, she throws herself into the arms of one teammate after another. She cries and hugs, and hugs and cries, and so do they.

Coach keeps knocking at the door, trying to roust the stragglers. Finally, he announces he is coming in, and what greets him is a roomful of girls who return his level gaze with eyes that are rheumy and red as they sputter "last . . . final . . . never again."

He looks right at them and says: "You're wrong. This isn't the last. There will be more basketball." His tone is conversational, almost adult to adult.

"But—" they start to say.

"I promise you. There will be lots more basketball."

Still they regard him with disbelief. They can't decipher his real message, at least not at this moment. They can't fathom how the word "basketball" might have more than one meaning.

Over. The game was over. On the way home, they watched a videotape of the game. Jen was stunned at how it had all fallen into place: We were so fluid it was scary. While they watched themselves, television viewers all over the state were witnessing recaps of the highlights and hearing the verdicts of professional commentators who claimed these girls had wandered into the wrong league: They shoulda been playing Calipari's men at U Mass; they coulda taught the Celtics a thing or two.

The girls would hear all that in the days to come, but at this moment they were mostly thinking about the present—when truth itself had become a dream. The bus was going backward, retracing its earlier path, down the Pike back through Palmer, where the only sense of abundance is in the fast-food stores, then through Bondsville with its gin mill and the sunken rusty playground with a metal fence, back through the center of Belchertown, a singularly flat stretch in a town with a singularly unfortunate name, and back in and out of Pelham—thanks to Jen, on the map at last.

Kathleen Poe wished that the whole team could sleep that night in the gym at the high school, the coziest, most homey, softest place she could now imagine, that they could all sink into its floor, become part of it forever. She kept trying out rhymes in her head, phrases popping into her mind like sudden rebounds: top and stop, pride and ride, forever and sever, heart, smart, true, you.

> Hoop Phi is of an intangible, untouchable breed,
> It satisfies the soul, and a life-long need.
> We represented our school, represented our sex,
> Now maybe both will get some well-earned respect.

No one really wanted the ride to end. The bare trees, the velvety night air, the cocoon of the bus itself.

At the town line there awaited another police escort, this time back into town. The cruiser was once again full of proud, slow ceremony. At the corner of Main and Triangle, the cruiser seemed to lurch right to take the short-cut back to the school, but then as if that was only a feint, it continued to move forward, so that the girls would be brought through town the long way.

The bus, boisterous in its very bigness, moved past the red-bricked Dickinson homestead with its top-heavy trees, tall and thin with a crown of green: *We're somebody; who are you?* Downtown was almost empty save for a couple of pizza eaters in the front window of Antonio's and a lone worker sweeping in the back shadows of Bart's Ice Cream. As the strobe lights from the cruiser bounced off the storefronts, the bus wheezed past St. Bridget's and the bagel place, turning right, then left, finally pulling into the school parking lot a few minutes shy of midnight.

All of a sudden one of the players shouted: "There are people there, waiting for us!" And, indeed, in the distance was a small crowd standing in the cold and in the dark, clapping. When the bus came to a stop, Coach stood up. "I promise it won't be mushy. There's just one thing you should know. When you're the state champions, the season never ever ends. I love you. Great job. And now, I'd like everybody else on the bus to please wait so that the team can get off first."

Often the Hurricanes will bound off a bus in a joyous squealing clump. On this night, they rose from their seats, slowly, in silence. *State champs!* For the final time this season, with great care bordering on tenderness, the teammates gathered their stuff, their uniforms, their shoes, their socks, their game faces and their courage. And then in a decision that was never actually articulated but seemed to have evolved as naturally as the parabola of a perfect three-pointer, the Hurricanes waited for captain Jen Pariseau to lead the way, which she did, and one by one the rest of the women followed, with captain Jamila Wideman the last of the Hurricanes to step off the bus into the swirling sea of well-wishers and winter coats.

Overhead the sky was as low-hanging and as opaque as it had been earlier in the evening, but it didn't need stars to make it shine.

 ## Author's Afterwords . . .

The basketball team idea came from my own backyard. One of the young ladies in the piece baby-sat for my kids. She would play basketball with my son and my daughter, and they loved her. When she talking about this team she was on, I realized the culture had changed and young women had a different idea of who they are and who they could be. I'm sure they all longed to be pretty and popular, but they put it aside for something more important. I was quite entranced.

We started going to see their games as a family at the beginning of the next season. I talked to my editor at the *Times Magazine* and he said he'd love to have a story on the team. I started out doing separate, private interviews with the young women about their lives. They loved that. It made them feel so grown up. They would gush things out about their lives, and I would make it clear that this was for an article—don't say anything you can't live with 20 years from now. I wanted them to feel comfortable with what they were saying. After all, they were children.

I really started the reporting in mid-season. I did a couple of sit-downs with the whole team, but I found that they would be showing off for each other or they'd have a private joke going. It was less productive than private interviews. But I also went to a lot of practices, and I rode with them to games on the bus. And on the bus, I never talked to them at all. I felt that by them seeing me on the bus as part of the landscape, I would become less alien.

Even before I started to write, I knew I wanted to capture a strong sense of place. I was writing about a team from a town I happen to be from and it is a place I care about. I've known it intimately since childhood. I also knew that I would be playing with the fact that these kids were taking part in a season, that it was also a season in their lives and that they live in a place with four seasons. I wanted to evoke the sense of time going by, a sense of life's cycles. Another theme in the story obviously is gender and how women are treated today as opposed to years ago. I also had an editorial point of view: these girls are better off being on a team playing a sport, than not. It was unbelievable when they actually won the state championship. The gods of journalism were on my side.

The story was fun to write, and they aren't all fun. But I've been interested in kids, in honoring them as people to write about, for a long time. These girls were just so sincere and excited. Reporting on them was like picking daisies. But I obsess during writing to the point where I can lose sleep over the right word. And whether something is fair or not fair to the people I'm writing about. The very thought that I've been unfair after they've opened their lives to me is extremely troubling.

When I start writing I think I don't have anything to say. And then I sit down and find out I do. When I start writing, I think everything I write is great. Then I look at it the next morning and see how clumsy or inarticulate it really is. I just keep trying and trying and trying. Sometimes, I can just tell I got it right, and it's a great feeling. But finally, I get to the point where I figure I've done my best. With writing, you can never be perfect. If you're waiting for that, you'll never get anything done.—M. B.

Zepp's Last Stand

There was indeed one of us who hesitated and did not want to fall into line. That was Joseph Behm, a plump, homely fellow. But he did allow himself to be persuaded, otherwise he would have been ostracized. And perhaps more of us thought as he did, but no one could very well stand out, because at that time even one's parents were ready with the word "coward."
——*All Quiet on the Western Front*
——Erich Maria Remarque

All his life Edward Zepp has wanted nothing so much as to go to the next world with a clear conscience. So on September 11 the old man, carrying a borrowed briefcase filled with papers, boarded an Amtrak train in Deerfield Beach, Florida, and headed north on the Silver Meteor to our nation's capital. As the porter showed him to his roomette, Ed Zepp kept saying, "I'm 83 years old. Eighty-three."

At 9:00 a.m. the next day, Zepp was to appear at the Pentagon for a hearing before the Board for Correction of Military Records. This was, he said, "the supreme effort, the final fight" in the private battle of Private Zepp, Company D, 323rd Machine Gun Battalion, veteran of World War I, discharged on November 9, 1919—with dishonor.

Something happens to people after a certain age, and the distinctions of youth disappear. The wrinkles conquer, like an army. In his old age, Zepp is bald. He wears fragile glasses. The shoulders are rounded. His pace is stooped and slow. It is hard, in a way, to remove 60 years, and picture him tall, lanky, a rebel.

The old man, wearing a carefully chosen business suit which he hoped would be appropriately subdued for the Pentagon, sat in the chair of his roomette as the train pulled out of Deerfield Beach. With a certain palsied eagerness he foraged his briefcase. Before the train reached full speed, he arranged on his lap the relics from his days at war. There were the dog tags and draft card, even his Department of War Risk life insurance policy. There was a letter to his mother written in 1919 in France, explaining why he was in the stockade. His fingers, curled with arthritis and in pain, attacked several documents. He unfurled the pages of a copy of the original court-martial proceedings which found him in violation of the 64th Article of War: failure to obey the command of a superior officer. There was also a copy of the rule book for Fort Leavenworth, where Zepp had been sentenced to 10 years at hard labor.

When Ed Zepp was drafted in 1917, he told his draft board he had conscientious objections to fighting overseas. The draft board told him his objections did not count; at the time only Quakers and Mennonites were routinely granted C.O. (conscientious objector) status. "As a Lutheran, I didn't cut any ice," he said. Zepp was one of 20,873 men between the ages of 21 and 31 who were classified as C.O.s but inducted nonetheless. Of those, only 3,999 made formal claims once they were in camp. Zepp's claim occurred on June 10, 1918, at Fort Merritt, New Jersey, the day before his battalion was scheduled for shipment overseas. Earlier, Zepp had tried to explain his position to a commanding officer, who told him he had a "damn fool belief." On June 10, Zepp was ordered to pack his barracks bag. When he refused, a sergeant—"Sergeant Hitchcock, a real hard-boiled guy, a Regular Army man"—held a gun to his head: "Pack that bag or I'll shoot."

"Shoot," said Zepp, "you son of a bitch."

Conscientious objection has always been a difficult issue for the military, but perhaps less difficult in 1917 than in recent times. Men who refused to fight were called "slackers" and "cowards." By the time the United States entered the war, the public had been subjected to a steady onslaught of "blatant propaganda," said Dr. Raymond O'Connor, professor of American history at the University of Miami.

The government found ways to erode the spirit of isolationism felt by many Americans, and replace it with a feeling of jubilant hostility against the Germans. It was patriotic to despise the Kaiser. It was patriotic to sing: *Over There; Oh, I Hate to Get Up in the Morning* and *Long Way to Tipperary*. A new recruiting poster pointed out that "Uncle Sam Wants You." The war's most important hero was Sergeant York, a conscientious objector who was later decorated for capturing Germans. They made a movie of Sergeant Alvin York's heroics.

They made an example of Private Edward Zepp, a kid from Cleveland.

Zepp was formally released from the Army 60 years and two days ago. But Zepp has never released the Army.

At his upcoming hearing at the Pentagon, Zepp was after a subtle distinction, two words really, "honorable discharge," meaningless to anybody but himself. It would be a victory that couldn't even be shared with the most important person in his life, his wife Christine, who died in 1977.

In 1952, Zepp appeared before the same military board. At that time the Army agreed that he was a sincere C.O. His discharge was upgraded to a "general discharge with honor." He became entitled to the same benefits as any other veteran, but he has never taken any money: "I have lived without their benefits all my life." The board refused to hear his case again; only a bureaucratic snafu and the intercession of Florida Congressman Daniel Mica paved the way to the hearing scheduled for September 12.

For 41 years Zepp worked as the money raiser for the Community Chest, now called The United Way, in Cleveland. He learned how to get things done, to get things from people.

For years, he has sought his due from the Pentagon. His persistence was not only heroic, but also a touch ornery. Here is a man who refused to fight in World War I but who takes a blackjack with him to ward off potential punks every time he leaves his Margate condominium at night. He talks about how there are just wars, and maybe we should have gone all out in Vietnam, "just like we did in Hiroshima, killing the whole city" and in the next breath he talks about the problems that occur when "the Church starts waving a flag."

It is impossible to tell how much of his fight is hobby and how much the passion of a man who says he cannot die—he literally cannot leave this earth—until his honor is fully restored.

To some, his refusal to fight meant cowardice; to Zepp, it represented heroism. It is an ethical no-man's-land. War leaves no room for subtle distinctions.

For his day in court, Ed Zepp was not taking any chances. His health is failing; he is at the age of illness and eulogy. He has an understandable preoccupation with his own debilities (proximal atrial fibrillations, coronary heart disease, pernicious anemia). Many of his references, especially his war stories, are to people now gone. At $270 for a round-trip train ticket, the plane would have been cheaper, but Zepp thought flying would be too risky; it might bring on a seizure, a blackout, something worse.

On the train the old man talked obsessively about what happened during the war. He told his story over and over and over—clack clack clack, like the train on the rails. Except for this constant talk, there was nothing about him that revealed his mission. As he hesitantly walked the narrow, shaking corridors, making his way from car to car, he did not have the air of a man headed for the crucial confrontation of his life. He looked like a nicely dressed elderly man who might be taking the train out of a preference for gravity or perhaps in sentimental memory of the glory days of railroading.

"This was the war to end war," Zepp said on the way to the dining car. "The war to make the world safe for democracy. *Democracy.* They gave me a kangaroo court-martial."

All his life, Zepp has believed he was denied the very freedoms he had been recruited to defend. He has nursed his grievances like an old war injury, which, on one level, is exactly what they are. "They murdered me, you know. They tried to, in a way." His refusal to fight turned him into a fighter: "I was cursed," he said. "It made a killer out of me, almost."

He said he was seeking only one thing: "My honor. My good name. I don't see how a great nation can stigmatize as dishonorable a person who was following the dictates of his conscience. When I die, I want it said of me, 'Well done, thou good and faithful servant.' "

Ed Zepp turned to the young waiter, in his starched white mess coat, who had been patiently waiting for him to order lunch. He ordered a turkey sandwich: "I can't eat much. My doctor says I should eat lightly. I take enzyme pills to help me digest."

September 1979, Sebring, Florida. Ed Zepp's light lunch has just been placed before him. September 1917, Cleveland, Ohio: Ed Zepp's appeals to the draft board have been rejected twice.

During any long trip, there is a distortion of landscape and time; the old man's talk echoed the feeling of suspension that comes with being on the road. The closer he got to the Pentagon, the closer he got to 1917.

Before he was drafted at the age of 21, Zepp had already earned a business, degree and worked as a clerk at Johns Manville. At the time, his native Cleveland was heavily industrialized, with much social and political unrest. Socialist Eugene Debs was a frequent visitor; Zepp says the man was "fire." He remembers listening to his speeches and once joined a Debs march, clear across town, to a large hall on the west side. Debs preached workers' rights and counseled against war. So did Zepp's pastor, who was censured by the Lutheran Church for his outspoken views against the war. "War," says Ed Zepp, "was an ocean away."

Zepp's parents were Polish immigrants, Michael and Louise Czepieus. His father was a blacksmith, "not the kind who made shoes for horses, but rather he made all the ironwork pertaining to a wagon." There were five children and all of them were sent to business school and ended up, says Zepp, "in the office world."

"I was a top-notch office man all my life," he says. In any family there is talk about somebody's lost promise, failed opportunity, and in the Zepp family, there was talk, principally among his sisters, about how, with his meticulous mind, he would have been a great lawyer, but for the war, but for what happened over there.

The waiter removed the empty plates from Zepp's table, and the next group of hungry passengers was seated.

Three p.m., Waldo, Florida, in the club car. Ed Zepp is nursing a soda, and on the table in front of him, like a deck of marked cards, are the original court-martial proceedings.

Eighty miles an hour.

The train was moving almost as fast as Edward Zepp is old, and he seemed impressed by that. "It is," he said, "a wonderful way to see the countryside." The world passed by in a blur.

Despite his ailments, there is something energetic and alert about Zepp; for two months before the hearing, he swam every day for half an hour to build stamina. Sipping his soda, he wondered whether he had chosen the correct clothes. His suit was brown and orange. He had a color-coordinated, clip-on tie and a beige shirt. "I have another suit that my wife, Christine, picked out for me, but it has all the colors of the rainbow, and I didn't want to show up at the Pentagon looking like a sport in front of all those monkeys. Oops. I'd better be careful. They probably wouldn't like it if I called them monkeys, would they?"

This trip was partly in memory of Christine, Zepp's third wife, whom he married in 1962, shortly before he retired to Florida. His first marriage was brief; during the second marriage he had two children, a son who died in his early 30s ("He served in Korea and he was a teacher.") and a daughter, now 46 years old, a psychiatric social worker who lives near Boston.

"Christine would want me to do this. She was a fighter, she was a real person. She was the only one I cared about. And what happened? She died. All the guys in my condominium thought I would be the first to go, but she passed away on May 1, 1977, two days before my 81st birthday. Do you know what she said to me before she died? 'I want to be buried with my wedding ring on.' I meet other women at the square dances at the senior center. One of them said, 'Ed, let's go to the Bahamas for a week. Get your mind off this. It's too much pressure.' But I couldn't go away. Christine and I are married, even in death."

When Ed Zepp speaks of his third wife, his face sometimes gets an odd look; there is a dream-like minute or so. The voice catches, the blue eyes become rheumy, his words come out in a higher pitch. Just as it seems as if he will break down and sob, composure returns. The same thing often happens when he speaks of what happened during the war.

"Anyone who reads this court-martial," said Zepp, "will acquaint himself with all the vital points of my case: how the draft board refused to listen; how the Army loused it up in Camp Sherman when they failed to inform me of General Order Number 28; how, at Fort Merritt, Sergeant Hitchcock held the gun to my head and forced me to pack, and then they

Shanghaied me out of the country on the SS *Carmania,* and in France
they gave me a kangaroo court-martial."

General Order Number 28, issued by the War Department on March
23, 1918, was an effort by the government in mid-war to expand the
definition of those who qualified for C.O. status. Men who had already
been drafted, but had sought C.O. status were supposed to be informed
by a "tactful and considerate" officer of their right to choose noncombatant service.

"General Order Number 28 was never read or posted during the time
I was at boot camp at Camp Sherman in Chillicothe, Ohio," Zepp
maintains. "This was how it was done—gospel truth: 250 of us were lined
up in retreat. Lieutenant Paul Herbert went through the ranks, asking
each man, 'Any objections to fighting the Germans?' Well, I thought they
were looking for pro-German sympathizers. I wasn't a pro-German
sympathizer. My parents were Polish. I did not speak up.

"Then at Fort Merritt, Sergeant Hitchcock, he was a hard-boiled
sergeant, put the gun on me. He never told the court-martial about that.
He approached me in a belligerent manner; there was no kindly and
courteous officer informing me of my rights as specified in General
Order Number 28.

"They shipped me overseas against my will, and for two months in
France I still didn't know what action would be taken against me for
defying Sergeant Hitchcock and Captain Faxon. They kept me busy with
regular military work. I helped erect a machine-gun range, I had rifle
practice, I learned how to break a person's arm in close combat.

"During that time Lieutenant Herbert propositioned me with a nice
soft easy job. He came up to me and he said, 'Zepp, how about calling
the whole thing off. I'll get you a nice soft easy job in the quarter-
master.'" Zepp repeated Herbert's words in the buttery tone of voice he
always uses when he repeats Herbert's words. "He tried to make a deal.
But I had no confidence. I smelled a rat. And to prove to you beyond a
shadow of a doubt it was not a sincere offer, find one word in the
court-martial proceedings that he offered me a job. He was trying to
make a deal. It was a trap.

"And then they shanghaied me out of the country and gave me a
kangaroo court-martial. I wasn't even allowed to face my accusers."
During Zepp's court-martial many of the basic facts which are part of
his litany are mentioned. The sergeant who held a gun to his head

testified, but no mention was made of that action. Captain C. W. Faxon said he believed Zepp had "sincere religious objections." Sergeant Steve Kozman admitted to giving the defendant "a few kicks in the behind" on his way to the SS *Carmania.*

In his testimony, Zepp told about how, the same evening he refused to pack his barracks bag, "Lieutenant Paul Herbert came up to me and spoke in a general way about my views and called them pro-German. He also asked me if I had a mother and I said, 'Yes,' and he asked me if I had a sister and I said, 'Yes,' and he said, 'Would you disgrace them by having your picture in the paper?' "

Zepp argued that in light of General Order Number 28 the Army had no right to ship him overseas without first offering noncombatant service. The heart of Zepp's case, as he spoke it before that tribunal long ago, showed his instinct for fine, if quixotic distinctions: "I did not willfully disobey two lawful orders, but I was compelled to willfully disobey two alleged lawful orders."

Seven p.m., Savannah, Georgia. The train had crossed state lines, and Zepp had just entered the dining car for an evening meal of fish and vegetables. His conversation once again crossed the borders of geography and time.

Even at dinner, it was impossible for him to abandon his topic.

"Let me tell you about what happened after the court-martial. They put me in a dungeon; there were rats running over me, the floor was wet, it was just a place to throw potatoes, except they'd all rot. It was later condemned as unfit for human habitation by the psychiatrists who interviewed me. That was a perfect opportunity to act crazy and get out of the whole thing. But I stuck by my conscience. I was not a coward. It's easier to take a chance with a bullet than stand up on your own two feet and defy."

He talked about how the Army discovered he had "office skills" and he spent much of his time as a clerk—"sergeant's work, or at least corporal's."

He said he was transferred to Army bases all over France during the year 1919; the best time was under Captain John Evans: "I had my own desk, and Captain Evans put a box of chocolates on it, which he shouldn't have because it turned me into a 250-pounder. I had the liberty of the city, and Captain Evans gave me an unsolicited recommendation." Zepp quoted it by heart: "Private Zepp has worked for me since January 3, 1919. During this time he has been my personal clerk, and anyone desiring a stenographer will find him trustworthy and with no mean ability."

In August of 1919, as part of his clerical duties, Zepp was "making out service records for boys to return home to the United States, and finally the time came for me to make one out for myself." In September he arrived in Fort Leavenworth where once again he served as a clerk: "They made me secretary to the chaplain, and I taught the boys how to operate a typewriter.

"Finally on November 9, 1919, they released me. I still don't know why I didn't serve the complete sentence. I never asked for their mercy. I think it must have been my mother, she must have gone to our pastor, and he intervened." Zepp paused, and his look became distant. There was that catch in his voice; he cried without tears.

Dinner was over.

Ten p.m., Florence, South Carolina. After nursing one beer in the club car, Zepp decided it was time to get some sleep. As he prepared to leave for his roomette, he said, "They tried to make Martin Luther recant, but he wouldn't. Remember: 'If they put you to shame or call you faithless, it is better that God call you faithful and honorable than that the world call you faithful and honorable.' Those are Luther's own words. 1526."

It was hard to sleep on the train; it rocked at high speeds and it made a number of jerking stops and churning starts in the middle of the night in small towns in North Carolina.

Ed Zepp asked the porter to wake him an hour before the 6:00 a.m. arrival in Washington, but his sleep was light and he awoke on his own at 4:00. He shaved, dressed, and then sat in the roomette, briefcase beside him. The train pulled in on time, before sunrise.

Wandering the almost-empty station, Zepp had a tall dignity, eye-glasses adding to his air of alertness. He sat by himself on a bench, waiting for his lawyer who was due at 7:00. Zepp's lawyer was a young fellow who had read about his client in *Liberty Magazine*. Thirty-four years old, John St. Landau works at the Center for Conscientious Objection in Philadelphia. Landau called the old man in Florida and volunteered his services. They made plans to meet at Union Station, and

Zepp told the lawyer, "Don't worry. You'll recognize me. I'll be the decrepit old man creeping down the platform."

Landau, himself a C.O. during the Vietnam War, arrived at the appointed hour. The two men found an empty coffee shop where they huddled at a table for about an hour. Zepp told his lawyer he had not brought his blackjack to Washington, and the lawyer said, smiling, "I take it you are no longer a C.O."

At 8:30 they left to take Metro, Washington's eerily modern subway system with computerized "farecards," to the Pentagon. Zepp was easily the oldest person on the commuter-filled subway. He did not try to speak above the roar. His was a vigil of silence. When the doors sliced open at the "Pentagon" stop, the hour of judgment was upon him.

"The gates of hell," he said, "shall not prevail."

It would be hard to surmise, given the enthusiasm of his recital, that Zepp was in Washington on not much more than a wing and a prayer. In April, the Pentagon had mistakenly promised him a hearing; it was a bureaucratic bungle. On May 9, he was told there had been an error; there was no new evidence in his case; therefore there should be no new hearing. On May 31, Rep. Mica wrote to the review board requesting a new hearing on the strength of his office. It was granted for September 12, but Zepp had been forewarned in a letter from the Pentagon that just because he was getting his hearing, he should not conclude from this concession that "the department" admits "any error or injustice now . . . in your records."

Just before Zepp was ushered into the small hearing room at 11:00, he gave himself a pep talk: "I am going to be real nice. Getting even doesn't do anything, punching someone around. I want to do things the Christian way. And I'll use the oil can. When I was at the Community Chest, I called all the women 'darlings' and I would polka with them at the parties. I used the oil can profusely."

Zepp departed for the hearing room.

The fate of the World War I veteran, defended by a Vietnam era lawyer, was to be decided by a panel of five—four veterans of World War II, one veteran of the Korean War. The chairman was Charles Woodside, who also served on the panel that heard the appeal of the widow of Private Eddie Slovik, the first deserter since the Civil War to be executed. Less than a week before Zepp's hearing, newspapers carried a story about how Slovik's widow, denied a pension by the Army, had finally died, penniless, in a nursing home.

Landau stated Zepp's case, saying that the defendant accepted the findings of the 1952 hearing, the findings which concluded Zepp had in fact been sincere: "The reason we're here is that we believe the general discharge ought to be upgraded to an honorable discharge. . . . What we see as the critical issue is the quality of [Mr. Zepp's] service."

The first witness was Martin Sovik, a member of the staff of the Office for Governmental Affairs of the Lutheran Church Council. Like Landau, Sovik had also been a C.O. during Vietnam. He confirmed that in 1969 the Lutheran Church in America supported individual members of the church, following their consciences, to oppose participation in war. One member of the panel asked Sovik how you can determine whether a person is in fact a C.O.

"That decision is made within a person's mind—obviously you can't know whether a person is a C.O. anymore than whether he is a Yankees' fan or an Orioles' fan except by his own affirmation."

Next, the old man took his turn. The panel urged him to remain seated during the testimony. The old man marshalled the highlights of his military experience: *Shanghaied, nice soft easy job, tactful and courteous officer, hard-boiled sergeant, gun at my head, face my accusers, unfit for human habitation, unsolicited recommendation.* The words tumbled out, a litany.

Every now and then Zepp's composure cracked, stalling the proceedings. "I'm sure it's hard to recall," said Woodside.

"It's not that," said the defendant. "I'm just living it. This was indelibly impressed, it is vivid on my mind, like something that happened yesterday."

At 1:00, a luncheon recess was called. Woodside promised that he would continue to listen with sympathy when the hearing resumed.

"Govern yourself by the facts," said Zepp. "Then we'll both be happy."

As they were leaving the hearing room, Zepp turned to Landau and Sovik and apologized for breaking down. "You're doing all right, you're doing just fine," said Sovik.

"I can't help it. Every now and then my voice breaks," said Zepp. "It touches me."

Sovik, putting his hand on the old man's arm, said: "It touches us all."

The afternoon was more of the same: *Light. Herbert was not making me a sincere offer, German sympathizer, disgrace your sisters, sincere religious objections.*

Finally, the executive secretary of the Corrections Board, Ray Williams, the man most familiar with Zepp's case, asked the defendant: "Mr. Zepp, since you received your general discharge under honorable conditions back in 1952 as a result of a recommendation of this board, have you ever applied to the V.A. for any benefits?"

Zepp: "No. I haven't."

Williams: "You understand you are entitled to all the benefits of an honorably discharged soldier."

Zepp: "That's right. The one thing that bothers me is my conscience, my allegiance to the Almighty. I have to see this thing through. . . . I don't think that a person who follows the dictates of his conscience and is a true Christian should be stigmatized as a dishonorable person. And I think he shouldn't even get a second-rate discharge."

Williams: "In all good conscience you can say that your discharge is under honorable conditions."

Zepp: "I personally feel it would behoove the United States of America, who believes in freedom of conscience, religion or the Bill of Rights, that a person who follows, truthfully follows, the dictates of his conscience, and you are obligated to follow that because you've got a relationship with God, and I don't think that we should stigmatize anybody like that as being a dishonorable person.

"And the reason I'm here at my advanced age—83, arthritis and all that—my inner self, my conscience, says, 'Now, here. You go to the board and make one last effort.' "

Zepp paused. He hunched forward and made ready to sling one final arrow: "In view of the fact, Mr. Williams, that there's not much difference, then why not make it honorable? There isn't much difference. Let's make it honorable and we'll all be happy."

Zepp's lawyer closed with this plea:

"The military has come a long way since 1918 in their dealing with these individuals who have religious scruples about continued military service. . . . I would contend that it's in part because of individuals like

Mr. Zepp who were willing to put their principles on the line many years ago . . . that it took individuals like that to finally work out a good system of dealing with conscientious objection. And that's what the military has now after many, many years. That, in its own right, is a very important service to the military."

The panel closed the proceedings. A decision was promised sometime within the next month.

Back at Union Station, waiting for the return trip: gone now the derelict emptiness of the early morning hours. In the evening the station was smart with purpose: well-dressed men and women, toting briefcases and newspapers, in long lines waiting for trains. The old man sat on a chair and reviewed the day. He smiled and his eyes were bright.

"I feel very confident. I sensed victory. I put all my cards on the table and I called a spade a spade. Did you see how I went up afterwards and I shook all their hands, just like they were my friends. I even shook the hands of Williams, my enemy, and I leaned over and I said to him, 'I love you, darling.' I acted as if I expected victory and I did not accept defeat. I used the oil can profusely."

He paused. Zepp looked up, seeming to study the ceiling. He cupped his chin with his left hand. The old man was silent. A college girl across from him watched him in his reverie, and she smiled a young smile. Finally, the old man spoke. He seemed shaken. His voice was soft, filled with fear, the earlier confidence gone. The thought had come, like a traitor, jabbing him in the heart:

"What next?

"I'll be lonesome without this. Here's my problem. Now that I don't have anything to battle for, what will I do? There's nothing I know of on the horizon to compete with that."

He paused. His face brightened. "Well, I can go swimming. And I can keep square dancing. Something happens to me when I square dance, it's the—what do they call it?—the adrenalin. I am a top form dancer. Maybe I can go back to being the treasurer of the Broward Community Senior Center. I did that before my wife became sick, but I quit to take care of her. I always was a fine office man. Maybe I'll become active in the Hope Lutheran Church. In other words, keep moving. Keep moving. That's the secret.

"All I know is that I could not face my departure from this earth if I had failed to put up this fight."

At 7:20, there came the boom of an announcement over the loud-speaker; the voice was anonymous and businesslike: "The Silver Meteor, bound for Miami, Florida, scheduled to depart at 7:40 is ready for boarding. All passengers may now board the Silver Meteor with stops in Alexandria . . . Richmond . . . Petersburg . . . Fayetteville . . . Florence . . . Charleston . . . Savannah . . . Jacksonville . . . Waldo . . . Ocala . . . Wildwood . . . Winter Haven . . . Sebring . . . West Palm Beach . . . Deerfield Beach . . . Fort Lauderdale . . . Hollywood . . . Miami."

Edward Zepp boarded the train, located his roomette and departed for home. Within minutes of leaving the station, exhausted by the day's excitement, he fell asleep.

On Tuesday, October 2, 1979, the Pentagon issued the following statement: "Having considered the additional findings, conclusions and recommendation of the Army Board for Correction of Military Records and under the provisions of 10 U.S.C. 1552, the action of the Secretary of the Army on 4 December 1952 is hereby amended insofar as the character of discharge is concerned, and it is directed: (1) That all Department of the Army records of Edward Zepp be corrected to show that he was separated from the Army of the United States on a Certificate of Honorable Discharge on November 1919. (2) That the Department of the Army issue to Edward Zepp a Certificate of Honorable Discharge from the Army of the United States dated 9 November 1919 in lieu of the General Discharge Certificate of the same date now held by him."

"In other words," said Edward Zepp. "I was right all along."

A week later, a copy of the Pentagon's decision arrived at Zepp's Margate condominium. He discovered the decision was not unanimous. One member, James Hise, had voted against him.

"I'm so mad I could kick the hell out of him. A guy like that shouldn't be sitting on the Board. I am going to write to the Pentagon and tell them he should be thrown off the panel. It would be better to have just a head up there loaded with concrete or sawdust than this guy Hise, who doesn't know the first thing about justice. If he can't judge better than that, he should be kicked off. He's a menace to justice in this world.

"I'd like to go up there and bust his head wide open."

Author's Afterwords . . .

Mr. Zepp had haunted Florida newsrooms up and down the coast for 10 or 15 years. He would come into a newsroom, and the youngest reporter would be assigned to hold his hand and be polite. Someone wrote my editor at *Tropic Magazine* about him and suggested doing a story. He bought the idea and asked me if I'd be interested in doing it. I was. I really didn't know much about World War I, and I thought this would be a good way to find out about it.

Mr. Zepp turned out to be a nettlesome person. I talked to him once and after that he was in touch with me incessantly. In every family there's someone who has a story to tell, and they keep telling it until everybody stops listening. Maybe there's some merit to the story, maybe not. That was Mr. Zepp.

The question people always have about this piece is, "How did you get him to tell his story?" There was no problem there. I had to listen to him tell it a million times. Yet early on, there was a puzzling element. Although he talked about pacifism, he was a belligerent and hostile person. So he instantly became a character in the way that a person in a novel is a character—somebody filled with conviction and absolute contradiction.

I took the train with him to Washington, D.C., and for 24 hours he went over and over his story. By the time we got to Washington, I felt fatigue mingled with despair. Maybe I had misjudged him, maybe there was no story, maybe he was simply pathetic. But still there was a stubborn valor to his quest. Even if they put him in Leavenworth simply because he was such a pain in the butt, there was something about the fact that he wouldn't give up that you had to admire. He was extremely elderly, yet he had this strength in that he bulldozed forward in the world.

The biggest lesson I learned on this story was that any piece of writing is really a journey from the writer's ignorance to the writer's enlightenment. What really fueled this piece was that this man was taking a journey into the past along with a journey from Florida to Washington. His story is told as present day journey, but it is totally driven by Mr. Zepp's past journey.

Several weeks of reporting went into the piece before I wrote. I located people who had known him, family members and friends. But I didn't clutter the piece with their quotes. I used them more for corroboration. It took me another couple weeks to write it. After three or four days, when I realized I had two intersecting journeys, the whole piece suddenly had its structure.

The piece baffled me at first because there's a lot of moral ambiguity in Mr. Zepp's life. He wasn't a pleasant, amiable person, which is what you might expect from a pacifist. Even after winning, he still objected to the decision. I thought, "Oh, my God!" And then it hit me, as they say, up side of the head: I can put this in the piece. It will explain him better than anything I could say. And so I wrote it in as the last paragraph, and that made the piece. Without it, the irony and ambiguity would have been missing. It was a happy ending that wasn't happy.—M. B.

Jeanne Marie Laskas

Jeanne Marie Laskas has written essays and articles for numerous publications including *GQ, Life, Allure, Glamour, Redbook* and the *Washington Post Magazine*. She is a columnist for *This Old House Magazine* and *Discovery Online*. She is the author of *The Balloon Lady and Other People I Know* (1996) and has taught writing at the University of Pittsburgh. She lives in Pittsburgh, Pennsylvania.

Each Other's Mirror

Selfness is an essential fact of life. The thought of nonselfness, precise sameness, is terrifying.

—Lewis Thomas

Isobel and Elizabeth Ingalls were born in the woods, 59 years ago, in a little Maryland bungalow situated on a tract of land named "Truth and Trust" by some forgotten settler. That night there was a blizzard, and their father walked six snowy and frantic miles to retrieve a doctor. They were a surprise: twins! Their father bundled them up in blankets, put them in a breadbasket and, fearing frostbite, set them like uncooked loaves behind the hot kitchen stove.

"The doctor came back the next day, and he said, 'Good Lord! Are they still breathing?' " says Betty. She enjoys telling this story told to her by her parents. So does Isobel. Given license to ramble, the two often get lost in happy chatter about their early years of life as the twin babies of Truth and Trust. Sometimes they wonder why their parents didn't just go ahead and name them Truth and Trust. That would have been so perfect. And they wonder just exactly where in southern Maryland that little tract of land called Truth and Trust actually is. They like to go hunt for it. They like to imagine it; paint pictures of it. They would certainly like to recapture it.

Home nowadays is Potomac, Maryland, where Isobel and Betty live with their respective husbands, Martel and Mackall Ricketts—who also happen to be identical twins. The two identical couples live next door to one another, in identical houses, connected porch-to-porch by a well-trod path. Inside, much of their furniture is identical, arranged in identical positions. Downstairs in their basements they have identical antique doll collections, and upstairs they have identical kitchens, right down to the General Electric dishwashers, the Black & Decker Space Maker toaster ovens and the no-wax linoleum floors made to look like brick to hide dirt.

They are wives, mothers, suburban homemakers in charge of split-levels. They are giddy about most of life, exuberant, generous, a little bumbling, a little naughty. They are best friends to a degree some people can scarcely fathom, indeed might prefer to overlook. When considering twins, the tendency is to gawk. When considering precise sameness, the tendency is to feel terrified. Much has been written about the bond that exists between twins, particularly identical twins. Singletons—people who are not twins—tend to search for clues to support a common hypothesis: that the twin bond can be so deep, so thickly rooted, that the two twins never become fully distinct and independent individuals.

Isobel: "Oh, we hate when people say that."

Betty: "Oh, we really hate that."

Usually Isobel and Betty use "we" to express likes, dislikes and opinions. Often they interrupt one another, politely and with ease, to finish the other's point, which turns out to be not exactly the point the first was trying to make, so she cuts back in, and then the other comes in, until finally both are lost in a tumble of questions: "Where were we? Now what was I going to say? It was good. It was interesting. Oh, my mind is blank again."

The paintings. That was it. They were talking about the paintings they did. "Would you like to see them?" asks Betty. The paintings are renditions of Truth and Trust. They made them together, with the help of their mother's memory. The pictures show an idyllic little house bordered by neat rows of flowers. They are identical pictures, still on easels, in Isobel's kitchen.

Betty: "I like your roof much better, Isobel."

Isobel: "Your tree is magnificent, Betty."

Betty: "I like your sky."

Isobel: "I like your blue windows."

Betty: "We always like each other's work better."

In unison: "Always."

Remarking on the similarity of their twin paintings, they begin considering the similarity of their twin persons, their twin lives, their twin husbands. Marty, who is married to Isobel, and Mackall, who is married to Betty, are partners in their own accounting firm—twin husbands with twin jobs—and the couples have three children apiece, all of them now grown.

Betty: "But see, that's it."

Isobel: "None of our life has been traumatic."

Betty: "Our lives—it's plural."

Isobel: "Oh, thank you, Betty. Really, it's all been very simple and not important. Hasn't it, Betty?"

Betty: "Um, I am trying to think. There have been some deaths and things."

Isobel: "Just like anybody else. We are just like anybody else."

In unison: "Except there's two."

Isobel: "And why shouldn't we be alike? I keep thinking, wouldn't it be more surprising if we were identical twins and we were totally unalike? Now that would be really something. See, it's just like you made a batch of cookies, and this cookie and this cookie are alike because they're from the same mixture."

And what about this issue of becoming distinct and independent individuals?

Betty: "We are!"

Isobel: "I think we are an individual person!"

In unison: "We are!"

How are they different? Isobel and Betty wear identical clothes, hairdos, eyeglasses, wristwatches. They are pretty women with deep chocolate eyes, black cherry hair and creamy complexions; distinguishing between the two is not easy, at first. After a while, though, you might notice that

Isobel has a slightly narrower face, a slightly tilted smile, and that Betty often holds her hands on her hips, that Isobel often fluffs up her puffed sleeves, and then, later, you might graduate to the finer details: Isobel has a glimmer of irony in her eyes, a way of twisting the world into a wholly humorous place. Betty is innocent, soft. Isobel is Lucy Ricardo. Betty is Ethel Mertz. They bounce off one another, ping-pong, ping-pong, laughing at themselves and entertaining anyone who cares to watch.

Always they dress alike, in crisp, careful costumes. One evening recently they were done up in pretty yellow dresses, fixed at the neck with a brooch shaped like a turtle. Before Isobel put her lipstick on, she looked at Betty's lips, to see what the night's color would be. Then it was time. They got up. They stood before a crowd of about 50 people at Phineas restaurant in Rockville, Maryland. Everyone else was eating cheese-cake, drinking Sanka; dinner was over, and Isobel and Betty had been invited to speak at this annual gathering of the Montgomery County Parents of Multiples organization. They told the story of their life.

Betty: "Our lives."

Isobel: "Oh. Thank you, Betty."

Not surprisingly, they began their talk with the story of Truth and Trust, which continues in rich romantic detail to scenes of being educated in a one-room schoolhouse, playing ball, "alley-oop" over the roof. At home, their father delighted in their similarities, never quite able to tell them apart. He would call them both Betty for a month, then Isobel for a month, then switch back to Betty again. They had an older brother, Huntley, who was fascinated by their accounts of similar dreams and their seemingly telepathic communications. Their mother took pleasure in making their twin clothes, and Betty always hated the ones that were pieced together from remnants of the first. Isobel didn't care. But Isobel would always put up a fuss, just for the sake of fussing, before surrendering to Betty's insistence on owning the finer garment. Once, Betty grabbed the better Easter bonnet just an instant before Isobel was ready to surrender.

Isobel: "And so I snatched the blasted bonnet and threw it on the floor and stomped it to pieces."

She had principles. She had a temper.

Betty was better in school. Isobel didn't care about studying. "I was too busy." In their yearbooks, underneath Betty's name, it says: "charm, long lustrous locks, smart, nice, eyelashes." Underneath Isobel's: "excitable, dramatic, fiery, peppy."

At the restaurant, before the crowd, the twin speakers finally got to the subject of marriage.

Betty: "Our husbands were raised in Bethesda. They were the only ones in their family, and, um, what else about them, anything important?"

Isobel: "No. When we were 19, Betty and I gave each other dancing lessons, and Marty and Mackall were taking dancing lessons at the same dancing school. And their instructor wanted us to meet so we could do an exhibition dance. We never did do the exhibition dance and we were not awfully interested in dating them because we had heard so many times someone say, 'You should marry twins!' We kind of got sick of hearing it."

Betty: "And besides that, a few months earlier, we had had a luncheon date with a set of twins, and it was okay, but Isobel sort of dumped all of her lunch on her lap."

Isobel: "See, well, I didn't know him anyhow . . . but anyway, we did meet our husbands at the dancing school, and I danced with my husband first, and she danced with her husband first, and we never changed. That's the way it was."

Betty: "And we did not want to give them a date, and I don't know how long they kept calling, and they asked did we like football, and we hated it, and did we like basketball, and we hated it, and did we like boxing, and we hated that, too."

Isobel: "We decided to give them one date and get it over with. It'll be 37 years, June the 15th, and we still haven't gotten it over with. But, wait a minute now, back to the—we dated for three and a half years while our husbands finished their college. We planned our double wedding. They're very, very reserved and they don't care for this sort of thing too much, but they went along with it . . . and . . . what next?"

Betty: "And our husbands were in the service."

Isobel: "Betty and I were separated for the first time while our husbands were on the tour of duty, and guess what? We survived without each other."

The decision to buy neighboring houses was one Isobel and Betty had to wheedle Mackall and Marty into. The wives thought: Why not?

They could baby-sit for one another. Grocery shop. Why not live next door to your best friend? The husbands thought: This is getting to be a bit much.

Betty: "And so my husband decreed it was okay to be in the same community, same development, but not next door. Then Isobel and I went out and picked out the lots. And we picked out lots with just one neighbor in the middle and the two of us on each side. Well, my husband said we couldn't do that because we'd be dragging lawn mowers back and forth, so then he consented to living next door to each other."

Decorating the homes, buying similar furniture, came quite naturally. When one shopped, she just bought two. It was an efficient arrangement. Isobel and Betty claim to have such similar tastes that it never much matters which one does the actual shopping. Eventually, the two houses became nearly identical inside, as well as out.

Isobel: "But the point is, we moved next door to each other because we planned it, not because we could not get along without each other. Very important point. Because that's a pet peeve. I'm up to pet peeves, aren't you, Betty?"

Betty: "Yeah."

Isobel: "Pet peeves. One of the pet peeves we have is this thing of saying which twin is the smartest."

Betty: "Or the prettiest."

Isobel: "And also, which one is the leader."

Betty: "And who's the oldest."

Isobel: "And we don't know because we're mixed up."

Betty: "And what difference does it make?"

Isobel: "Which one is the smartest—that's a real bad one. It's a stereotype that one twin is smarter than the other."

Betty: "And it's usually not true."

Isobel: "It's usually me that's not the smartest."

Betty: "And there are a few more pet peeves."

Isobel: "Oh, uh, what were we going to say? Uh, a lot of pet peeves that we thought of. There's another one, I forgot it. It'll come in a minute—we draw a couple blanks. Um, we are open for questions."

Betty: "Except one thing, some pluses."

Isobel: "Oh."

Betty: "There are a lot of pluses. Like when we had our kitchens redone last fall, or whenever it was, the people who installed it, you know, sometimes you can work a deal that way."

Isobel: "You can."

Betty: "Because they installed five appliances in her house, and five in mine, and they only had to make one trip, and they loved it. They said they wished they could have some more days like that."

Isobel: "You need to take advantage of being twins, you see, and we have. And we thought it over carefully. Just like the dressing thing. You know, we dress alike."

They didn't always. For 11 years, early during their marriages, they tried not to.

Isobel: "Everyone told us we were grown and married now so you don't dress alike. And so we conferred very carefully and tried not to."

Betty: "It was awful."

Isobel: "We hated it."

Betty: "And we really don't care."

Isobel: "We don't care if people think it's unusual or odd that we dress alike. That's really not our problem. That's everybody else's problem."

In unison: "Yeah."

The decision was to celebrate their similarity, not hide it. Their decision was to assert their individuality by becoming the same.

Weekends, during the summer, all the twins go to the summer house. Marty and Mackall drive down together, and Isobel and Betty arrive later on. Marty and Mackall do not dress alike, do not have matching haircuts, cars, desks or wristwatches. They are not what you would call enthusiastic about the idea of being identical twins. They prefer to remain a shadow in the background of any picture depicting them. They prefer not to be looked on as freaks. Isobel wonders if it has anything to do with their being accountants.

Isobel: "And you know they always drive the speed limit, too."

Mornings at the summer house, everybody goes out on bikes. Marty and Mackall take off at about 6:30, riding 10-speeds that do not match, while Isobel and Betty go out later on, riding identical blue Raleighs. They wear matching blue culottes, matching yellow tops, support hose, sneakers, visors and, attached to their handlebars, matching cans of mace, just in case of dogs. Gum Spring is the name of their summer place, and the two couples share it. It is in St. Mary's County, a stone's throw away from two waterfront lots where the couples plan to build neighboring retirement homes.

For Marty and Mackall, Gum Spring has become a place to feel like Boy Scouts, pals, fishermen, a place to tinker with tools in the garage and fetch crab traps from the shed. They bought a boat and named it Isobeth. Betty and Isobel don't like that sort of stuff. They bring sewing. They wish the men would install more air conditioners. Sure, they like the bay, but they like to look at it from the house. And sure, they like crab—the kind you get out of the freezer. Why go to all the trouble of catching it? The men gave up.

Not surprisingly, the idea to buy matching retirement lots was Isobel and Betty's. They had a vision: They could end their lives just as they began them, on a tract of land they could call Truth and Trust. They could return, at least metaphorically, to their warm place of origin. They have planned this: When the retirement houses are built, Betty's will be named Truth, Isobel's will be Trust. Sometimes they like to go looking for the original Truth and Trust. Not coincidentally, it is located just a few miles from Gum Spring, and, on a hot and muggy Sunday afternoon, Betty and Isobel are out searching. They are in Betty's station wagon, driving down a wooded road, with their necks craned.

Betty: "Is that it?"

Isobel: "Back in there. I think there is a possible chance it could be back in there."

Once, they found Truth and Trust, when their brother Huntley joined them on the search. Huntley found the spring from which the family once drank, and the stone that once formed their back doorstep. All agreed to one day retrieve that stone. It was nestled deep in the woods, and Betty and Isobel believe they have just now stumbled upon the path leading back to it.

Betty: "There's no way we could walk all the way back there. It's very far."

Isobel: "Oh, Betty, look at the pine trees. And the lovely holly. And the whippoorwill was down here, remember?"

Betty: "There is absolutely no way we could get back there. And I don't know how we could get that stone. It's huge. Oh, Lord, you couldn't carry it."

Isobel: "Remember? It sounded just like that, 'whip or will.' And now what does that sign say? 'No Trespassing?' I do suppose it does."

They hop out of the car. They climb over the wire barrier that swings across the path. They begin walking, exploring, talking, and their sneakers get soggy in the mud. It starts raining, a drizzle at first, then harder, but neither bothers to mention it, so engrossed are they in their walking and talking. They muse on the past, anticipate the future. What will happen when it's over? What will happen when one of them dies?

Betty: "I'll tell you what—I'd just as soon as we both die at the same time. I don't think it's going to be so good."

Isobel: "Probably we'll draw on the past a lot."

Betty: "But why shouldn't we enjoy each other while we have each other?"

Isobel: "That's the point."

Isobel sees a bush, tells Betty to look at it. They don't know what kind of plant it is, exactly, but they remember they used to eat it. Isobel takes some leaves, pops them in her mouth. Betty follows suit. They chew.

Betty: "It's a little bitter."

Isobel: "But that's the same taste."

In unison: "Exactly."

Just then, the rain comes down on them with a great mean crack.

Isobel: "This is getting interesting, Betty."

Betty: "Really interesting."

They surrender, turn around. Truth and Trust is simply too far away. They can't make it back there, can't carry the stone of their origin to the home of their future. Some things are just impossible. And why bother trying?

Isobel: "I do not know. I do not know why we are so interested in this Truth and Trust story. Mother and Daddy talked about it constantly, all growing up we heard Truth and Trust."

And whip or wills, and one another's beating hearts.

Isobel: "Oh, Betty, we look wretched."
Betty looks at Isobel.
Betty: "Oh, Isobel, we really do."

▮ Author's Afterword . . .

I didn't go into this story hoping to make the observation that these
were two people who understood each other as well as they understood
themselves. Or that this was something we all yearn for. That discovery
was borne of spending time with these women.

I found Isobel and Betty when I was reading local papers that
highlight people in the community. I saw this story about these women
and their fantastic doll collections. As I read the story, I realized they
were twins, and that they had twin doll collections. Then I learned they
lived next door to each other in identical houses and were married to
identical twins. I thought, "Boy, there might be more to this." I figured
I'd go spend some time with them. I worried that perhaps I wouldn't be
able to stand them—that this was going to be too weird.

I got there, and I hadn't done research on twins. I just wanted to
meet the women. And they were wonderful, just the most delightful
people. They were aware of how bizarre their situation was and yet asked,
"Wouldn't it be even more strange if we *weren't* alike? We were born at
the same time and spent all of our lives together." Suddenly, they were
educating me about what kind of world I lived in as a "singleton." I got
to see what it would be like to have someone who pretty much agreed
with everything I thought, who understood and accepted me just as I
was because they were just like me. A perfect mirror and a perfect friend.
And I thought, "God, that would be so great."

I visited them twice, probably four days each time. I went to a doll
show with them, for a bike ride Sunday morning. We sat around the
kitchen and talked. I taped the conversations and the dialogue is
verbatim. That was important because there was no way I could have
re-created that. It was like music.

The husbands were part of my original idea for the story, but they
were two very shy men. It just didn't work. And that was okay. I always
tell myself, if it's not happening, then what *is* happening? I didn't see

the idea that they were each other's mirror early on. I was just reporting. Pretty soon, I started noticing I was in a good mood when I was around them. I'm having fun! I pay attention to that kind of thing. Other stories I've done, I've realized I just felt sick, dirty. That usually means something icky is going on with the people I'm interviewing.

Sometimes, I'm aware of where the story is going thematically, but often I'm not. I sit down with all the material and start looking at it. The first thing I do is listen to the tapes. That's the long way around. It's tedious. But for me the whole ritual of listening to everything I've experienced is part of the writing process. I probably had 15 hours of tape on this story. That's a week of transcribing.

I go into this trance when I'm transcribing. And I take naps. I have to take naps, a couple a day. It's embarrassing. But I honor the process and say, "Well, that's how I clean out." Maybe 15 or 20 minutes of sleep, and I wake up refreshed. I do it while writing, too. How do you explain that if you're working in a newsroom and it's this macho rhythm of "grab that story"? You don't explain it. You trust yourself. This is not laziness. This is what gets you there, what unlocks you. A lot of answers come that way.

The discovery comes in the writing. After I transcribe, I read everything over and highlight what's important. I almost never know where I'm headed when I start. I just start writing scenes. Or I'll start with what I think will be a lead, but 90% of the time it's not. I've talked to people who, if they can't get that beginning right, they can't go on. I start better if I jump into the middle. It's like jumping into a pool. If I can get all wet, I'm not so afraid of the water. When I re-read this story now, I'm surprised at how easy it is to read, which usually means it was hard to write. It has a kind of effortless quality, like it had to be written this way.

I usually give myself a two-week period to write once the transcription is done. I will crank out a sloppy draft and that's the difficult part. It takes about a week. Then I'm obsessed and can't put it down for the next week. And it is so much fun! I don't do anything else. I know the story's going to work at that point, and I'm shaping it. For me, that's the payoff—not having my name in a magazine or getting a check at the end. The payoff is that week. I don't return phone calls, my friends know I'm not available to go have fun. I'm not doing laundry, the house gets messy. Sometimes, I'll wake up at 3:00 in the morning and go, "Oh, my God, I got it! Why didn't I think of that before?" And I'll get up and work in the middle of the night. It's a trancelike state.

The joy of it doesn't last that long, and it's a hellish road to get there. But it's fun while it lasts. That's the drug. It's what keeps me doing it.—J. M. L.

Richard Ben Cramer

Richard Ben Cramer has worked as a reporter on the *Philadelphia Inquirer,* where he won a Pulitzer Prize for his coverage of the Middle East. He is the author of *What It Takes* (1992), about which *New York Times* columnist Russell Baker wrote, "Cramer does for American politics what Marcel Proust did for the cookie. . . . I just cannot stop reading." He is also the author of *Bob Dole* (1995). He is at work on a biography of Joe DiMaggio and lives on Maryland's Eastern Shore.

11

How The World Turns in West Philadelphia

Chapter 1

When Russell Monroe saw the blind man groping, lost, in the middle of the unemployment office, he did not speak but laid his strong hand gently on the blind man's arm. Of such small and natural graces is Russell Monroe possessed. Witness his walk, springy, subtly powerful, slowed now to match the blind man's pace as they moved off toward the proper window, the blind man no longer floundering but strolling, eased by Monroe's steady left hand. Witness also his grace at the counter where checks are issued, under a sign that read "5000 to 9999," halting the blind man with subtle hand pressure, placing the man's forearm against the counter, but not on it, so as not to jog his grip on the cane.

"There ain't no one there," said a young woman with corn-rowed hair. She stood behind the counter at the adjoining window, marked "000 to 4999." She stared at Monroe and the blind man, chewing her gum. It was clear she would not move one window to help. Monroe stood his ground.

"He said he wanted 5000 to 9999."

"Well, that ain't nothing," the young woman said, then bent her head once again to the file cards she was shuffling at her counter.

"This man said . . .," Monroe began, but the young woman was not listening. Monroe's foot thudded into the base of the counter. His black hand gripped the pale Formica so hard it seemed something would break. Jerkily, he strode from the counter, leaving the blind man at the window, leaving, too, some of his grace at 5000 to 9999.

By such small and futile rages is Russell Monroe also possessed.

Myrtle Lane in West Philadelphia, hard by the Penn Central's Main Line tracks, is a street of two-story rowhouses that hunker under summer heat in a sweaty squat. The house already was hot and airless that morning when Monroe woke and carried the color TV set downstairs to the living room, where it would play for the next 16 hours. Connie Monroe, his wife, came down moments later and asked him to turn the water on. The main valve into the house is kept shut to prevent the leaky plumbing from further damaging the walls. Mrs. Monroe made the rounds of the living and dining room furniture, collecting the clothes that had been left out to dry. Monroe, in the basement, threw the valve.

All five children were up, by the sound of it. Russell Jr., three, and Paul, one and a half, were running and giggling in the second-floor hall. Andrea, eight, came downstairs, rubbing her eyes under her glasses and asking her mother for cereal. Carla, 15, and Cathy, 13, were waiting upstairs for the water to reach the bathroom.

Cathy . . . graduation . . . dress . . . Cathy . . .

Cathy and her dress were on top of the mountain of his worries as Monroe sipped his coffee and lit his first Kool in the dining room. Her graduation from the eighth grade at Lamberton School was one day away. One day to get the dress. One day to get $20. . . . Monroe called his uncle to ask about using the uncle's Sears charge card to pay for Cathy's dress. "He said the charge was already up to $800," Monroe said after the call. "He said it would have to wait till next week. But kids, you know . . ." Monroe stared into his coffee. "Cathy wouldn't understand that."

On the big color screen, swiveled now to face the dining table, David Hartman was golly-wowing: a square watermelon in Japan, a man-powered flying machine in Britain, 110-degree temperatures in Palm Springs, California. . . . Monroe, 27, stared without seeing. He was not going to Japan. If he was lucky that day, he was going to another uncle's house to work on cleaning and carpentry, to ask thereafter for $20 or so to pay for a new dress for Cathy.

There was laughter in the house now, children's squeals of delight as little Russ got tickled by an older sister, as Paul stuck his tiny foot into his father's big workboot and called out, "Da! Ssoos!"

Monroe didn't notice for a minute, his thoughts occupied with making it; making it past Cathy's graduation, past the shut-off on the water bill, making it up to the next of Connie's welfare checks, making it through Sunday when the church would need his weekly $10, or into the Fourth of July with enough money, say $20, to take his wife and their five children *somewhere* for *something;* no, this was not the making it that most Philadelphians contemplate and scheme for.

And if the mornings were easier now—no burning in the stomach walls, none of the eyepain of vodka-bright light, none of the mystifying and reproachful looks from Connie and Carla and Cathy (the others were too young to understand), now that drink did not companion his darkness—did this not leave his nights close and fearful, without release from his evening horrors, that tomorrow would offer nothing for food, that dawn would reveal disaster encamped like a gas-man on the broken doorstep, that, even now, the bell of the ice cream truck (how he hated that steady, cheery bell!) would send his children squalling at him, calling for quarters and finding. . . ?

Ding, d-ding-ding. "Come and get it," cried the cheery blond mommy to her freckle-faced brood and the screen of the television was filled with the eye-catching label of her lemonade mix. . .

"Da! Ssoos!"

"Nothing . . .," Monroe said, from out of nowhere.

"Da!"

"Russell," his wife said from the kitchen, where she was wiping up after Andrea's breakfast cornflakes. "Look at Paul."

"All right, Paul, bring it here." Monroe held out his arms to his son, who had grabbed the boot with both little hands and was teetering across the floor toward the table.

"That kid loves shoes," Monroe said. "He's gonna be a shoe sales-man."

Paul, with an air of accomplishment, dropped the shoe at his father's feet. Monroe reached down and swept his son into a battered highchair at the table. With a humorless chuckle, he added: "Better be a shoe manufacturer."

In the living room, Russell Jr. fell against a chair and wailed in pain. Paul discovered himself in his highchair and started screaming: "Da! Get out!" Then the phone rang, and, for the first time in months, Monroe was offered a job referral. Monroe got off the phone and sat silently in the living room for a moment.

"That was a guy from the unemployment," he said to his wife. "They got a job at a warehouse, but it's only $3 an hour."

Constance Monroe had learned not to push. Still, expectant, she sat across from her husband, waiting.

"We'll have to report it," Monroe said.

Mrs. Monroe just sat, looking anxious, not wanting to seem too eager.

"Da! Get out! Da!"

There was no answer from the living room.

"At first, we kept asking ourselves how we had made our son do this, what had made him . . ." Several parents whose children were homosexuals were confiding in Phil Donahue. Monroe had unconsciously swiveled the TV set to face the living room as he passed.

"You want me to take it?" he asked.

Connie Monroe paused, looking up at her husband through lowered lashes. "Well, how do you feel about it?"

He said, sharply, "I feel about like you feel about it."

She looked up at him and decided to plunge. "Well, I'd take it."

Monroe looked annoyed, as if his doubts had been confirmed.

"No, I mean for me," Mrs. Monroe said, hurriedly. "I mean, I'd take it . . . if I could . . . for me." But she didn't mean for her.

"Okay," said Monroe and he stood suddenly. Mrs. Monroe got up to iron a clean T-shirt for his interview. She detoured toward the kitchen to release Paul, still screaming, from his confining highchair.

By the time Monroe came downstairs, redressed, to leave for the unemployment office, the talk shows and game shows had given way to the first of the soaps. As he crossed the living room, he paused, watching a tense, hoarsely whispered scene between two brothers, one good, one bad. The bad one had a gun. The good one, pleading, feared for his life. The show was called *Search for Tomorrow,* but that didn't really matter.

In the close, gray living room of the Monroe house, the soaps—or the stories, as the family calls them—run into one another in an endless stream of hot domestic quarrels and melting kisses, stealthy infidelity and misdirected love, psychological venom and occasional violence. Now, Cathy and Carla sat wordlessly watching the brothers caught in the horrid but painstakingly intelligible consequences of the bad one's unhappy childhood. Now, Mrs. Monroe interrupted her housework to watch. Now, Monroe stood, the hour for his interview crowding closer. Few words are spoken on most afternoons between the members of the Monroe household. So important are the stories.

So important is that television that fills and at times subsumes this house that its cost will be borne whatever the family income. The family that watched those brothers quarrel was living mainly on Mrs. Monroe's welfare benefits, a twice-monthly check of $250. The television set, a rental ("we don't have the down-payment to buy"), costs more than $60 a month. And yet, what price silence in that household where conversation seldom becomes recreation? And what price the loss of connection to a world that is larger, prettier, but still related to the lives of the family in that house?

"Did you hear?" Carla said to Cathy at breakfast. "Miz Chambers showed her face to Liz yesterday!"

Miz Chambers? Liz?

"It's in a story," Carla explained.

Yes, there was the connection, and more. For if their own lives were of the same stuff, it seemed paler somehow, as if held at one remove, like music heard through a wall, with its highest and most painful notes buffered out. Oh, the troubles in those stories! Nick was up to his ears with the Mafia; Paige was in mortal danger from a sniper; courts and parents had frustrated the marriage of Scotty and Laura; Heather's anonymous, threatening phone calls were all but driving Diana mad. Even now, the bad brother screamed through tears: "I can't do it. I can't kill you. You're my brother. I can't." Then he smashed his gun butt onto his brother's head.

"Mmm, ain't that a shame!" Carla said.

And if the stories had no resolution, what was resolved on Myrtle Lane? The characters made it by each day while somewhere (here, too, life seemed paler) a just hand made sure that the bad suffered, each in his own way, while the good seemed headed for some better thing. And there was some comfort in the slogging sameness, for the known face, fading now to the accompaniment of the show's theme song, would be back tomorrow and next year.

Monroe stopped at the front door and called his wife over to look. "Hey Connie, don't you know this black cop?" Two plainclothes policemen, one white, one black, were pounding at a door across Myrtle Lane. Their black city car was parked at the corner.

"Jerry's in there," Mrs. Monroe said. "I just saw him go in. Just now. Somebody must have called him and tipped him off."

"I know that black detective," Monroe said. "He busted me one time."

The cops gave up after a while and got back in their car. Monroe let them turn the corner at the end of the block before he stepped out to the street.

The unemployment office on Lansdowne Avenue is a big room of pale green, half-filled with pale men behind metal desks and peopled in its other half with black men and women sitting in rows of green chairs or standing in lines leading up to the counters. The bleakness of the office felt foreign to Monroe, although he had been there many times. He had registered for job referrals six months before. He had spent a few long days in the green chairs, waiting for the next job to turn up—even though, as he had reminded Connie, it would have to be reported to the welfare people and would cut into her check, and even though he had little inclination for the kinds of work he knew would be offered here. Then he learned there was no point in hanging around. As winter passed to spring and summer, he stayed home, and there had been few calls.

There seemed to be no excitement in him as he arrived, even though the day might bring a job and it had been a long time between jobs. But no matter, for the office on Lansdowne Avenue was a place to drain excitement from any man. It seemed to suck the energy from all who entered, past the tired guard at the front desk, past the signs that hawked savings bonds, into lines that seemed neither to grow nor to diminish.

The anger Monroe showed at the counter, when the blind man seeking his check was rebuffed, was no match for that weary government green. The anger was sucked up in the blank fluorescence, and Monroe, like everyone else inside, looked stripped and somehow smaller than he might have been outside. Now, killing time, waiting for his caseworker to finish a coffee break, Monroe showed nothing but insensate unease, flicking Kool ash onto the tiles, staring absently ahead. On his third foray through the stand of desks, Monroe found that the caseworker, John Ryan, had returned.

"You're Russell . . ." Ryan looked down at his file card, "Monroe? Have a seat."

Ryan started filling out the card. He was a man with one withered arm. His face, tending toward the white of his file cards, seemed pulled tight around the eyes. A little limp flag, once bright green, now tending toward the green that surrounded it, proclaimed Erin Go Bragh and distinguished his desk from its neighbors. Monroe leaned over the desk, trying to get Ryan to look up for a moment. The man attended to his card.

"Uh, is anybody else sent out on this job?" Monroe said, finally.

Ryan looked up at the interruption. "*I* didn't send anybody else," he said.

"I don't want to be smart," Monroe said. "I just want to find out what my chances are." He looked as if he hated himself for saying that. He slumped back in his chair.

Ryan lifted his card and his head at the same time. "Now," he said, formally, "it's warehousing, distribution and general stock work. . . . Pennsy Distributors . . . Mr. Gene Simms, he's the foreman, or Mr. Steinman, he's the owner. You'll probably be working under Simms. . . ." The caseworker paced this recitation with taps of his pen point on the file card. "Now, how much will it cost you to get there?"

Monroe paused only briefly. He would be getting a ride to the warehouse. But, out loud, he computed the cost of two bus trips, with transfers, at $1.10.

"And how much was it to get here?"

No pause this time. "Fifty-five."

"Okay, $1.10 and 55¢, that's $1.65. Wait there and I'll get you the carfare," Ryan said, and he moved off toward a corner of the room. The forms for $1.65 took about three minutes. Ryan returned with a clipboard and the money. Monroe signed for the carfare.

"If I get the job," he said, "do you give the carfare?"

"Yeah," Ryan said. "If you get the job, you come back and I'll give you the carfare."

Outside, in the car, Monroe multiplied the bus fares he could get in advance. "Two weeks, I think they'll give you two weeks. Let's see, 10 days, $1.10 a day . . ." He fell silent, computing, trying to imagine: Would $11 buy a graduation dress?

Connie Monroe tore eagerly at the envelope from Harrisburg.

The check for $41.40 was a retroactive increase in her welfare payment, bringing it up-to-date from March, when she had left her job at a home for the elderly. Standing near the front door, in the half-light filtered through thin curtains, Mrs. Monroe bent her scarved head close to the print on the check stub. The television played on mindlessly, coloring a corner of the gray living room. *"Don't you see, Larry Joe? I had to tell him I loved him or he'd be suspicious!"*

"There's a TV payment," she said, tentatively, holding the check in both hands as if to gauge its heft against the stack of payments-due she kept filed in her head. "But I want to put money aside for church on Sunday," she said, and her long face filled with the sweet smile she gets whenever she mentions the Church or the Lord. Mrs. Monroe was born again, at 30, last year. Her four oldest children played on the steamy street outside. Paul was beginning a well deserved nap. With a sigh, she sat down in the dining room and considered the family finances.

She started slowly. "There's the water bill . . .," she said. But as she dived into the complications of the water bill (for there is no simple way to pay a $702 water bill from a semimonthly welfare check of $250), she scattered such a spray of numbers and programs, notices and offices and cutoff dates that her tale became as intractable as the bills themselves. ". . . But the water bill," she was saying, "we're supposed to give them the check we get at the end of the month. That's the welfare, we're supposed to turn that over to them. . . ."

The whole check?

She nodded. "They don't care. You see, really, for four years, we haven't paid the water. With this broken plumbing, from the bathtub, you know—we know what it is, but the parts are $20—we were losing a lot more water than we used. So Russell called and explained this to the water company man and he said they couldn't fix it for us but he . . . could make some kind of arrangement on the bill. So, the water company came out twice. They left those little cards that they leave. But, I don't know. We never called them. We took water for granted, really. It ought to be free anyway. Then, three weeks ago, we got the immediate-cutoff notice. We went to the Community Legal Services; the woman's name, I think, is Tracy. She called up the water department. No, she called up the HEW to negotiate with the water company. . . ." Mrs. Monroe paused, trying to remember, one hand unconsciously smoothing the check on the dining room table.

"You see, first, we went to the water department. They said, '$300 or we cut it off.' Then we had to go to the mayor's office in City Hall, the complaint office, and then they told us about the Community Legal Services and sent us to 52nd and Chestnut. Then, the lawyer, Tracy, she arranged with the HEW to negotiate with the water company so they wouldn't cut it off. It must have been the end of April, because—that's another thing we talked to the lawyer about. We took Carla to the youth job desk at the unemployment office. You see, she's 15, and without the work papers, the only jobs you get are from that youth desk. But they looked at her card and they said she had a different Social Security number on her medical card from her Social Security card. It's the computer, probably, but they said they couldn't sign her up with the different numbers because the Social Security card didn't jibe with the medical card.

"So, in the first week in May, the caseworker from the welfare came around on his regular visit and we told him about Carla's card. He says he'll take care of it. But he didn't. We called him twice and then we both went to the office, the welfare office, and we showed him the cards and it must have been their computer that put the wrong number on the medical card. But the caseworker said we have to go to Social Security to get it straightened out. So, Russell called the Social Security to ask could he get it done the same day. They said it would take awhile. I don't know, just 'awhile.' I think they said four to six weeks.

"It got to the point, we just forfeited the idea of getting her a job because it was past the time. But we told Tracy about it and she called the welfare right there and told them they had to change the cards. They must have been saying that the cards were forged because I remember her saying, 'No, it looks like a regular Social Security card to me.' She said that over and over. And right there and then, she got us an appointment to have the cards changed. I think I gave you the wrong dates. We must have been in May in Tracy's office. . . ."

Mrs. Monroe tried to remember. "When were the checks, the 15th and 30th in May? No, the 14th and 29th. . . . So, that's right. May. Because it was the cutoff for the fuel program. That's a program that if you get a shut-off notice from the gas or electric, they pay, directly to the utility, up to $250.

"No, we didn't get it. We didn't have a shut-off notice. We got one now, but it's too late. It was the middle of May and I went to the public-assistance office. It's in the welfare office, but it's still an independent program. The man, it was another man, not the welfare caseworker, he said I had to present a shut-off notice. I had an electric bill of $77. We thought the water was applicable, too, but that's not under the Public Utility Commissions authority, so we didn't fit in for the program.

"I asked could I call the electric and get a shut-off notice, but the man said, 'You'll never get it from the computer.' Then, at the Community Legal Services, we found out that program, the fuel program, was extended. But it was only extended to June 15 and we got the shut-off notice June 19. We made an arrangement with them, though. We have to pay $50 before July 2. That's on a total bill now of $111."

Mrs. Monroe looked up as the front screen door banged shut. Russell Jr. came trudging in from the street and climbed onto a dining room chair. "Mom, I want some juice," he said.

"You can have some water," she said and continued her monologue from the kitchen. "It goes pretty bad for us around the third week because we start running out of food. The stamps are $149 a month, but the bills are more like $250. So we have to take cash money to buy food, or borrow money, you know, for food or for Pampers, for necessities. . . ."

"I want some potato chips," Rusty said.

"Then, you know, when the ice cream truck comes around, the kids want ice cream. And I feel, I know both of us feel bad saying no. You know, they're kids. They don't understand. So, if we have a couple of dollars, we go ahead and get ice cream, and it's 35¢ a cone."

Mrs. Monroe handed Rusty his ice water.

"We try to buy Popsicles when we get groceries," she said. "But Rusty doesn't like them." Rusty confirmed that with a 3-year-old's gravity. And, still solemnly nodding, he added: "I want some potato chips."

Mrs. Monroe's gaze strayed back to the check on the table. Slowly, the smile filled her face again. "We'll use $20 for the church this week," she said. "There's $10 for the Family Day this Sunday and $10 for the regular tithe. The tithe is supposed to be 10 percent of your earnings. We do the tithe every week because we do believe that everything we get comes from the Lord. Like if Russell gets the job, you know. So, the more you can give back to the Lord . . .

"It's trust," she said. "Even if you give your last $10, you know you're trusting in the Lord to meet your every need. We don't just sit back. We try to channel that money that we get the best we can. If we have these bills, we try to pay that worst bill that we have. But we have to trust in the Lord to supply our every need."

Only after grace was said over the steaming chicken stew did Monroe get to tell of his triumph. He was bound to be offhand about it, but there was pride in the set of his shoulders, even as he bent to prayer. Mrs. Monroe's eyes gleamed as she listened. She had piled her husband's plate so high his first forkful threatened an avalanche.

"When I got there, there was this other guy ahead of me," Monroe said. "He had a big hat, cocked to the side, sneakers on, you know, hands in his pockets, maybe about 19 or 20. Hoodlumish, you know? So, I was only there a couple of minutes when this other guy got the brushoff." Monroe let two forkfuls pass silently, in deference to hunger and dramatic effect.

"*Coming up next on* Eyewitness News . . .," said a face on the screen, now swiveled to beam at the table once again.

"It looked like a nickel-and-dime operation. That's what it looked like," Monroe said. "Everything was crammed into one room, window shades everywhere and mats and those bamboo-type shades. A lot of old machinery. Outdated. There was that mom-and-pop atmosphere. It is a father-and-son outfit. I just felt it was a sure thing. The type of work they're doing, I mean, a fourth-grader could do.

"So, the foreman, Simms, comes out of the office, a little glass-walled dispatcher-type office, and he gives this other guy carfare and says, you know, 'Sorry.' Simms is a thin guy, black guy. He looks like a drinker. That place is his whole life, you can tell. He reminds me of a guy who shines shoes, and he sees a little spot and goes over it again, you know. He's real meticulous about his little work.

"We go in the back and he shows me a ruler and a tape measure, just to see if I could use them. Like, 'Where's seven and three-quarters and where's eleven and two-thirds?' Then we go into the real back of the place and he shows me a box of venetian blinds and a box of accordion folding doors and all you do is match the labels on the boxes to the bill of lading.

"Then he shows me a U.P.S. stamping machine and one of those wire wrapping machines and I tell him I've used them both before. That's when he stopped using 'ifs.' He says, 'When you start' and 'If you work out after two weeks,' and things like that, and starts telling me about days off. I didn't tell him about wanting to start with school again in September. . . . He just started telling me. . . . Anyways, I start Monday, 8:30."

"Thank the Lord," said Mrs. Monroe.

Monroe was nonchalant. "The only thing good about it is all the stuff I can get on discount. I'm going to get one of those padded toilet seats for the bathroom and some of those shades for the front. . . ." He stopped and looked up at his wife looking at him, and her smile started him smiling. And when he tried to stop smiling, he had to laugh, and then they both laughed, for a moment, until Paul started screaming to get out of his highchair. After dinner, Mrs. Monroe brought her husband his coffee in the living room, then set to work with Cathy on the graduation dress that was too small.

Yes, Monroe had got the dress: marked down at Wanamakers from $36 to $7.98, $8 and change with the taxes, plus $1.10 for SEPTA fares, and more than $1 left in his pocket.

He did not worry about the size. Connie would make it fit. He lapsed into a placid sleep in front of a raucous game show and only woke hours later when the distant bell of the ice cream truck brought his children in a stampede through the front screen door, asking in unison for quarters.

Chapter 2

When the talk shows replace the stories in the late afternoons, Myrtle Lane sparkles with fireplug water that has floated candy wrappers and cigarette butts and drawn every child to a bright, cool freshet to slop and splash and scream. Then, with the houses still hot from the day's sun, sinking through haze onto the facing roofline, the early-working fathers return to close the hydrants, the girls give up jacks and gossip for gossip and jump-rope, the boys wring out their shirts and, still drying, chalk the drying street for a game of tops. Then, Connie Monroe takes her ease on the front stoop. Behind her, house cleaned, children fed, clothes ironed or perhaps a day spent weaving her strained, delicate web of programs and centers, grants and offices, officials, applications and ID cards. Ahead, dinner to be cooked, washing dishes, washing children, washing clothes and, finally, when Russell carries the TV upstairs, a bit of late movie and a short sleep. Russell would be home soon. She wanted dinner ready for him. It was her husband's first week of work in the warehouse.

The tops game—looking something like hopscotch without hopping—was in full cry. The "men," tar-filled tops from mayonnaise jars, were tossed into the chalked squares on the street. *"Git ya hands off, that's my man!" "Ah'ma slide you, man!" "Ah got my man in two awready." "Did not!" "Ah'ma slide you!" "Did not, you! . . ."*

Little Russell Jr., three, ran out toward the game in the street. "Russell!" his mother called. She remembered she had to sew his jeans. . . . Andrea broke her glasses on that telephone pole . . . got to get those glasses fixed . . . Russell would be home soon. . . .

The girls had two ropes whirling in a fast rhythm. *"Rockin' robin, tweet, tweet, tweet . . . rockin' robin, tweet, tweedleedeet . . ."*

"My mother used to hate to see me jump rope," Mrs. Monroe mused through a cloud of Kool smoke. "She'd say, 'Connie, you're wearin' out my shoes!'" She laughed at the sound of herself sounding like her mother. "I never had much childhood. . . ." She was 16 when she had her own first child, Carla, almost 16 years ago. "I was so young," she said. "There's still a lot of little girl in me. . . ."

And she jumped up, straight and slender in her jeans, and tossed her Kool in the gutter as she ran toward the center of the ropes flicking on the asphalt. *Flickatikatikatikatikatika.* Mrs. Monroe jumped in. "One! *Tikatikatikatikatikatika* Two! *Tikatiktik.*" Her daughters and their friends called out the cadence. They could not chant, they were laughing so hard. "Go, Mom!" Cathy yelled. The rope caught her feet at "Eight!" Connie Monroe came back grinning broadly.

"See that?" she said on the way to the kitchen.

The front screen door bangs shut perhaps 100 times a day. Most often, it heralds a child who comes back toward the kitchen, calling out, "Mom, can I have . . .?"

"There is none," Mrs. Monroe has to say. She always offers a substitute. But who has the words to explain to a child that not for two weeks (a child's eon) will the food stamps come from Harrisburg, and then, if they stretch, there will be juice? And when the child shuffles, head hung, sniffling, out of the kitchen, back toward the street, without his juice, and his mother watches his shoulders heave and her eyes tighten with the pain in him, whose words comfort her?

Near the front door where the children bang in and out, there is a photograph of a friend, who inscribed it to the Monroes: "To Russell, a man . . . To Connie, a rock . . ."

Mrs. Monroe was pleased with that. Strong Connie, savvy Connie, able Connie, Christian Connie, each is a facet of this rock, and who gets inside (who tries?) to see if there is perhaps something softer, more desirous, more fearful, something to be cared for, something like a child? She could cry, if no one were around, or sit pensive, worn down by meagerness sometimes, but when someone asks if, perhaps, there is something. . . ?

"I'm okay," Mrs. Monroe replies and brightens.

She has posted on her refrigerator her favorite Bible verse, Matthew, Chapter 6, Verse 33: *"But seek ye first the kingdom of God, and his righteousness; and all these things shall be added unto you."* The plaque-makers left off a previous verse that identifies "all these things": *"Therefore take no thought, saying, What shall we eat? or, What shall we drink? or, Wherewithal shall we be clothed?"*

"Yes, sometimes it hits me, truthfully," she said one night when she was the only one in the house. "But that's only when I really get inside myself. And it's just feeling sorry for myself, really. . . . It doesn't feel good, no. Because, after I delve into myself like that, I feel guilty. It's like—if I can bring Christianity in again—it's like the devil coming to me to say, 'Hey, you know, you're young! You don't have to put up with this.' " She looked up, smiling bashfully. But then, the Holy Spirit comes and says, 'These are your children. The Lord has given you these children, and this husband, and this house, and you've got to work, and . . . be at peace.' "

For two hours, Connie Monroe waited at the Community Legal Services center: She looked at a mural of famous black jurists, then she looked at the wall; she pored, with a furrow in her forehead, over a notice on the changes in food stamps, then she carefully folded that notice into her purse with 100 other papers; she gave information to a Puerto Rican woman who was screening the clients, filling out the same eligibility form that another screening clerk had filled out on Mrs. Monroe two weeks before; she inspected her long fingernails; mostly, she smiled at other women's children and worried about her own, at home. She did not get cross, or even impatient. She said nothing untoward.

"The Lord has taught me to bridle my tongue," she said as she looked toward the reception desk where she had been signed in more than an hour before, ". . . for my family."

All that week, she had risen early, by 7:45, she had served coffee, ironed clothes and seen her husband off to his new job. Then, after the children had been fed and the house cleaned, Mrs. Monroe had left to do business:

• She spent a couple of hours at the office of the Philadelphia Anti-Poverty Action Commission, seeking a referral for emergency food, but her qualifications had to be cross-checked and Mrs. Monroe was told to come back another time.

• She waited for almost an hour at the state welfare office to ask for the newly required food-stamp card. Her caseworker told her she wouldn't need the card for 10 more days, so she would have to come back at that time.

• She spent a day on the WIC (Women, Infants, Children) program—traveling to Jefferson Hospital to obtain six computer cards that entitled her to free milk, cheese, eggs, cereal and juice for her two youngest children. But when she got to the Acme supermarket on Lancaster Avenue (the program allows clients to visit only one store), she found out so many WIC cards had been issued that the store had none of the cereals and juices allowed by her computer cards.

"I almost said something there," she confessed.

This morning, she began with the Number 10 trolley, swaying up Lansdowne Avenue toward the 3-2 Center, where welfare checks are issued and cashed. Most of the passengers in the trolley were going for their "digits," or checks. Mrs. Monroe held herself aloof from the general air of festivity. Two women seated near the back door talked about a shopping trip, to begin after they picked up their checks. A heavy woman with a seat to herself and bare arms of rippling chocolate brown stopped fanning herself with her *Daily News* and dipped a hand into the pocketbook beside her. She produced a wrinkled paper bag with the neck of a small bottle protruding, and, with the daintiness some women display handling their powder compacts, she opened, drank from and replaced the bottle and took up her newspaper fan again. A discussion between a man and woman in the second-last seat was growing steadily louder. The man, accusing, told the woman he could never trust her again.

"Get outa here!" she replied. "You had lots of women, too."

"Yeah?" the man said, now with anger. "But I found you in *my bed* with that . . .!"

A few of the women were still laughing about that as they climbed out in the 6000 block of Lansdowne. On the corner, outside a tavern, a half-dozen men lounged against cars, each waiting for his girlfriend to pick up her check. Mrs. Monroe passed by them quickly, looking neither right nor left. "I hate it," she said when she was out of earshot. "These people don't have no scruples for themselves—cursing and drinking—guys trying to impress women." She shook her head. "They don't even have a pot to pee-pee in."

In the 3-2 Center, Mrs. Monroe waited while, from behind thick plexiglass, her face was checked by clerks and recorded by closed-circuit cameras. She asked that $230, all but $20 of her welfare payment, be converted to a money order, to be paid to the City Water Department.

The $230 money order would forestall a water shutoff notice. But it meant that she would have no money for the next 15 days' food until her monthly food stamps arrived. She knew that a Catholic organization gave food from the Springfield Avenue convent of St. Francis DeSales. She also knew that any such grant would require referrals. So, with her money order tucked in her purse, she boarded a trolley and then a bus to Chestnut Street, to the office of Community Legal Services, to ask for a letter vouching for her penury.

Then, she waited.

After 26 minutes, she was called into "intake." Inez Pruebas, a plump woman with hair of many colors and wearing cork heels worn down to their last four inches, had a kindly lilt of Caribbean in her voice as she said, brightly: "Yes?"

Mrs. Monroe produced her money order. "I picked up our check today, and . . ."

"Our check?"

"Yes, our welfare check," Mrs. Monroe said. She sounded as if she was gritting her teeth. She does not like the word *welfare*. She pressed on. "We have to pay $230 to the mortgage company, I mean the water company, and the lawyer, Tracy, told me to come in to get some emergency food."

"We don't give any food."

"No, I mean a letter to this office on Springfield Avenue for emergency food."

"Oh," Mrs. Pruebas said. She sat back, stumped. She had started work at the office on Chestnut Street two weeks before. "I'll have to call her and ask. I don't know where that is." She dialed. "Hello? Tracy? This is Inez at intake and I have here a Mrs. . . . ." She turned to her for guidance.

"Monroe," said Mrs. Monroe.

"Monroe," said Mrs. Pruebas. She reported, word for word, what Mrs. Monroe had told her. "Okay, okay I'll have to fill out an application for welfare section because I don't have time to be writing letters . . . okay, okay . . . Bye-bye."

She produced a dense, multipart form.

"Name again?" she said, pencil poised. "Address? . . . Single home? . . . Own? . . . Telephone? . . . Number? . . ."

Mrs. Monroe sat forward, uneasy. She gave answers too fast. She had to repeat them for transcription.

"Children?"

"Yes, five . . ."

"Married?"

"Yes!"

"Living together?"

"Yes!"

"Do you happen to have your medical card?"

Mrs. Monroe rooted nervously among the forms and papers in her purse.

"It's all right," Mrs. Pruebas said. "Take your time." She took the card that Mrs. Monroe proffered and decided, after a study, that it was not right. "It should have your name, too."

Mrs. Monroe explained the family's medical cards. Mrs. Pruebas nodded. She studied the card again, then bent to her form.

"Sign your name here, please," she said a couple of minutes later, pushing the form across the desk. "Just requesting legal services." Mrs. Pruebas looked around the office for a list of food distribution centers. There was none. She turned to her phone. Mrs. Monroe stuffed her card among her papers. Mrs. Pruebas was on the phone: "Yes, and could you get me an address?"

Mrs. Monroe was trying to get her attention. "I can tell them where the food center is."

"Okay," Mrs. Pruebas said into the phone. ". . . Anti-Poverty . . . Action . . . Commission . . . Yes, and do you know the address? No? Okay, okay, I'll call. Bye-bye."

"Excuse me," Mrs. Monroe said, "but I can tell them where the food center is."

Mrs. Pruebas was getting harried. "Well, you were talking and they were talking and they were talking and I can't talk to all people at the same time. . . . Do you know the exact address?"

"It's at 45th and Springfield," Mrs. Monroe said. "But I don't know the exact name. It's affiliated with the Catholic Church, St. Francis DeSales."

"Maybe one of the other intake people knows," Mrs. Pruebas said, and she was off on the phone again. She tried two numbers and got no answer. She was flustered now. "Excuse me," she said, and she stood up to leave. She said, over her shoulder, at the door, "I want to know where I'm sending you."

Mrs. Monroe sat back in her chair with a sigh. She was silent for more than a minute. "These people are really deep," she said, finally. "You know their job better than they do, and they work here."

Mrs. Pruebas came back to her desk. "He doesn't know," she said. "Let me call Miss Tracy again. Is Tracy there? . . . Tracy, I hate to keep bugging you. This is Inez. The client stated that you gave her an address at 45th and Springfield where she could get emergency food. . . ."

Across the desk, Mrs. Monroe was shaking her head. A different lawyer had mentioned the address. Mrs. Monroe said nothing.

"No . . . No . . . You don't know? Okay then, sorry." She turned to Mrs. Monroe: "She said she did not give you that address. I am just relaying what she said."

"I know," Mrs. Monroe said. "What is the name of the lawyer, the thin white guy with the glasses?"

"I don't know." Mrs. Pruebas turned to her telephone again.

Mrs. Monroe left the room, walked five steps to the reception desk and returned to announce: "His name is Jack Means."

"Oh, okay," Mrs. Pruebas said. "I'll call him." She called. "They say he's downstairs here, somewhere," she said when she hung up. She left the office again. This time, she was gone five minutes. "He's with a client now and he's very busy," she said when she came back. "He says he has the address, but he'll have to go up to his office to get it . . . so what I want you to do is to just go outside here, and just . . . have a seat."

Back in her chair in the reception room, Mrs. Monroe looked at the wall some more, then her nails, then the notices advising clients what services would have to be obtained elsewhere, then the wall some more. A couple of girls, seven and eight, were running noisily between the chairs, water cooler and restroom. They stopped at Mrs. Monroe's chair as if magnetized. She has a special smile for children, a big, transforming smile that draws them close without words and makes them quiet, almost confidential. Next to her, the two girls sat and started patty-cake. The older one, in a flouncy pale-blue skirt and precocious high heels, kicked her skinny legs back and forth, back and forth, keeping rhythm with the slapping of palms and her husky woman's voice as she sang:

> Grandma in the kitchen, cookin' rice.
> Father roun' the corner, shootin' dice.
> Brother in jail, raisin' hell.
> Sister on the corner, sellin' fruit cocktail!
> Rockin' robin, tweet, tweet, tweet.
> Rockin' robin, tweet, tweedleedeet . . .

From the end of the reception room, her mother's ratchet voice cut in: "That's enough of that rockin' robin. You don't shut up your mouth right now, you're gonna meet this belt again!"

The girl glanced across at her mother and, leaning closer to Mrs. Monroe, a bit more quietly, started another verse: *"Mama in the kitchen, cookin' soup . . ."*

Mrs. Monroe looked at the girl with a tiny, cautioning eye movement. The little girl fell silent. "If it's bad, you shouldn't sing it," Mrs. Monroe said. The girl nodded to show she understood. She looked a little solemn. Mrs. Monroe flashed her smile. "Can you walk in those shoes?" she said.

"Uh-huh," the girl said, eagerly, and jumped up to show off her high-heeled strut.

Jack Means, the thin, busy lawyer, who had the address Mrs. Monroe needed, walked through the reception room, carrying papers. Mrs. Monroe sat up in her chair. Means walked through without stopping. She sat back again, a little lower in the chair. She said, after a moment's pause, "I'd like to get off this welfare business." She had a job offer from a Head Start program center. She could start in September at $3.90 an hour—after taxes, more than $500 a month. "I can't afford to," she said.

She listed all that she would lose:

• Her welfare checks brought in $500 a month.

• The food stamps brought the equivalent of $149 more. And she expected her food stamp grant to be raised to $200 a month this summer.

• And then there was the value of Medicaid, the medical cards.

"This month," she said, "Russ had one doctor's appointment, Cathy had two. The dentist would have been at least $15. No. More. Andrea went to the dentist twice this month. She had root-canal work done on one tooth. That's up in the money. I think $50, or more. Then, the white fillings are $20 and the silver ones $15. The doctor for Cathy would have been $15 or $20 or more. With growing children, you don't know when they're going to be sick. And if you don't have the money . . ." She shook her head at the prospect. She crumpled up the little paper on which she had been adding figures. It showed that she would lose at least $250 for every month she worked.

"I'd like the social work. I like to do *something*. I like to feel that I'm contributing to somebody's welfare. Of course, with the children, I like to think I'm doing that. But I get a little bored sometimes. . . ."

Means came back, looking for Mrs. Monroe this time. He paused only seconds at her chair. "Hi. All right, same problem as before, huh?"

She nodded.

"I'll get a letter typed up." And he left the room again.

A small smile grew on Mrs. Monroe's lips. "I used to say, if patience was a virtue, then I'm not a virtuous woman," she said wryly. "But I'm learning."

The wet, gray heat of the afternoon hit Mrs. Monroe as she walked toward a bus stop on Chestnut Street, armed with her letter. Only five SEPTA rides and a few bouts of waiting remained before she would get home with her groceries.

The front screen door banged behind Mrs. Monroe as she struggled through with her grocery bags. Her three youngest children ganged up with requests. "Mom, a sandwich . . . water-ice . . . juice . . ."—this last from Paul, who, at one and a half, had learned that persistence brought results. "Ma, juice! Ma, juice! Ma . . . Ma!" Paul broke into a wail of protest that rose to a high shriek.

"Paul, do you want a bottle?" Mrs. Monroe said. The Catholic group had included powdered milk in its grant.

"Juice?" Paul said, through tears.

"We don't have juice, Paul," his mother said. Paul cried. "Mama will get some soon."

She started to fix him a bottle of milk. Carla came in from the street. "Mom, where you been?" she said. Carla had been watching the younger children all day. She said, with a 15-year-old's drama: "I almost died being bored." Paul got a bottle and Mrs. Monroe moved on to peanut butter sandwiches for Andrea and Russell Jr. Andrea took hers back out to the street. Rusty dropped his on the living-room carpet.

Mrs. Monroe moved around the house quickly, straightening here and there, working against the day's five-child havoc. The theme song from *Eyewitness News*, blaring in the living room, told her she was late. No time for the front steps. Russell would be home soon. She unpacked the groceries and started on dinner, ground meat laced in swirls through mashed potatoes.

Andrea ran into the house to tell her mother about the big boys teasing little Russ. Mrs. Monroe went out to the street to stop it. On her way back in, she paused to survey the living room—two chairs and a sofa facing the television set, arranged on stained and near-colorless carpet. For a moment, Mrs. Monroe saw it as she would like it: deep-brown carpet, perhaps a shag, flecked with strands of orange or rust, off-white walls bouncing sunlight onto lots of houseplants. *"But seek ye first the kingdom of God, and his righteousness; and all these things shall be added unto you."* She thought of her husband on his way home. God willing, she thought, his job would go well. Perhaps he would like it well enough to stay. . . .

She hurriedly emptied a couple of ashtrays and set them straight near the sofa and a chair. She wanted everything to be right for him. She barely got back to the kitchen before her husband wearily banged through the door, called a greeting toward her and sank into the chair closest to the TV set. Little Russ followed his father in.

"Dad, you got money?" he asked, cocking his head ingenuously. "I want some potato chips."

"Russ, we're going to have dinner soon," Mrs. Monroe told her son. She edged around her husband's outstretched legs and lowered herself onto his lap. Monroe craned his neck up to reach her face with a kiss, then slumped back uncomfortably and said with a little laugh "Hey, Connie, really. Cut me a break, huh?" She lifted herself off his lap.

Grace and supper lasted barely 20 minutes, barely through the sports and weather reports and attendant car commercials. All the talk came from the big color screen. Finally, as she cleared the plates, Connie asked Russell about the day at work.

"It's just a hump. It's all humping," Russell said. "They don't want you to think." He said he had been asked that day to fill his first outgoing order. He had gone to the back room and pulled the items specified on the bill of lading. "Then this guy, Sam, a Southern guy, says, 'Hey, you filled that too fast.'" Monroe's voice held a hint of disgust.

"So, I say, 'Well, what am I supposed to do now?' He says, 'Just hang around for a while, and then go back up front.' I mean, the work that they're doing a fourth-grader could do. A monkey could do it." He shook his head.

"It's all right. Free coffee all day. Friendly. The whites call the blacks 'nigger.' The blacks call the whites 'honky m. f.'s.' I mean, the place is pretty decent. After lunch, I looked for the guy I was working with. He was upstairs sleepin' with the elevator doors open so no one could get up there. I said, 'Hey, it's time.' He says, 'Hey, slow down. Wake me up in a half-hour.' It's a place I could get along. But I can't see staying there very long."

Mrs. Monroe bridled her tongue.

She finally got out to the stoop at dusk. Behind her, the sound of a siren wailed from the television through the living room. In front, the stark geometry of Myrtle Lane was softening in the graying light. Her own children played on the sidewalk in front of her. "Mom, watch this!" Rusty called and he jumped the final two steps to the pavement. Mrs. Monroe smiled at him and nodded. Rusty ran off to find a friend. Every child on the block was outside. For perhaps half an hour, Mrs. Monroe watched the street, a little smile on her face all the while, a big smile for all the children who came by and said, "Hi, Miz Connie." The tops game was called because of darkness. The jump rope flicked on. The noise, it seemed, only increased.

Yolanda, a little girl with green yarn on her pigtails, ran by three or four times screaming, "AAAAAAEEEEEE," just to hear herself. Christopher, six, the mad tricyclist, roared by every three or four minutes, the plastic wheels of his Hot Wheels trike rumbling on the pavement, his own voice wailing like a demon race car. WDAS from two radios vied with WHAT booming from a speaker across the street. Tony, the next-door neighbor, came out to take his evening seat on his stoop, no more than three feet away. He brought out his own radio and his habitual short glass of Scotch. A few doors down, Linda, the most active hostess on the block, entertained another gentleman caller on her own front stoop.

Cathy called from the street for her mother to come and try skipping rope. Mrs. Monroe stayed seated, smoking. For a while, she refereed the footraces between Andrea and Yolanda and between Rusty and his friend Diane. "On your knees . . .," she called out. The children bent to the cement. "Ready to sneeze . . ." The children giggled. "Ahhhhhhh CHOO!" The children took off down the sidewalk. The streetlights flickered on and grew steady, brighter, each illuminating its own wet aureole of misty, sickly yellow. Mrs. Monroe stood and brushed off her jeans. Nighttime was not her street time. In the darkness, the young men inherited the street, gathering under the harsh lights to swear and swap lies and act as big as they could without cars. Even now, a young man on a bicycle approached a group of his friends at the curb. "F——— you and you and you and you," he said by way of greeting.

"It's too noisy and polluted with cursing," Mrs. Monroe said softly as she turned toward the door. "I don't feel too good about it. We try to keep that out of our house." She called her younger children in and locked the screen door behind them. Inside, the TV set drowned out all other noise. The wan, mottled carpet was washed with splashes of color from the screen, which provided the only light in the room. Andrea went upstairs with her jacks. Little Russ asked "Mom, you got money?" He cocked his head cutely again. "I want some water-ice."

"No," she said, simply. Rusty sulked, then asked "Where's Dad?" His father was in the basement, elbow-deep in the washing machine, agitating the soaking clothes to make up for a broken washer part.

"Russell's good about that wash," Mrs. Monroe said. "I always feel bad when he has to do that."

Downstairs, Monroe sweated over the machine. He said he only minded the work when his forearms cramped in the water. "Someone has to do it," he said, jerking his head toward the stairs that led up to the living room. "And she's ready to drop up there." He, too, said there was no money. Rusty began to cry.

"Russ!" his father snapped. "Get upstairs."

In the dark living room, Mrs. Monroe called to Rusty with her special children's smile. She held her arms out to him and he climbed onto her, wrapping his arms tightly around her neck. The lurid red and blue flashes from the television screen showed his little hands slowly slackening on her back as his breathing grew regular, then shallow. Fifteen minutes later, a bleach commercial threw a shaft of bright white across the room and for a moment lit Mrs. Monroe's face as it leaned lightly against her child's warm head, her brow smooth, her lips just parted, her eyes, like his, now closed.

Chapter 3

Russell Monroe got his first Friday paycheck, $94.82 after taxes, and stopped off to drink a bit of it. His wife was sitting on the front-stoop, waiting to go to choir practice. She knew when she saw him approaching. She saw the bold imperiousness in his orders to their children, who ran down Myrtle Lane to meet him. She knew that hint of swagger in his walk. She knew Russell, whose worst bouts with alcohol he and she had curbed. Those bouts had all but disappeared since Connie and Russell turned to God and Church in the spring of last year.

She had known drink before that, from her first husband, whom she had married when she was 16, and who, only a few years later, dived into a bottle and never came out. She had learned about drink and she had learned about loss. On her own, with two daughters, she had had to learn how to take care of herself. But Connie always had been capable. She came from a big family—five brothers and three sisters, and there had been more. One brother was shot dead in a dispute with his landlord. Another was beaten to death by a gang of whites in Southwest Philadelphia. Yes, she had known loss.

Now, on the stoop of her rowhouse, her face set in unfamiliar, hard lines. She would not without a fight know that loss again.

By now, she also had learned how to fight. She spoke and her voice was strained, but soft. "Hi, Russell," she said. "Tired?"

She hurried the children into the house and through preparations for the trip to the church. She reminded Russell, once, softly, that they would have to leave right away. She did not ask Russell where he had been, or with whom, or why. When the family assembled outdoors for the trip, Connie remembered the bottle for Paul. She ran in to fix it and re-emerged, still screwing on the top. "Hey," said Russell, challenging, "weren't you the one just hurrying me up out of the house? Weren't you?"

Connie held her peace.

When they met, Russell had just returned from a Job Corps program in Kentucky. Connie was older than he by four years, by two children and one bad marriage. Both were living in West Philadelphia, past University City, where Walnut Street rolls for miles carrying a steady stream of cars out to Delaware County.

"We had mutual friends, you know," Russell recalls now. "But when I met her, she didn't even know I was alive. I was maybe 19, and, anyway, we parted company. When we got into the singing group is when it really happened." The group ("one or two people might know the melody, someone else knew the words—we didn't have any sheet music") didn't last long enough to get a name. But Russell and Connie left together after an evening rehearsal and they have been together ever since.

"He wrote songs for me," Connie recalls now. "I still have 'em, too. You know, 'You are the sun, the moon and the stars to me. . . .' I can't remember all of it. . . ." She giggles. "But it was *deep*." For her part, Connie celebrated Russell in prose. She still has her first essay from college (a year and a half at Community, majoring in police science). She shows the paper with shy pride. It still bears the red-pen praise of the instructor at the top: *Excellent. Attractive style. Original description. Good introduction.*

"Russ is a guy I'd love to have around our house, small in stature but ranking high in everything else. Weighing in at or around 155 pounds. *(His)* Height 5', 11". *(He has)* A beautiful brown complexion that goes extremely well with big brown eyes that seem to speak back at you. His nose is really cute, reminding me of a ski slope *(very good)* because of its point upward *(upturned tip)*. He has a smile that is a proud one, for while he is smiling, his big head is held high and very proud. . . . His walk is very proud and sort of sexy, *(Read about semicolon use in* Handbook of Basic English Skills) his derriere protrudes just enough, making the back part of him look really good. Conservative in dress as well as personality, Russ's main interest is me! *(And a very good closing!)*"

Connie still marvels at how her life changed when she met Russell. "I stopped hangin' out so much, partying. I changed my friends. It was a relief, in a sense," she says. "I felt secure. And it takes two parents to raise a child. To be committed to someone who cares about you, it was just fulfilling. . . . I think the girls were happy, too. But I didn't do it for them."

Russell talks about his life before Connie as if it belonged to another man. "I was in a lot of things I wish I could forget," he says. "It was a bad scene, I can tell you that. I was still into hangin' out with the boys. I had to go out, you know, to a club or a party. It was an obsession with partying. I was a basketball freak during the week. I wasn't working."

There were chances, plenty of chances. He finished high school in the Job Corps in Kentucky; he did well there and took some courses at the University of Kentucky, but he never made proper application to continue studying there. He came back to a Postal Service job; they liked him at the post office and urged him to take the test for permanent employment, but he balked. "I just thought I hadn't studied enough to pass it the first time." He went back to hanging out, living on odd jobs and hustles. Sometimes, when he needed money, he went to a center city clinic and, there, sold his blood. When he and Connie moved in together, Russell found he liked family life. "It was something I never had before. You feel proud," he says. "To be protective, you know, to take that step in life, to cut all the bad habits and the bad influences loose . . . It gave me a sense of responsibility."

In nine years, there have been three more children, and a few fine times, like trips to New York when both were working and money was at hand, back when they bought their house. And, more often, simple joys, like days in the park with a bag of sandwiches and a quart of beer. There have been very bad times as well, like 1977, when there was almost no money at all and Russell was drinking hard. Then Connie and her oldest daughters learned fear as well, when Russell would come home spoiling for a fight. That ended last year, when they found the Lord. Connie began it by going to church and by taking a new interest in the Bible. Soon, Russell joined her for a Sunday service, and, weeping, they answered the call of the preacher to give over their lives to Christ.

"Everything changed," Russell says. "Then, we *had* something. . . ."

"We have God's promise," Connie says.

"We have our guidance spelled out," Russell says. "For every situation, it's right in the Bible."

"And," Connie says, "we have our church home."

They joined the First Evangelical Church, which they knew little about. The church was also far from home, at least 40 minutes' bus ride into North Philadelphia. But Russell's uncle is the pastor. Russell's grandfather is assistant pastor. Another uncle is President. An aunt runs the choir. By joining the church, they rejoined the Monroes. Their sense of belonging was doubled. And there was a sense of responsibility, for the Church was something larger than their own lives, a care that lifted them, as nothing else could (as nothing else was permitted to), out of their own household pressures.

And there was more than concern to lift them from their routine of poverty. For there was the feeling of something noble, something altogether larger than this life, under the high, flaking white ceiling of that old stone church. There was in the ritual something stately, something elaborate, something garnished with all the ornament that Myrtle Lane and its life lacked.

So, every Wednesday was prayer meeting night, and every Sunday, school and service. There were board and committee meetings and Youth

Forum sessions to be planned, and there were excursions to promote and to join, church suppers and sales, church business, church gossip. And every Friday, a rigorous practice in the choir, in front of Aunt Evelyn.

"Not 7:15, but 7:00!" Aunt Evelyn was saying to the choir, like a schoolmarm threatening to keep everybody after class. On this Friday evening, her hair pulled severely back on her head, her chin jutting out over the neck of her T-shirt, she started practice with a 10-minute tongue-lashing. "When we say 7:00 that means you come at 7:00 or before! I put in too much effort for this. I keep trying to impress upon you that you are performing a ministry."

In the front row of the choirbox, Connie looked down at her shoes. The church was very quiet. From the back row, tenor section, Russell piped up: "I have an excuse. I'm late."

It was supposed to be a joke. No one laughed. Aunt Evelyn glared. She turned to her piano. But she was mad now. "And when you come," she said, looking up again, "try to look like you're coming to the House of the Lord. Some of you look just like you're in the service of the devil!" Her eyes, flat and baleful, rested on Russell, tipsy and grinning in the back row. She turned again to her piano:

> Spirit of the living God
> Fall fresh on me.
> Melt me . . .

The rich sound of 20 voices seemed to swell the church.

> Mold me . . .

The pastor's son, at the organ, added treble tracery that fluttered over and around the hymn like tuneful cherubim.

> Fill-l-l me . . .

The choir members lifted their faces toward the back balcony of the church and the music came down from the white ceiling in a flood over the 12 empty, dully shining pews. Then it stopped. Russell had his hand up. "Would you play the tenor part again?" Evelyn played it. The choir waited while Russell satisfied himself as to the tune.

> Praise God from whom all blessings flow.
> Praise Him all creatures here below.
> Hallelujah,
> Hallelu-u-u-jah . . .

Aunt Evelyn cut them off with a hand wave. "Tenors!" she said sharply. "Now, listen." She sang their part.

> Hallelujah,
> Hallelu-u-u . . .

Russell's voice was sailing up the register on a solo flight. Evelyn cut them off again, then again. Perhaps 10 times the choir sang its hallelujahs. Sometimes the altos sang alone, sometimes the bass section. Too often, Russell alone.

"Wait," he said, his hand in the air again. "Where are you?"

She played his part as she wanted it sung.

"That's not what the music says," Russell said.

Evelyn slammed her hand on the piano. "We have spent 20 minutes on something very simple," she said. "Now, we either have to have an organized group or no choir at all. I can't deal with individuals."

When Russell raised his hand again, she ignored him. He was sullen on the long ride home to West Philadelphia. Connie was careful to say nothing upsetting. Back home in the dark living room, when the children all had gone outside, Russell told Connie he'd been treated unfairly. "What Evelyn was doing was, she was puttin' me down," he said. "You know, most Sundays, I'm the only tenor they really have. And I put up my hand, and I say, 'It's important,' and she says, 'I don't want to hear it.' "

He turned on the television and threw himself onto the couch. Anger had put a scowl on his face. "She was puttin' me down," he said. He turned to Connie again. "Is there anything that can be cooked fast?" He knew there was not.

"We have chicken and fish, but frozen," she said softly.

Russell said, more truculently, "Is there anything that can be cooked? Fast."

"Soup?" she said.

"A meal."

Connie sent Carla to the store for tuna fish. She came back to the living room and glanced at Russell, nursing his wounded pride on the couch. Suddenly, she wheeled and put up her fists. "Come on, you want to fight?" she said, bouncing like a boxer and bobbing her biggest grin in his face. Her feet scuffled back and forth on the rug in an imitation of the Ali shuffle. "Come on," she said, laughing now. "You got frustration? Come on!"

Slowly, a smile spread on Russell's face. "Yeah, we can bring back 1977," he said.

Connie laughed. "Please Lord, no," she said. And she dropped her dukes and headed for the kitchen.

Russell was still grinning as he settled back to watch TV.

Sunday, the Russell Monroes got to church early. The children sat in on Sunday school. The parents went upstairs to put on choir robes. At 11:00 a.m., Russell's uncle, Pastor M. Harold Monroe, a big, balding, square-shouldered man with strong features under glasses and beard, entered and stood at his rostrum. In the assistant's chair, the Reverend Paul H. Monroe, older, grayer, rounder than his son, sat placidly listening while Gene Monroe, his slim grandson, played the organ prelude. Clinton (Ike) Monroe, the pastor's brother, dapper in his dark-blue designer suit, made the church announcements. There were about 100 parishioners in the tall stone church, children upstairs, adults below, eight lady ushers in white hats and dresses roaming between the smooth old pews, all present bathed in soft sunlight that filtered through simple stained-glass windows and bounced off the white walls and ceiling. The choir members, resplendent in new maroon robes, lined up in the church's central aisle. Suddenly, their music filled the church.

> Spirit of the living God,
> Fall fresh on me . . .

Slowly, with decorum, the choir filed in front of the congregation and into the box to the right of the pulpit.

Melt me . . .

The organ was cranked up in power now and its bass notes registered not in the ear but in the viscera.

Mold me . . .

In the front row, Connie's face shone with a smile from somewhere deep within her, a smile of transport that seemed almost to lift her from the floor.

Fill-l-l me . . .

Russell was not in the choir.

U-u-use me.

"Mom said Russell's not feeling good," Carla said to her neighbor in a rear pew. Then all stood for responsive reading. The service was long and loving, intricately filigreed with song and gospel, each act of worship elaborated, elongated and embellished to accord it honor and weight. The choir sang a hymn. A choir member took a solo on a verse of the hymn. Pastor Monroe discoursed on the theme of the hymn. Behind him, the choir kept humming the hymn. In front of him, the audience reacted to his strongest points with punctuating cries, "Yes!" "That's right!" Jackie, a thin soprano with an other-worldly stare, sang the verses: *Earnestly, tenderly, Jesus is calling* . . .

"Yes, Jesus is calling to you and to me," said Pastor Monroe. He warmed to his own words, to the sound of his voice resonating throughout the church while the choir hummed and swayed. His voice rose as he talked of the devil, not an abstract, textbook devil but a living, ineluctable devil who could be, could *be* right here in this church. "But, Jesus *calls* to all sinners, calls them to Him, to say His name, to say His name . . . Jesus . . . how sweet the name," he said. Then softly "Jesus, how sweet the name . . . Jesus . . ." Now stronger his voice rising: "How sweet the name!"

"JESUS!" screamed Jackie who broke from the solemn swaying of the choir and began to shake with the force inside her. "JESUS THANK

YOU JESUS, LORD," she screamed. "THANK YOU JESUS, THANK YOU THANK YOU JESUS." She slumped. Two ushers and a fellow choir member helped ease her onto a chair. The ushers fanned her with little paper fans that advertise the name of a Broad Street mortuary. "Ohhhhhh," Jackie moaned and her voice rose again. "Thank you for being there when no one else was, oh, Jesus, thank you, Lord Jesus. . . ."

The congregation smiled upon her. The ushers fanned. Around her, the choir continued humming. The preacher talked of the forgiveness of sin. Slowly, the tall church picked up the heat of midday, the pastor's voice became gravelly from preaching and reading the gospel to his flock. The whole congregation took communion, received the benediction and an invitation to the evening service. As the worship ended, the members embraced and wished God's blessings upon one another. Then the families of First Evangelical started home for Sunday dinner.

Connie shed her choir robe upstairs but kept for most of the hot trip home her remote, ethereal air. Only when the bus left Fairmount Park for the asphalt hills of West Philadelphia did her face fall and furrow, and she confided her worry: Russell, she said, had been suspended from the choir. The pastor had told Russell before the service: He was to be disciplined for entering the church with alcohol on his breath last Friday. Briefly, there were words. Russell left in a fury.

Now, Connie walked the children up Myrtle Lane and anxiously scanned the front of her house for signs of activity inside. There were none. The door was locked. Russell had not come home.

He got home drunk, obviously drunk, and sore from hours on the basketball courts. The courts always had been his release. In his old life, before he and Connie settled, he and his friends almost lived for playing ball. In those days, there was always a game, of course, but the courts were also his place to sing with his friends, to have a sip of wine, "have a taste" of something stronger, to settle any arguments that came up, or simply to get away. That Sunday, after he left the church, he played until his legs wobbled and then he played more. Still, it was not enough. It did not dissipate that bubble of rage that threatened to rise and choke him. He drank and the bubble got larger, hotter inside him. Back home, his voice boomed through the house. "Andrea, don't you hear right? What did I tell you? I told you no candy. Right? RIGHT? Give it here."

The oldest daughters gave Russell a wide berth. Were they reminded of 1977? Did they remember their own father in similar moods when they were much younger? In the basement, where they sought refuge, Carla looked up at the ceiling as Russell's voice filtered through from above. She turned to Cathy and remarked: "Don't he be getting evil?"

Russell had a telephone shouting match with his uncle, the pastor. The assistant pastor and his wife, Russell's grandfather and grandmother, showed up at the house to try to make peace. Russell was adamant. He acknowledged wrongdoing, but, he claimed, the punishment dwarfed his crime. He claimed he was a political victim, offered up as an example to the congregation that a Monroe who had transgressed would be treated as harshly as a non-Monroe. Connie, Russell and his grandparents settled around the dining room table. Russell banished the rest of the family from the room.

"I'm going to make my point," he was saying loudly as the group sat down.

"But you don't listen. That's your problem, you don't listen," his grandfather told him sternly.

"I'm going to have my say," Russell said, even louder, cutting off protests. "I've listened to you and Uncle Harold for a long time." Downstairs, the ceiling thudded as Russell pounded the table. "You can listen to me, now. . . ."

He was calmer after his grandparents left. He went upstairs to lie down. Connie and he talked a little then. But there wasn't much to say. She knew what was trapped in that bubble inside. He had said it so many times before. His relatives kept thinking he was the little Monroe, the junior member, the next generation. They didn't understand that such things don't last. The little Monroe was now just as big as they. Yes, there had been fights before. As bitter as this? Perhaps. After time passed, wary time, the wounds got covered over and the rage inside Russell shrank.

"They're going to put me on probation," Russell said. He often talked of them this way, as cops or inquisitors. "Or," he added, "they're going to try." Then, and he said this twice, to make sure she understood him, "They can't do nothing to an absentee."

Downstairs, in the kitchen, fixing sandwiches to make up for the lost Sunday dinner, Connie said she would not follow Russell if he chose to leave the Church. She could not force him to go back, she said. ("All we can do is pray for him.") But neither could she force herself to leave on his account. She would go back, within hours, to put on her robe and sing in praise. "It's a feeling I can't lose," she said. There had been times when she, like Jackie, had lost herself in an ecstasy, calling out Jesus's name in a strange voice that owed nothing to her will. On her way to the basement water valve, Connie paused, trying to describe that feeling. "Freedom," she said, finally. "It's like, like a great burden's been lifted and there's no one else but you and the Lord. I don't know. Would *oblivious* be the right word?"

Chapter 4

Dusk on that stoop seemed to last forever; the last light tantalized with the illusory promise of cool and quiet on Myrtle Lane. The ice cream truck had clangored through, beset on its halting way by a swarm of children feeding. Now, those children ran toward their houses, licking at the goo that rolled toward their clenched hands. Now, the young men clumped in small groups around big radios, and soon the small groups would coalesce and the street would be theirs for the night.

Still, Connie Monroe stayed on her cement steps, which, she reflected, she was too tired to sweep. She stayed out longer, stayed out on purpose, trying to give some breathing space to Russell, her husband, stretched out in the front room before the TV set. Her daughter Carla fidgeted next to her. All day she had watched the younger children. All day she had watched the stories on TV. Her summer stretched out ahead like a desert. It was July 3 and there was no hope of a job. "Bored to death," she said, whenever she was asked. And then she would shift her newly rounding form (astir, too alive at 15) on the couch or chair, or the front stoop, and stare off to the side, her chin on one hand, as if she were too miserable to talk more. She would go in now to watch *Emergency,* but Russell was there and Russell was in a mood.

"He been *so* evil," Carla said.

The pressure on Russell had squeezed the household. Since Sunday, his fight with the church had roiled inside him. He had stopped off each night on the way home from work for "a quick one," as he called it.

Tonight, there was something more on his mind: Independence Day, a holiday, a whole day to celebrate, and what could seven people do with $10 or $15? He turned his face from the bright TV screen and he felt the next day pressing on him, tightening, heating up that bubble of frustration he had carried in his gut since Sunday. He would have broken something if something were at hand. He might have talked to Connie but what would talking do? Instead, wordlessly, awkwardly, he stepped outdoors, past Connie and Carla, and over the little iron dividing rail to his neighbor's front door, behind which, he knew, the evening's drinking had begun.

Russell was still next door when Carla got her mother's permission to take a ride with a friend. Russell might not have allowed it, not without knowing the destination, companions and the time of return. Russell ruled by fiat and Connie by persuasion.

"I talk to my girls straight," she said. "Because I was 16, *so* naive. I didn't know anything about sex, making love. . . . You know, I ask her. I say to her, 'Well, what would you do if James asked you to, you know, go to bed? If he said, you know, to show you really loved him, like that?' James, that's the boy she talks with. She says, 'Mom! I don't *know!*'" I said, 'Well, why don't you tell him just that you don't have to go to bed with him to show you love him. And if he really loved you he wouldn't ask you to, not for right now.'

"I guess she listens," Connie said. "I don't know, both girls are coming into that age now, 13 to 15, where things can really turn their heads. Especially boys. I figure if they can get to 16, they have a better chance. So, I tell them now. I didn't have no childhood at all. I wish I could grab it back." Connie sighed. "I hope she listens."

In the car, Carla said she'd heard all that. "Yeah, they're always talking. Let's go." She turned up the radio as the car swung out, and she said in a singsong that seemed to include the whole street. "Goodbye, boring people!" Carla directed the car straight to North Philadelphia, to the house of her friend Liz. When she got close, she hung out the window of the car, seeing and being seen by people who should know that she was riding through.

"Lemme hold your cigarette," she said, and smoked it down to a yellow half-inch. Then she asked for another, not mentioning that the cigarettes, like the trip to North Philadelphia, were forbidden by her parents. She talked nonstop, more words than she had spoken in a week at home, all about smoking cigarettes and boys smoking reefer and drinking at parties and how her parents wouldn't let her go to parties anymore. She fizzed like shaken soda.

"I thought I was going to go crazy today," she said through a mouthful of smoke. "You see how evil I was gettin', just sittin' there all day." She slouched at ease in the passenger seat, savoring her lungfuls of independence. "Liz! Get in!" she called when the car turned into the little street near 30th and Erie. Liz screamed when she saw her friend. It was a rare treat when one or the other could make it from West to North Philadelphia, or from North to West. And a car! Liz and her friend Tina got in.

"Where is he?" Carla said at once. She meant James, who lived nearby. Round the square, treeless blocks, they searched the front porches and the sidewalks and finally spotted James at the house of his friend Elijah.

"Liz!" Carla said, conspiratorially. "Go in and tell him I'm out here." There was giggling, plotting, planning. Liz got out to pass the word. James and Eli joined the group.

Then they rode and rode through the night, Eli in the back between Carla's two friends, Carla in the front seat, so close to James. They rode down Ridge—past the bars leaking music and patrons onto the street— and into center city, where James had to lean out and yell smart things to the well-dressed women on the sidewalks.

"Hey, baby, ain't you fine!" he yelled to a woman on Pine Street. Carla swiveled away from him as if it were no matter to her. He did it only once or twice more. James had seen more of life than Carla. At one point, he turned to the backseat and said, "Hey, Tina, you pregnant?"

"No!" she said.

"Whew!" James said, with a dramatic wipe of his brow. "That's a relief." Then, in a burst of candor, he said to the car at large: "I saw this dude say that to a girl. It was funny, man." And he repeated the exchange as the dude had done it, which sounded pretty much the same. For her part, Carla wanted it known that she had lived longer and harder than James might think. "Liz, tell him, don't I hang out?"

On their way back north, they passed the Benjamin Franklin Parkway, where the median was alive with rides and stands and people were getting the jump on celebrations of Independence Day. Carla leaned forward and turned up the radio. Carla asked for a cigarette as the car wound north toward Lehigh Avenue. It was early July 4 by the time they pulled up at the Monroe house. "Ooh, that's my song!" Carla said, and sat listening to the car radio. Then: "Ooh, that's my song, too!" The driver finally had to put her out of the car and make sure she went into the house.

July 4 had been pressing on him for a long time now—in the back of his mind as he handed over July's television rental money, or in his eye, like that big flag hanging at the bank, where he paid half his salary on the electric bill. How could a man saving nickels for SEPTA fares celebrate independence? What independence? That much had leaked out from him during the last few days. Mostly, Russell didn't talk much. One time, he had almost seemed himself when the subject of the Fourth came up. "You know what I'd really like to do?" Connie said, casually, dreamily. "I'd just like to get away for a day or two. Anywhere. The Marriott on City Line would be fine. I don't *care* where." She chuckled pleasurably at the thought.

And Russell, picking up on the idea, said, "You want to? When?"

"Russell, we don't have the money for that." She said it before she had thought. And when she saw the hurt in his face at the harsh truth that had no place in that dreamy talk, she tried to change the subject, but Russell already was silent again. What would talking do? But now, as Carla banged through the door, Russell was talking, yelling almost, his face bent forward toward his wife across the room, and he was mad. Carla barely stopped to say hello. She headed upstairs at a trot. *"Declare your independence, with a gas-stingy Toyota from . . ."*

Connie sat stone-faced near the TV, her profile washed darkly with its colors, her eye unwavering upon the screen. Still, Russell talked.

"What are seven people going to do? I mean, since it's a holiday and the kids get half-fare, I mean, I guess we can get somewhere and back. But is that a holiday? Really?" *"Hey, kids, baseball cards at Burger King! Hey, it's Pete Rose . . ."*

"I guess there's a lot of free stuff downtown," Russell said, more quietly. "But we can't all eat one hot dog all day. I mean, the kids. I don't have to eat. . . . I got the day off, that's my holiday. . . ."

As he talked, something hovered in his plaint. Was this his holiday? Was the nation cause for celebration? If Russell rooted for the United States, very much as he did for the Phillies; if he snarled at the

Eyewitness News films of the OPEC ministers meeting to raise prices
("We ought to go over and show those OPECs"), still, he had not attained
the American dream of a car. If he voted, and reported proudly that he
voted; if he put no stock in black mayoral candidate Charles Bowser's
claims of electoral miscarriage ("Bowser wasn't ready to be mayor—he
was only out for the blacks"), he could not believe that his child might
grow up to be president. If he was not racist, and never spoke of racist
whites; if he claimed that it made no difference whether one dealt with
white or black ("When it comes to their money, the only color is green"),
he knew, of course, that there were no white families left on Myrtle Lane.
Was this national dream his? Or did it somehow fall short of belonging
to him as he seemed to fall short of belonging in it?

"Hey," Russell said abruptly, waving all abstraction away. "We dig the
country. Better than China, huh? I mean, I'm just talking about getting
$20 to take the kids out somewhere."

It was afternoon before the family set out, through gray mist and empty
streets, toward center city to find its holiday. Russell had been glad of
the cold and drizzle; it was easier to stay indoors. Easier for the kids to
stay in, for Russell had been out early that day, visiting the neighbors,
collecting little debts, cigarette money he had lent last week, or a little
consideration for the beers he had bought same months back. He didn't
like to do it, but the day had come. Through the morning, the family had
gone on as if it were just another day. Donahue commiserated with
fathers whose wives had left them. *"Really, Phil, single parenthood has
its rewards."* The morning newscast showed minicam pictures of hardy
picnickers braving the rain.

"Mom, what are we going to do?"

"I don't know, Andrea."

"Sharon Beckler, come on DOWN!" A frowsy California woman
bounced toward the camera, ready to seek her fortune on *The New Price
Is Right*. Connie ironed. Carla put her hair in pincurls. The game shows
gave way to the first of the stories.

When Russell came back, he had assembled $20, from neighbors,
friends, Connie and his pockets. Carla was the last one out of the living
room. Her finger lingered on the TV power switch. *"Oh, Johnny, don't
leave me. I'm so scared. . . ."*

"I wish we could stay and watch this," Carla said.

The Monroes landed in an empty center city, glistening with rain and eerily quiet. "This is dead," Connie said.

Much of the money dropped at Burger King: six hamburgers for the seven people, a big order of french fries and some Cokes to split. Paul, Rusty and Andrea got little three-packs of Phillies baseball cards. And after the Burger King, for a while, there was nothing.

But there was a certain pleasure in the empty city. In the glittery Penn Center section, so foreign to Myrtle Lane, the children looked with big eyes toward the tops of the buildings, and, with no one else around to claim them, it was almost as if those buildings were theirs. The children swapped penny candy and used the whole width of the broad sidewalks, making sure not to step on cracks. They walked up the Parkway, past little groups of marching band members who were complaining about the damp cold. Cathy and Andrea ran up the Franklin Institute steps and found at the top that the doors were locked. But then Cathy came down the steps, giggling, arms raised in triumph, like Rocky. Andrea picked up on that. Soon, Rusty and Carla, too, ran to pose and play on the steps. They came down, warmed and lively. Andrea turned a walk back toward Market Street into a musical strut: *"Come, ease on down, ease on down the ro-oad. Come . . ."*

Connie and Rusty picked up the song and the Monroes danced down 20th Street. Little Paul, holding his bottle in one hand, pumped his arms and swayed his taut belly, his face round with his biggest grin. He danced just for the pleasure of moving in the city's big, gray spaces.

The parade started up. The rain resumed. No matter. The Monroes found a Chestnut Street bus shelter where they could watch the floats and bands pass by. Afterward, they spent their last: coffee and sodas at McDonald's. They emerged to drying streets and, finally, to crowds. The fireworks at the Art Museum drew thousands to the Parkway. The bursts of color in the sky, the crackles and great booms, made the smaller children gasp.

"Mom, wasn't it pretty?" Andrea said on the long walk back up the Parkway.

"I liked that last one," Cathy said.

The Monroes moved among the thousands, all talking about the fireworks. Carla looked at the couples strolling and said she wished she were there with her boyfriend. But she couldn't get much anguish into the complaint. Russell and Connie each carried one sleeping son. A child can get heavy on a 15-block walk. But there was, too, a certain triumph in making a day full enough to knock a child out. And when the long walk ended at the subway-surface car, Russell may have meant something larger than that walk when he set down Rusty and said to his wife: "Well, we made it."

At the house, the television set went on right away. The children were revved up from the ride. Andrea got out her jacks and played in the middle of the living-room carpet. Rusty flopped and flipped on the floor, practicing his newest trick, somersaults. Connie's grilled-cheese sandwiches silenced the talk and laughter for a while and the noise from the big color screen took over. Mannix was driving around sunny California, two fellows rode competing brands of tractor lawnmowers over their acres of grass, a couple in Italy found romance over their brand of wine. . . . The Monroes watched blank-eyed and silent.

Then, *"Hey, kids, baseball cards at Burger King!"*

"Yes," Andrea said with proprietary nonchalance. "They better show Danny Ozark, cause that's what we got."

"Yeah," said Rusty, excited, "that's what we got!"

"Hey, you better show Danny Ozark," Andrea said to the screen, with all the right of command. She had, after all, those same cards that the kids in the commercial had. Those cards, that hamburger, even those smiles, all belonged to her, now. When she was sent to bed, minutes later, she declined to let her mother hold the cards for her. She carefully placed them in the pocket of her shirt and paused, on the second floor, by the bright bathroom bulb, to look at them again. She still had them in her hand when she scooted toward her bedroom at the sound of lights clicking off below and Russell's little grunt as he lifted the TV set to take it upstairs.

Chapter 5

On Saturdays, of course, there are no stories (can troubles take the weekends off?) and the Monroes were gathered in the late afternoon, watching *Fangs of the Living Dead*.

"My kind of movie," Russell said. He was, as Connie said, a little high.

Russell had just dressed (white shirt, black tie) for a catering job. He waited tables on nights or weekends to pull in a little extra money.

Connie called a cab for Russell and dispatched Cathy to the corner store for some small supper groceries. Carla made a cup of strong coffee and set it down for Russell on the dining room table.

"Hey, Dad, want to see?" Russ Jr. was showing off his new running somersault on the living-room carpet.

"That's good, Russ," his father said. He lit a Kool and settled back on the couch, killing time until his cab arrived. Cathy banged through the door with the bag of groceries. Her mother bent over the bag. "D'you get the mayonnaise?" she was saying when the screams from the dining room paralyzed . . .

"*Paul!*" Russell yelled. He and Connie bolted for the dining room at the same instant. Paul, their youngest, one and a half, stood by the dining room table, screaming, his little fists flailing at air, at nothing, and he screamed with an anguish they had never heard. The coffee cup, empty of its scalding load, rolled around at his feet. Russell grabbed Paul by a shoulder and, with the palm of his hand, started to wipe the burning coffee off Paul's bare tummy. Paul's fists beat at his father's face and chest. "Paul!" Russell yelled, again. But this was pain Paul could not understand. Something told him to fight, to beat it to death. He punched at his father with all his might.

Connie had a towel from the kitchen. "Russell, get it off him," she said, imploring. Russell wiped Paul's tummy gently, from his chest to the waistband of his Pamper. Paul screamed. His father had to hold his wrists.

Only after a minute did Russell and Connie figure out that the coffee had spilled into the Pamper, holding Paul's genitals in a scalding puddle. "Oh, God, get it off him," Connie begged. She and Russell tugged at the diaper, opened it and gently brought it away. Layers of skin fell away and shriveled when the air hit the burns inside the Pamper.

"Oh, Jesus," Connie called out, and she ran (she still does not know why) upstairs to the bathroom, calling "Oh, Jesus, Jesus, Lord Jesus." She called out before the bathroom mirror. With her eyes to the ceiling and her fists raised above her head, she stood for perhaps a minute, just calling, "Jesus, *Jesus! Jesus!*"

Then she ran back to call an ambulance. The cab came first, and Russell carried Paul by the feet, holding the feet apart like the points of a forked stick so nothing would rub the raw, red, underflesh at the juncture of that fork. Carefully, he eased into the cab. Paul still screamed and flailed, trying to beat at the pain. The ambulance pulled up behind and Russell eased back out of the cab and carried Paul around to the open rear doors. The medics laid Paul out with pads under and around his legs. Russell and Connie squeezed in the back doors.

"Hey," yelled the cab driver. "You're not going to take the cab? Hey, you called a cab. Hey!"

At Children's Hospital, Paul, still screaming, was wheeled at once into an operating room. A resident came out a few minutes later to tell Russell and Connie that Paul was to be admitted. The resident called the burns on Paul's penis "second-degree, probably." Russell nodded, silent, at the news. Connie saw suddenly that Russell was stone sober. She let herself cry, then.

They spent most of the next week at the hospital. Connie went early, as soon as her house was clean. Russell joined her after work. Together, they sat with Paul on the fifth floor of the hospital, watching him, always watching, and handing him toys, feeding him juice, rocking him, crooning, talking, laughing, holding him, changing his diaper that burned so when it got wet. They sat with him on little stools in the playroom, or on creaking plastic chairs in the room where he slept. He was one of four children in the room. One was a baby who coughed and moaned. Another had a burn on her arm. The other had water on the brain; her skull, twice its normal size, was misshapen and furrowed with the strain like a crazy, overripe fruit. They sat with him in the parents' lounge, where they could smoke, and where Paul, when he felt well enough, would climb up on a broad windowsill to look down into the hospital atrium, at the fountain that splashed and glistened, and say "Da! Fire-Plug."

He improved slowly. He cried often. He ate little. His genitals were still raw, under a stinking plaster of pigskin. He still fussed and whimpered every time he was laid on his back to be changed. He still kept his eyes open each evening as long as he could, longer than anyone thought he could, because, when he slept, his parents went home. Russell and Connie grew drawn and grim. He had eight hours of hot, hard labor behind him when he got to the hospital. She had four children to care for at home after she left the hospital.

"They ought to call this The Tombs," Connie said one night in the parents' lounge.

"Yeah, or Attica," Russell said.

"But you know, I feel lucky. This makes you feel how lucky you are. These poor children, some of them. . . . Five pregnancies . . .," she said, and a smile began to form on her lips. ". . . and five healthy children. You really never know how much you have to thank the Lord for."

At home in the early evenings, Carla took her ease on the stoop. She lit the day's last clandestine cigarette. She watched the street and listened for the younger children with eyes and ears almost as practiced as her mother's. For more than a week, she had watched the younger children, made sure they had their sandwiches and Kool-Aid, made sure the bigger kids on the block laid off Rusty and Andrea.

Bored?

"It's not so bad," she said. "It's nice being here alone."

Of course, she was not alone, for there were 100 children on the block. The mad tricyclist roared by on the sidewalk, a tops game flourished in the street. A couple of older boys lay in ambush with a bucket of fireplug water, waiting for an unwary friend to walk by. But she was singly in charge, this week, and the status became her. She seemed not so restless now. It seemed for the first time in a long time that she belonged just where she was. Perhaps the change had started that day when Russell came home just after noon. His boss had sent him out in a car to hunt for a tank of gasoline.

"Carla'd been saying that she was miserable," Russell said. "I went upstairs and knocked." Carla was staring out the window with a look that proclaimed the world was against her.

"I know you don't like the situation," Russell began, to the back of her head. "But while you're here, you have to do what we say, and there's no two ways about that. . . . When I was a teenager," Russell said, more softly, "there was the same things goin' on. There was reefer. There was sex. Maybe the clothes looked a little different, but it was the whole kit and caboodle. So I know what's going on now. You know, you don't have to make your friends think you're so tough. If they want to act ignorant out there, come in the house. Watch TV that night, or do your hair. Do anything.

"Y'understand?" Carla did not turn to him.

"Understand?" Russell left not knowing whether Carla understood. She nodded, but she would not talk.

The next night, Russell and Connie came home to find that Carla had made their supper. "And it was *good,*" Connie recalls with a chuckle. And Russell made sure to tell Carla how good it was. It was that night, too, when Connie was sitting on the stoop, that Carla came by to say: "Mom, lend me a quarter."

"Lend!" Connie said, laughing. "Girl, you owe for 15½ years!"

"Mom," Carla said, wheedling, "when I get to be a doctor, or a legal secretary or something, I'll pay you back."

"Hah," Connie said, extending the quarter, "you'll be takin' care of your man."

"No, I won't," Carla said, turning toward the store. But she grinned in spite of herself at the sound of "your man."

Now, her parents all but lived at the hospital for a second week, and Carla seemed at ease. Anyway, there was plenty to keep her mind at work. She was in a fight with a 16-year-old girl on the street. "She came up here," Carla was saying. "I was standin' right on the steps. . . . She start shoutin' and runnin' her mouth, saying, 'I'm going to whip your ass.' I told her, 'Get off my property.' She kept runnin' her mouth, gettin' in my face. . . . 'I'm going to whip your ass.' Like that, you know, and my mother came out to look. And right in front of my mother, she said, 'You better keep Carla in the house, 'cause she come out I'm gonna whip her ass!' I didn't say nothin' to her then, but, next day, I came out with two shirts on and my sneakers on and my hair all up so she couldn't pull it. I was ready," Carla said with a laugh.

The result?

"I beat her ass," Carla said, simply. "I didn't like her runnin' her mouth to my mother."

At Children's Hospital, doctors roam in packs. The parents sit by, sometimes for hours, waiting for the medical team to appear.

Russell and Connie were waiting on edge. The doctors had said that Paul was almost ready to leave the hospital. They had said in their last visit that they would look under the pigskin today and examine the skin underneath.

"Paul, you want juice?" Russell was saying as he pointed a bottle toward Paul's mouth. Paul, teeth clenched, shook his head. Russell gave up on the bottle. In the next chair, Connie hung her head, silent. She was weary and worried. That morning, she had learned that her father was in the hospital, too. He had pneumonia, her sister had said. Since then, Connie had heard nothing more.

"I wish they'd come," Connie said. And, as if she had willed them into being, the doctors rounded the corner of the hall.

"Okay, Paul, let's go in the room now," Russell said. Paul protested with a little whimper. It still scared him to have his diapers removed. "It's okay, it won't hurt," Russell said into Paul's ear. He laid Paul gently on the bed and stood away while a nurse peeled the diaper tapes. Eight hospital personnel were clumped at the bedside.

"His culture showed the presence of staph (bacteria) but it took a week to develop into anything," a resident said to the physician in charge. "We don't think it's significant, yet."

"Let's have a look," the surgeon said, and he bent to Paul's bandages with a small scissors.

"It's much better," Connie said as the gauze came away to reveal Paul's genitals, still shocking pink. "It's still flesh-colored, though." A woman resident looked up at Connie quizzically, wondering, perhaps, why Connie would label such a hue "flesh-colored."

"Uh-huh," the physician in charge was saying. He looked at Paul's chart. "Temperature steady? . . . Uh-huh . . ."

"It's up in the afternoons," the chief nurse said.

"Let's culture him again," said the physician in charge. Then he turned to Russell and Connie, across the bed, and said, "We'll get back to you." The pack moved down the hall.

Russell smoothed down Paul's new diaper. "See? That didn't hurt, did it?" He shouldered Paul and moved off with Connie toward the lounge for a smoke.

"When did they mean that they'd tell us?" Connie said.

"I don't know," Russell said. "Guess we just wait."

Anyway, Paul was not ready to sleep. He climbed up on the wide windowsill and stared into the atrium. "Water fountain," he said.

"Hey," Russell said. "He doesn't call it fireplug anymore."

"Right," Connie said with a smile. "You think we got an illiterate kid?"

"Da! Bottle?" Paul said.

"Want to go home, Paul?" Connie said.

"Yes," Paul said, and Connie laughed.

For hours then, as the light dimmed on the skylights of the atrium, the Monroes sat up with Paul, waiting for the doctors to return. Paul got cranky, Russell got more tired. Connie tried her sister twice, without luck, from the pay phone. Finally, Russell ruled that it was time and he took Paul back to his room. Silently, he rocked in a plastic chair, with Paul's face lying gently on his shoulder, while the light from the big window disappeared and the room grew dark and quiet. Cautiously, he stood, with Paul still held gently on his chest, and he bent, slowly, smoothly, to lay Paul on the bed. Paul stirred when his father's hands left him. Russell leaned back over his son, propping himself on his elbows so that Paul could feel his father's form, warm and close on him. Motionless as only a strong man can be, Russell hung in that unnatural stance, while he listened to Paul breathe, slowly . . . quietly . . . asleep. Then he straightened, stood by the bed and, silently, edged from the room. Connie was on the other side of the hall, nodding as two doctors talked. Finally, the word had come. Paul could go home tomorrow.

"I think it's going to be all right," Connie told her other children as she came in the door. "Paul will be home tomorrow, thank the Lord." She bustled through the living room, straightening as she went, spotting the little untidinesses by the light of the TV set. *"Jennifer, you've got to tell him. You can't let him think . . ."*

A hard rain had washed the street clear of children. The living room was loud with play. Connie smiled after Carla, who, released, went upstairs to do her hair. Russell had to check the windows upstairs. Then, in the basement, he turned on the water. He returned to the dining room and flopped into a chair, waiting for a bit of supper from Connie.

"Yeah, it'll be all right . . . for a while," he said wearily. It seemed to him that he was always tired. "It's like, over and over," he said. Often he dreamed, staring at nothing, and seeing . . . ? "Another life," he said. "I think about that a lot. I mean, if I had $2 million. Well, I'd probably give a million to the Lord, right away. But—I'll put it this way. The majority would go to the kids, right away, their education and then living expenses for when they grow up. Probably get a new house . . . and transportation . . . but right now, schools for the kids. And I know we'd take a vacation. That's something we haven't been able to do until now." He glanced up toward Connie, opening soup in the kitchen. "I think about it a lot," he said. "She doesn't like me to think that way. Calls it dreaming . . ."

But he dreams.

"Making it, I mean, making it wouldn't have to be all that," he said. "I just want to be successful, for my family to be comfortable, not to have to go without the necessities. Cause we've had to . . ." Connie put a bowl of soup in front of him. He looked up at her as if to say something, but she had turned back to the kitchen. ". . . To get clothes," he said, "to get the proper schooling for the kids, to have a few dollars in the bank. To be successful doesn't really mean rich, just to be current with the bills, not to rob Peter to pay Paul. . . . "We're making it, really. I mean, getting by. But we're making it poor."

He paused through a couple of spoonfuls of soup. And the dream pressed in on him again. "Man, a house with some land around it. Not a lot of land, but maybe two houses on my side of the street . . ." Connie came back with her own bowl of soup. Russell stopped talking of dreams. Thunder rolled over Myrtle Lane and the lightning crackled in the television's sound.

"Making it, to me . . .," Connie considered for a moment. "We're not just talking about money, right?"

She looked across the table at Russell. "When I have matured to the point where I can give everybody, Russell and the children, room to grow," she said. "When I can really accept Russell, as he is, and still love him. There's always a part of me that is trying to change him. . . . A lot of arguments we have, at those times, they could be my fault," she said. "If Russell comes in a little tipsy, or something . . . but if I'm humble, you know, submissive, and don't pick, he's usually pretty cool." Connie looked bashful, talking about Russell straight out, like that. Russell jumped in, maybe trying to help her out, perhaps with something he wanted to say. "The thing is," he said, "there's . . ."

A barrage of thunder overwhelmed all sound. The lights died. The TV set went blank. The house was tar black and, for a moment, strangely, perfectly silent. Then Andrea screamed. Rusty started calling, "Mom? Mom!"

"It's all right," their father called out. "Just be cool."

He started toward the stairs and the fusebox. Cathy came in from the street and said all the lights on the block were out. So Russell edged his way through the kitchen and felt in a cupboard for the candles. Three thick stubs were left from the time the electric company had shut off the lights. The children took a candle out on the steps, in view of the reassuring glow from the next block. Russell came back to the table. Now it was clear he had something to say.

"The thing is," he said, "there's a lot of things I was into that I knew I wanted to change, just to be worthy of her." He paused and looked at Connie through the candlelight. "My goal is to please her anyway." Now, he looked bashful. He pressed on. "The church. The church thing," he said, and this was what he wanted to say. "It's not a thing, well . . . I don't want her to worry. I don't want anybody to worry. I mean, well . . . It's not a thing where I will be gone for any length of time. I mean, I'll probably be back this week. Or maybe next week at the latest." He looked across at Connie again and saw her, silent, her face turned intently on him, glowing softly in the candle flicker. "Most probably this week," Russell said. Then, in the silence, the bashfulness got him and he said he thought he'd see how the kids were doing on the step.

Connie stayed quiet at the table. The house was so still. She shifted in her chair. "Mmm, no radio or anything," she said. Then, staring at her own hand playing in the candlewax, a little smile at the corners of her mouth, she said, "It's a lot of pain in growing. It's a lot of pain in growing strong in Christ. But if you see God, you really see God, he won't let you down. Russell's growing," she said, still staring into the flame. "That's what I meant when I said 'making it,' letting others grow. Even if I would do it a different way. . . .

"We've come a long way. The Lord has brought us a long way, even when we didn't know the Lord. . . . Uh-huh, it seems to have come a circle now, but it's not just over and over." Connie looked up and the little candle flames leapt up in her eyes. She said, "We're living. I feel good about today. And if the Lord wakes me up, tomorrow, I'll feel good."

The lights came on with a glare and the *Rockford Files* jumped into the room. A raucous cheer came from the steps, from Russell and the neighbors, who were sitting together. Was that the high tinkle of ice in short glasses? The children slammed in in a pack through the front door. The phone rang behind Connie and she turned to pick it up.

"Oh, hi," she said into the mouthpiece. "Did you see Dad?" Connie listened while her sister spoke on the other end of the wire. Carla was talking to her at the same time, asking permission to go for a ride. "What time can we go to see him tomorrow?" Connie said into the phone. She nodded silently to Carla, who turned and ran out the door. Rusty walked into the dining room asking for a sandwich. Connie cut short her talk with her sister and started on Rusty's peanut butter sandwich. She was humming a pretty little ribbon of gospel tune as she reached into the cupboard for the bread. Not until the following morning would she get the call telling her of her father's death. Outside, Carla slammed the car door behind her.

"Goodbye, boring people," she said.

Epilogue

Now, it is three months—no, longer—since Russell and Connie Monroe first found a reporter encamped on their doorstep, like a gas-man ("Should we answer?").

Now, Connie's father is buried.

Now, Russell is back at church.

Now, Paul, his burns healed, romps through the house with shouts of glee.

Now, Carla, her sins of tobacco and romance revealed in this story, hangs, bored to death, in the house, "on punishment."

Yes, the Monroes have seen this story, followed their progress and troubles on the page as once they pursued them alive and unrestricted (but watched) in real life. And here, too, life seemed paler. The story, cruel and unchangeable print, jumped out at them, upsetting, infuriating, unfair.

"We look awful."

"You got to change the names."

"Yeah, change the names."

"Isn't there a better word for welfare?" Russell said.

"I look like all I care about is money," Connie said.

"Why'd you *write* all that?" Carla said.

The reporter answered with his editor's words. The words don't sound as noble on Myrtle Lane. "Some feeling," he was saying, "for how

one family in West Philadelphia is making it in a hard summer, a
recession summer, you know, we're always writing about the middle class
and . . ."

What he meant (why can't he say this?) is that they, the Monroes,
these people we have called the Monroes, are a story, like those stories
on the color screen. Yes, there is connection here. Oh, the troubles in
those stories! But, in West Philadelphia (is this why?), troubles don't
take the weekends off. That's what Russell must have meant (it didn't
seem important at the time) when he said, "Hey, we're *in* it." There are
no more chapters, but this story goes on.

Author's Afterwords . . .

An editor had the idea that we were going to be in for a long hot
summer in the city and that we should be ready to write about it. We
decided I'd move in with a family for the summer. I called a lot of city
ministers and explained the story. It took a few weeks, but when I found
the Monroes, they seemed right. I moved into their house, literally
sleeping in their basement.

I was terribly alarmed that nothing would happen in their house for
days at a time. When you think about it, that's pretty much how life goes,
but I was frantic—there's nothing happening here! I'd done stories on
ordinary people in the Middle East to explicate the issues of the region,
but the exotica of their customs and religions could all be used to create
the feeling that something strange and wonderful was going on. But a
poor American family wasn't exotic. I would sit in their house and watch
soap operas with them. Ten days and I still didn't see a story.

But little by little, I saw that the story had to be like a soap opera.
It didn't have to be war and cataclysm. It had to be bite-sized bits of life
that connected one to the other. I often just lived out the evening with
them and then went downstairs and wrote out some notes. Everybody at
the paper thought I was nuts. The newsroom people were saying, "Good
luck, Cramer."

I'm a suburban kid and I had expected a lot of action on the street.
After all, the premise was "the long hot summer." But it was the slow,
slow summer. I saw that life in what we pigeon-hole as the ghetto wasn't

what we write about. If you thought life there was like you read about it in the newspapers, which is how I thought about it, you'd figure it was constant drive-by shootings. It's not like that at all. The story clicked when I went with Connie on her rounds to register for all these damned programs. I saw that this woman was doing high-level bureaucratic maneuvering just to get a bag of groceries. When I saw the actual texture of her life, I knew I had a story that never gets covered.

After awhile, I was just there. The hardest thing was not fixing stuff. Hell, Russell needs 20 bucks to take his family out on Independence Day. I needed all my power to not whip out a 20 and say, "Here, just do it." For god sakes, the little boy wants juice. I wanted to go get him a bottle of juice, but I couldn't.

When I sat down to write, it was a big mess. I thought I wanted to open with the soap operas, because TV was such a central part of their lives. It was only after noodling around during two all-nighters that I realized the beginning had to be about Russell and the job, because that's what was changing as I walked in the door. The second section had to be about Connie struggling with getting along. Once I figured that out, I had a story to write.

I would spend the day and into the evening with them until the kids would go to sleep. Then I'd jump in the car and go back to the office. I would write all night, go out for breakfast, and go back to their house and take a nap and start again. The story took about three weeks to write that way.

I had told the Monroes that I'd be a boarder in their house, but that I'd also write about the neighborhood. So when I told them it was going to be a story about them, they were a little freaked out. I just thought to be fair I had to show them the story. I wanted it all out on the table so I wouldn't feel like I had ripped anything off from them and switched signals and screwed them in the newspaper. I left it with them and came back the next day, and they were shaky. I'd used their real names.

I didn't want to ram the story down their throats, but I also didn't want to have worked for several months for nothing. So I said, "What if I change the names?" And they said, "Oh, that's fine." At the paper, they wanted the family's agreement for fear of violating their privacy. The lawyers were relieved when the family signed off as long as we didn't use their names.

When I read it years later, I don't like how choppy it is. But I like that it was an attempt to show what life was like for poor people. I like the spirit of the piece better than the execution. Although sometimes the words are not so pretty, I like that we took readers someplace they don't usually go.—R. B. C.

Mike Sager

Mike Sager has worked as a reporter for the *Washington Post* and written for numerous magazines, including *Esquire* and *Playboy*. He has been a contributing editor and columnist for *Rolling Stone* and is now a Writer-at-Large for *GQ*. He lives in Southern California.

Death in Venice

Lil' Gato and Tequila are hanging with Yogi, all three sitting on his bed. The room is dark, narrow, smoky. A towel is jammed against the bottom of the door.

"I forgot to tell you," says Yogi, "Big Gato called."

"Yeah?" says Lil' Gato.

"He asked what have we done to pay back Culver City."

"Pay 'em back for what?"

"You know, man. The drive-by at the park. Those *vatos* who shot at us."

Lil' Gato chews his thumb. He thinks. The TV screen flickers, the radio plays rap, a table fan moves air back and forth. After a minute, he knocks his girl, Tequila, on the knee. "When this happen?" he asks. Tequila's eyes pan slowly toward his face. She is wearing a necklace of hickeys, a black miniskirt, a pair of three-inch heels she bought two weeks ago on her 14th birthday. Her hair is shoulder length, crowned at the front with a stiff, thick pompadour four inches high, a tiara of bangs combed skyward and encased in Aqua Net. She blinks. She shrugs.

Some of the names and identifying details in this story have been changed.

Lil' Gato chews his thumb some more. The skin at the tip, just below the nail, is burned and crusty, a condition the homeboys call Bic thumb. Like Yogi, he is 19. He is wearing a nylon sweat suit and high-top Adidases. His hair is black, clipped short and oiled straight back from a widow's peak. His lashes are long and curly, his eyes are bloodshot, a front tooth is missing. He was arrested first when he was six, for stealing a TV from his grammar school. Last year, he was arrested 11 times for using heroin and two times for using PCP, a drug he likes because "when you do it, it be hard for you to walk and think."

As days in the neighborhood go, this one started off pretty well. At 10:00 this morning, Lil' Gato and Tequila ran into a crack dealer they know. He gave them some "love," free drugs, the dregs of last night's stash: a couple of $5 and $10 rocks and a lot of crumbs. They went immediately to Yogi's and smoked it all in 15 minutes. Now they need more. Especially Lil' Gato. Sitting on the edge of the bed, Lil' Gato is a ramrod. His mouth is pulled back in a tight grimace, and above his lip, among the faint stirrings of a mustache, are little drops of sweat. His teeth are clenched, and you can see the strain in the muscles of his jaw and in the cords of his neck, upon which is tattooed, in big blue letters, the logo of his gang, V-13. Lil' Gato plucks an ice cube from his glass. He holds it up, regards it in the light, turns it over, then over again.

"Wouldn't you like a rock this size?" he says.

"Yea-ah!" says Yogi.

"What would you say this was, a 50?"

"A righteous five-oh," says Yogi.

Lil' Gato loses himself in his daydream, and hope pops like a flashbulb in his eyes, and then the light recedes, and his attention drifts to the carpet. There are lots of little white pieces of paper and lint and cloth and cigarette ash down there. To him, each piece looks like a rock. Could be a rock. He has an urge to reach down with his index finger. He knows there are no rocks on the carpet; he's too methodical to have dropped anything, but it doesn't matter, because something strong makes him want to get down on his hands and knees on the filthy rug in the dark, narrow room and touch each little piece of paper and lint and cloth and ash and test its composition. There are no crumbs. He knows that, but it doesn't matter. Just a few minutes ago, he tried to smoke a sesame seed in a pipe made of aluminum foil.

"So what are we going to do about Culver City?" asks Yogi. "Big Gato say that if we down for the neighborhood, we got to pay them back."

Lil' Gato looks up from the floor. He's remembering something. The neighborhood. The gang. The tradition. He and Yogi are members of V-13, the Venice Gang, among the oldest of the 400 gangs in Los Angeles. Theirs is a gang with history. For more than 30 years, Chicano homeboys have claimed this neighborhood, one square mile of palm trees and poverty in the middle of Venice, California, a little piece of barrio in the heart of the California lifestyle. Ten years ago, when Yogi and Lil' Gato were just coming up, war was raging in the neighborhood; V-13 was battling all the gangs that surrounded it. The Venice gang fought the Shoreline Crips, Santa Monica, Culver City, anyone, everyone. In March 1979, the *Los Angeles Times* devoted a special section to the unrest in Venice, or more specifically in Oakwood, as their barrio is officially named. DEATH, DAILY VIOLENCE BECOME WAY OF LIFE FOR NEIGH-BORHOOD, said the lead headline, one of 12 screamers in the 12-page pullout. The Los Angeles police department's now-famous CRASH unit (Community Resources Against Street Hoodlums) cut its teeth here, back when it numbered 21 instead of the present 143. The National Guard walked the streets for a period, too, and a whole generation of Venice homeboys went to jail, or became addicted to heroin, or died.

These days, Venice still gets its CRASH sweeps, low-key Tuesday- and Thursday-night affairs, and the pop of automatic-weapons fire is still part of the everyday soundtrack of squealing tires, cursing homeboys, laughing children, thumping rap. But aside from Popo, the homeboy who lost his cool during a burglary and slit the throat of L.A. city councilwoman Ruth Galanter, Venice hasn't been in the news at all. South-Central L.A. is where the action is now. There, black gangs like the Bloods and the Crips have begun a reign of entrepreneurial terror that has turned the L.A. gang culture inside out. For 30 years, the poor and the powerless of Southern California have banded together in gangs to fight for the safety of their neighborhoods, for some measure of self-respect. In those days, the Chicanos owned the streets of L.A., and gangs like Venice were strong and proud. Today, everything is different. Gangs are no longer about turf and respect. Instead, they are about drugs and money.

Last year, there were 387 reported gang killings in Los Angeles County, a good many of them in the district called South Central, 60% of them claiming the lives of innocent bystanders. This year, according to the L.A. County Sheriff's Department, that total could rise to as many as 450. Following the death last January of a 27-year-old woman who was caught in the cross fire of a gang fight outside a tony restaurant in Westwood Village, the L.A. County Board of Supervisors appropriated $1.5 million to halt the epidemic of gang violence. Since then, the police have been working overtime, battering doors, arresting hundreds, seizing ounce after ounce of crack. The press, for its part, has made sure the public has kept in step along the way, providing bang-bang footage from a war where the front lines are America's own streets.

But behind the lines of the drug war, in the Venice barrio, crack is doing to V-13 what the police and the National Guard and other gangs have been trying to do for years. If horrible can get worse, that is what has happened to Venice. Spend time there, and what you see is the real raw footage, the daily pictures of lives being burned through a tinfoil tube.

The drive-by happened two nights ago, on Tuesday, at the park. Yogi and Lil' Gato and Tequila were there, and so were their friends Wormy and Linda and a couple other *vatos* and *heinas*. They were kickin' it, hanging out on a field behind Broadway Elementary, in the middle of their neighborhood, on their own turf. Someone had bought a *pisto*, a bottle of Colt 45, and someone had *yeska*, Mexican pot. Everyone was shermed out, high on *frios*, which are menthol cigarettes dipped in a bottle of liquid PCP. Some of them were shermed worse than others, and three or four of them were prone. Yogi and Lil' Gato and Panther were taking turns crouching behind a wall, doing blasts, taking hits of crack. Near midnight, Wormy had been smoking a *frio*, telling about the time, in jail, that he was stabbed in the head. After that, he began talking about his father, a white guy who is doing time in prison. When the *frio* was finished, he got quiet.

Then he went off. He smashed a bottle on the sidewalk, uttered incantations to the devil, danced around in the grass. Then he focused on the white guy who was with them. He stood over the guy and shook his fists and bellowed, "Prejudice!" over and over and over again. Then he got quiet.

All of a sudden, an old two-toned Chevy rattled out of the darkness toward the park. Shots. Six, seven, eight, nine, 10. Quick, loud pops from a .22-caliber semi. Bullets whizzed overhead. Yogi rolled on top of Linda.

Tequila gasped and rolled on top of Lil' Gato. Everyone else hit the dirt. Five seconds later it was over. They watched a single taillight recede from their territory.

"There go those motherfuckers from Culver City again!" said Wormy.

"Cheese eaters!" said Yogi.

"Uh-oh!" exclaimed Tequila, pointing across the field.

Big Gato. Approaching at a dead run, Gato is 27, an older homeboy, a leader. He's got a thick scar across his cheek, two bullet holes in his side, another in his shoulder. To this day, he carries a shotgun pellet in his penis. He calls it his Mexican Tickler. At the moment he's pissed.

"What the fuck was that, homes?" screamed Big Gato.

"Just some of those cheese eaters from Culver City," said Yogi.

"Those motherfuckers again!" screamed Big Gato. "They drivin' by your ass again? Why don't you do something? They disrespecting you, homes!"

Nobody said a word.

Gato shook his head, clenched his fists at his sides. Lately, he thinks, everything is fucked up in Venice, everything is changed. These younger homeboys know as well as he does that if someone disrespects you—if he calls you a name, if he mad-dogs you, if he owes you money, if he shoots at you, if he talks shit about your old lady, if he makes you angry about anything at all—there is only one thing you're supposed to do. You get your gun, you hunt him down, you cap him. Or, if you can't find him, you cap one of his homeboys. You don't drive by. That's for cheese eaters. That's something new. For years Venice and Culver City have been shooting each other, but it was always done face to face. Those have always been the rules: never do you shoot from a car, never do you shoot at a house, never do you jeopardize children, moms or dads. A few years ago, one of the Venice homeboys shot into a church and killed a mom and a child from Culver City. As soon as they heard, the Venice homeboys beat up the *vato*, banished him from the neighborhood. Now Big Gato surveyed the youngsters before him. He spit on the ground.

"Somebody better do something soon."

Since 1900, when "Venice of America" was built, complete with canals, as a sort of residential theme park by the beach, the Oakwood section has been poor and predominantly nonwhite, one of the few ghettos of its kind along the pricey Southern California coast. By 1970, according to U.S.-census figures, Oakwood's population of 8,000 was 43% black, 33% Latin and 46% white. By 1975, Latins were up to 46% as workers from Mexico, both documented and illegal, began to swell across the borders and into Venice, drawn north by the promise of good pay and plentiful jobs in restaurants and light industry. Today the population is about 9,000. Almost 50% is Chicano.

The neighborhood claimed by V-13 is a ramshackle collection of bungalows with front and back yards, most with several big American cars, in various states of repair, in the driveway, and maybe an old stove dumped around the side, and walls covered with graffiti, the stylized markings of the gang and the male occupants of the house.

The insides of the houses are tidy, the furnishings cheap but clean. The TV is always on. Horror, action, gang movies play on the VCR. Usually a house has a big living room with lots of sofas and chairs, and a kitchen near that, and an iron skillet of beans on the stove, some tortillas on the table. Every other room, including the back porch, is used as a bedroom. Typically, four or five generations of relatives live in one house. Great-grandma's daughter and her daughter will share one bedroom. Grandma and an orphan great-niece will share another. A high-ranking daughter—the one with the best job—will have a room to herself. A young couple will also have a room. If they have a small child, the child will sleep with the ranking female, usually his grandma, who is usually a woman of about 34. The females of the clan share an elaborate network of responsibilities. Everyone cooks, cleans, takes care of the kids. Young couples have the fewest responsibilities. They are encouraged to sleep alone, to sleep late, to make more kids.

Inside the house, the women run things. Grandma or Great-grandma holds the lease and heads the house, and all the women work, many off the books so they can still collect from the government. Because the homeboys live at the pleasure of their wife or girlfriend's mother or grandmother and because many have no job and no intention of getting one, they are, in the sense of family ranking, pretty low in the pecking order. They do as they're told and are treated not so differently from the children.

Maybe this is why honor, their own particular brand of honor, has always been so important to the homeboys of Venice, and maybe this is why Big Gato is so upset about the lack of action on the part of the youngsters. Until recently, the homeboys never considered themselves a gang. Gang was something the police called them, something the newspapers called them. To themselves, they were, have always been, just a neighborhood: people who live in a place where they've lived all their lives, where a lot of their parents have lived all their lives. It doesn't matter that they own not an acre or a brick or a stucco wall. To some 4,100 Chicanos in Oakwood, this one square mile is their village, their home, their world, a society within society.

Here in the barrio, most everyone knows everyone, and they have known one another from the time they were born. So when somebody disrespects the neighborhood, when somebody from Culver City hits Lutie's mom on the head with a bumper jack or takes a knife to Beaver, or a bat to Tavo, or shoots Sleeper in the back, well, then the neighborhood is supposed to make sure that somebody from Culver City is bumper-jacked or knifed or clubbed or shot. It is the job of the men to protect the honor of the neighborhood; they have to be, as they say, down for the 'hood.

Lately, the youngsters like Yogi and Lil' Gato have been forgetting this. Culver City—a longtime rival gang of Chicanos who live in the government projects nearby—has taken potshots at Venice two or three times in the last 10 days. The youngsters have done nothing to pay them back. If young homies like Yogi and Lil' Gato are going to claim the neighborhood, call themselves members, they must, as Big Gato says, be willing to bust a grape. That is the tradition. Back in the '70s, there were no questions about what should be done.

"I remember the Venice from when I was gang banging," says Marianne Diaz, 29, an outreach worker with Community Youth Gang Services Project, a county- and city-funded program that works to defuse gang tensions and rehabilitate members. Diaz is a former member of Compadres, another Chicano gang in Los Angeles. "Venice is such a big, old gang. Even back then they had, like, maybe 1,000 homeboys. They were down. People respected them. Venice, Lennox, South Los and 18th Street. Those were your four big gangs. Everyone has heard of Venice. I mean, if you got busted, you were gonna see 20 or 30 of them down in the pen, and they were the ones running things. Just about every older Venice homeboy I meet is a *veterano.*"

In Venice, just about every homeboy over 15 has been to jail, which is why, perhaps, the chance for anything resembling a better life pretty much evaporates while he's still young. He figures the system is against him, and no one wants to give him a chance, and anyway, he might die tomorrow. Lil' Gato has done a total of four years so far; Yogi is about to go off and serve one. Oddly, many *veteranos* went to jail for crimes they didn't commit. As one has said, "I figured I'd already done about 30 or 40 burglaries, so they had to get me for one of them, even if I didn't do it." Being respected for going to jail is only one aspect of a curious system of beliefs in Venice. It seems as if the social stigma that most of America attaches to things like killing, going to jail and being addicted to drugs is not attached to such things here.

Take the Gonzales family. A Saturday night in the living room with popcorn and a video, the adults, the kids. Three people in the room are nodding out from heroin, somebody is smoking *yeska,* and the daughter's boyfriend and his friends are running in and out from the back yard, doing crack. Nobody pays much attention. Great-grandma looks up from the video. She laughs, "Oh, Thumper. I know you are doing that shit again," she says. "You are sprunger than a motherfucker! Oh, ho, ho, ho, ho!"

Of course, the homeboys' parents disapprove—they wring their hands, they wonder what they can do about their wayward kids. But in the end, it seems their actions speak more of loyalty than of disapproval. Over the years, one 27-year-old homeboy's father, a $22,000-a-year city employee, has borrowed $40,000 to bail out and defend his son for various crimes. Another's father took a week off from work to help his son kick his heroin habit.

As a homeboy gets older, however, chances are he learns to like being out of jail. By the time he's 25, if he lives that long, he's slowed down considerably. Some homeboys get jobs—in city sanitation, city maintenance, city deliveries, the best shots for ex-cons. Almost all have children, and they value the lives they've created, so they're not going to go shoot anyone unless they really get mad.

So now it's up to the younger homeboys. Times being what they are—with gang membership in L.A. County estimated at 70,000, with gangs of Samoans and Asians and blacks and whites and peewees and wanna-bes and never-bes running around the streets packing semiautomatic weapons—the younger homeboys have a big load on their shoulders. They haven't been carrying it.

As Diaz says, "The older homeboys are saying that the younger homeboys, all they care about is getting high. They're telling them, 'You like to wear Venice on your hat, you like to write your name on the walls and throw up a hand sign and get tattoos all over your body, but you won't bust a grape for nobody.' "

In the '40s and '50s, says Diaz, the Chicano gangs that emerged in Southern California were "more or less derived from the Hispanic culture." Descendants of the Mexican *banditos,* and later of the zoot suiters, they inherited a macho culture dedicated to the preservation of territory and respect. "Now," says Diaz, "things are changing. The rock cocaine has come in, and the blacks have taken over the gang thing. My partner—and he's black—says, 'My people took your ideas and totally bent it and turned it around and took away any of the pride or the respect that was in a gang.' That's what he says. It's like before, in the old days, the leader of a gang was the homeboy who was downest. Now it's the homeboy who is richest. Other things are more important now than the 'hood. Getting high. Staying high. Getting that rock. That rock."

"PSSSSST. PSSSSSSST!"

Yogi starts. His eyes go wide. "What was that?" he whispers.

"What?" asks Lil' Gato.

"That noise," says Yogi. He eases off the narrow bed, stands, turns down the radio, switches off the fan, cocks an ear.

"What noise?" asks Lil' Gato.

"Pssssst! Hey! Yogi! Yogi! Let me in!"

Yogi looks up, pulls back the curtain on the window over his bed. Outside there is daylight. The palms rustle in the breeze, and into the room come the scents of blue sea and pink hydrangeas, of refried beans and the exhaust from old Chevys. Panther is outside. He holds up a $20 rock the size of a marble. Homeboys are all the time trooping into Yogi's, especially members of the Little Banditos, a 12-member *cliqua* within the V-13 gang, which numbers roughly 300. A *cliqua* is an age-affinity group of homies who were all jumped into the larger gang at the same time. Currently in the 'hood, there are *cliquas*—of homeboys from their early teens to their late 20s—called the Banditos, the Little Banditos, the Tiny Banditos and the Midget Banditos. Likewise there are *cliquas* of Locos, Winos, Chucos and Dukes, all of them with subgroups ranging from Midgets to Bigs.

At any rate, when the Little Banditos come by, they check first with Yogi at the window, then go around the front and knock politely at the door, enter, exchange pleasantries with Yogi's mom and grandfather and little sister in the front room, then head down the hallway to the back room, where Yogi spends all his time. Yogi's mom thinks they're watching television back there, at least that's what Yogi says. In the last month, since he got his tax-refund check (he did some gardening for his uncle's company last summer), Yogi has not been away from his room for longer than an hour. That's what happens when you do crack, and at the moment, that is what Yogi and Panther and Lil' Gato are getting ready to do.

"I get first hit!" calls Yogi.

"No, I do!" says Panther. "It's my rock."

"Yeah," says Yogi, "but it's my room."

Panther hands over the rock, and Yogi breaks it with a razor blade, then puts a piece the size of a small aquarium stone into a tinfoil tube. He melts it a little with a Bic lighter, and then he blows out the air in his lungs and takes a blast. He inhales, holds, exhales. It is light, clean smoke that smells like ether. Yogi sits back, closes his eyes. Lil' Gato takes the pipe from his hand, then he and Panther begin to argue over who's next.

Meanwhile, Yogi hears nothing. As soon as he exhales, there is an instant explosion of pleasure inside his head, a rush, he says, that drills a hole from the top of his scalp down to his groin and another between his ears, a kind of ecstatic, physical, electric sign of the cross. He hears a buzz in his brain, his sight blurs, he smiles. Then, after a minute or so, the smile recedes, the feeling goes. He begins thinking about the next hit.

The next hit. One more hit. That's all he can think about, all he cares about. His teeth clench, his jaw muscles stand, his throat tightens. Everything inside tightens. His dick shrivels, his veins constrict, his heart pounds. He chainsmokes cigarettes.

The problem is that with each subsequent hit, the rush is less intense but the desire is more intense. It's like a heroin habit, except you acquire it instantly instead of over weeks or months. Heroin is a twice-a-day obligation. You fix morning and night and forget about it. Crack, though, is moment to moment. You hit it, rush, think about getting more. It doesn't last that long. If you could wait 30 minutes and forget about it, it could be all over; you'd be straight again. But you can't *not* think about it. Your every thought is focused on the next hit, and the next hit is never very good, but you don't care. You get, as they say around here, *sprung*.

"So what are we gonna do?" asks Yogi, sitting on the bed in his narrow room. It is just about noon, and the drugs are gone, again. Panther has left to try and get some money some *vato* owes him.

"Let's go get a rock," says Lil' Gato.

"You got any money?"

"No."

"You do so."

"I do not."

"You do so."

The way you get a rock in the neighborhood is you walk out of your house, turn left or right. Day or night, you can buy rock cocaine from men or women, boys or girls, on the corners, in the alleys, in windows of houses, in apartment buildings, in classic cars, in sports cars, in Cadillacs, on bicycles, on front porches. The dealers don't use cute little glassine packages here. They sell the *pedasos*, the rocks, loose. They stash them in their socks, in their hands, in bags and beneath their tongues, a place the cops haven't learned yet to look.

There is constant commerce, and the curbside dealers range from businesslike slickers with theme songs ("I'm Billy D.!/ You stick with me!") to skinny, skinny rockheads, who by 6:00 in the morning are walking around like extras from *Night of the Living Dead*, trying to sell another rock to go score more. Drive into Venice to buy at this time of day, a time that the neighborhood is usually crowded with *gavachos*, white people, in their nice rides, and the rock creatures come staggering and rushing out from the curbs, sticking their hands inside the car, jockeying and fending for position, vibrating, clenching, exhorting, "Take mine!" "Me!" "I got you!"

Most of the dealers are *miatas*, blacks, members of the Shoreline Crip gang. The Shorelines coexist in the square mile of turf that is claimed by the Chicanos of V-13. There is a truce here now, but Big Gato remembers the days when things were different. He moved here with his parents from Arizona when he was a baby, and he doesn't remember a time when there weren't *cholos,* gang members, in the neighborhood. But, he says, things really began heating up in the '70s, when he was in his prime.

"Nineteen seventy-seven was the first I remember somebody getting killed that I knew," he says. "And then soon there were, like, 10, 12 shootings a week. I mean, when we walked down the street, we carried a gun. We wore the whole outfit, the khakis and the Pendletons, the hairnets, the bandannas, the hats, the overcoats, the whole bit. We was clean, five creases in every shirt, and we ironed them ourselves. Between me, my brother and my father, we used to go through two cans of spray starch a week. I sometimes carried a 12-gauge under my overcoat. And when we saw a car come with an open window, we automatically ducked. It was like the wild, wild West, man. You'd have homeboys on the roof, homeboys behind the trees, guns everywhere. For a while, the National Guard had the streets barricaded. You couldn't get in except by police escort. The fire department, if a house got burned, they wouldn't go in until sunrise. It was up to you to put it out. That was a bad time, homeboy. A hell of a war. We was little, but we was down, homeboy, wasn't nobody meaner."

And so it went in Venice, and by 1979 the media figured out that there was a gang problem by the sea, and in March the *Los Angeles Times* did its special report. There were stories of stray bullets, innocent victims, grieving mothers, shattered lives and midnight death. The trouble in Oakwood, read a subhead on the front page, followed by this summation: "Swept by smog-free ocean breezes, bordered on the south by the affluent playground called Marina del Rey . . . Oakwood is a strangely incongruous center of poverty and tragedy. While crime and gang violence tear at the community from within, mounting coastal real-estate values threaten to crush it from without."

If this all sounds familiar, sounds like newspaper articles being written today, nine years later, it is because, to an outside eye at least, things are pretty much the same. But if you listen to Big Gato and the older homeboys, if you look around, you see that things have changed as the drugs have changed. In the old days, *chiva* and PCP were the drugs of choice in the neighborhood. *Chiva* is slang for "goat" in Spanish. In Venice, *chiva* is heroin. Black, gummy Mexican tar. When *chiva* was the thing, a lot of the Chicanos were doing business, and not just the homeboys, either. One woman, the head of a household who works as a secretary for a Century City law firm, used to bankroll a small-time heroin operation that was run by her daughter and her son-in-law. In those days, it was the Chicanos with the cars and the money and the guns.

In the last few years, however, since crack came to the 'hood, the *miatas* have been in control. If you forget about Rock, a greedy, small-time dealer who's currently in jail, you find that unlike the Chicano homeboys in Culver City and Lennox, Venice homeboys don't sell crack. Many, however, smoke it, and homeboys like Yogi and Lil' Gato and dozens of others do it every day. Because they don't work and don't have any money, every day is the same. In the morning, grown men go beg their mothers or their old ladies for $5 or $10. They say they have to get a new driver's license or use some other official-sounding excuse. Or they say they need a new asthma inhaler or some other small, expensive thing that they can rip off and produce later to back up their story. Scam done, they buy two hits. They do those two hits, then immediately start scamming to get more. Sometimes they can get a *miata* to kick them down to a free rock.

If they can't get any love, the homeboys look around for something to sell. Many have sold their tools and their father's tools. There are great deals floating around Venice at 3:00 in the morning. Whole automotive tuneup kits for under $50. VCRs for $25. Many in Venice have even sold their guns, which is probably another reason that the Venice homeboys have been doing less capping lately. You can get a .22-caliber semiautomatic Ruger rifle for the price of a dove, which is what they call a $20 rock.

If they can't find something of value to sell, homeboys may go do a crime, perhaps a burglary or a robbery, but for the most part crimes take too long, and when you're sprung, as they say, any time is too long. Faster to scam $10 from your old lady. This is what crack does to you, and this, more than anything else, is the reason for change in the neighborhood. Proud Venice is slipping. Other neighborhoods are disrespecting, and no one can bring himself to do anything about it.

Today, thanks to crack, the homeboys have nothing left. In the old days, no matter how bad all the killing was, at least the homeboys had self-respect; that, any social worker will agree, is something to work from. Today the young homeboys are down for nothing. Nothing, that is, besides rock.

"The worst thing about it," says Joe Alarcon, a former Lennox gang member who now works for Youth Gang Services, "is that at this point we don't have much to offer Venice. The real problems are in South Central. Down there we're getting, like, five homicides a week. The black areas are really bad. On a daily basis, something like 85 to 90% of all crimes are being committed by Bloods and Crips. Those guys are crazy; they don't care. As far as everybody sees things right now, the Hispanic gangs like Venice are not a big problem. Because our resources are limited, we have to concentrate on the areas that are the worst. We kind of have to let Venice fall through the cracks."

"Really, now," says Lil' Gato, "how much *fedia* you got?"

"Two dollars."

"I got two, too," says Lil' Gato. Really, he has five. "You got any *fedia*?" Lil' Gato asks Tequila.

Tequila leans back and works three crumpled dollar bills out of the front pocket of her mini. She holds them up.

"Well, we got six," says Lil' Gato.

"Seven," says Yogi.

"What?"

"Seven. We got seven. Two, two and three. Seven."

Just now they hear footsteps coming down the hall, down the steps. A hard knock. Yogi rockets to the door. He leans his sweaty nose to the crack, then asks, sweetly, "Who's there?"

"Me, motherfucker!"

Big Gato!

Yogi and Tequila trade looks. Lil' Gato's eyes bulge. The time has come. He has to answer to Big Gato. Five years ago, when Lil' Gato was still known as David, he went one day to Big Gato and asked if he could have his name. Gato was honored. Gato was willing. But there was a problem. Another homeboy was already calling himself Lil' Gato, though as it turned out, he was a cheese eater. If David wanted the handle for himself, Gato told him, he would have to earn it. David beat up the guy and took his name. Thereafter, he was known as Lil' Gato. And therefore he owed allegiance to Big. Yesterday, the day after the drive-by at the park, Big Gato called his namesake out of Yogi's. This is what he told him: "Look, homeboy, I been thinkin'. We can't have Culver City disrespecting us. We can't have that, *ese*. No, you do something, or I'm gonna have to. And if I have to, you're fucked, homeboy. You hear me, homeboy? You're fucked." Now Big Gato is here to get the report, and Lil' Gato has nothing to say. He chews his thumb. He looks at Yogi.

"Open the door," Lil' Gato says.

"So what have you got to tell me?" asks Big Gato.

"What?" says Lil' Gato.

"What you mean, 'What?' You done anything yet?"

"I ain't gonna do nothing," says Lil' Gato.

"We ain't gonna do nothing," repeats Yogi.

Tequila shrugs.

Big Gato looks at them in disbelief. He stares for a minute. A full minute. Then he explodes. "You got shot at the other day, homeboy! You got shot at three times in the last week. Do I have to go mess with those motherfuckers myself? Is there something wrong with you? Are you peeing in your pants? Are you fucked up or what?"

"Why should I do anything?" asks Lil' Gato. He shrugs.

Yogi shrugs.

Tequila shrugs.

A few moments pass. Big Gato stares. His mouth is pulled back in a tight grimace, and above his lip are little drops of sweat. His teeth are clenched, and you can see the strain in the muscles of his jaw. Then his eyes drift to the carpet. There are lots of little white pieces of paper and lint and cloth and cigarette ash down there. To him, each piece looks like a rock. Could be a rock.

"Gimme a blast," says Big Gato.

"We was just going to get a 10 from Binky," says Yogi.

"A 10?" says Big Gato. He chews his thumb. He thinks. "A 10?"

"Yeah," says Yogi, warming. "We were gonna go get a 10."

"Well, go get it," says Big Gato.

"What about Culver City?" asks Tequila.

"Culver City?" asks Big Gato. "Oh. We'll get them later."

Author's Afterwords . . .

By the time I wrote this story, I felt like I'd spent years in the ghetto interpreting minority subculture for white readers. It started with night police at the *Washington Post* when they'd send me out to talk to the mothers of murdered 15-year-old boys, and I'd say, "Sorry to bother you at a time like this, but . . ."

The Venice Beach piece is taking it all way out there. It's full of information both observed and researched through books, articles, novels and movies, although I tend to do the background research after I've been to the scene. I don't want to be shaped by anyone else's views. I find that most reporting isn't done in-depth enough. I always come back to my favorite line from *Absence of Malice* in which the subject tells the reporter she has ruined his life with a story that was accurate but not true.

Gangs and crack were just starting and the reportage was coming out of the ghetto by people who'd run in and get a quote and run out before dark. They painted these people as a lower species of human, people who had no feelings, no familial ties, no reason for being. Just drugs and guns and degradation. The stories didn't have the feeling you get when you stand at a street corner waiting for the light to change and you look around and remind yourself that each of these people has a complex interwoven life with family and friends and things that are important to them and systems of belief and gossamer rationalizations.

That's the approach I take. While the ghetto is a scary place, there are also human beings living there. I approach people in the ancient Oriental fashion, with my palms pressed prayerfully together before my forehead and my eyes averted, and I say, "Teach me about your world. You are the master of your world. I am but a guest." You must park your educated, judgmental, holier-than-thou, insecure self in the car.

People have called me a method writer, and in a way I am. These guys had no money and I did. So I declared myself bankrupt and went, as the homeboys say, to the curb. I allowed myself no money for food or cigarettes. I have a pack-a-day habit, and before long I was looking on the floor for quarters and butts and bumming cigarettes. If I wanted to eat, I did what the homeboys did, I showed up at somebody's house around dinner time.

After four days, I actually remember looking at some white people on the street and thinking, "I could rob those mothers and take their money and then I'd have money." For one second, I could feel myself considering it. I wasn't trying to *be* these gang guys, but I was trying to feel something of what it's like to be them, what it's like to be inside their skins.

The biggest fault of journalism isn't getting a quote wrong. It's judging people without looking deeply enough at them. If you can subvert your ego to the lives of others for a period of time to realize that their pain or joy is something like this other pain or joy that you've felt before, then maybe you can make readers understand them. That's the goal.

I wasn't obtrusive when I hung out with these guys. I spent 75% of my time just watching. Then I sat them down and talked specifics I figured I might use in my story. I asked stupid things, and I warned them that I would, told them what's normal to them wasn't normal to me. "What kind of shoes are those Tequila has on? They're new to me." It was all done in a familiar, natural way. I always tell young journalists to be better people than they are. *Listen!* Don't be Mr. Columbia J. School Grad. Be yourself.

When you write, you have to make the leap. You mull it all over for a day or two, leave your notes in the other room and start writing. See what leaps out, let the story appear to you. Let your subjects become characters in a drama you are creating.

What really happened in the soap opera of these people's lives? Well, here's these guys who are supposed to go on a drive-by shooting because this other gang has disrespected them. They can't because they're all on crack and can't get their business straight. That became not only metaphor, but theme and story line. In 20 years of doing this, theme and metaphor and story have always come together. They have to. Meaning is implicit in human experience. But you have to be ready to see it, to receive it.

You have to get out from under the material, shed the craft long enough to see the story and let it flow from your head and heart out through your fingers. The key is to get your tools honed to such an extent that the tools do their job without too much thought. Then your head is freed to do its job. Master technique and then listen to your heart. You don't need just brains, but guts—a visceral feeling for subjects. And you have to have confidence enough in yourself and the process to know that if you throw yourself into a story, something will come out of it.—M. S.

Walt Harrington

Walt Harrington has worked as a staff writer for the *Allentown Morning Call* and the *Washington Post Magazine*. He is the author of *American Profiles* (1992), *Crossings: A White Man's Journey Into Black America* (1993) and *At the Heart of It* (1996). He is a Professor of Journalism at the University of Illinois at Urbana-Champaign.

True Detective

A man goes 22 years without being afraid, without giving his own death a glance, without worrying that the map of the city's criminal ways and rhythms that he has always carried in his head might be obsolete. A man goes 22 years climbing the ladder from beat cop to blue-boy elite, to homicide detective. A man goes 22 years to earn a reputation as a "90%er"—a detective who puts the souls of nearly all his victims to rest by closing the book on their murders. A man goes 22 years, and then the waters he inhabits shift and roil with unpredictable currents, until murder isn't murder anymore, isn't a biblical sentence that friends and lovers and fathers and sons impose on each other in storms of rage and recrimination. A man goes 22 years and finds himself leaning casually over a corpse on Halley Terrace in Southeast Washington, D.C., about to be made aware. That man—Detective Victor "V. I." Smith—flips back the dead man's coat and sees a blue-black machine gun, an Uzi, cocked and ready to fire.

Detective V. I. Smith is fearless, at least his police buddies think he's fearless. He has waltzed into Barry Farms, one of the roughest housing projects in Washington, at 4:00 in the morning, disappeared for an hour and returned with his suspect in tow. He has raided crack houses alone, lined up the drug heads and sweated them for reconnaissance on the spot. V. I.'s cop friends can't imagine him being afraid of anything. But tonight, after Halley Terrace, V. I. talks and talks about his shock at seeing that Uzi. About how six of his last seven murder victims have been packing guns. He doesn't reveal it to his comrades, but V. I. realizes that for the first time in 22 years as a Washington cop, he was afraid. Oh, maybe he'd been afraid before and hadn't realized it, imagined his feeling was excitement or readiness or the flow of adrenaline. But there's no mistaking or denying the emotion that surged through V. I. Smith on Halley Terrace tonight: It was fear.

Two years later . . . everything squeaks. The heavy doors squeak. The metal swivel chairs squeak. The drawers in the metal desks squeak. The file drawers squeak. The keys of the old manual upright squeak. The room—No. 5058, dubbed Homicide North because it is isolated two floors above D.C.'s other homicide offices in the city's Municipal Center—is a concerto of squeaks. Its other noises—the hollering voices, the clamoring phones, the electric typewriters, *Gilligan's Island* laugh-tracking on the beat-up TV, the two coffeepots spitting mud, the hand-held walkie-talkies belching static—all add layer upon layer of volume, creating finally a kind of jangled symphony.

What will stop this din and turn the entire room of nine men prayerfully silent are three words their ears are tuned to as if they were set on a private frequency: "stabbing" or "shooting" or "homicide." When the police radio dispatcher speaks any of these words, everything stops, hands reach for tiny volume knobs on radios and everybody waits. Usually, it's a false alarm and, just as abruptly, the noise once again envelops the momentary silence like a stadium cheer after the crack of a long ball.

The men in Homicide North are tonight "on the bubble"—cop talk meaning that their squad of detectives is on call to investigate the city's next murder. Detective Jeff Mayberry, a short, wiry, close-cropped, jet-propelled 34-year-old in a tight blue sports coat, is riding the top of the bubble in his rotation as lead investigator on whatever horror is next offered up from the bowels of the city. He has ridden the bubble aloft for four duty days now—and no murder. At least none on his 3-to-11 shift.

"You believe it?" he asks in frustration. No murder in a town that sees almost four murders every three days!

"You're bad luck," comes the rejoinder of his partner, Joe Fox, a respected and bearded 41-year-old bear of a detective who has a compulsive squint that constantly edges his wire-rimmed glasses up the bridge of his nose. He is called neither "Joe" nor "Fox." He is called "Joefox."

"Screw you, Joefox," Mayberry says.

Seated at the end of a row of desks in a corner under a wash of fluorescent light in front of pale curtains that hang off their track is V. I. Smith, looking out of place in this seedy domain. At age 46, he's quiet and self-contained, talking softly into the receiver of the old phone atop his desk, which isn't unkempt like most of the others. He's chatting with a woman who lives on W Street NW. She has been peeking out her window tonight to see if the drug boys V. I. wants to bust and shake down for tips about a recent murder are hanging on the street. They aren't.

Leaning on his elbows at his desk, talking into the phone, V. I. looks less like a tough city cop than, say, a prosecuting attorney or an FBI agent. He's 6' 4". Naked on the scale, he goes a trim and powerful 230, only 10 pounds over the weight he carried as a freshman basketball star at Howard University nearly three decades ago.

His face is wide and handsome, chiseled. It smiles rarely. In temperament, V. I. is terminally cool, never nervous or edgy. The more excited he gets, the more deliberately he speaks. And the more deliberately he speaks, the more trouble whomever he's speaking to is probably in. Even V. I.'s laugh is deliberate, with each "hah" in his slow "hah-hah-hah" being fully enunciated. In dress and style, he resembles a new-breed jazz player: His hair and mustache are short and neat, his shirt is crisp, his tie is knotted tightly and never yanked loose at his neck, and his suit, usually bought at Raleighs, is always well-tailored and never cheap. Unlike some of his detective pals, V. I. would never wear brown shoes with a blue suit. He dresses to the nines because, having grown up on the streets of black Washington, he knows that a man who dresses well is ascribed a dose of respect in that world, and every small advantage counts, especially these days.

The guys in the office call V. I. "the Ghost," because they rarely know what he's doing from minute to minute. With his reputation as one of Washington's best homicide detectives, V. I. comes and goes at Room 5058 pretty much as he pleases. But if the radio calls out a murder, he's on the scene, appearing as if from nowhere, like an apparition. Of Washington's 65 homicide detectives, V. I. Smith figures he's the only one without a regular partner. That's because Joefox, who came with V. I. to homicide seven years ago on the same cold Tuesday in February, used to be his partner, until the green and gung-ho Mayberry arrived from uniform four years ago and was assigned to Joefox for diapering.

Joefox and V. I. eventually took the kid aside and told him how it was going to be: The three of them would be partners, meaning that any one man's case was also the case of the other two. If Mayberry listened and studied and showed respect, he would learn the art and science of unraveling the darkest of human behaviors from two of the masters. And that's how it came down, with Mayberry now a fine detective in his own right. So when Mayberry is riding the bubble, Joefox and the Ghost are riding with him.

When the bubble seems to burst tonight, it's no thriller. A man named Willis Fields, who lived in a Washington boarding house, died at the Washington Hospital Center burn unit today, and the death was passed on to Detective C. J. Thomas, whose job it is to investigate and certify natural deaths. But in the hospital file he discovered that the 56-year-old man had told a nurse that "they" had poured alcohol on him and set him afire. Willis Fields was in the hospital 10 days, but his story fell through the cracks. Nobody called the police about his allegation, which means the inquiry will start nearly two weeks cold, no leads, only an address.

"C. J., why is it every one a these things you do, you always get us?" asks Mayberry. "Remember that guy on Suitland Parkway? Been there two years? Six shots to the head?"

"And what did you tell me?" C. J. asks.

"Man, that's a natural!"

"Well, here we go," says V. I., in his smooth, lyrical baritone as he palms a radio, unconsciously pats his right breast coat pocket for evidence of his ID wallet, pats his left breast coat pocket for evidence of his notebook and heads out the door in his athlete's saunter, a stylized and liquid stroll, a modern cakewalk.

The address for Willis Fields is wrong—2119 11th St. NW is a vacant lot. "They probably got it turned around," V. I. says, as the threesome mills about the grassy lot, looking lamely around, shrugging. It's just before dusk and the hot summer day has begun to cool, but except for a man staring at them intently from the sidewalk in front of the Soul Saving Center Church of God across the street, the block is empty of people, quiet. V. I. knows this neighborhood. He spent years living nearby as a kid, attending Garnet-Patterson Junior High over at 10th and U streets, Bell High School at Hiatt Place and Park Road and Cardozo High just up the hill at 13th and Clifton streets. This block of 11th Street isn't Beverly Hills, but it's a stable block that doesn't fit V. I.'s image of the crime at hand. An old man is more likely to be set on fire on a block where guys hang out drinking liquor, where there's a lot of street action. He nods down the road. That sounds more like the block back at 11th and U, with a corner market and a liquor store nearby. Sure enough, when the office checks the address the detectives were given, it's wrong. Willis Fields lived at 1929—near the corner of 11th and U.

Being in his old neighborhood makes V. I. nostalgic. As a boy, he seemed to live everywhere in Washington—Southeast, Northeast, here in North-west, as his mother and father struggled and moved up from dumpy apartment to less dumpy apartment. Sometimes, he and his brothers sacked out four to a mattress. But in the '50s, V. I.'s daddy—a laborer by day, a cabby by night—bought a big old house on Adams Street in LeDroit Park, near First and W streets Northwest, and the kids finally slept two to a room.

The man who grew up to be a cop was no choirboy. He didn't worry about his grades, he cut classes to play basketball, he learned to palm loaded dice, he hustled pool. By age 16, V. I. was frequenting the now defunct Birdland and Rio nightclubs on 14th Street with his older buddies. And it was at one such club that his friend Jimmy got killed. They were hanging with a fool of a friend, who flipped his cigarette butt toward the bar and hit a dude in the neck. When the guy flicked out the narrow blade with the pearl handle, everybody scrambled, but Jimmy didn't scramble fast enough. He took the knife deep in his back, stumbled outside and bled out his life on the sidewalk.

After that, V. I. was more judicious about the company he kept. A lot of guys he hung with eventually went bad in the ways kids went bad in those days—stealing purses, robbing people on the street. But not V. I. For some reason—maybe because his daddy was so strict—V. I. was always afraid of the police. While other guys figured the cops would never catch them, V. I. figured the cops would always catch him.

One incident had frightened him good: A woman was raped in his neighborhood, and the police rounded up anybody on the street close to the rapist's description and took them to the old 10th Precinct. V. I. sat in a holding room until 3:00 a.m., when the cops told him he could go home—they'd caught their man. That night made V. I. a believer in the "wrong place, wrong time" theory of city life. A guy had to think ahead, anticipate, cut trouble off at the pass, stay off the streets and away from guys bound for infamy. Or go down, too.

After a stint in the military, after attending Howard University, after becoming a basketball celebrity on the playgrounds of Washington and before graduating from American University, V. I. was sworn in as one of the city's early black cops. Only a few days later, he attended the funeral of a boyhood friend, a kid nicknamed Porgy, a kid V. I. had learned to avoid. Porgy had graduated from purses to stickups, and he was killed in a gun battle with police. Almost 25 years later, V. I. has never stopped believing that with a few unlucky breaks, a few poor choices, he, too, could have gone down the toilet like Porgy. To this day, he can arrive on a street corner and find a young man who has just bled out his life on the sidewalk, and think: *But for the grace of God* . . .

At 1929 11th St., nobody answers the door. So the detectives spread out and canvass the street, talking to neighbors. They have the office run the license plates of nearby parked cars, checking for the name Willis Fields. When an elderly man walks into the yard at 1929, Mayberry asks if he knows him.

"Yeah, I know 'im."

"When's the last time you talked to Willie?"

"The Sunday 'fore last."

"Who's he hang with?"

"He works at Ben's Chili Bowl."

"Where you live?"

It turns out the man lives in the room next to the one once occupied by Willis Fields. He says Fields has no girlfriend and few male friends, that nobody ever visits his room and that he smokes cigars and hits the bottle hard. The detectives want to get inside Fields's room to check for signs of a fire, because if he was burned in his room—fell asleep smoking and drinking liquor on the bed—it would show that he could have gotten burned on his back by accident, not malicious design. But the man says Fields's room is locked and that the landlady is out.

"What happened to 'im?" the man asks.

"He didn't tell ya?" asks V. I., careful to reveal no information likely to make its way into the street gossip mill.

"Hell if I know."

At Ben's Chili Bowl a block away on U Street, they ask their questions again. The whole time, V. I. is building scenarios, theories, in his mind. Say Fields had a buddy who often came to visit him at Ben's, but who hasn't stopped by in the last couple weeks. Good chance that guy knows something. Or say a woman always seemed to visit Fields on his payday. She's a good possibility. Or maybe Fields complained to a co-worker about somebody who'd been bothering him. Or mentioned somebody who owed him money. Whatever the story, V. I. knows from experience that men like Fields usually lead very simple lives. They go from their rooms to their jobs to the liquor store and back to their rooms. So that's the bird dog's trail. Unfortunately, nobody at Ben's knows much about Fields either, except that he has been missing.

"Ooohhh, booooy!" says Mayberry.

As a murder, this case has "unsolved" written all over it. And unless V. I., Mayberry and Joefox declare it a homicide, it will likely be forgotten. There's been no publicity, no relatives or political heavyweights demanding action. If Fields's death were declared a natural, his demise would slip into bureaucratic oblivion. It wouldn't take up their time or mess up their statistics with an unsolved murder. It would—poof—disappear. Except for one detail: Some dirtbag might have turned Willis Fields into a human torch, and catching the scum would bring great satisfaction. The idea is downright inspirational. Because in an era when most of the homicides V. I. gets are drug boys wasting drug boys, bandits beefing each other through the nose of a 9 mm, or hotheads retaliating after some trivial insult, this Willis Fields case is, well, intriguing, a puzzle with most of the pieces missing. The men need to hit 1929 again, talk to the landlady, get into Fields's room. But in the meantime—since Willis Fields is still not an official homicide—Mayberry, Joefox and the Ghost are back on the bubble.

The call comes at 9:50 p.m. . . .

When the men arrive at Rhode Island Avenue and Brentwood Road NE, the scene, as it always does, seems not real, somehow outside of time and place, like a page brought to life from a paperback novel: The shooting ground is cordoned off in a triangle of yellow plastic tape (POLICE LINE DO NOT CROSS), and squad cars and cruisers are parked every which way, as if they'd landed as randomly as dice thrown in a tornado's game of craps. The crowd of mostly women and youngsters is congregated in the vague and dreamy light of street lamps beneath huge and gnarled trees in the scrub-grass yard of the L-shaped Brookland Manor apartments. A police helicopter flutters overhead, its searchlight scorching a block nearby. The cops know this stretch of Rhode Island as a drug market, and that's the first scenario V. I.'s mind starts to build. One shot, large caliber, left side of the head. That's all he knows.

V. I. steps into the triangle and begins to think in the language of the scene before him. On the sidewalk begins the pool of blood, not red, but a thick, syrupy black. The blood has cascaded over the curb and run southwest with gravity for about five feet, where a pile of leaves and debris has dammed its flow. The young man who was shot was alive when the ambulance left, but this is a large pool of blood, and V. I. figures Mayberry is off the bubble. On the sidewalk is a footprint in blood. Could be that of the victim, the shooter, a witness, a passerby, an ambulance attendant. A few feet away is a lonely quarter, heads up. On a waist-high embankment, where the sidewalk meets the yard about six feet from the street, stand a Mountain Dew bottle and a can of Red Bull malt liquor.

The details seem trivial, but a homicide detective's life is a sea of details, a collage of unconnected dots gathered and collated. In the end, most will turn out to be insignificant. But at the time, a detective cannot know the revelatory from the inconsequential. He must try to see them all, then hold them in his mind in abeyance until the few details that matter rise forth from the ocean to reveal themselves. V. I. begins to link the dots in the scene before him. For instance, a man who is shot at such close range was either hit by someone he trusted or by someone who sneaked up on him. Maybe the Mountain Dew and the Red Bull belonged to the victim and to one of his friends, who were sitting on the embankment looking toward the street, talking, laughing. From the darkened yard behind them the shooter moved in. The victim fell forward, his head landing at the curb and spurting blood with each heartbeat. His buddy bolted. If the dots are connected correctly, that buddy is a witness. If not, he could be the shooter.

Suddenly, from the crowd in the dreamy light on the scrub-grass yard, comes a long, awful scream. In five seconds, it comes again. And then a woman runs wildly through the crowd, crashing into people as she goes. She disappears into a door at the elbow of the L-shaped Brookland Manor.

On the chance that this might be a drug-boy shooting, V. I., Mayberry and Joefox will not wander through the crowd or canvass the apartments looking for witnesses tonight. Until a few years ago, it was virtually unheard of for witnesses to be killed, but today they are crossed off like bad debts. Witnesses know it, cops know it, shooters know it. It's simply too dangerous for witnesses to be seen talking to the cops after a shooting, especially at night when the drug boys are out. V. I. plans to return tomorrow afternoon to do his canvass. But after hearing the woman scream, he invokes another law of experience: "You get people cryin', they gonna tell ya somethin'."

With this in mind, V. I. saunters toward the door at the building's elbow and the crowd parts and murmurs as he passes. On the darkened stairs up to the second floor, a place filled with the smells of a dozen dinners cooking, he finds the woman's mother, who says her daughter knew the victim but doesn't want to talk to the police. V. I. doesn't push. He gets the daughter's name, her apartment number. One of the problems these days is that victims and suspects are usually known on the streets only by nicknames that the cops don't know. So V. I. asks if the victim had a nickname. The mother says, "KK."

The wanton killings of the last few years have changed everything. From 1964 to 1987, the number of Washington homicides fluctuated between 132 and 287, with 225 posted in 1987. In their first two years as detectives, the eager V. I. and Joefox drove around with their radio microphone in hand so they could lay claim to any murder as soon as it came down. Then, in 1988, homicides skyrocketed to 369—then 434, 474 and 483 in the following years, with the pace flagging only slightly so far this year. The police closure rate plummeted: By the end of 1991, only 65% of homicides from 1990 and 54% from 1991 had been closed by police, compared with 80% of homicides from 1986.

As homicides have gone berserk, so have the lives of V. I. and his fellow detectives. A cop used to have time to investigate his murders, interview everybody, build a case. In the old days, murder was more often a domestic affair, and a victim's killer was often found among his family. But by 1991, only 4% of Washington homicides were domestics, while more than three-quarters were attributed to drugs, robberies, burglaries, arguments or non-drug-related retaliations. All of which means that for most homicides today, detectives no longer have a neat list of identifiable suspects but a barrage of friends, enemies, business partners and competitors to investigate. Even with more detectives, the cases are constantly rolling over one another, with new murders arriving before old ones are solved. Sometimes, V. I. sits down and pores through his old files so he doesn't plain forget a case.

And the drug-boy and bandit killings are so much more complicated than the old "mom-and-pop murders." V. I. has a case in far Northeast, where a bunch of guys opened fire on a crowd one evening, killing a young man and wounding three others. On its face, it looks like a drug-boy shooting. But the chain of events is also intertwined with the lives, loves, personalities and values of an array of individuals. The case began, according to the tips V. I. has collected from informants, a week before the shooting, when a woman friend of a suspected drug dealer was beaten by another woman. The suspected drug dealer went gunning for his friend's assailant, but shot the wrong woman. A male friend of the woman who was mistakenly shot then interceded in her behalf with the shooter, who apparently took this as a threat. With several buddies, he sought out and killed the male friend of the woman who had been mistakenly shot, before the guy could ice him. And that's a simple case.

V. I. has had cases that intertwine with as many as a dozen other murders—shootings, retaliations, shootings, retaliations. He has cases where families have been wiped out. A young man was killed, and his brother was set to testify against the shooter and then the brother was killed. Another brother was set to testify against that brother's shooter and he was killed. A sister was set to testify against that brother's shooter and she, too, was shot. There's little moral outrage about many killings because of what V. I. calls "victim participation"—meaning the victims are often as sleazy as their killers. Nowadays, half the battle is finding some reason to lock up a suspected killer on another charge to get him off the street so witnesses will cooperate and so they will be safe. This onslaught has erupted in only a few years.

But that's not the worst of it: Worse yet is what has happened inside V. I.'s heart and his head. He goes to the home of dead kids these days, knocks on the door and tells a mother and father that their child has been killed, and they say, "Yeah, okay." Without a hint of emotion, they close the door. The homicide detective's code of honor has always been that he identifies with the dead, swears to find the killer. These days, that's harder and harder. It's hard to get worked up over the injustice of a dead man who may have killed one or two or three people himself.

But that's not the worst of it: Worse yet is that V. I. has had witnesses he promised to protect get killed. After he promised! So, after 24 years of putting his honor and duty on the line at any time, night or day, V. I. Smith stopped promising. He began saying only that he would do what he could. He has been forced to make his own moral choices outside the expectations of the law: He has let murderers stay free rather than risk the lives of more witnesses.

But even that's not the worst of it: Worse yet is that in the last few years, V. I. Smith—tough, cool, brave—has ridden home late at night and broken down in tears of private bereavement: The fabric of the city where he grew up, the city he loves, has been shredded, destroyed. People on the outside haven't grasped this yet, haven't felt the deadening weight of this sadness, this heartsickness.

From Brookland Manor, V. I. takes only a nickname. He is famous for crashing cases at the scene, not waiting until tomorrow to investigate. He theorizes from the dots and pushes every lead to the limit. He can't interview witnesses tonight, but maybe the detectives dispatched to the hospital have a lead he can push. Maybe a brother or the mother or father of the victim named names, knew somebody who was beefing with the victim, gave the cops a line. V. I. heads back out the door, through the parting crowd, to see what Mayberry and Joefox have learned.

"He's gonna live," Mayberry says.

"That right?" V. I. asks without emotion. He glances at the pool of blood: KK is one lucky dude. Then he heads for his cruiser. He will not spend one more millisecond connecting the dots of this picture. It is an attempted murder now, another cop's glory, another cop's worry. They are still on the bubble. . . .

At 1929 11th St., the landlady is home. She seems to stop breathing when they tell her Willis Fields is dead. With her hands covering her cheeks she leads the detectives up an oddly tinted turquoise stairway to his dowdy, sweltering room. One life, one room. A round white clock on the wall reads 10:55. On the dingy carpet lie one razor blade, a bottle cap and a few toothpicks. Half a dozen shirts hang on a rack, along with a single pair of pants, dirty. A lamp without a cover, an unmade bed, a small bottle of Listerine, nearly empty, three unopened bars of soap, a loaf of Wonder Bread. On the wall are a calendar and a newspaper photo of a woman in black hat, underwear and stockings. Atop the television are three pens, a pencil, a nail clipper, a wristwatch, six cigars and two packs of matches. On the nightstand is a red address book. In it are the names of people listed as owing Fields money.

"Whatever happened didn't happen here," says V. I., which means the death of Fields is probably a murder. V. I. starts theorizing, figuring maybe Fields went on a drinking binge and demanded money from one of his debtors, who went off. Lighting someone on fire isn't an efficient way to kill; it's more a murder of passion. As the detectives are about to leave, call it a day's work at 11:35 p.m., the landlady's brother arrives.

On the last Saturday of Willis Fields's life, the brother says, he had come out of the apartment he shares with his sister, headed to catch a plane for vacation. He found Fields passed out drunk on the exterior steps going up to his room. He mentions two men—Robert and Theodore, whom Fields often hung out with on the street. He talks for a long time and the detectives are about to leave when the brother, in an aside, says, "He was layin' right there in the doorway, and this old fag was tryin' to frisk him." Mayberry, Joefox and V. I. look at each other in wonder at what people can forget to mention.

"You know his name?" Joefox asks.

"Naw, he be down the street."

"Did Fields go in the house then?" V. I. asks.

"Stump can answer that," the brother says, explaining that he left Willis Fields in the care of one of Fields's friends, who happened along the Saturday before last, a man nicknamed Stump. V. I. knows that none of the people mentioned or interviewed so far tonight is a suspect, and he figures Stump isn't either, but a trail's a trail. He says of Stump, "That's where we gotta start."

For days more, Mayberry, Joefox and the Ghost are on the bubble. *Amazing!* Still no murders on 3-to-11. Just the luck of the draw. But when a man and his squad are on the bubble, it's hard to do much police work, because when the call comes, everything else must be dropped. V. I. has nonetheless arranged for the squad to squeeze in a quick raid one night, sweep in with some uniformed cops in marked cruisers and hit the drug boys hanging on W Street, where his source is still peeking out the window and reporting back. Two guys argued on that street a while back and one ended up killing the other. At least that's how V. I.'s informants have explained the murder, but he has "no eyes"—no witnesses willing to testify.

His plan is to sweep in, make everybody hug the ground, scare up some guns and drugs, drag the crew downtown and start sweatin' 'em about the murder. When a guy's looking at 5-to-10 on a federal firearms rap, his memory can improve dramatically. Very little planning goes into such a raid. Eat some pizza, watch the Redskins, or *Top Cops,* or *Road Warrior*—then hop in the cars and do it. Although V. I. figures maybe a quarter of the guys on that street will be strapped with guns or have a gun hidden nearby, no detective will wear a bulletproof vest. All in a day's work. But night after night, the drug boys don't cooperate, and the street stays empty. Word comes back to V. I. through the drug boys' girlfriends that pals of the dead man are planning a retaliatory drive-by shooting and everybody is staying scarce.

While on the bubble, V. I. works his case in far Northeast. He conspicuously cruises the neighborhood, which is a signal to his informants that he wants them to call. V. I. will collect reconnaissance as well as spread rumors—gossip that will get more people talking so his real informants will have cover, gossip that may make the shooter fear his own friends and allies are turning against him. Some guys will flag down V. I. in the street and talk to him. These are young men who have their own troubles with the law and who can tell their friends they were discussing their cases, asking V. I. to put in a good word with a judge or a prosecutor. V. I. often does. But the way the game is played, he wants payback—the names of potential witnesses, the name of a shooter, the details of the Byzantine events that often lead up to a killing.

"You owe me big time," V. I. tells one young man.

"That last thing didn't work. They done me."

V. I. is unmoved. "I can't save you twice. But I did it the first time. So stay in touch. I can make it worth your while. I gotta get some eyes."

It seems that nobody helps the cops anymore just because it's the right thing to do. "You ain't got nobody helpin' ya now," V. I. says. "Nobody gives a crap. You gotta make everybody do what you want 'em to do. And you gotta be real mean to get results." The drug-boy killings have spooked everybody. V. I. can't blame folks. But that has meant more and more of his encounters with potential witnesses are hostile. More and more, he has to threaten people to get their cooperation. He has to get them subpoenaed before the grand jury and then warn them that they can be charged with perjury if they don't tell the truth. And these are innocent people. He has even hinted that a witness's name might leak out before a suspected shooter has been jailed, unless that witness agrees to testify after the guy is locked up. He must sometimes act threatening to even the most harmless of people, which is what happens on the Saturday afternoon V. I. swings by the home of the last man known to have seen Willis Fields alive. Stump, a 64-year-old man whose real name is Earl Johnson, is off his porch and headed for his front door the instant V. I.'s cruiser pulls to the curb. V. I. halts the retreat.

"Need to talk to you. Detective Smith, Homicide."

"You wanta come inside?"

"No, sir, you gonna have ta come with me." V. I. opens the creaking front-yard gate and gestures toward his cruiser.

Stump is disoriented. "I gotta tell my wife."

"You can call her from downtown."

"I don't know nothin'."

"We gonna just talk about it."

"I don't know nothin'."

Stump looks up at his wife, who is peering down from a second-story window. V. I. could have interviewed Stump at home, but he believes people are a lot like animals: They're more comfortable in their own territory. He wants them uncomfortable, so they drive off toward the station. Suddenly, the word "stabbing" squawks from the cruiser radio.

"You got a condition?" V. I. asks the dispatcher.

"I didn't do nothin'," Stump says from the backseat.

"Hey, Stump, we know you all right, man." V. I. says this in a more friendly tone, trying to calm the man down. Then he heads for the scene of the stabbing, doing 85 mph on the Southwest Freeway. He arrives at M and Half streets SW. The victim is gone and only a dab of blood stains the sidewalk. He will live.

Still on the bubble . . .

Seated back at Homicide North, staring into the middle distance and wringing thick and worn hands, Stump is not a happy camper. He's a short man with a good belly, a mustache and short graying hair. He wears his blue-and-white cap backwards. He wears blue work pants and a white short-sleeved shirt. A ring of keys hangs off his belt.

"Never did a crime in my life," Stump says to the air.

"You know Fields?" V. I. asks.

"Right. But what happened to him, I don't know."

As these things often go, however, Stump knows more than he knows he knows. He says that before the detectives came around asking questions, a man nicknamed Bo had told him that Fields had been set on fire. V. I. knows from the hospital report that an unidentified person drove Fields to the hospital. He figures Fields must have told that person what happened. And he figures that person might have told others.

"You can't set me up for no murder," Stump says.

"I'm not tryin' ta charge you with murder," V. I. says, knowing that indeed Stump is not a suspect. "Did you ask Bo how he knew Fields got burned?"

"He said it was over on 18th Street."

"Did he tell ya who Fields was with?"

"He never did tell me that."

"How'd he know about it?"

"I don't know."

"You know who lives up on 18th?"

"I don't."

V. I. then takes Stump out cruising the neighborhood for Bo, but they don't find him. "I wanta go home," Stump says.

"That's where we're on the way to."

Says V. I., "Bo is the next guy to talk with."

Back at the office, V. I. find Joefox and Mayberry yukking it up. As V. I. has been working the fringes of other cases while riding the bubble, they, too, have been working other cases. Joefox is telling about his informant who called and said his mother was sick in another city and that he needed $300 for airfare to visit her. He said he hated to be a snitch, but that his mother was very sick. Then he gave Joefox the address of a shooter Joefox was after. Even before patrolmen could make the arrest, Joefox's informant walked into the office looking for his finder's fee.

"They're still out tryin' ta get 'im," Joefox said.

With that, the informant picked up Joefox's phone, rang a number and asked for the shooter by name. They chatted. "See, I told ya he's still there," the man said after hanging up.

"Man, they got caller ID?" asked an incredulous Joefox.

"Ah, I don't think so."

Anyway, the cops got a shooter, the informant got his cash, and presumably, a sick mother got a visit from a devoted son.

It's unimaginable that Mayberry, Joefox and the Ghost won't draw a murder tonight, Saturday night. But in the meantime, before the intrigues of darkness set in, V. I. heads out to Northeast Washington to meet Detective J. O. Johnson. They're off to look for Tony Boyce and Eldee Edwards, who are wanted for obstruction of justice for allegedly threatening a witness scheduled to testify in a grand jury investigation into a murder in which Edwards is a suspect.

The detectives cruise East Capitol near 17th Street, where Tony lives. They hope to find him on the street. It's safer to make an arrest outside. Besides, if they raid the men's homes and come up empty, the men will learn the cops are on their tails and maybe take an extended vacation. V. I. interviewed Tony a couple days ago, hoping to get him to give up his buddy Eldee, but Tony hung tough. He told them to bug off, that if they were gonna arrest him, then arrest him. And call his lawyer. He wasn't tellin' 'em anything. V. I. let Tony go. But he doesn't like it when cops are treated rudely, and he's back today with a warrant. Because it's late afternoon on Saturday, there will be no judges available to process Tony's case until Monday, which means he'll cool in jail for at least the weekend. When they finally spot Tony walking up East Capitol, V. I. pulls a U-turn and hops out.

"How ya doin'?" V. I. asks in a friendly voice.

"I'm fine," says Tony, momentarily confused. He's a short, thin 31-year-old man wearing a white Champion T-shirt, blue jeans shorts and lavender Saucony running shoes. He has a dark blue wrap on his hair. His nails are long, his body lithe and taut.

"I got a warrant for ya."

"For my arrest?"

"Yep."

V. I. is downright cheerful. He gently turns Tony toward the trunk of a car, has him lay down the leather-bound Bible he's carrying and clamps the cuffs on him behind his back. A man walks up and gruffly asks what's happening.

"They arrestin' me!" Tony says, emotional now, with an edge of fear in his high-pitched voice. "I don't know why."

V. I.'s entire manner changes. "Sir!" he says to the man in a deep and suddenly ominous voice, stepping toward him with the full authority of his 230 pounds. "You wanta walk wherever you walkin', because you gonna be the next one that's locked up." The man opens his mouth to speak, but before the words emerge, V. I. says, "*Walk wherever you walkin'!* I don't wanta hear 'bout it." The man does not move, and V. I. goes stone calm. "Turn and go," he says in almost a whisper. "Turn and go." And the man does. Just then, a woman arrives and says she is Tony's mother. Because she is polite, because a mother has the right to worry about her son, V. I. is polite in return.

"I'll call you," he says.

After Tony is taken away in a paddy wagon, J. O. and V. I. head for the last known address for Eldee Edwards. Now that Tony has been taken, there's no hope of surprising his friend. J. O. goes to cover the back door and V. I. climbs the steep steps to the row house's front porch. To his right is a gray cat sunning itself on a stone railing. To his left, beneath a striped awning, sits an old man in a green metal chair. V. I. asks if he has seen Eldee, and the old man nods.

"Where's he at? In the house?"

"No."

"When's the last time you saw 'im?"

"Two days ago, three days ago."

"Who's home now?"

"My daughter."

"How old's she?"

"Forty."

Walking into a strange house is a dangerous play, and V. I. has asked the old man these questions as reconnaissance. He believes the old man is telling the truth, although he has learned not to rely too heavily on his intuition in such matters because any cop who thinks he can't be successfully lied to is a fool. V. I. has been tricked more times than he cares to remember. "Lookin' at a jail sentence," he says, "makes people great liars." He knocks hard on the door eight times. No answer. He waits, opens the door, knocks hard nine times and hollers, "Hello!" No answer. He walks in the door. A narrow hallway leads back to a kitchen, rooms are off to the left, a stairway rises on the right. On the floor are two unopened gallons of fresh paint.

The place brings a flash of déjà vu, because it was in just this kind of house that, as a young uniformed cop, V. I. had decided to play hero when he got a report of a burglary in progress. When nobody answered the door in the darkened house, he didn't announce that he was a policeman for fear of warning the burglar, and he walked in. When he flicked on the light, he looked up the stairway to see an old woman huddled terrified on her knees and an old man standing resolutely with a shotgun aimed down the stairwell's tunnel at the intruder—Patrolman V. I. Smith.

"Hello!" he hollers again, and his voice rings like a trumpet in the cavernous hallway. No answer. He waits four seconds and hollers "Hello" again. He waits six seconds and yells, "Anybody home?" He waits five more seconds and yells "Hello," louder this time. His back pressed against the wall, his gun still in the holster, he starts slowly up the stairs. As he goes, he glances calmly back and forth from the first to second floors. Finally, a woman appears on the upstairs landing, and V. I. introduces himself as a policeman.

"I'm looking for Eldee."

"Eldee has not lived here in four or five years," she says, seeming miffed at the question.

"How frequently you see him?"

"Maybe three times a week."

"You got a phone number?"

"No. He lives in Southeast. That's all I can tell ya."

J. O. Johnson has joined them in the foyer now, and he isn't happy with what he's hearing. "I talked to you the other day myself, and I had a little confidence in what you was tellin' me, but now you make me think that you're not bein' truthful."

The woman starts to interrupt, "You know . . ."

J. O. cuts her off, "We're tryin' to be nice about it."

The woman snickers.

"We haven't been here at four o'clock in the mornin' and wake everybody up in the house and turn the house upside down lookin' for Eldee. I'm sure you don't want us to do that."

"I don't think that you supposed to be doin' that."

"You don't know what we *supposed to be doin'*. I'm askin' you to get in touch with him and have him call me. Tonight."

"Okay," she says, clearly angry.

In the car, V. I. says, "He's probably in and outta there."

"I can tell ya one thing," J. O. says, "when I break back in here 'bout 4:00 in the morning . . ."

Says V. I., "She doesn't believe."

When Eldee doesn't call later that night, J. O. will take his warrant and a crew of cops and hit the last known address of Eldee Edwards in the early morning hours. He will get everybody out of bed, secure them downstairs and search for Eldee. He will not find him. But afterward, V. I. will figure the folks in that house will be more likely to lean heavily on Eldee to turn himself in. They will have been made believers.

But right now, back at Homicide North, V. I. looks straight into the eyes of Tony Boyce, who is sitting with his right elbow on his knee, his chin on his fist and his left hand cuffed to his chair. V. I. says nothing. He gets a cup of coffee, checks the score of the Eagles-Jets game on the tube. Then he reads Tony his rights and tells him he'll be arraigned Monday morning.

"Monday morning?" Tony asks, shocked. "Does my lawyer know?"

V. I. asks Tony if he has his lawyer's phone number.

"Not here."

V. I. shrugs.

"Why didn't you arrest me yesterday?" Tony asks, finally realizing that he'll spend at least the weekend in jail.

V. I. shrugs again.

After the paperwork is done and Mayberry takes Tony, who has abandoned his cool and loosed a blast of obscenity, down to a cell, Joefox says, "He'll have a lotta company down there."

"Saturday in the big house!" says V. I. And then, out of character, he throws back his head and roars with laughter.

Incredibly, 11:00 comes and goes. They are still on the bubble. . . .

Over the years, V. I. has had some spectacular cases. Soon after he came to Homicide in 1986, when he was barely off the natural death detail, he solved a series of killings in which a man in a dark van was abducting women and murdering them. The seven-year-old brother of one dead woman had mentioned to V. I. that his sister kept her boyfriends' phone numbers on the back of matchbooks and that they were spread all over the house. V. I. had the boy collect them in a bag, and the next day he began calling numbers, posing as a doctor tracking a case of venereal disease. After 17 calls, V. I. found a man who had seen the woman the night she died. Before the day was over, V. I. had interviewed him, discovered the name of another man the dead woman had been with that night, located his dark van and gone with his squad to arrest him.

Just last winter, V. I. and Joefox were assigned by Chief Isaac Fulwood Jr. himself to handle a high-publicity multiple murder on P Street NW, in which a man, woman and child were found slain in a car. They were a brother and sister and her two-year-old son. When the body of the child, who had been suffocated, was taken from the backseat, it looked to V. I. as if the boy were only asleep. He felt the righteousness rise in him, felt his revulsion for the random injustice, felt as if this could happen to his own family, his own friends. There was no "victim participation." And when V. I. and Joefox went to the home of the dead to inform their parents, who were also the boy's grandparents, the family cried, sobbed as humans should, must, if they are to be human. V. I., Joefox and Mayberry, the entire squad, worked day and night for four days. As their reward, as affirmation of their own humanity, they locked up the alleged son-of-a-bitch killer, who's now awaiting trial and facing the possibility of life in prison.

That's what has changed. So many murders seem to count for nothing today. They don't embody the eternals of love and devotion and loss, recall the immeasurable value of one life, no matter how seemingly insignificant, announce through quick justice that living is safe and predictable and violence an aberration, thereby cauterizing the psychic wounds of the living. No, these murders trumpet the evil, insidious reverse: Life is cheap, easily forgotten, humanity is a fraud. At the front lines of this diminution, V. I. Smith feels his own humanity under assault, feels the fire of indignation in his belly going cold. His deep fear is that, at the front lines, he is taking only the early hit for an entire society. Because what's happening to V. I. Smith is happening to everyone who reads the paper or watches the TV news. His numbed heart is but an early warning.

"If you see the motives for why people are killing people out there now, you say to yourself, 'How can you do anything about somebody who's thinkin' like this?' It's valueless. You go into a crack house two or three months after it's got rollin' and find a family with young girls 15, 16 years old who have lost everything. They've lost their dignity. They've lost their will. They've lost themselves.

"And what have you accomplished being a policeman? You're on TV: 'We got one of the biggest cocaine raids we've had and locked up two New Yorkers.' But you've left the victimized family devastated and haven't given them any alternative. But I don't have time to worry about people anymore. And it's a goddamned shame. I've gotten to the point where I'm not really comfortable doing what I do anymore. I've gotten to the point where I sense fear. And I've never done that before. You can't predict who's out there anymore. Everything has gone to extremes."

On the next 3-to-11 shift, with Joefox home sick, the bubble finally bursts at 5:30 p.m., probably too early for a drug-boy killing. On the way to the scene in an apartment on 29th Street SE, just off Pennsylvania Avenue, V. I. starts theorizing. *Female victim, inside her apartment, shot once in the head.* When a person is killed inside her home, the case is usually easier, because it's a snap to discover the last person to see the victim alive. It's also daylight, which makes any investigation easier still, and most promising, this killing is in a normally quiet neighborhood, which hints at an old-fashioned, mom-and-pop murder, a murder of passion. When Mayberry and V. I. walk into the door of apartment 101, they find half a dozen cops, like gawkers at a car crash, milling around. Mayberry orders everybody out.

The dead woman is lying in the middle of the room, halfway between the front door and the rear patio doors, one of which has been knocked off its track. It is an ugly scene, with brain and skull splattered on the wall and floor. The room is dark, but they don't touch the light switches for fear of smudging any prints. They wander the apartment with flashlights and find a framed photo of a woman. Mayberry flashes a light on the dead woman's face to be certain it is her.

In a matter of minutes, the dots are made whole: The woman, Crystal Johnson-Kinzer, and a male friend had walked in the door and been attacked. The male friend had escaped as shots were fired. The woman did not. Outside the patio balcony, detectives scour the yard and garbage cans for clues. They find a footprint with a distinctive circle in the tread imprinted on the hood of a gray Toyota parked beneath the balcony.

When the victim's family arrives, there is—as there should be—great anguish. For months, they say, Crystal had been harassed by her husband, from whom she was separated. She'd quit a job, moved across town to this apartment, gotten a court order for him to stay away. Crystal's brother is screaming at the police: "She called y'all! And now look! Y'all come when it's too late!" He is weeping and hitting his forehead with his fist. Crystal's father, wearing the gray uniform of a working man, stands perfectly still, stunned silent. Her mother, with a rose bandanna wrapped on her head, shuffles about without expression, wiping her face again and again with a tissue. The fiancee of Crystal's brother—a woman who is a look-alike for Crystal, a woman who was often mistaken for her twin—is holding a diapered baby and sobbing.

Amid this horror, V. I. is invigorated, renewed. *This poor woman!* She could have been *his* sister, *his* daughter! A sweet 22-year-old girl with a good job as a telephone operator. She loved smooth jazz, John Coltrane. She was studying cosmetology at night. She came from a nice, protective family. She had stopped at her apartment to change clothes and head out for a picnic at her brother's. She does not deserve this. This murder is "real"—with a good guy and a bad guy. Crystal's death must be avenged.

Says V. I., "You don't get many like this anymore."

Back at Homicide North, the details are gathered and collated, family and friends are interviewed, the husband's undistinguished police record is pulled. At 12:17 a.m., V. I. has finished writing the arrest warrant for Kodie Cotrell Kinzer, age 21, last known address in Silver Spring. It's the home of Kinzer's grandmother, and V. I. figures it's probably where he ran to, because that's just what shooters usually do.

"They wanta go home," V. I. says.

"We gotta start the hunt!" says Mayberry, excited.

When they arrive at the Georgetown home of the judge who will sign the arrest warrant, V. I. notices for the first time that it is a lovely, perfectly clear and starry night, cool, with a light breeze. The Georgetown street is quiet, except for the soothing mantra of crickets and the conversation of what look to be two drunken college boys stumbling home. As V. I. walks through the manicured garden courtyard to the judge's town house, he sees yard after yard marked with signs that read "Electronic Security by Night Owl." It's the kind of neighborhood V. I.

hasn't seen much of in his job. As the judge puts down his book and reads the warrant, V. I. studies the high, elegant ceilings in the judge's home. "You wouldn't be needin' our services too often in this neighborhood," he says, and the judge laughs, although V. I. is not joking.

The Montgomery County police are waiting for the three-car caravan of detectives that arrives about 2:00 in the morning. Taking down a suspected murderer is still an exotic event in suburban Montgomery, and the sergeant on duty is talking about whether he should call in the SWAT team and waiting for a captain to arrive to take responsibility for the decisions.

"They don't get to do this much," Mayberry whispers.

"It's comin'," V. I. answers ominously. "Believe me, it's comin'."

Despite the delay, the detectives will not complain. V. I. doesn't want neighboring police telling stories about how Washington's cowboy cops came out and broke protocol or acted arrogant. So they wait . . . and wait . . . and wait. Finally, it is decided that several more cars of Montgomery cops, all of whom don bulletproof vests, will surround the apartment, and V. I. will call in on a telephone and announce the raid. This gentlemanly approach runs against every grain in Mayberry and V. I., who back home would take a couple of uniformed cops and knock on the damned door. On the phone, V. I. talks to a young man who says Kodie Kinzer isn't home and that Kinzer's grandmother is too frail to be awakened with the shock of a police raid. V. I. asks the youth to come outside, which he does. He's a nice kid, clean-cut, polite.

"Did you see Kodie last night?" V. I. asks gently.

"I came in like *late,* 'bout 1:00 or 2:00."

"Was he in bed?"

"Yes, sir."

"Where does he usually sleep?"

"Huh?"

"Where does he usually sleep?"

"He sleeps on the couch."

"He doesn't have a room?"

"No, he's like a pass-through."

"You know of any girlfriends he might be stayin' with?"

"I couldn't tell ya."

"How old is Kodie's grandmother?"

"She's 'bout 70."

"Is she in pretty good health?"

"Ah, not really, that's why I say I didn't wanta scare her."

"Do you expect him to come back tonight?"

"Uhm, I don't think so."

"Why not?"

"Huh?"

"Why not?"

"Ah, 'cause, ah, he was, uhm, talkin' about he was gonna go over his friend's house or somethin'."

"You ever meet his wife?"

"Nah, I never met her. I heard of her name before."

V. I. looks at Mayberry. "Think we oughta wake Grandma up?" Mayberry shrugs, but he is thinking of a line from the movie *Dirty Harry*: "I gots ta know." And he knows V. I. is thinking the same thing. The kid seems honest, but V. I. has learned not to always trust his intuition. They didn't come all the way out here with seven, eight police cars to be talked away at the door. V. I. is being gentle, getting the kid used to the idea.

"Captain, whataya think?" V. I. asks, bringing the Montgomery brass into a decision that he has already made. The captain nods, and V. I. turns back to the youth. "Think it would be a problem if we talk to Kodie's grandmother?"

The young man looks suddenly shaky. "See, all these people . . ."

V. I. cuts him off. "There ain't gonna be all these people."

"I don't, I don't know . . ."

V. I. cuts him off again, this time in a voice that has once again gone stone calm: "Look, man, this is somethin' we gotta do. Prolongin' the situation isn't gonna do any good. Let's go."

Inside, buried beneath a pile of blankets, they find Kodie Kinzer. Minutes later, he's led away, his head tilted downward mournfully. He's wearing yellow shorts, a white T-shirt, white socks and no shoes. When V. I. leaves the apartment, he's carrying a pair of black Adidas with three white stripes adorning the uppers and a distinctive circle on the sole. It will be up to Forensics to evaluate whether they could have left that footprint on the car beneath Crystal Johnson-Kinzer's balcony. But V. I. says, "I remember that tread."

It is nearly dawn by the time V. I. and Mayberry finish interviewing Kodie Kinzer, who denies that he killed Crystal. When the detectives head back to Homicide North, leaving Kinzer in a Montgomery cell awaiting extradition to Washington, the city is just waking up. The sky is brightening in the east, and people are standing at bus stops in twos and threes. A laundry truck is picking up, a Coke truck is dropping off, and the lights of sleeping cars are awakening along the roads. Outside police headquarters, a rat scurries along the sidewalk, stops, gazes about at the emerging daylight and dives into the bushes for cover.

Life as it should be.

In the next few weeks, V. I. will keep tugging at threads in his murder case in far Northeast—the one that began when a suspected drug dealer shot the wrong woman. Before that chain of misery and foolishness concludes, five people will end up shot. He'll keep working the murder of Willis Fields, never finding Bo, the man who told Stump that Fields was attacked on 18th Street. But no matter. Bo was simply repeating street rumor passed on by lots of other people. V. I. will discover that somebody who lives on 18th Street owed Fields money. But it will be a long time, if ever, before that murder is avenged. In the meantime, Tony Boyce will stay in jail for weeks and be indicted for obstruction of justice. Eldee Edwards will be arrested and indicted for murder. In a few days, Kodie Kinzer will arrive at the D.C. jail, where he will await trial after his indictment for murder. Soon, Mayberry, Joefox and the Ghost will collect half a dozen new homicides, all of which will look like drug-boy killings.

But that's all in the future. This morning, just back from the hunt, V. I. and Mayberry still have their damned paperwork to do. And in Room 5058, the coffee is cold. But that's okay. It has been a good night—an old-fashioned night, a night that affirmed the world's predictability, justice and humanity, that healed the psychic wounds of the living, that again brought feeling to the numbed heart of Detective Victor "V. I." Smith. This horrific night has made him feel better. It has made him feel human again.

▓ Author's Afterwords . . .

I had wanted to profile a homicide detective for more than a decade and never managed to find one I liked well enough at the same time I was working for an editor who wanted the story. When the two converged, I jumped at the chance.

The weekend before I started reporting the piece, I stayed home and read a half-dozen mystery novels in which the main characters were homicide detectives. I realized that what made those books work was the extraordinarily detailed quality of the description. So I decided I'd work even harder at collecting that kind of material in my reporting. I tape-recorded more than 20 hours of actual police conversation on the street, in the squad room, in the police cruiser, interrogations of suspects, the hollering and chaos during raids. I took dozens of photos, including close-up shots of the blood flowing down the street and pictures of a victim's boarding house room. Later, I studied them with a magnifying glass for details.

I reported the story traditionally, simply hanging out and riding around with V. I. and his partners. If they worked until 11:00 p.m., so did I. If they worked until dawn, so did I. Although I seem unobtrusive in the story, I was actually asking nonstop questions and one cop finally dubbed me "the why-guy."

I did long sit-down interviews with V. I., who talked about his life and childhood and how he became a cop. Naturally, I assumed several murders would occur in my two weeks of tagging along, but none did. I had little choice but to make that part of the story. I quickly realized that the boom in drug-related murders had changed V. I.'s job and his outlook on his work and life.

It seemed to me that he was going through a more intense version of what anybody who watches the six o'clock news was going through— shock, anger, resignation, fear and, finally, cynicism. I wanted that thematic idea to connect readers' lives with V. I.'s life. When on my final night with him an "old-fashioned" murder took place—a murder with an innocent victim—and V. I. felt the old juice of righteous indignation rising in him, the crime gave me the chance to tie that theme to a real event.

When I sat down to write, I consciously wanted the story to evoke the feeling of a paperback cop novel or a TV show like *Homicide*. So I tried hard to keep the story moving from scene to scene, using contemporaneous events for my narrative structure and working in V. I.'s background and outlook around that story line. I wanted the piece to have a gritty tone, and so I had the coffee pot "spitting mud" and the police radios "belching static."

I didn't begin writing the story while I was reporting it. I had no idea where it was going to go and I tried to relax, collect everything I could through as many senses as I could, then figure out the story later. When I did begin writing, I wanted to capture V. I.'s tough-guy personae without making him into a caricature. I used a lot of repetition in the story trying to evoke that tough-guy feeling. Looking back, I might have gone overboard. I also left the impression with some readers that V. I. was afraid on the streets, when he actually had for the first time *realized* he was sometimes afraid. That's a subtle difference, and I wish I'd made the distinction clearer, although V. I. didn't complain.—W. H.

When Daddy Comes Home

Georgia had never seen her father naked.

Certainly not when he was young and prideful, walking with a bantam swagger that she and her sisters called "the strut"—a walk at once jaunty and commanding, with an unforgiving posture softened by a long, friendly gait and made theatrical by arms that pumped confidently from rolling shoulders. *Make a path, folks, here comes the reverend, the Reverend James A. Holman.* Georgia's older sister, Leila, when she was a girl, would feign exhaustion just so Daddy would hoist her onto his chest and shoulder, where she'd pretend to be asleep, all the while watching with fascination over his back as his legs, like tiny rockets, launched him and her off the sidewalk with each dancing, prancing step.

That legendary strut, where was it now? When Georgia first touched his skin in the hospital, helped turn his body in bed or helped change his diaper, she nearly recoiled, as if meeting these intimate needs for her sick 80-year-old father were unnatural acts, a violation of all human hierarchy. She thought to herself: *This is not my father.*

It was not the father who had mesmerized huge revival crowds with his stunning "Take Up the Cross" sermon. It was not the father who had signed men out of jail on his word alone. It was not the father who had always arrived with pennies for her piggy bank. And, surely, it was not the father who had sat on the front porch rocking her on hot summer nights while he recited poetry.

This frail man's bones poked at his skin like sticks prodding soft leather. This man didn't recognize her, called her "Cat," the nickname for her dead sister, Catherine. This man rambled deliriously about a Reverend Johnson, asked the name of the street where his own former church stood and insisted that one of the nurses was his dead wife, Anna Pearl. This man seemed afraid. All hours, Georgia and Leila sat beside him, his body as light and fragile as settled dust, his skin dark against the ocean of white sheets into which Georgia was sure he was about to disappear.

She wondered, Where are his dreams taking him tonight? She wrote in her diary: "This, the man who held my hand."

But Daddy didn't die . . . For months, Georgia Kaiser, who is now 50, and Leila Davies, who is now 58, took turns driving or riding the bus back and forth from their homes in Silver Spring and Chevy Chase, Maryland, to Augusta, Georgia, where Daddy had left the hospital and was staying with a friend. The commuting was exhausting and expensive. Georgia and Leila were schoolteachers with only so many days off, and they had children and husbands who needed their time. In theory, they had two choices: Put Daddy in a nursing home or take him into their own homes. But like many elderly people, their father had let it be known that he'd rather die than go into a nursing home. In a sermon Georgia remembered him preaching when she was a girl, he said, "Some people marry their cross. Some people give birth to their cross. And some people put their cross in a nursing home." The sisters really had only one choice.

That was four years ago, just before Georgia cleaned out a room and Daddy moved into her house. When he was strong enough, he began splitting his time between Georgia's and Leila's, only a few miles away. The women's decision to take their father into their homes seemed to Georgia a private choice. But such private choices will be occurring more and more often in the years to come. By 2025, nearly 20% of the population will be 65 or older. In 1900, only an estimated one in 10 married couples between the ages of 40 and 60 had two or more parents alive. Today, thanks to a U.S. life expectancy that has risen by about 25 years in the 20th century, more than half of America's middle-age couples are estimated to have two or more parents living. Despite the

myth that modern children dump their parents into nursing homes, only
5% of people over 65 are in such facilities, and nearly three-quarters of
the nation's frail elderly are cared for by family members who live in the
same residence. The numbers are daunting: In 1985, there were about
6.5 million dependent elderly in various living arrangements. By 2020,
there will be an estimated 14.3 million. Hardly a family in America will
be untouched.

But Georgia Kaiser wasn't thinking about other families. First came
her duty to her father. Beyond that, she worried how her own life and
her own family would be changed. Deep down, she childishly wished her
father hadn't gotten feeble. Then she felt guilty for feeling this. As
Georgia packed his things for the move to Washington, she stuffed her
father's old family photos and memorabilia in a brown box and put it all
away, unable even to look. She thought, *This is all that's left of him.* In
her diary, she wrote: "If you should go and I remain, whatever shall I do?"

Looking back now, looking at her family as a human laboratory for
what is about to touch so many lives, Georgia believes life with Daddy has
turned out to be a bittersweet blessing for her, Leila, their children,
their husbands—and for Daddy. Don't get Georgia wrong, it has been no
picnic for any of them. But it has been no horror show either. It has
made her feel good to know she has returned what was given her as a
child, and it has created a time tunnel through which she, her family,
even her father have looked back and ahead at their own lives. She puts
it simply.

"I feel more grown up."

They are brother relics: the reverend and the curio. He is 84. The
curio—a dark wooden cabinet with a curving glass front, three shelves,
feet that are carved into animal paws and a horizontal mirror that rests
on a warping top—is probably that old, too. The reverend was only 15,
working as a delivery boy at a dry goods store in his home town of
Americus, Georgia, when he heard two sisters from the family that owned
the store mention that they were selling the curio to make room for a
new piece of furniture. The boy spoke up, saying he'd love to buy it as a
gift for his mother, and the deal was struck: 50¢ from the boy's $3 weekly
wage for 40 weeks—$20, a lot of money in 1925. The boy borrowed a
truck and delivered the prize to his mother, who was elated. Sixty-four
years passed. And when Georgia was packing her father's books and

roll-top desk and a few other belongings, the curio was the only item he asked her to bring along.

"If you can," he said.

The curio and the boy, now antiques.

The reverend sits in a tall, flowered wing chair to the left of his curio. He is a militantly dignified man, his shoulders still erect, his head bald and buffed on top, his remaining hair short and snowy white against his skin. He shaves himself and does a good job, leaving only a few patches of gray beard. His face, like his body, is taut and lean, his cheeks high and hollow, his forehead remarkably unwrinkled. As always, he wears a white shirt and a tie, this day dark blue with a diagonal gray stripe and held in place with a gold tie bar. When he was young, he required two starched and ironed white shirts a day, which his wife, Anna Pearl, delivered without fail. He crosses his thin left leg over his right leg at the knee, adjusts his wooden cane against his side, plants his elbows on the chair's armrests and steeples his fingers. He rubs his palms together softly, barely touching, then plays with the change in his pocket. For a moment, he taps his cane with the nail of his finger, then lightly rubs his thigh with his right palm.

He does not squirm, but rather makes each move with a methodical, self-conscious elegance. He holds his hands at his chest and rubs them together slowly, as if working lotion into his skin. The hands are large, with long, expressive fingers that curl upward after their middle joints. On the bridge of each hand is a spider web of wrinkles that record his many years like the rings of an old tree. But his palms are as smooth and glassy as pebbles drawn from a running creek. Unlike a laboring man's, his hands were not his most precious tool.

"Let me tell you a story," he always says, his coarse, gravel voice animated by an array of rising and falling volumes and pitches and a masterful range of poetic rhythms, hesitations and inflections. "I was sitting in the house, the telephone rang and it was a young lady whose husband was a Pullman redcap. . . ."

This is not the man who moved into Georgia's house four years ago. After what doctors called a "seizure," that man's memory was wrecked and he had to be taught to walk again. That man was so frail and confused, he spent the early days at Georgia's house in bed, not knowing where he was. He constantly apologized for being in the way. At night, he rambled about the house knocking on doors, saying, "Time to go, anybody taking me to work?" One night he got up and packed his bag for a trip he'd gone on years before. He couldn't take himself to the bathroom. He had to be reminded to eat. He had to be told, "Daddy, here's your shirt, put this on." Night after night, he asked, "Where am I?" And Georgia answered, "Daddy, you're with me." And he asked, "Now, who are you?" When Georgia returned from a brief trip, he told her that the man and the girls in the house had been very nice to him.

"Daddy, that's my husband."

"Your husband?"

"Daddy, that's Carl and those are my children."

"Those two girls? Well, they certainly were nice to me." It was almost more than Georgia could bear. "This is my father!" She couldn't get past her perception that he was now the child, she the parent. She remembered her mother nursing her 93-year-old father. "I'm taking care of Papa," her mother would say. She remembered her father's mother, who lived to be 104, sitting on the porch of the family home in Americus, where she lived with two daughters. She remembered Uncle Willie, crazy with dementia and sick with cancer, who lived with his wife until he finally died. She remembered Uncle Robert, never quite right after returning from World War II, who lived with his sisters for the rest of his life.

Georgia was a grown woman, but she couldn't accept that it was now her turn. "I was in charge of *him*," she says. "I've got to tell this man what to do. . . . This is my father, who would tell *me*." She balked at the profound gap between saying, "Daddy, dinner's ready," and saying, "Daddy, come eat dinner now."

"I just hadn't grown up to that."

Her father's illness also threw Georgia into renewed mourning for her mother, who had died three years earlier. "It just made a microscopic image of the fact that she's dead, and he's alone. . . . All the things that had been, never would be again." Then, in the midst of it all, her father angrily accused her of trying to steal his money. "It hurt me," she says. "I was angry. How dare he!" She sometimes thought: "I wish he were not here. I don't mean dead . . . I don't wish he were in a nursing home. But I wish it hadn't happened. That's what I wish. I wish it hadn't happened." Georgia even found herself wondering if her enfeebled father wouldn't be better off dead. But each morning, when she went to awaken him, she worried that he might actually be dead. Then it hit her: *What if Karen or Lisa finds him dead?* From then on, she made sure waking up Grandpa wasn't one of her daughters' chores.

The oddest things irritated her. On the first evening that her father was well enough to eat at the dining room table, he happened to sit in Georgia's chair. "That night I let him," Georgia says. But she was astounded how much his sitting in her chair annoyed her. It was silly, irrational. She knew that. But she couldn't help herself. Then she remembered something her father had told families he counseled as a minister: "People argue about what they're not angry about." Of course. It wasn't the chair: Daddy was here and her life was forever changed. She wasn't angry at him but at her helplessness in the face of it all. After about a week of stewing, Georgia politely said, "Daddy, you're going to sit here now." Daddy did, never knowing the little psychodrama that had unfolded, and Georgia reclaimed her place at the table.

Summer 1954, Georgia is a little girl. . . . It's hot and dusty in rural north Georgia, in the towns of Gainesville and Dahlonega, before air conditioning, a time of straw hats and cardboard fans, a time when sweaty shirts drew no disapprobation. Little Georgia, with her pretty cotton dress, is the apple of everyone's eye—the Reverend Holman's daughter, the youngest by eight years, spoiled by his undivided attention, the daughter who most takes after his outgoing manner, who, like him, loves books and poetry, a good speaker, too, and polite to a fault. When the reverend comes to town on the dirt-road revival circuit, often carrying little Georgia along, the church women pretend to bicker over who'll get her for the day—for sewing or fishing or, just for fun, a stint picking cotton. She is a princess because Daddy is a king.

Every night, Georgia takes her place in the front pew. If Daddy's revival is set to start at 7:00, it starts at 7:00, not a minute or 30 minutes after. In a world of dynamic Southern preachers, the Reverend James A. Holman always held his own. He'd graduated from Atlanta's Gammon Theological Seminary and in 58 years of ministering rose to become a presiding elder in the Christian Methodist Episcopal Church. He ran his churches like a benevolent dictator, not only giving the sermon but picking the choir music, too. And no chatter in the pews, no droning on about fund-raising picnics. No, Daddy was a choreographer of spiritual emotion. To Georgia, it was as if the whole congregation went into a magical trance, left themselves behind and entered a realm of Daddy's making. He could "line a hymn" like nobody—prayerfully announce or echo each line, turning a hymn into a sermon in itself.

Says Georgia now, "It was a *big* life."

But three decades later, living in her home, he shuffled along the walls, his hand bracing him as he went. He stuffed bread into his pockets at the dinner table and was terrified to be alone, afraid an intruder would kill him. He picked up schoolbooks, magazines, pens, pencils and hoarded them. He hid soiled and stinking clothing in the corners of his room. When Georgia read him their favorite poem from her childhood, Rosa Hartwick Thorpe's "Curfew Must Not Ring Tonight," he did not recall it.

Again, Georgia is a girl . . . It is 1:00 in the morning and she wakes up instinctively, waiting for her father to return from his weeknight job as a waiter at the Buckhead Elks Club. She hears the door open and close and, as footsteps come down the hall, "Where's my baby?" Then, predictable as dawn, she hears her mother say, "James, don't wake her up." When the bedroom door opens, Georgia feigns sleep until her daddy says, "Here's some pennies I brought you. Put them in your bank and get back in bed."

Another time . . . Georgia comes home from junior high school three days in a row and thoughtlessly lets the screen door slam. Each day, her father tells her not to let it slam. After the third day, he stops her and says she's in trouble. Then he makes her go in and out the door five times without slamming the screen.

Sunday night, suitor night . . . Georgia's teenage boyfriend comes to the house and sits in the parlor with his beloved and they watch television. At 10 o'clock Daddy comes in to watch his favorite half-hour of TV, *The Loretta Young Show,* and sees the boy give Georgia a little kiss on his way out the door. Daddy says nothing, but the next morning tells Georgia that for a boy to kiss her in her father's home is an act of disrespect. She is not to see the boy again. Every day, Georgia sneaks around the corner and calls the boy on a pay phone. After a week, her father says, "You don't have to call on the phone around there. We've got a phone, and he can come back."

But three decades later, living in Georgia's home, her father didn't always recognize her. She wrote in her diary: "Not the man that I remember."

Sitting in the tall, flowered wing chair to the left of his curio, the reverend tells his story about the phone call from a young lady whose husband was a Pullman redcap. She asked the reverend to do an anniversary service and he agreed. He says he got down on his knees and asked God for guidance with his sermon. He thought of the Bible story about a man on his way to Jericho who fell among thieves and was left for dead. The man was passed by a priest and a Levite, before a Samaritan took pity on him, bound up his wounds, took him to an inn and paid his way. Jesus said, "Go, and do thou likewise." In this Bible story the reverend found a good message for train porters, who, like the Samaritan, had many chances to do a traveler good. "When I preach," the reverend says, "I aim at something just like I'm shooting at a bird." He says he didn't just preach God is love. He always laid down a challenge, a tough challenge. He pauses, leans forward, cocks his head and smiles.

"I'm sorry if I bored you."

The reverend sits on the edge of the piano bench. In movements so deliberate they seem sculpted, he shifts his cane from his right hand to his left, turns to his right and lowers the arm of the record player onto Frankie Laine's version of "I Believe." Behind him on the chalkboard is printed, "God Is Our Refuge." At the Holy Cross Hospital Adult Day Care Center, where he and about 30 others go every weekday, the reverend's Tuesday morning prayer meeting is about to begin. The congregants arrive slowly—two in wheelchairs, four with canes, one who is blind, one who is nearly blind, one with her chin bent violently to her chest, one with a gnarled hand, one who bobs her head repeatedly as if responding to a conversation only she can hear, one elegant old woman dressed in a bright green jacket and looking as if she's about to play golf at the country club.

The reverend, still the choreographer of spiritual emotion, intones, "We humbly ask you to give us your attention for these few minutes." His voice is tranquil, soothing, confident. He stands, leans on his cane with his right hand. With his left hand, he gestures in a half moon, his long, dexterous fingers wide and open and seeming to trail behind the sweep of his palm like the spreading tail of a comet. "Whatever else you have to discuss, social matters, jokes, let's forget them now . . . Our theme here is 'God Is Our Refuge' . . . This is a prayer meeting."

An old woman begins to read the 91st Psalm from her Bible, and the reverend gently touches her shoulder and whispers, "Not now," as Frankie Laine sings: *"I believe that somewhere in the darkest night, a candle glows . . ."* And the reverend, conjuring the magical trance Georgia remembers from childhood, lines the hymn.

> *I believe above the storm the smallest prayer . . .*

"Above the storm . . ."

> *Will still be heard . . .*

"Do you believe that?"

> *Every time I hear a newborn baby cry . . .*

"You believe it . . ."

> *Or touch a leaf . . .*

"Touch a leaf . . ."

> *Or see the sky . . .*

"That's belief . . ."

> *Then I know why, I believe.*

"You hear those words? You know why you believe."

The reverend pauses for a long moment. Everyone is silent. One woman has tears in her eyes, two other women hold hands. He switches his cane from his right hand to his left, reaches out and again touches the shoulder of the old woman with her Bible open to the 91st Psalm. He nods to her and says, "Now."

It took about six months after Daddy moved into Georgia's house before she realized she had her father back. After the first few months, he'd begun spending half his time at Leila's, which gave Georgia a respite. His memory was much clearer, he bathed and dressed himself, although even today his clothes must be laid out every morning or he might put on yesterday's dirty clothes. Eventually, he agreed to wear Depends, which made his occasional accidents only a nuisance. His sharp humor returned, and he and Georgia spent many evenings reminiscing, he telling her stories she did not recall and she telling him stories he did not recall. Georgia was once more able to think of those childhood moments with her father—when he made her go in and out the screen door five times or brought her those pennies or banished her boyfriend—without mourning that he was no longer the same man. She took out the brown box filled with her father's old pictures and memorabilia, the box she had put away, and pored over the material, laughing and crying joyful tears as she went.

Because Daddy was the same man, but only in flashes. When he cracked a joke about Georgia's driving: "Too bad the brakes on my side didn't work." When he asked to be taken to Metro's Kiss & Ride so he, too, could get a kiss. When he got sad after reading that a stray bullet had killed a child. When he put on his black fedora at that certain rakish angle, stopped, glanced back over his shoulder, touched the brim and smiled. When Georgia took a different route to Holy Cross and he asked, "Where are we going?" and she said, "I couldn't lose you, could I?" and he beamed. "It makes me feel that, yes, family and love and care will make a difference," Georgia says. "He's so much better." And, "I'm definitely a better person. I'm a more tolerant person . . . the change in me that I didn't think I needed to have."

Daddy had always been a hard man to live with. As a minister, he was accustomed to the spotlight, craved and demanded it. His wife, Anna Pearl, also had spoiled him rotten—not only supplying his starched shirts but getting up to fetch him a glass of water or a snack whenever he asked. Decades ago, when he smoked Camel cigarettes, no ashtray was ever so close that he wouldn't summon Anna Pearl to move it closer. Once, just after the reverend had left home for a tour of the Holy Land with a group of ministers, she hopped in the car, sped after the bus, beeped her horn and motioned the driver to the roadside: The reverend had forgotten his favorite hat.

But Georgia soon realized that if she had changed her life to accommodate Daddy, he, too, had changed. For instance, he'd always been a finicky eater. A woman on the revival circuit had once packed him a lunch and later found him down the road feeding it to the hogs. But now Daddy ate everything without complaint. All his life, Daddy had refused to eat garlic, but now he did. All his life, Daddy had refused to eat chicken. Now he did. Leila even believed he'd come to like chicken. Privately, the reverend still detests it. He laughs. "I'm looking to be as easy as I can."

The changes went beyond food. Growing up in the Old South, Daddy always had a deep fear and distrust of white people, but he went to the integrated Holy Cross center and became good friends with many whites, even deferring to one white woman's insistent requests for an occasional peck on the lips. Daddy'd had a temper as a young man, but he had almost no temper now. He'd also had an opinion about everything. So when he arrived, Georgia never yelled at her daughters in front of him, sometimes took them out to the car for scolding, afraid her father would judge her a bad mother. But he never said a critical word about how she and Carl raised the girls, and he never said a bad word about the girls either, only praised them. When Georgia was embarrassed by one daughter's temper tantrum, he said calmly, "We all get angry. . . . They're doing fine." Daddy also had always hated cats, but now he loved Georgia's cat, sat petting it, even let it sleep on his bed. In his own way, Georgia realized, her father was trying hard to fit into the family. At his age, over the hill, he was still growing.

Even Carl, Georgia's husband, who hadn't felt close to Georgia's father and who believed he was too domineering and self-centered, came to admire him. He loved the wise aphorisms the reverend dropped from time to time. Carl's favorite: "Just because you didn't mean to step on my toe, doesn't mean it didn't hurt." Carl had always cooked most of the family meals, and he quickly added softer fare to accommodate the reverend. He cooked the reverend's breakfast and freely pitched in to help Georgia with the new workload. That made life easier for her, but it also had an unexpected benefit: It deepened Georgia's already deep affection for her husband of 21 years.

Georgia's and Leila's greatest fear was what Daddy would do with his time while they and their husbands were at work. Then a neighbor told Georgia about the Holy Cross day care center, which saved the day. Because the reverend's only income was $568 a month in Social Security, he qualified for Medicaid to pay the center's $51-a-day cost. Georgia and Leila worried that Daddy wouldn't go—he had always refused to socialize with old people and was still nervous around whites. But again, he surprised them. He said, "The people there, I could be a morale-builder for them." Soon, the reverend was center stage at the center, eager to arrive before 8:30 so he could greet everyone in the morning, always inviting one of the women to dip a finger in his coffee to sweeten it up, always asking at the morning gathering, "What's for lunch?" And when he began his Tuesday morning prayer meetings, he was again able to do his life's work. Having people pay attention to him and listen to him, making a contribution again, being accorded special respect and status enlivened him.

The reverend's condition improved, but Georgia still struggled with her grief at her father's decline, still felt ashamed that she wished he didn't need her care, still felt guilty that his presence in the house grated on her. *He's not doing anything to bother me,* she thought, *but he's still getting on my nerves doing it.* She began attending the center's group counseling sessions, where she saw that her emotions were downright mundane, as she heard others caring for elderly loved ones gripe about the same kind of irritations. She thought, *Hallelujah, somebody feels the same way!* She saw that her burden was neither unique nor the heaviest to bear. At her last session, a man explained that his wife couldn't remember where anything went in the house they'd lived in for 50 years. Another man said his elderly wife had become so incontinent that even with adult diapers, the church choir had finally asked that she retire. A woman said of her stroke-victim husband, "He's like a dummy sitting there . . . I don't know how I do it. It's getting harder and harder."

When the center's director, Bob Grossman, said that as many as half the people over age 85 have some form of dementia, Georgia felt suddenly blessed by the clarity of her father's memory. When he explained that people caring for the elderly often suspect that their charges are pretending frailty to get more attention, Georgia felt relief: She was not an ungrateful daughter, she was only human. Georgia learned that beyond the confines of the center was a full spectrum of elderly life—elderly people living independently, those living in group homes with special assistance, those living bedridden in relatives' homes with help of professional aides and nurses, those living in nursing homes. The sad truth is, few elderly people die today without some period of dependency. Georgia's father could be in better health, but he also could be in worse health. For that, Georgia was grateful.

And she realized she'd been wrong: She had not become the parent, her father the child. A needful child will become less needful, grow in strength and self-mastery, and a parent burdened with the demands and irritations of constant care knows this, anticipates it. That anticipated future is part of the joy. In Daddy's case, the joy was strictly in the here and now, because the longer he lives the more he will decline. The more jokes he will be unable to finish, the more often he will repeatedly ask Georgia what time a favorite TV show starts, the more often he will hang his dirty clothes in the closet, the more often he will not know what day of the week it is, the more often he will apologize for boring his listeners. But there will be satisfaction later, after his death, in knowing she was a good daughter. "When I look into his casket," Georgia says, "I want to know my mother is looking here, saying that I did a good job. And I want to be able to say, 'I did a good job.' "

Leila never attended the counseling sessions, and it amazes Georgia that her sister didn't agonize over their father moving in. Leila is a practical-minded, matter-of-fact woman. "We have little things that bother us, but so what?" she says. "This is life." Leila enjoyed hearing Daddy's stories about her childhood. She loved it that her husband, Langston, and Daddy would sit for hours talking about the Bible. She glowed with pride that he always found the strength and concentration to comport himself with dignity at her church's Sunday services, a couple of times even giving a decent sermon or prayer.

Leila took her father's presence in stride, while Georgia struggled with it. Perhaps because Georgia was the youngest by so many years, had been babied and spoiled in that role, had shared a love of books and poetry, she saw more of herself in her father. Who knows? At the counseling sessions, seeing the wide range of people's ways of dealing with their aging parents and spouses, Georgia realized there was no right way to respond.

She says, "It lifted a lot off my shoulders."

Back at his Tuesday morning prayer meeting, the reverend leads in reciting the 23rd Psalm—"The Lord is my shepherd . . ."—and then, his voice strong, his eyes closed, he prays: "Father in heaven . . . here we are now. Our heads are white with the frost of many winters, our faces are wrinkled with the furrows of age and our bodies are bent beneath the weight of years, but in spite of all that, You have sustained us and kept us in the evening of our lives . . ." And the voice of Frankie Laine again rises: *"I believe that somewhere in the darkest night . . ."*

He is in his room at Georgia's house. It is evening. He often secludes himself here, no phone, no bother. In this room, with a blend of prayer and conversation, he talks to his wife, hears her voice when she says of their daughters, "Stand by them. They're all you have." He reads from the scores of religious books he has collected, searching for themes and passages for his Tuesday prayer meeting. For next week, he selects a stanza of poetry originally written in ancient Sanskrit: "Look to this day, for it is life, the very breath of life." He sits on his bed, a big bed covered with a brown and white quilt, in a small, darkly paneled room. Around him: a picture of Jesus, a bronze relief of the Last Supper, a sepia-toned photo of his father, a handsome man with mustache, white shirt, dark jacket and old-fashioned necktie, a photo of Anna Pearl, his roll-top desk, which is cluttered with pens and pencils, its top drawer holding the false teeth he no longer wears, his last automobile license plate—DDR 207—posted on the wall, two ties already tied hanging from a hanger on a hook near the closet. Everything washed with light turned a vague amber through a tan shade.

The reverend studies and then presses a button on the tape recorder next to him on the bed, inserts a tape, to do what he enjoys so much: listening to his old sermons, some dating back 20 years. When Georgia moved away, she asked him to tape them and send them to her so she could hear them. Now it is he who hears them. Sometimes he gets ready for bed and climbs under the covers to listen. Sometimes he paces the room, gesturing along, moving his lips to his own words. Sometimes he lines the hymns out loud. He thinks of himself as an old preacher listening to a young preacher. He is not that man anymore, but still he is.

"I'm that preacher. I'm doing that speaking now."

"That's me."

"I haven't changed."

"I still have the same philosophy."

"I was"—he hesitates—"*good.*"

"Something that I did that turned out to be magnificent."

"Be that it made some contribution."

The voice on the tape is more than the voice of the Tuesday prayer meeting, layers more. A deep, powerful, chest-rumbling voice, preaching and singing at once, a voice somewhere between that of a whispering prayer-giver and that of a bellowing auctioneer: "*Anybody* can live good when there ain't nobody botherin' ya! *Anybody* can live good when they got a good job! *Anybody* can live good when there ain't nobody pickin' at your wife! *Anybody* can live good when the money is right!" In that church decades ago, amens and laughter arose.

"But if you stand with God when the chips are down! Everybody! Because it's a cross."

"Jesus, keep me near the cross."

On his bed, a white handkerchief held to his face like a mask, his dark hand silhouetted against it, the reverend cries.

Living with Grandpa has been a complicated ride for his three grand-daughters. Leila's son, Paul, was 22 when he arrived, and he took the change in stride. He wasn't home much and eventually married and moved out of his folks' home. But for Leila's daughter, Ursula, then 18, and Georgia's daughters, Karen and Lisa, 15 and 14 at the time, their grandfather's arrival loomed larger. Politeness is an enforced virtue in both families, and the girls were never rude to their grandfather, but inside they often fumed as they struggled to understand his place in their lives.

"I couldn't understand why he was coming all the way here," says Ursula, now 22. "I worried about having to stay home and baby-sit him. I don't mean to sound selfish, but I had my life, too. I couldn't understand why they didn't put him in a nursing home nearby and we could go visit him."

It was Ursula's job to clean the downstairs bathroom and it irked her that her grandfather didn't always hit the mark. The idea of sharing the same bathtub with an old man also annoyed her, and she always sanitized the tub before she bathed. He put half-consumed cans of soda back in the fridge. He sometimes used Ursula's drinking cup. He interrupted conversations and told the same jokes and stories repeatedly. He asked, "Ursula, you heard this one?" She answered, "Yes, Granddaddy." Then he told the joke anyway. But worst of all, Ursula was embarrassed for her friends to meet him. He was so, well, so *old*.

"It was just not cool," Ursula says. "Only in the last year have I started to pay attention to him." She has learned to put away her drinking cup so he won't use it by mistake. She has learned to say, "That's a good one, Granddaddy," when he interrupts with a joke that she has heard before, and then go back to her conversation. She has tried to imagine what it will be like to someday ask her own father, "Daddy, did you go to the bathroom?" before they walk out the door. She has listened to her grandfather tell horrible stories about life for blacks in the Old South, and she has resolved to complain less and appreciate more the opportunities open to her today. From her grandfather, she has taken this lesson: "Even though he has aches and pains and can be forgetful and had his wife die, he still seems to enjoy life."

Sometimes, Ursula will be in a hurry in the morning, running out the door, trying to get her grandfather off to the day care center and herself off to Howard University, and he will step outside and say, "Look at the sky, not a cloud! And the grass is so green." That makes Ursula stop in her rush, look at the sky and the grass and see that he is exactly right.

She says, "It's an inspiration."

Karen and Lisa, 19 and 18 today, tell of similar journeys. In the early days, Karen couldn't help but be amused when her grandfather got up in the middle of the night and knocked on doors—it was just so weird! It bugged Lisa that he claimed a chair in the TV room as his own, when nobody had ever had assigned chairs in the TV room. When she sat in it, he shuffled around nearby, hoping she'd get up. But she didn't. Not unless he asked, which he rarely did.

Georgia didn't have as much time for the girls and that bothered them. But once again, it was the trivial irritants that irked them the most. New, unpleasant odors filled the house. Grandpa left the toilet seat up. He tilted lamp shades to read and left them crooked. It angered Karen terribly that she and her sister had to squeeze their chairs on one side of the dinner table. He went up and down the stairs so slowly when Lisa was behind him that she became convinced he did it to annoy her. Both girls believed their grandfather acted more feeble than he was so they'd wait on him—get him a drink, a snack, a newspaper—just as Grandma had always done. Karen harbored the deepest resentment, which she kept to herself until just last year, when she talked with Georgia about what she had come to see as her irrational anger at her grandfather. "He didn't do anything, really," Karen says. "It was me." Karen felt gypped. "I wanted grandparents like my friends' who took them shopping and on trips and to a play." She believed her grandfather's infirmity was something he'd done to himself. "I couldn't see that he was just old," she says. Karen also was angered by stories that her grandmother had waited on her grandfather "hand and foot." Unlike her mother, Karen saw nothing quaint in this. She thought, "Why should a woman have to do that?" When her grandfather seemed to expect Karen to do him small favors, she couldn't help but think he was treating her the same way, like a servant. "It disturbed me for so long," she says. "I didn't know the context.

"Looking back, I just wasn't at all compassionate. . . . Now I realize he didn't like being so dependent. That's something I've thought about: What if I couldn't do anything by myself? I wouldn't feel good about it, and I'm sure he didn't either. What if I were paralyzed in a car accident? I realized that's how he must feel."

Last year, Karen began to sit in the yard and talk with her grandfather. Without being asked, she did his laundry occasionally and was surprised at how the smell of his soiled clothing no longer sickened her. She found herself listening intently as her mother and grandfather told old stories on each other and found herself imagining her own children and grandchildren someday sitting with her, an old woman, talking about the life she was living right now. And she saw herself in their stories, realized that her grandfather had seemed to act so strict when her mother was a girl but was actually quite indulgent—a carbon copy of how Georgia had raised her and her sister.

"We're all pretty much alike, as much as I'd like to think I'm different," Karen says. "But pretty much I'm not." Lisa's resentment of her grandfather was never as deep as Karen's, and she says only that she has learned patience from living with him. But Karen's silent anger was once so fierce that she still sometimes asks God to forgive her for it. She has had long talks with the man she dates about how when her parents get old, she will expect to take them into her home. Like her cousin Ursula, when her grandfather moved in, Karen couldn't understand why they didn't just put him in a nursing home. Now Karen understands. "I know it would hurt him to know we put him out. . . . I also wouldn't want him to think I was the kind of person to put him out. I'm glad I grew up."

The reverend's room at Leila's house is larger and brighter, though it is still cluttered with his books. He sits on a stiff-backed chair, stiff-backed himself, rubs the palm of one hand lightly along his thigh and with his other hand plays with the change in his pants pocket. A person has to understand: The *feeling* the reverend got while preaching was the most powerful emotion of his life. More powerful even than his love of his wife or his children. That's why listening to his old sermons and conducting his prayer meeting at the center mean so much to him. They touch the old emotion—the power, the joy, the intimacy with God—that he felt every Sunday and every revival for half a century. Like an aging athlete who still feels as if he should be able to make the mark but cannot get his body to cooperate, the reverend still feels like a young man, although his mind and body won't cooperate.

"I feel like I have something to offer. . . . I'm afraid people don't want to hear it. . . . It's difficult for me to come to that place, but the only way not to come to that place is to die. . . . You adjust. You wake up on Sunday morning and say, 'Now if I was in Americus, I would have a place to preach this morning.' I don't have a place. So I put on my clothes and go to church."

The reverend, in his deliberate way, brushing his face lightly with one hand, tapping his cane with the nail of a finger, says it has been a joy to live with his daughters and their families, seeing his grandkids grow up, seeing how competent his daughters are as mothers and wives, seeing how decent are their husbands. "I had a wife who was almost a mother to me," he says. "I was known as a spoiled brat." But as an old man, living with his daughters, he has learned something about compromise, about not always getting his own way. It may have been a long time coming, but the reverend says, "I learned how to get along with people." He acknowledges that, yes, he does make little demands on his family just to get attention. He asks for juice or cookies, asks someone to recite a poem or listen to him recite a poem. "I just abhor loneliness," he says. "I do like babies, I cry." He smiles. "I need attention. I need to feel like they need me."

When the reverend was a young minister, he would go to the home of an elderly preacher he knew to help him bathe, make sure he got a haircut when he needed it. He ran errands, picked up the old man's spending money at the bank. "That man had something to offer," the reverend says, "but he needed help to do it." Once again, he tells the entire story of his sermon in honor of the Pullman redcap, which reminded the baggage handlers that they had many chances to do a traveler good. The message: "Everyone can make a contribution." At Holy Cross, the reverend knows elderly men who say little, are perhaps locked in their loneliness or debilitations. So he talks to them, compliments them, because he believes he knows what they want and need—attention. Because if a person doesn't get attention, it's as if he has disappeared.

"The ones I ask," the reverend says of Georgia and Leila, "are the ones I gave glasses of water to when they couldn't get them. Reciprocity is the order of the day. . . . I feel like my daughters are obligated. . . . I need it done and I feel like they ought to know I need it done." It's harder to get up and get a drink, he says, than young people realize. It's harder to take a glass down from the shelf for fear of breaking it. It's harder to pour a hot cup of coffee, and it's harder to clean up the crumbs after making a sandwich. And every day, it gets harder to remember what pants and shirt he wore yesterday. "I shouldn't have to admit that I can't do at 84 what I did before. You ought to know it. . . . Maybe when they get to be my age, they'll say, 'I know what he means.' But I'll be molding in the grave." Maybe 25 years from now, he says, Georgia or Leila will think back on their dead dad. "And they can be more tolerant of their own children."

He tells a story: When he was a minister in Augusta, he had elderly congregants who couldn't get out of bed to eat or go to the bathroom. "If you have one on your hands," he says, "don't make them concede they have the problem. They know. Don't frown every time they call. Turnabout is fair play. Time is passing for me, but it's also passing for you. . . . I'd hate to have Leila or Georgia put me in the bathtub when I was naked. I'd hate that. I still have my pride. . . . I don't worry about it, but I think about it. And I believe if I come to that place, they'd do it. . . . I believe this is life. You have to take it as you find it." The reverend sits forward in his chair, straightens his back, says, "There's one thing you have to know." As he speaks, his voice goes deep and clear and his arms gesture in grand designs.

> My latest sun is sinking fast,
> My race is nearly run.
> My strongest trials now are past,
> My triumph is begun.
> I know I'm nearing the holy ranks
> Of friend and kindred dear.
> I brush the dew on Jordan's banks;
> The crossing must be near.

The reverend stops. "I may be here tomorrow. I may not." He leans forward, cocks his head and smiles.

"I'm sorry if I bored you."

Author's Afterwords . . .

It was my editor's idea to write about what life was like for a family sharing a house with an elderly parent. I spent a week interviewing anthropologists and social scientists who had studied how family members respond to that living arrangement. Then I contacted social service agencies for the elderly and elder day care centers to find a family. I interviewed at least a half a dozen families over the phone. My main concern was finding a family in which the elderly parent was frail enough that his or her needs complicated the lives of other family members but who was still mentally alert enough to share insights in interviews. Reverend Holman fit perfectly. It helped that his daughter had a good memory for detail and that she was also comfortable talking about her emotions, not embarrassed at admitting she wasn't completely happy that her father was back in her house.

Then I spent the next three weeks with the family. I interviewed Reverend Holman's daughters several times for several hours, and I interviewed their husbands and children in single two-hour interview sessions. Then I focused on Reverend Holman and his daughter Georgia, who was more interested in taking part in the story. I had Georgia dig out old photo albums and poems she had written and the material spurred her memories. I spent several days with Reverend Holman at the elder care center, just watching and taking notes and tape-recording conversations. I sat through a counseling session with Georgia and other adults caring for sick family members. At night back at their house, I sat in Reverend Holman's bedroom for several evenings talking with him, listening to his old sermons with him, talking with him about the Bible. I taped many of these conversations and took detailed notes on the deliberate way he moved his hands and body, his facial expressions. Then I interviewed Georgia and her father together so I could flesh out stories they'd told about each other.

When I sat down to write, I kept thinking of something a social scientist had told me in my early interviews before I'd met Reverend Holman. She'd said that everyone thinks it's the younger members of the family who must adjust when a parent moves into their home, but that the elderly person, too, must adjust. Even in old age, she'd said, people change and grow. I had seen that in Reverend Holman, and I wanted to capture it in my story. I wanted to portray him as a complete individual, despite his age and his infirmities, as a person still evolving.

Beyond that, I wanted to show how the entire family had changed and grown. I wanted to evoke what I believed Reverend Holman and his family had learned: that getting old and watching a loved one get old is part of life's full circle.—W. H.

The Shape of Her Dreaming

Bed, where are you flying to?
—A line jotted in a notebook in 1980 by
Rita Dove, United States poet laureate

February 5, 1995, 5:35 p.m.

Twilight is not the time Rita Dove prefers to work. Much better are the crystal hours between midnight and 5:00 a.m., her writing hours when she lived in Ireland the summer of 1978, before her daughter was born, and Rita was young, with only a handful of poems published, before the Pulitzer Prize, before she became poet laureate of the United States. In Ireland, she and her husband, Fred Viebahn, a German novelist, would spend the late afternoons selecting dinner at the fish market, filling their sherry bottle from the merchant's oak cask, strolling Dublin's streets. They would cook dinner, write letters, read, talk, make love, watch TV into the late night, and then Rita would write, or do what people *call* writing, until the milkman arrived at sunrise and it was time to go off to sleep.

No more, not with her 12-year-old daughter, Aviva, the trips to Washington, the phone and fax, the letters, speeches, interviews, the traveling—oh, the traveling. It's the worst. It doesn't respect a poet's frame of mind. Rita can't go off chasing a shard of thought about the three-legged telescope her father once bought, or why it is that hosts in southern Germany fill up a guest's wineglass before it is empty, or whether a forest's leaves can be both mute and riotous at once (they can, of course). While traveling, Rita must catch a plane, look both ways, always muster the dedicated, logical mind of a banker or a plumber.

But this afternoon, for the first time in a while, she sits at her desk in her new writing cabin, which stands down a sharp slope from the back door of her house in the countrified suburbs of Charlottesville, Virginia, where she teaches at the University of Virginia. The cabin is small—12 by 20, a storage shed with insulation and drywall, a skylight so tiny it's more like the thought of a skylight, a wall of windows whose mullions create miniature portraits of the woods, pond, mountains and sunset to the west. No phone, fax, TV, no bathroom or running water, hardly any books by others and certainly no copies of her own nine books: "They're done. They have nothing to do with the moment of writing a poem." On a small stereo, she plays music without words—lately, Bach's Brandenburg concertos and Keith Jarrett's jazz piano.

The last few days, Rita has been thinking about three poems she'd like to write—"Meditation," "Parlor" and "Sweet Dreams." She began to ponder the last poem after she reread a few lines she'd scribbled in a notebook in 1980. For 15 years, she had looked at those lines every couple of months and thought, "No, I can't do it yet." She wrote 300 other poems instead. But just seven weeks from today, Rita Dove will consider "Sweet Dreams" done—with a new title, new lines, new images and a new meaning the poet herself will not recognize until the poem is nearly finished.

It will be a curious, enlightening journey: one poem, one act of creation, evoked from a thousand private choices, embedded in breath and heartbeat, music, meter and rhyme, in the logic of thought and the intuition of emotion, in the confluence of the two, in the mystery of art and the labor of craft, which will transform random journal notations, bodiless images, unanchored thoughts, orphan lines of poetry and meticulously kept records of times and dates into something more. Words with dictionary meanings will become words that mean only what the experiences of others will make of them, words no longer spoken in Rita's voice but in whispering voices heard only inside the heads of those who pause to read her poem.

In 1980, living in a $50-a-month, one-room walk-up in West Berlin, Rita was sick in bed one day. For light reading, she picked up *Das Bett*, a German book about the place of the bed in history. She was leafing page to page, when she came upon this sentence: "Vergleiche man die Waende der Wohnung mit einer Nusschale, so waere das Bett jene feine Haut um den Nusskern, den Menschen." She stopped. She loved the sentence, its meaning—if the walls of an apartment are like a nutshell, then the apartment's bed is like the fine, delicate skin around the kernel, which is the human being. But she also loved the sentence's sound. In the way that the sensuous glissando of a harp, the haunting blue note of a trumpet or the hypnotic percussion of a drum can touch a person's mood, Rita's mood was touched by the sound of the German words said together in their sentence. As a composer might hear a bird twittering and a woodpecker pecking and suddenly hear instead a melody, Rita suddenly felt "the cadence of thought."

The sentence said something beautiful and it sounded beautiful: "And that is the essence of poetry." It is language as idea and sensation at once: "the clay that makes the pot." She copied the German sentence into her notebook and wrote, "Bed, where are you flying to?" She imagined the bed as a home, the bed as a magic carpet, the bed as a world: "That's the inspiration. I have no idea what the leap is." Soon after, she wrote:

> **sic itur ad astra**
> (such is the way to the stars, or to immortality)
>
> Bed, where are you flying to?
> I went to sleep
> an hour ago, now
> I'm on a porch
> open to the world.
>
> I don't remember a thing,
> not even dreaming.
>
> and Chagall shall play
> his piebald violin.
>
> we'll throw away
> the books and play
> sea-diver in the sheets—
> for aren't we all children

in our over-size shirts (clothes),
white priests of the night!

Rita enjoyed the lines, especially the first stanza. Like the sentence in *Das Bett,* it seemed to have a music all its own and to carry the exuberance and spontaneity of a child's dream, although the stanza also baffled Rita: "I wasn't quite sure what it meant."

Rita has, after a fashion, a filing system—plastic folders in yellow, blue, red, purple, green, pink, peach or clear. She doesn't file her nascent poems by subject or title, as a scientist or historian might file documents. She files poems by the way they *feel* to her. Red attracts poems about war and violence. Purple, Rita's favorite color, accumulates introspective poems. Yellow likes sunshine. Blue likes the sky. Green likes nature. Pink—after a line she wrote about her daughter: "We're in the pink/ and the pink's in us"—is a magnet for poems about mothers and daughters. But the categories aren't fixed: Blue is the color of sky, but blue is also the color of the Virgin Mary's robe.

Rita's flying bed poem went in the clear folder, which holds very little: "The clear folder wants to be pure thought." A perfect, clear, pure lyrical poem: "It was a daunting folder. Very few things ever made it out of that folder."

But when Rita sits down at her desk this fifth of February, as she goes through her ritual of laying out her folders, looking at each and waiting for the door to her intuition to swing open and reveal to her which she should pick up and thumb through, she reaches for the clear folder, reads the old poem and thinks: "Maybe I can do it now." Maybe in this cabin, clean and fresh and pure as a lyrical poem, she can finally finish it. "It was now or never."

At 5:35, she writes:

SWEET DREAMS
  —*Sic itur ad astra. (Such is the way to the stars.)*

Bed, where are you flying to?
I went to sleep nearly
an hour ago—now I'm on a porch
open to the stars!

I don't remember a thing,
not the crease in the sheet,

the neighbor's washing machine.
I'm a child again, barefoot, catching
my death of cold,

in my oversized nightshirt
and stocking cap . . .
but so are all the others,
eyes wide, arms outstretched in greeting—
white priests of the night!

Rita is fiddling, playing, just seeing where her mind takes her words. She has changed the poem's title to "Sweet Dreams." She has lost Chagall and his piebald violin, the sea-diver in the sheets. She has gained the neighbor's washing machine, the crease in the sheet and the barefoot child catching her death of cold. She has altered punctuation. But as she rereads the poem, it is the stanza she wrote 15 years ago that grabs her—the porch open to the world has become the porch open to the stars: "It changed without me even thinking about it." What did that mean?

She jots these notes on her poem: "The original impulse of the poem—it was meant to be magic, pure impossible magic. The speaker goes to sleep & wakes into a journey—is it a dream or the lost feeling when you wake & don't know where you are? . . . How to capture the ecstasy, the spontaneity?"

Rita now enters a strange and magical place in the creation of her poetry, as she begins to carry on a kind of conversation with her poem, as she tries to actually listen to what the poem she has written is trying to tell her, the poet.

And the poem begins to create itself.

Rita uses this analogy: One of her favorite books as a girl was *Harold and the Purple Crayon*. With his crayon, Harold drew before him on the blank page the places he wanted to go—a street, a hill, a house. He created the world into which he then entered. But once inside that world, it was real, not an illusion. For Rita, writing a poem is like Harold drawing his way through life: Once a line is written she can step out onto it. The line is like a train and she a passenger curious to learn its destination. Each line is an idea that carries her to the next idea. Yes, she is taking the poem somewhere, but the poem is also taking her.

Some people's minds run from point A to point B with the linear de-
termination of an express bus roaring from stop to distant stop.
Theirs are minds trained to avoid detours, to cut a path past the alleys
and side streets of distraction. Rita's mind is more like the water of
a stream swirling randomly, chaotically and unpredictably over the
stones below as it still flows resolutely downstream: "It's hard to describe
your own mind, but I am really interested in the process of thought.
Sometimes I catch myself observing my own thoughts and think, 'Boy,
that's kinda strange how that works.' " Rita is not like those who see
tangential thoughts as distracting digressions: "I'm interested in the
sidetracking."

When her poem's first stanza was written, for instance, its character
was in a dream, flying on a bed, feeling a child's excitement—"open to
the world." Perhaps, Rita asks herself, she unthinkingly changed "world"
to "stars" in a later version not as a simple slip of the pen, but because
the world is really what her dreamer wants to leave behind? Perhaps the
stars—or immortality, the word Rita wrote beneath the poem's title
15 years ago—are her character's real destination? And, she tells herself, that isn't just exciting but also frightening, meaning that "Sweet
Dreams" was never meant to be only a joyful, childlike poem.

"That's what had stopped me all these years."

February 10, 4:30 p.m.

In her cabin, Rita stands at the *Schreibpult,* the stand-up writing
desk that her father, an amateur woodworker, built as a surprise for
her two years ago when she turned 40. While visiting her folks, Rita saw
the desk in their basement. She came upstairs and said to her father,
"That's a pretty nice desk down there." And he said, "Well, when your
birthday comes you can take it home." It had been a decade since Rita
had mentioned to her father that she'd like such a desk: "It was
astonishing."

Rita is sick today, coughing and feverish, but the jobs of wife, mother,
professor and poet laureate go on, with the job of poet taking a backseat.
It has been a satisfying and grueling time that will ease this summer
when her two-year tenure as laureate expires, but the fame that it has
brought will forever change her life. She can no longer write in her
university office, because someone will stop by to visit. She can no longer
sit in an outdoor cafe in town and read, because someone will recognize

her. Some days she hasn't the time to make a single entry in her notebook—not a fragment of conversation, a recipe, a fresh word. She has a new book of poetry just out, *Mother Love,* but still feels a creative emptiness in the face of so many demands, is afraid of losing the human connection to the clay that makes the pot: "It's harder and harder. Fame is very seductive. I'm tired of hearing the sound of my own voice. I want to be silent." Often, she has asked herself, "Was I writing for prizes? No. I wrote because of those moments when something happens in a poem." She once wrote these lines: "He used to sleep like a glass of water/ held up in the hand of a very young girl."

"That was a great moment."

Rita loves the image, although she doesn't know exactly what it means or even feel the need to know. She remembers a line written by poet Stanley Kunitz: "The night nailed like an orange to my brow." Kunitz once said that for years he lived in fear that someone would ask him to explain that line. He didn't understand the image, Rita says, but he wasn't going to touch it. "Sometimes you have those moments. Those are the moments you live for. There are some that change your life. When I write, I feel like I am learning something new every second. But I'm also *feeling* something more deeply. You don't know where you've been. That's the mystery of it. And then to be able to put it down so that someone else can feel it! I feel incredibly alive."

Outside Rita's cabin windows, two Canada geese are nesting at the pond beneath the little pier Fred built last year. Never before has she had so comforting a view from the windows of a study. The years she and Fred spent in Europe, they lived in dark apartments that looked out onto concrete. In Arizona, she gazed out at a decaying swimming pool in the backyard.

This cabin is doing something *to* Rita. When she was a 10-year-old girl, a few months before her first period, she daydreamed a house for herself: "It was small, one room . . . This dream house would stand in the backyard, away from the house with its clinging odors but close enough to run back—just in case." Her cabin is eerily reminiscent of the fantasy. And like Harold's purple crayon, like a poem that begins to create itself, the cabin is casting its own role in Rita's life. When she comes here, even for an hour, she writes at least a line or two. In this cabin, even in the middle of the day, it seems like the crystal hours from midnight to 5:00 a.m.

"It's a harkening back."

On her desk, Rita has put the tiniest clock she could find, and she has decorated her bulletin board with pictures. A photo of a Colorado sand dune that resembles the torso of a woman: "I just love this. I don't know why I love it." A postcard depicting a solarium (her grandmother's house had a solarium) in which sits a violoncello, an instrument Rita played as a girl: "It's a room I'd like to be in." A snapshot of Rita and her daughter, who is almost totally obscured by shadows, standing in a dry riverbed in Arizona: "You can barely see her, but I know she's there." What do the pictures mean? Rita has no idea. "These are things that make me start to dream. They open my mind."

She writes in her journal: "What I love about my cabin—what I always forget that I love until I open the door and step into it—is the absolute quiet. Oh, not the dead silence of a studio, a silence so physical that you begin to gasp for air; and it's not the allegorical silence of an empty apartment, with its creaks and sniffles and traffic a dull roar below, and the neighbors' muffled treading overhead. No, this is the silence of the world: birds shifting weight on branches, the branches squeaking against other twigs, the deer *hooosching* through the woods . . . It's a silence where you can hear your blood in your chest, if you choose to listen."

February 20, 5:45 p.m.

Rita has identified her problem: She's like an opera singer who must—without exercising her voice, humming a bar, hearing a note struck on a keyboard—hit a perfect B-flat. She has been away from the first stanza of "Sweet Dreams" so long, she likes it so much, that it's like one of her published books—it's *done.* She can't read the lines and rekindle the emotions that created the lines in the first place—and so she can't hitch a ride on those emotions into the rest of the poem. In the language of the poetry craft, she can't "make the turn" from the first stanza to the next. So she ignores the first stanza, begins without it.

In her cabin, she writes:

> I'm a child again, barefoot,
> catching my death of cold
> in a nightshirt I've never seen before
> fluttering white as a sail . . .

> moonlight cool as peaches above me,
> below,—but I won't look below.
>
> Bed, come back (here), I need you!
> I don't know my way back.
> Bed, at least leave me my pillow

Rita is writing lines and stepping out onto them. She decides to break away from "the tyranny of the typewritten page." In the margins, at odd angles, she writes: "purple crayon," "blow," "languid," "fluid," "landings," "whispering, happy landings." She is searching for the feeling of flying. Suddenly, she's frustrated: "Can I fly? If I could only remember! How does one remember?" She continues to scribble: "I've lost my feet," "with its garden of smells," "aromas," "crushed smells," "its petals whispering happy landings." She picks up a book of poetry by Wallace Stevens, thumbs through the pages and jots down words that strike her: "confusion," "hermit," "fetched." She scrawls: "purple hermit of dream." At 6:02, she writes:

> I'm a child again, barefoot,
> catching my death of cold
> in a nightshirt I've never seen before
> fluttering white as a sail.
>
> Above me, moonlight cool as peaches.
> Below . . . but I won't look below . . .
>
> Come here bed, I need you!
> I don't know my way back.
> At least leave me my pillow
> with its crushed aromas, its
> garden of dreams, its purple petals
> whispering *Happy landings*

"I'm a child again." Too explanatory. The poem should have the feeling of childhood without needing to announce it.

"Catching my death of cold." It goes on too long. This poem must be a collage of fleeting images, as in a dream. But Rita likes the line and would like to find a way to keep it.

"Moonlight cool as peaches." She likes that line, too, may use it someday in another poem, but to mention food while in flight is too corporeal, too earthly. Still, she'll leave it in for now.

"In a nightshirt I've never seen before." The image is too surreal, gives the sensation that the poem is a real dream rather than the sensation that it is like a dream.

"I won't look below." Not believable. Her poem's character wouldn't need to remind herself not to look below at the world. She's yearning to leave it behind—for a ride to the stars.

"Come here bed, I need you!" Wait, the poem is talking to Rita again: Its traveler is ambivalent about her journey. She craves the stars but, like a child, also the comfort of her bed.

"I don't know my way back." The word "back" is too narrow, too referential to the world. This traveler isn't worried about the way "back," but the way to the stars, the future, immortality.

"Garden of dreams," "purple petals," "Happy landings." "Yech!" "Awful!" "Disgusting!" But Rita doesn't stop to change them. They are place holders for the poem's cadence. New words will come.

On and on it goes—each line, each word examined. At 6:10, 6:15, 7:33 and 7:44, Rita begins new versions. She now believes that the complicated emotions in her poem can no longer be described as "Sweet Dreams." She hates it that people always accuse poets of being "hermetic"—hard to understand, obscure—but she goes back to the original Latin title from 1980 anyway. Unlike an essayist, who must keep in mind readers' tastes, interests, biases and education the better to convince them, Rita never thinks of her readers: "That sounds awful, I know. But to me a poem can't possibly be honest if I'm thinking about my readers."

It is a paradox: Rita has a better chance of reaching the emotions of her readers if she doesn't consciously try to reach them, if she doesn't worry about how people will respond to a certain poem. Pondering that would put a kind of emotional membrane between herself and her material, making it less authentic and more distant from the unmediated emotion she is trying to feel and then evoke, reinvent, in her readers: "If I start thinking about the world and about the reception of this poem in the world, then I'm lost. I'm lost. It's not gonna be a poem."

Rita deletes "crushed aromas" because the word aroma is too "thick," not simple enough. That allows her to replace "garden of dreams," a cliché, with "garden of smells." She likes that change, because a smell, unlike an aroma, can be either pleasant or sickening. "Purple petals," which probably referred back to Harold's purple crayon, is excised. It's, well, too purple. Now, without "crushed aromas" and "purple petals," she adds "crushed petals." She plays with the poem's enjambment—the way sentences run on or break from line to line—looking for meanings that she didn't see at first: "Catching my death/ of cold in a fluttering nightshirt," for instance, can mean something far different from "catching my death of cold/ in a fluttering nightshirt."

At 7:44, with Keith Jarrett playing, she writes:

SIC ITUR AD ASTRA
—Thus is the way to the stars.

Bed, where are you flying to?
I went to sleep nearly
an hour ago, and now
I'm on a porch open
to the stars—barefoot,

catching my death of cold,
in a fluttering nightshirt
white as a sail. Above me,
moonlight cool as peaches.
Bed, come back here,

I need you! I don't know
my way. At least leave me
my pillow, with its garden of smells,
its crushed petals whispering
Lay back. Relax. Gentle landings.

On the poem she jots: "dreams" and "worries of the day," reminding herself not to lose the poem's dreamlike feeling and to add the idea that traveling to the stars is also a way to leave the trivial bothers of daily life behind.

February 24, 5:35 p.m.

In her journal, Rita writes: "I want more intriguing, surprising metaphors. . . . I want the language to imitate the clarity of children's literature. . . . I'm looking for an image as wild and apt, as wonderfully penetrating yet impenetrable, as Gabriel Garcia Marquez': ' . . . and death began to flow through his bones like a river of ashes.' If I could catch a fish like that, I'd be ready to die. No, not really. But the contentment would be immense and would last my entire life."

But not so others can read the line and admire her as she admires Marquez, but so she can *feel* the line's creation. It's an addictive joy, a feeling of exhilaration, yes, but not of pride. It's beyond pride, or maybe before it: "I feel very humble: Thank you, line. I don't know where you came from, but you're greater than I am.' You have those moments. They're the ones that keep you writing. You're always after the next fish."

It is 6:20 now, sundown out the cabin window. Rita takes up a new pen and writes: "Now we'll see how this pen works. Sungown. Dundown. The light quenched. Oh, fennel bloom. Another ladybug—perennially cute, ladybug, body and name. Too many make a plague of luck. Ah shame on you, duckie: You've lost your quack. For an ounce of your prattle I'd hang up my traveling shoes."

What does it mean? Who knows.

Gone fishing.

March 13, 4:23 p.m.

Rita was going through old notebooks earlier today, trying to unclog her mind, searching for inspiration hidden in a line or even a word: "A word that will knock this damn poem back on line." It was a beautiful 73° day outside, but Rita was at her desk imagining the sensations of flying on a bed at night: "The absence of incidental white noise, the smells and the cool feelings that night floats up in us, almost like the earth is emitting a faint subterranean sigh." She wants to write this poem, but the world is relentless: *USA Weekend* has asked the U.S.A. poet laureate for an original poem to publish, she must plan her laureate's farewell poetry reading at the Library of Congress, organize the panels for an upcoming literature conference, write the opening remarks for the Nobel Laureates in Literature convocation, finish writing her lecture for the university faculty colloquium and write the foreword to an anthology of stories written by children. That's for starters.

But then, going through a tiny black and red notebook, Rita comes across a snatch of forgotten poetry she jotted down while at a conference in Morelia, Mexico, in January 1994.

READING BEFORE SLEEP

Bed, where are you flying to?
One minute ago I climbed

```
          into the cool
     waters of night & now
          (end of day)
     I'm on a porch
     open to the sky
          world!
     If I close my eyes
     I'll sink back
     into the day, made
          strange—
     but no, my eyes are open
     and I am falling it
          seems
     forward
```

Rita is amazed. Just the other day, she made a note to remind herself to add to her poem the idea that traveling to the stars was also a way to escape daily life—"the worries of the day." Now she finds, in the forgotten Mexico notations, these lines: "If I close my eyes/ I'll sink back/ into the day." She thinks, "This thing has been haunting me for all these years." She writes in her journal: "Somewhere there's a few lines about melancholy . . . Where is that sheet of paper?" Then, dutifully, she spends the afternoon and the evening working on a poem for *USA Weekend*.

March 17, 5:47 p.m.
Fred has asked Rita to go with him and Aviva to the stable where Aviva keeps her horse. Rita, who hasn't been out to the stable in months, hears Fred's plea and agrees, although she plans to sit in the car, watch Aviva and her horse trot around the track and work on "Sic Itur." But once she gets to the stable, she can't capture the poem's mood. The grounds are too much of the earth, not the stars. So Rita works on "Parlor," one of the three unfinished poems she considered working on way back on February 5. She works for an hour, scribbling additions and deletions and notations on her copy. Then Fred climbs into the car, out of the cold and turns on the radio news.

"Does that disturb you?" he asks.

"No," Rita says, lying. "I think I'll just stretch my legs."

Walking out along the fence line in the descending darkness, Rita asks herself, "I've had all this time to write. Why can't I give up this few minutes?" She wants to be in her cabin writing, but she wants to be with

Fred and Aviva. She wants to be with Fred and Aviva, but she wants to be poet laureate of the United States: "I want to fly as a poet." She takes out her notebook and writes, "Sic Itur Ad Astra: You don't want to come down. Immortality—it's loneliness. You long for the pillow's smells, the earth you are leaving but that's all you can take—the recycled breath, the memory—into the rarefied air. . . . The dear worries, the sweet troubles of dailiness."

And it has happened.

Rita's poem is creating itself—it is a train, she its passenger: "For the first time since I wrote that stupid title down I realized I wrote it down because it had that line about the way to immortality. I realized I was talking about fame." Naturally, people reading Rita's poem will know none of this. They'll see the poem's themes through the lens of their own ambivalent feelings about whatever are the conflicting demands in their lives. But the tension Rita feels between the satisfactions of fame and accomplishment and the joys of everyday life is *her* particular lens—and the emotional juice of her poem. Because a new meaning has emerged for that first line written in Rita's sickbed in Germany in 1980, before her life had become a dream ride from earth to the stars: "I want 'em both."

"It's just that I've felt lonely."

"Where's my life? I want a life."

March 19, 4:30 p.m.

It comes quickly. Yesterday, the Brandenburg concertos playing for two hours, Rita ripped through four versions of "Sic Itur." Today, the Brandenburg concertos still playing, she whips through five versions. She has found her old musings on melancholy, cribbed an image—"tiny dismissals"—and combined it with the lines on life's trivial irritations from her Mexico notations: "If I close/ my eyes, I'll sink back into/ the day's tiny dismissals." Rita has turned a corner. Forced to work on her poem for *USA Weekend,* impelled to work on "Parlor" at the stable, her mind was somehow freed, her attention distracted momentarily from "Sic Itur," which, inexplicably, allowed Rita to finally see her poem clearly. These so-called distractions cleared a path so that her poem could happen to her, as if she is not the creator of insight, but its recipient. Rita keeps a single quote, in German, tacked to her cabin's bulletin board, the wisdom of Austrian poet Rainer Maria Rilke: *It is not enough for a poet to have memories. You must have very great patience and be able to wait until the memories come again.* Memories remain, but the poet changes: "You have to wait until it all comes back in a different form to find the meaning." Rita is loose now, playing—with words, images, punctuation, enjambment and stanza size. She writes a line, walks out onto it, looks ahead, continues or steps back, tries another. For the first time, she can hear the rhythm of her poem before its words are written, as in a song that doesn't yet have lyrics.

"It's very weird."

She writes:

> Bed, where are you flying to?
> I went to sleep nearly
> an hour ago, and now
> I'm on a porch open
> to the stars! If I close
> my eyes, I'll sink back into
>
> the day's tiny dismissals—
> bagged lunch, the tiny dismissal of a glance—
> but no, I'm wide-eyed and barefoot,
> catching my death of cold,
> nightshirt fluttering white as a sail.
>
> Bed, come back here, I need you!
> I don't know my way.
> At least leave me my pillow
> to remind me what I've rested my dreams on—
> my dear/crushed pillow, with its garden of smells.

Rita is suddenly hit with an image that grows from the lines she wrote way back on February 5: "I don't remember a thing,/ not the crease in the sheets."

She writes:

> What will they do when they come in
> and find me missing, just the shape
> of my dreaming creased in the sheets?

The lines make Rita shiver in the way she once shivered when she wrote, "He used to sleep like a glass of water/ held up in the hand of a very young girl." That *feeling*. So much of writing a poem is less like

saying a prayer than it is putting together the weekly shopping list. Then
comes a sacred moment. . . . For Rita, these lines are a fish to keep—a
rare poet's epiphany in the muck of craft: "I don't know where it came
from. It just came." Then:

> Bed, where are you flying to?
> I went to sleep nearly
> an hour ago, and now
> I'm on a porch
> open to the stars—barefoot,
> catching my death of a cold
> in a nightshirt fluttering white
>
> as a sail. Come here, bed,
> I need you! I don't know my way.
> If I close my eyes, I sink back
> into the day's bagged smiles,
> the tiny dismissal of a stranger's glance . . .
>
> Oh, what will they do
> when they find me missing,
> just the shape of my dreaming
> creased in the sheets?
> Who will tell them what it's like here?
> No one else knows but my pillow—
>
> my poor, crushed pillow with its garden of smells!

Then:

> Bed, where are you flying to?
> I went to sleep
> nearly an hour ago,
> and now I'm on a porch
> open to the stars!
>
> Close my eyes
> and I sink back into the day's
> tiny dismissals; eyes wide
> and I'm barefoot, in a nightshirt
> fluttering white as a sail.
>
> Come here, bed,
> I need you!
> I don't know my way.
> What will they say

when they find me missing,
just the shape of my dreaming

creasing the sheets?
At least leave me
my pillow to remind me
what misery I've fled—
my poor, crushed pillow

with its garden of smells!

Out Rita's window, the sun is lingering three inches above the mountains. The days are longer now, but she has been too busy even to notice that it is spring: "Why is spring a she? What gender are the other seasons? Summer is female, surely. And winter, too. Fall? Actually, they're all female." Rita's mind, again, is swirling like water over stones in a stream.

"I had given up on this poem."

"It's a great feeling."

"I'm rolling!"

Rita has deleted the sappy line, "*Lay back. Relax. Gentle landings.*" She has again included "catching my death of cold" but then excised it as too "cutesy-wootsy." "Bagged lunch" has gone in, become "bagged smiles" and gone out: "I don't know what a bagged smile is." She has finally taken out "moonlight cool as peaches," and the cliché "wide-eyed" has become "eyes wide" and will later become simply "open wide." She has added "the tiny dismissal of a glance," which has become "the tiny dismissal of a stranger's glance," a cliché she hates, and which has now become simply "the day's tiny dismissals." She loves the sneering sound of the *hiss* in the word dismissals. The line "Bed, come back here" has become the more direct "Come here, bed."

Remembering her notation to emphasize that this poem should have the feeling of a dream, Rita has added, "I've rested on my dreams," which she hates as a cliché. But she thinks, "Oh, hell, I'm just gonna put the dreams in and see what happens." Working from her epiphanic flash, the lines have become "just the shape/ of my dreaming creased in the sheets," which have now become "just the shape of my dreaming/ creasing the sheets." Rita also has added a stanza space between "just the shape of my dreaming" and "creasing the sheets." That space will force a reader to pause after the word "dreaming," float in the space and ponder the image before moving on to the next line. The newly added gerundive i-n-g ending on the word "dream" also carries action—and the sense that the act of dreaming, not the dream itself, is leaving its impression on the bed of real life. As with her poetry, the product is inseparable from the process. In the words of Yeats: "How can we know the dancer from the dance?"

Rita has added "my dear/ crushed pillow," although she knows it's too corny. She has quickly changed it to "my poor, crushed pillow." Despite the truism that a poet should never use two adjectives when one will do, she wants two adjectives to precede the word pillow. Less for the words than for the double *beat* of emphasis, which is meant to mimic the intense affection of a child for a blanket, toy or pillow: "It's not always the words themselves that bring you the nostalgia but the sound and the rhythm of the words."

This is Rita's ideal: She wants to take a reader to the place she would go as a girl when she read a poem and suddenly felt her breathing begin to synchronize with the poem's cadence: "Before you know it, your body's rhythm is the rhythm of the poem. That's one of the things poems do. You don't even notice that it's happening. But what convinces you is the way the poem influences your breathing, your heartbeat. It becomes a physical thing. You want people to get there."

Rita has realized that the final sentiment of her poem is mundane. After visiting the stars, her traveler discovers the wonder of what she has left behind: "my poor, crushed pillow/ with its garden of smells!"—meaning her ordinary life with Fred and Aviva, the days Rita cooks those quick meals of frozen fish fillets, sliced fried potatoes and salad with Caesar dressing, the evenings they all plop down at the TV and watch Aviva's favorite show, *Star Trek: Voyager,* and then Rita quizzes Aviva for her test on earthquakes and volcanoes, and Aviva is curled up on the chair and in the silence between Rita's questions and Aviva's answers, Rita can hear the sound of the leather creaking as her daughter adjusts her body, which makes Rita think to herself, "There's no sound in the poem. Is there sound in dreams? Sound does funny things in dreams—it's like telepathy."

Of her yearning to travel to the stars and her irritation with daily life, Rita asks herself, "Where you gonna go? Is there anything really better than this?" And how else to be a poet? Aren't the trivial, even irritating distractions of life the wellspring, the clay that makes the pot?

A poet free from "the day's tiny dismissals," living only among the stars, will not be a poet for long: "It sounds like the old, corny notion, 'Love will bring you back,' but you know that's what it is. How many different plots do we have in this world? Not many."

For the first time, Rita stops to analyze the poem's rhyme and discovers a surprising array of rhymes, half-rhymes and "cousins" of rhymes: barefoot/nightshirt, my way/they say, creasing/sheets, fled/bed, smells/dismissals, sail/smell. Although a reader wouldn't consciously notice the rhymes, they still weave the poem together, like the reprising melodies of a minuet. "Okay, I'm ready!"

Rita has been writing versions of "Sic Itur" with different stanza configurations—experimenting, seeing if stanza breaks at different lines carry meanings she hasn't recognized, in the same way that playing with a poem's enjambment can reveal a new insight. But now she realizes how she wants the stanzas constructed: "It's really, really picky." But if "Sic Itur" is a journey *up* to the stars and back *down* to earth, it demands a narrow, vertical silhouette on the page: "To lift you up in the sky." And if it is to evoke the simplicity of childhood, it also must look clean and pure on the page. The idea is to reach people not only through words, ideas, images, sounds, rhythms and rhymes, but also through the pattern of ink their eyes see on the page. She goes through tightening lines to narrow the poem's width and extend its height. Then she adjusts the number of lines in each stanza. From top to bottom: a 1½-line title, 5-line stanza, 6-line stanza, 6-line stanza, 5-line stanza, 1-line stanza: "It's like a mirror image," which makes the tug of the stars and the pull of the world equal in visual weight on the page.

At 5:24, she writes

> **SIC ITUR AD ASTRA**
> *Thus is the way to the stars.*
>
> Bed, where are you flying to?
> I went to sleep
> nearly an hour ago—
> and now I'm on a porch
> open to the stars!
>
> Close my eyes
> and sink back to
> day's tiny dismissals;

open wide and I'm
barefoot, in a nightshirt
fluttering white as a sail.

Come here, bed,
I need you!
I don't know my way.
What will they say
when they find me missing,
just the shape of my dreaming

creasing the sheets?
At least leave me
my pillow to remind me
what misery I've fled . . .
my poor, crushed pillow

with its garden of smells!

Rita has a few nits . . .

"I'm dotting the i's."

She worries about the word "fluttering" in the line "fluttering white as a sail." Is it necessary? Does it add enough for the space it takes? Unlike prose, which Rita compares to walking through the woods and describing everything you see, poetry is like walking through the woods, coming upon an old, deep well and describing only what you see as you stare down its casing. Poetry is a narrow world made wide. So every word, every line in a poem must stand on its own. But without the word "fluttering," the line is lame: "white as a sail." Pick any line: "just the shape of my dreaming" or "and sink back to." Each adds something—action, an image, lyricism, intrigue, an idea. But wait . . . that one line: "At least leave me." What does it add? Nothing: "It just sits there."

"This line and I are going to battle."

Rita's also not sure about those three i-n-gs in a row—missing, dreaming, creasing. And she's not sure about the line "Close my eyes"— she might add a comma. Today, she's not even sure about the title— maybe she should go back to "Sweet Dreams," which now carries a touch of irony. But adding "Sweet Dreams" would put too much type at the top of the poem and muck up her mirror-image construction of the stanzas. And for the poem to make sense she still needs the Latin and its translation—"Thus is the way to the stars." Come to think of it, maybe she should go back to translating "thus" as "such"—"Such is the way to the stars." Less pedantic. And she'd better look up the quotation. Turns out to be from Virgil's *Aeneid,* which she didn't know: "Oh, shame!" She must attribute it. No room for "Sweet Dreams" now.

Maybe she should move down "Come here, bed, I need you" and move up "just the shape of my dreaming creasing the sheets," so the poem's character flies from sky to earth, earth to sky, sky to earth—a trip that ends back home, where Rita has realized she wants to be. But then she'd lose the spatial pause between "just the shape of my dreaming" and "creasing the sheets." And that word "misery"! Rita wants it to be self-mocking. "What misery I've fled . . ." is supposed to mean that her daily life wasn't misery at all. But the word is too strong. "I think there's a different word that won't ring as many bells. One word. And it should be three syllables, but it might end up having to be two."

March 26, 1:43 a.m.

After allowing herself a week of distractions, a week for her poem to simmer, Rita writes:

> **SIC ITUR AD ASTRA**
> *Thus is the way to the stars.*
> —Virgil
>
> Bed, where are you flying to?
> I went to sleep
> nearly an hour ago,
> and now I'm on a porch
> open to the stars!
>
> Close my eyes
> and sink back to
> day's tiny dismissals;
> open wide and I'm
> barefoot, nightshirt
> fluttering white as a sail.
>
> What will they say
> when they find me
> missing—just
> the shape of my dreaming

creasing the sheets?
Come here, bed,

I need you! I don't know my way.
At least leave my pillow
behind to remind me
what affliction I've fled—
my poor, crushed pillow

with its garden of smells!

"A poem is never done. You just let it go."

In her cabin, Rita hears the distant woof of a dog. Outside the open
window is a faint wind: "The sound of air moving—not quite a breeze,
but a sighing—all that the word *zephyr* implies." She remembers a time
as a girl when her father said that word. At a gas station, as the attendant
filled his tank, her father stood and stretched, faced off into the horizon
and said as naturally as if he were asking for the time, "What a lovely
zephyr today." Young Rita never forgot the baffled look on the attendant's face.

Where are those few words she jotted?

Ah, here they are:

Meek, this fallen leaf
reminds me of a word
my father used to say—
zephyr, tilting back to
gaze up under his brimmed fedora
as if to coax the air along
his brow: "What a lovely zephyr
today." And the gas station
attendant scratched himself,
instantly ashamed

And once again, Rita steps out onto the lines . . .

 Author's Afterwords . . .

The Rita Dove piece started out as one kind of story and ended up
another. My original idea was to write a lyrical 1,500-word article about
how a poet—any notable poet—went about writing a poem. I was in

Washington, D.C., and so I first approached the then-poet laureate of the United States to see if she was interested in taking part in the story. She was. I told her the poem needed to be short so we could reproduce it in the *Post Magazine*. I suggested that she keep a journal of her thoughts as she was working on the poem and that she keep its various versions.

Several months went by before Rita called to say she'd finished the poem, and I went to visit her at her house in Charlottesville, Virginia. Soon after we sat down, I knew I had far more story than I'd anticipated. She'd kept a journal, vividly written and filled with telling details, about not only her thoughts but the weather conditions outside her study as she worked on her poem. She'd also kept dozens of versions of her poem along with notations on the exact time she'd begun to type them into her computer. I stacked the versions in chronological order and we worked our way through them one after the other. I asked questions about every line, every word, every changed comma. Why had she made the changes? What had she been thinking and feeling? What had she been trying to accomplish?

I encouraged Rita to go off on tangents about her life, background and experiences. I asked questions about the items on her desk, the pictures on her walls, what they meant to her. We talked for seven hours that day, and I tape-recorded the entire conversation. I also took photographs of Rita, the inside of her study, the top her desk, the view she saw out her window.

As I drove the three hours home that evening, I was euphoric. I knew I'd been granted a rare glimpse into the process of creativity itself. I spent the next few days transcribing my tapes and reading Rita's previous books of poetry as well as articles she'd written about herself and her craft.

The writing challenge was to convey the hard work of her craft with pin-point precision and also the more mystical and essentially unknowable character of her creativity. I wanted to demystify the craft while evoking the mystery of her mind. At first, I planned to write the story as if it was all happening inside her head, without quotations. I wanted the piece to have a dreamlike feeling that would, I hoped, evoke in readers the sensation that they were in Rita's study overhearing her thoughts.

I didn't want the attribution "she said" to be constantly reminding readers that she was recalling her thoughts and actions after the fact, that she was retelling them to a third party. How to do that? Normally, to put a reader inside the head of a subject I'd paraphrase her remarks to give the impression she was *thinking* them to herself. But I couldn't do that with Rita Dove, because her comments were simply too well stated to be paraphrased. Not surprisingly, the poet was better with words than the reporter.

Then I remembered that in her book *In These Girls, Hope Is a Muscle* Madeleine Blais had managed to convey the sensation that she was inside her teenage subjects' heads at the same time she was quoting their words. I pulled the book off the shelf and saw that she'd accomplished this by introducing the girls' quotations with colons rather than using traditional attributions. I borrowed the technique, which virtually eliminated invasive attributions.

I piled all my material—versions of the poem, Rita's journal entries, her remarks about them—in chronological order and began writing my story from the top of the pile. It came quickly. The entire piece was written in a week. It's still one my favorite pieces. I've never seen a story quite like it.—W. H.

Notes:
Prologue and A Writer's Essay

Will Durant quote: "Civilization is a stream. . .": "Historian Will Durant Dies," *New York Times,* Nov. 9, 1981, A1.

Page xi: Pete Hamill quote: "Writers are rememberers. . ." "A Writer Under the Influence," *Boston Globe,* David Mehegan, Jan. 31, 1994, Living 30.

Page xii: Herbert Gans quote: "How ordinary people work. . .": "What Is This Thing Called News?" *Washington Post,* Richard Harwood, March 12, 1994, A21.

Page xii: "Life its ownself. . .": Dan Jenkins, *Life Its Ownself* Simon and Schuster, 1984.

Page xix: The "feeling of a living experience" and "felt life": William Stott, *Documentary Expression and Thirties America,* Oxford University Press, 1973, 11, 153.

Page xx: Nelson Algren quote: "I try to write accurately. . .": "Hers," *New York Times,* Maxine Hong Kingston, Aug. 3, 1978, C2.

Page xxi: Mark Twain quote: "What a wee little part. . .": Justin Kaplan, "The Real Life," *Studies in Biography,* edited by Daniel Aaron, Harvard University Press, 1978, 4.

Page xxiv: "In classic journalism. . .": "Who is the Journalist's Client?" Media Ethics, Stephen Bates, Vol. 7, No. 1, Fall 1995.

Page xxv: Henry Adams quote: understanding is "not a fact but a feeling": Stott, 12.

Pages xxxii, xxxiii: William Carlos Williams quotes: "I try to put myself. . .", "I'll go on my rounds. . .", "Things I noticed. . ."; Robert Coles quote: "How do we place our. . .": Robert Coles, *The Call of Service,* Houghton Mifflin Company, 1993, 24-26.

Page xxxiii: "Plaster saints, glass jewels. . .": William Carlos Williams, *Paterson,* New Directions Publishing Company edition, 1963, 51. Originally published by W. C. Williams, 1946.

Page xxxiv: Walker Evans quote: "It's as though. . .": "The Artist in Black-and-White," *Washington Post,* Jonathan Yardley, June 7, 1995, C2, quoting Belinda Rathbone's *Walker Evans: A Biography,* Houghton Mifflin, 1995.

Page xxxvi: "James Agee borrowed and changed the poetry of Hart Crane. . .": Stott, 295.

Page xxxvi: "Writin' is fightin'. . .": Ishmael Reed, *Writing' Is Fightin',* Atheneum, 1988.

Page xl: Allen Stringfellow quote: "I work by music. . .": "The Texture of Success," American Visions, Curtia James, Oct./Nov. 1995, 17.

Acknowledgments

This book was 20 years in the making. It took shape in piles of articles I'd toss into a file cabinet for some vague later reference. It took shape in letters I wrote to colleagues, in talks I gave at conferences or to handfuls of journalism students and in feature writing classes taught at the University of Maryland. It took shape in passionate discussions with journalists of a similar bent and in debates with journalists of a different bent. It took shape in earlier essays I wrote for an earlier book titled *American Profiles*, which was published by the University of Missouri Press and edited by Beverly Jarrett and Jane Lago.

But mostly it took shape in the advanced feature seminars I led for reporters and editors at the *Washington Post*, where over the years 100 or so colleagues put up with my insistence that I give formal presentations. Most people pretended to listen intently, and I thank them for that. But it was the *Post's* Yvonne Lamb, a journalist turned educator, who first asked me to lead the seminars and who must accept the largest thank you for putting me in a situation that forced me to get my ideas together.

Thanks also to Robert Kaiser, the *Post's* managing editor, who oversaw the seminars and put his stature behind them. Thanks to *Post* Executive Editor Leonard Downie Jr., who touted the sessions to colleagues. Thanks to Suzanne Phelps Weir, who helped me find a home for the project, and thanks to Andy Winston, who gave me helpful suggestions. Thanks to Chip Scanlan at the Poynter Institute for Media Studies for giving me the wonderful quote from historian Will Durant that introduces the book. Thanks to Madeleine Blais for the Pete Hamill quote. Thanks to Richard Cunningham at New York University. At the National Workshop on the Teaching of Ethics in Journalism at the University of Missouri-Columbia more than a decade ago, he told a gathering that an article I had written was based on a kind of "intimate reporting." It was the first time I'd heard that reference.

Thanks to Norman Sims at the University of Massachusetts, Patsy Sims (no relation) at the University of Pittsburgh, and Steve Weinberg and Jan Colbert at the University of Missouri for thoughtful comments on my introductory essays. Thanks to John Cotter, Tom Frail, Liza Mundy and Bob Thompson at the *Washington Post Magazine*; David Hirshey at *Esquire*; John V. R. Bull at the *Philadelphia Inquirer*; John Carroll and Laura Gamble at the *Baltimore Sun*; and Jackie Paciulan, Jennifer Morgan, Linda Gray, and Astrid Virding at Sage. Special thanks to my Sage editor Margaret Seawell, whose enthusiasm for the book was instrumental in getting it done. Thanks to my agent, Amanda Urban, and to my old friends and colleagues whose advice is always invaluable— Edmund Lambeth at the University of Missouri and Joyce Hoffmann at Old Dominion University.

Thanks to my wife, Keran, and my children, Matthew and Kyle, who remind me every day that life is about more than the normal journalistic diet of public policy, politics and celebrity. Thanks to the writers and institutions who let me reprint their stories. And, finally, thanks to the people who let us write about them.

About the Editor

Walt Harrington was for nearly 15 years an award-winning staff writer for the *Washington Post Magazine*. He is the author of *Crossings: A White Man's Journey Into Black America,* the story of his 25,000-mile excursion through black America. Harrington, 46, is also the author of *American Profiles: Somebodies and Nobodies Who Matter* and *At the Heart of It: Ordinary People, Extraordinary Lives.* Over the years, Harrington has written benchmark profiles of George Bush, Jesse Jackson, Jerry Falwell, Lynda Bird Johnson Robb and Carl Bernstein, as well as numerous in-depth articles on ordinary people. He holds master's degrees in journalism and sociology from the University of Missouri. He is now a Professor of Journalism at the University of Illinois at Urbana-Champaign. His E-mail address is wharring@uiuc.edu.